JFK
For a New Generation

JFK
For a New Generation

CONOVER HUNT

THE SIXTH FLOOR MUSEUM

and

SOUTHERN METHODIST UNIVERSITY PRESS

Dallas, Texas

Copyright © 1996, Conover Hunt
All rights reserved

Published by
The Sixth Floor Museum and
Southern Methodist University Press

Requests for permission to reproduce material from this work
should be sent to:
    Rights and Permissions
    The Sixth Floor Museum
    411 Elm Street, Suite 120
    Dallas, Texas 75202-3301
    214-653-6659

Design by Tom Dawson Graphic Design, Dallas, Texas
Printed by Authentic Press, Arlington, Texas
Zapruder Film: © 1967 (Renewed 1995) LMH Co. c/o James Lorin Silverberg, Esq.
    Washington, DC 202-332-7978. All Rights Reserved.

Library of Congress Cataloging-in-Publication Data

Hunt-Jones, Conover.
    JFK for a new generation / Conover Hunt.
       p. cm.
    Includes bibliographical references and index.
    ISBN 0-87074-415-1 (cloth) — ISBN 0-87074-395-3 (paper)
    1. Kennedy, John F. (John Fitzgerald), 1917–1963—
Assassination.   2. United States—Politics and
government—1961–1963.   I. Title.
E842.9.H835   1996
973.922—dc20   96-14750

Printed in the United States of America on acid-free paper

10 9 8 7 6 5 4 3 2 1

COVER:
John F. Kennedy, captured during a pensive moment in the
Oval Office. *George Tames, courtesy George Tames/THE NEW YORK TIMES*

FRONTISPIECE:
The Kennedys shown after mass on Sunday. Americans avidly followed
the activities of the youthful presidential family. *UPI/Corbis-Bettmann*

CONTENTS

TO THE FOLLOWING SPECIAL MEMBERS
OF THE NEW GENERATION:

Sam and True Claycombe
Julia Collins
Desirée Dieste
Virginia Fain
Walt Fields
Paige Furr and Elizabeth Vint
Bill and Steven Hunt
Kelly and Lindsay Lawson
Erynn Montgomery
Charlie Powell
Chase and Corley Sadacca
Will Seale

ACKNOWLEDGMENTS

"Where there is sorrow there is holy ground," wrote Oscar Wilde in 1905. There is sorrow attached to the legacy of John Fitzgerald Kennedy. Those who do not remember 1963 sense the sadness in others; they also know that Kennedy has become a legend in the popular mind. He is holy ground. This book deals with that sorrow, and it treads on holy ground.

Dozens of people have helped with this project. For most of them the memory of JFK remains quite painful, making their contributions even more remarkable. Thank you all. The idea for an interim history of JFK took shape during the 1980's. Since its inception, *JFK for a New Generation* has been nurtured by the leadership of The Sixth Floor Museum. I wish to thank the present and former members of the board of directors of the Dallas County Historical Foundation, parent organization of the museum, for their vision, their tenacity, and their wisdom. Special thanks are due to organization founder Lindalyn B. Adams, to former president Walter S. Blake, to President William A. McKenzie, and to former board member Dr. Glenn Linden, the professional historian who oversaw the preparation of the original manuscript. Former Director Bob Hays took the prospectus to the board; Executive Director Jeff West drove the project to completion. I thank them for their sensitivity, their professionalism, and their energetic support. Archivist Gary Mack was relentlessly precise and invariably supportive; I am deeply in his debt. Museum staff members Janice Babineaux, Larissa Church, Stacy Conaway, Sue Hilty, Dr. Marian Ann Montgomery, Bob Porter, Cheryl Price, and Karen Wiley worked diligently to make the project a reality.

Many friends provided support and advice during the preparation of the manuscript. I particularly wish to thank Nancy and Bill Ackley, Tony Bass, Barbara Charles, Bruce Claycombe, Lois and Rick Cobleigh, John Crain, Mary Ellen Degnan, Joe DePetris, Martha and Tony Dieste, Bill and Kathy Erwin, Margaret Hackney, and Bill Howze. Lisa Alfieri, Stevelynne Brown, Kathie Frantom, Sheryl Nelon, and the other fine people at Spectrum Real Estate Services were uniformly helpful, as were Lytt Mahone, Allen and Cynthia Mondell, Keats Mullikin, Meg Read, the late Sylvia Richardson, Sharron Sadacca, Frederick Schmid, Maryln Schwartz, Bob Staples, and the regulars at Bob Allen's place. Ron Schulz deserves a medal. Carolina Pace provided sage professional insights and warm personal support at every stage of the project.

I am grateful to the following professional colleagues who took the time to review and correct the manuscript or provided suggestions for its improvement: Matthew Abbate,

Professor G. Robert Blakey, Dr. Paul Boller, Mary Ferrell, Dr. Paul Geisel, Dr. James Pennebaker, Marjory Philp, Dr. Robert Remini, Hilary Scott, and Lonn Taylor. The owners of photographs and the staffs of public archives used in this publication were uniformly generous in sharing their resources. Keith Gregory, Freddie Jane Goff, and Bradley Hundley from the SMU Press also provided keen insights and valuable support.

The majority of the research for this book took place between 1978 and 1994. Chuck Briggs, Amy Porter, Adah Leah Wolf, Cosy McLemore, and Carl Henry were most helpful during the years between 1987 and 1989. Cynthia Nichols assisted in research during 1993. Dallas historian Jackie McElhaney cheerfully combed libraries for more than six years, gathering materials that would throw light on the legacy of JFK and the evolution of Dealey Plaza and its environs. I am grateful to Ed Bearss, Jim Charleton, John E. Cook, Neil Mangum, and Richard Sellars, all of the National Park Service, to Jim Steeley of the Texas Historical Commission, to Trudy O'Reilly and Jim Anderson of the City of Dallas Landmarks Commission, and to Phil Huey (retired) and Ralph Mendez of the Dallas Park Department, for assisting in research on the assassination site.

Jane Grant was always there to sort things out when I needed her. Virginia Fain, my assistant since 1990, tracked the endless details of the project, ordered the photographs, and provided sage insights into the informational needs of those who do not remember JFK. Thank you, Virginia. My editors, Dr. Mike Hazel, D. Teddy Diggs, and SMU Press's Kathryn Lang, as well as indexer Paul Spragens, all made significant contributions to the final book. Finally, I owe a tremendous debt to Chip Johnson, who has provided elegant office space, efficient clerical services, and generous personal support to me since 1989.

John Kennedy's history remains clouded by controversy; on the matter of his assassination in particular, there is bitter debate. Most of the research for *JFK for a New Generation* relied on materials published before 1995; many publications that have appeared in print since that date were not consulted in the preparation of this book. I accept responsibility for any errors of fact and will gladly correct them. Some will disagree with my interpretation of JFK's legacy; it is their right to do so. This book is a history distorted by the emotionalism of firsthand memory; it is designed to lay a foundation of understanding for a new generation of Americans who will interpret JFK and his legacy dispassionately and according to their own unique vision.

Conover Hunt
Caddo Lake, January 1996

FOREWORD

The death of John Kennedy seared the nation's soul and will live forever in our history, a moment of violence that in the strange way of such events wrought a transcending strength and grace. The first two chapters of this book provide a clear and compelling account of those hours in Dallas and the School Book Depository. Understanding this timeless drama begins with the people, the place and the day, so well focused and recorded here.

During those first jubilant hours in Dallas on the campaign trail with John and Jacqueline Kennedy we reporters concerned ourselves with the little things of politics and people. Were Texas Governor John Connally and Senator Ralph Yarborough still feuding? Yep, with frosty glances. How come red roses for Jackie at the ramp instead of Texas's legendary yellow roses? Goof, couldn't find any at the moment.

I'd seen JFK work the fence, but witnessing Jackie on such a political assignment was a rarity. I followed her for novelty. She didn't much like the fence duty and it was plain. She inched along as if to lessen the contact. My mind wandered. Let's see, was her suit a shocking pink or a mulberry color? Both, actually, so I called it pink mulberry. Smile frozen most of the time, but now and then thawing in front of a child, even to a light laugh, but she did not let anyone get a firm grip on her gloved hand.

I made notes of sunshine and cheers and not a hint of a major disruption, physical or otherwise, within my sight or earshot. There was the rush for the motorcade limousines, Jackie looking relieved and handing the roses off to the guards.

People were sometimes ten deep along the curbs, delighted to give a little of the lunch hour to such glamorous visitors. Jackie sneaked a quick look at the Neiman-Marcus store facade. An acquisitor knows a quality marketplace. The caravan crept on, turned a corner, turned another, and Kennedy's limousine slid down the bright street toward an underpass as our press bus grunted and jerked forward.

Three reports. Like shots, I supposed, though I had no idea what shots fired in the middle of a joyous city should sound like. Not shots, I guessed. Couldn't be. Presidents don't get assassinated in the United States these days, at least not in glorious sunshine. Must be backfires or construction noises. Yet, they were loud bangs straight ahead and up above. I settled back into my motorcade slump for a split second, trying to rewind and set my mind on idle again. Then I bolted upright. My eyes crossed the troubled glances of other reporters. Something was dreadfully wrong on the low slopes of Dealey Plaza.

Two, three seconds. No more. The pigeons flapped and swooped obscenely. Motorcade cops went mad, leaping curbs, gunning their engines, spewing clouds of blue-gray exhaust into the air. At the corner finally I saw the first section of the motorcade fade over a small hill. It was like a snake chopped in two, both parts seething and writhing. I saw people on the grassy knoll pressed to the ground as if some gigantic wind had toppled them all at once. A young man with an arm cradling his small son was pounding the earth with the other in anger and horror.

Then came the surreal ritual of confirmation of death at Parkland Memorial Hospital. Stunned security men washed the blood and brains off the limousine seats. The red roses lay there—broken and crushed. The security men came out later, still walking like robots. The words they later denied saying tumbled out as if they were programmed. "He's dead all right." That was the flash. Death in the Dallas afternoon. A man and a friend killed, a president murdered, the end of the New Frontier, an era brought to a sordid close. I watched Deputy Press Secretary Malcolm Kilduff make the official announcement of Kennedy's death reading from a scrap of paper that fluttered like a leaf in the wind in his hand, and then fell on his desk when he had finished and he stared at it in horror. I stood with him a few seconds, alone and walled off from the deadline turmoil in the next room. Words started, then failed, then started, then failed, then came. "Oh, what they did to that man. You cannot believe."

But we had to—and we did, though no one on that afternoon could get his mind around it all. I watched the frantic movements of police and Secret Service guards, the comings and goings of the White House aides. Some too mute to talk, too destroyed to nod. The great, youthful adventure of John Kennedy was closed. Suddenly we were all old. I scribbled notes which today are incomprehensible. Then with two friends I walked aimlessly through the hospital, not knowing why or where I was going.

Unexpectedly we were at the hospital loading dock. Kennedy's body was being wheeled down the ramp toward a hearse. Aides walked beside the casket. Jackie rested her hand on it as if holding desperately to some final wisp of meaning on this shattered afternoon. Her suit was splotched with dark stains. Oh, God, now what color was it, soiled with a president's blood? She walked with her chin up and her face streaked with dried tears, eyes on some distant horizon. Somehow I knew that most of the world was watching and caring and feeling and that none of us would ever forget.

Hugh Sidey
May 1996

INTRODUCTION

This book was written primarily for Americans born after 1960, the *new* generation that does not remember John F. Kennedy. The strong mythology of JFK and the enduring controversy surrounding his death have made *not* remembering a dilemma for this growing audience, which is removed from any firsthand knowledge of the man and his era.

The memory of Kennedy remains a powerful force in American society. Hundreds of books and articles have been written about his life, hundreds more about his death. Television regularly produces documentaries and docudramas about him.

American leaders since his death have been compared to him, often with poor results. Dan Quayle is unlikely to forget Lloyd Bentsen's admonition during the vice presidential debate in 1988: "Senator, you're no Jack Kennedy." The Kennedy family, its next generation now grown, continues to interest Americans who recall the 1960's, or at least members of the media who focus attention on it. What *is* the basis for this strange attachment?

Those who remember John F. Kennedy tend to speak of him kindly today, but many will admit that they did not support his politics while he lived, a fascinating time of music, revolution, violence, promise, and change. Is Kennedy really a part of the Sixties, or did the decade take shape after his death? Woodstock seems light-years away from Camelot.

Rememberers still claim peculiar ownership rights to JFK. Ask people who were over the age of five or six in 1963, and they can probably tell you where they were and what they were doing when they heard the awful news that Kennedy had been shot and killed in Dallas, Texas. Even after all these years, people still *remember vividly*. Some talk about it; others do not. Strong emotions linger in the memory.

What does Kennedy's legacy mean to *you*? Wasn't he just another politician? You know the visual and audio symbols of the time: JFK with crowds; JFK alone on the beach at Hyannis Port; scenes with a smiling Jackie; the Kennedy children romping in the Oval Office; Kennedy walking with his brother Robert during the Cuban missile crisis; endless repeats of the inaugural address, "Ask not what your country can do for you . . ."

And then there is the final weekend: bits from Abraham Zapruder's famous film, which recorded the shooting in Dealey Plaza; the photograph of LBJ being sworn in aboard *Air Force One*, with a stricken Jackie Kennedy standing at his side. You've heard the sound of muffled drums along the route to the Capitol and observed the skittishness of that riderless horse, symbol of a fallen leader. You've seen Caroline kneel at the funeral bier, and you're familiar with the image of young John Kennedy, Jr., saluting his father after the funeral mass.

We have all watched reruns of the Kennedy state funeral, and I still wince when I hear the bugler blow the high note in "Taps." Perhaps you've visited JFK's grave site overlooking the Lincoln Memorial at Arlington National Cemetery and seen the eternal flame that Jacqueline Kennedy lit there. She's dead now, buried beside her husband on the same hill. We rememberers still tend to speak of her as young and beautiful. Why?

Knowing *about* JFK is one thing; understanding him is another. Historians, journalists, and political scientists have written about Kennedy's life and career, but these books rarely focus on the details of his death. There is broad disagreement about his accomplishments and even his character. Was he a good president? The record was so short, only 1,037 days in office. Much of the recent literature is extremely specialized—JFK and Vietnam, JFK and the missile crisis, JFK and the Peace Corps, JFK as a family man, JFK the philanderer. Where is the *big* picture of the whole man and his era?

The assassination remains in its own category, discussed more by journalists and specialized researchers than by historians. Arthur Schlesinger's Pulitzer Prize–winning biography of Kennedy, *A Thousand Days*, did not even mention the accused murderer, Lee Harvey Oswald, by name.[1] Why have historians stayed away from studies of JFK's death? Are the journalists and assassination researchers qualified to be the official voices for this important event?

The new generation's knowledge and understanding of JFK was obtained after he died, when his career, life, and death had fallen into separate categories. Perhaps you have read conspiracy books—pro or con—on the subject of the assassination and seen documentaries on TV that profess to answer at least some of the questions that linger about JFK's tragic death. Like the historical books on Kennedy himself, the assassination literature has created a jigsaw puzzle of specialized information. Those of us who remember JFK in all of his facets have left it to the new generation to compile a portrait from segmented, even contradictory, pieces.

How is it that the most powerful nation on earth has been unable to explain the assassination to the satisfaction of the majority of its own people? What *did* happen in Dealey Plaza? Did the government plan the crime and then cover it up after the fact? And if so, *why*? Who *was* Lee Harvey Oswald? Was he just a patsy, as he said, or was he, as the government has asserted, a disgruntled left-wing loner who committed the crime of the century all by himself?

For the new generation, John F. Kennedy, alive and dead, is history, as distant as the Greeks, Abraham Lincoln, or World War II. This is a book *about* history, but it is not *the* history of JFK's legacy, because history is reinterpreted by every generation that studies it. Also, history is biased by memory, and objectivity is what historiography seeks in analyzing the past.

For the people who recall 1963, Kennedy is a personal and a collective memory. This book seeks to shed light on that memory. Few people alive and aware of their surroundings will dispute the fact that the assassination of President Kennedy remains a subject of bitter controversy. This book tries to explain how the controversy was born and to suggest why it survives. Most of all, this book is about change; for history, memory, and the nature of the controversy about Kennedy's death have all changed significantly since 1963.

Your generation will write its own histories of John F. Kennedy, histories that are free from the emotionalism of firsthand memory. Ownership will someday pass to you. I invite you to use this book as an introduction written by a rememberer.

I was fourteen years old when Kennedy won the 1960 election, seventeen and a senior in high school when he died. I was born less than a year after the death of President Franklin Roosevelt and about six months after the end of World War II. Statisticians consider me one of the first baby boomers, that group of Americans who were born between 1946 and 1960.[2] There were more than eight hundred students in my senior class at Hampton High School in Virginia.

When I was growing up, my parents and my teachers seemed to forget that I was not old enough to remember Roosevelt and World War II. I never took a secondary-school history course that continued past World War I; in fact, most of my knowledge of the World War II era has come from PBS documentaries, books, movies, and the recollections of others. My mental picture of that time remains piecemeal, like a jigsaw puzzle without the picture on the box.

At the time that JFK ran for election in 1960, Americans had to be at least twenty-one years old to vote. I watched the Nixon-Kennedy debates on television, viewed footage of the inauguration on that freezing day in January 1961, and was inspired by the new president's challenge for me to get involved with America. I read all the magazine articles in *Life*, *Look*, and the *Saturday Evening Post* that described the Kennedy family, their activities, their sense of style, and their love of fun.

Being a woman, I paid attention to Jacqueline Kennedy's fashions, hair, and mannerisms. I was scared to death during the endless days of the Cuban missile crisis. I grew up believing that communism was evil and that the Soviet Union might blow us all away with nuclear weapons.

I remember exactly where I was and what I was doing when I heard the news that Kennedy had been shot.

The rest of the weekend remains blurred, with my memory lit by visual images and solemn pronouncements, almost all of which have been repeated again and again during the past three decades. Like 96% of the rest of the country, I spent the weekend watching television as the drama unfolded.[3] The memory runs in black-and-white; the magazines offered color pictures in those days, but color television was not yet the norm in most American homes.

I was satisfied with the Warren Commission *Report* when it was released in 1964 but felt growing dismay during the years that followed as more and more discrepancies about the investigation were brought to light. I was a student at Newcomb College at Tulane University in New Orleans in 1969 when District Attorney Jim Garrison conducted the Clay Shaw conspiracy trial there. At the time I thought the district attorney was more style than substance.

The case did not interest me much; I was more concerned that my male contemporaries were being sent to Vietnam by the thousands. Some avoided the draft by getting married and having children, a few hid in Canada, and others joined the Peace Corps. Many of us thought something was wrong with that war.

In 1969 few argued that women should be allowed to fight in combat. After graduate school, I became a public historian specializing in museums, worked in Richmond, Virginia, for a few years, and then moved to Washington, D.C. I walked the short distance from the DAR (Daughters of the American Revolution) Museum to the White House in August 1974, to stand at the gates there on the day that President Richard M. Nixon announced his resignation. Watergate has helped to shape your attitude toward the office of the presidency. You may not remember when people held it in respect.

During the mid-1970's, Jacqueline Kennedy Onassis started her editing career at Viking Press in New York City. She talked her publisher into taking on a book about the role of women during the American Revolution. Titled *Remember the Ladies: Women in America, 1750–1815*, it was one of her first editing projects, and it was the first book I wrote, with academic historian Linda Grant DePauw as coauthor.[4]

After I moved to Dallas during the late 1970's, I received a call from a colleague, asking if I would advise Dallas County about an appropriate use for the sixth floor of the old Texas School Book Depository, a decayed warehouse in the downtown county government complex. It was from that site that Lee Harvey Oswald had allegedly fired the shots that killed President Kennedy and wounded Texas Governor John B. Connally fifteen years before. I was repulsed by the memory of 1963, but I agreed to meet with county officials.

Between 1978 and 1989, I worked with a group of talented museum professionals, academics, and preservationists to assist Dallas County and some courageous community leaders in creating a historical museum dealing with the life, times, death, and legacy of John F. Kennedy. After The Sixth Floor Museum opened to positive reviews in

1989, I continued as a consultant to the museum for an additional six years. I prepared the draft application to designate the assassination site as a National Historic Landmark. Former Texas First Lady Nellie Connally dedicated the bronze plaque in a ceremony at Dealey Plaza on November 22, 1993.

During the seventeen years that I was involved with the museum, I spoke with hundreds of the thousands of people who wandered around Dealey Plaza every year. I realized that the rememberers had unresolved emotional feelings about John F. Kennedy while the new generation was genuinely confused about his legacy. My authority to speak on the topic of JFK and his legacy comes from my involvement with the Dallas project.

What do I believe about JFK and his legacy? I believe that his life and his death had a profound influence on my generation and a significant effect on people everywhere at the time. The biggest impact was on the people who were between the ages of twelve and twenty-five in 1963.[5] I also believe that this age group, because it contains many of your parents, exerts a strong influence on your generation. I believe that valid historical analysis of Kennedy's life and his tragic death awaits the full declassification of all pertinent documents. Finally, I believe that better histories will be written by nonrememberers who are freed from the emotionalism of having "known" the man and having experienced the trauma of his death.

This book is not intended to sway you to a particular point of view, nor does it go into great depth about John F. Kennedy's life and legacy. This is not academic history but a historic introduction to a complicated subject. This book is a basic guide, written with the conviction that the members of the new generation have the common sense to make up their own minds about important issues, historic or contemporary, and that some will want to read a few of the many books and articles that I have used in compiling this narrative summary. What *you* make of John Fitzgerald Kennedy, his era, and his legacy is *your* decision. Because you are freed from the stricture of memory, your search can be truly historic. I wish you luck.

CHAPTER 1

Being There: November 22, 1963

People everywhere visit historic sites in an attempt to experience history firsthand. These sites, when accurately preserved or restored, provide a physical context for past events; they are valid, palpable, and *real.* Dealey Plaza is such a site, largely unchanged in appearance since 1963. So please come with me on a journey back in time and to another place. The date is November 22, 1963, the Friday before Thanksgiving. The place is Dallas, Texas.

When you wake up around 7:30 A.M. (CST) it is raining.[1] Will they cancel the parade for President Kennedy? You hope not because you plan to try to catch a glimpse of JFK and his wife during their three-hour visit to the city. Dallas is not Washington or New York; a visit from the president is a special occasion. And this trip will include other notable dignitaries—Vice President Lyndon B. Johnson and his wife, Lady Bird, Texas Governor John B. Connally and his wife, Nellie, members of the Texas congressional delegation, and other leading lights.

The two local papers, *The Dallas Morning News* and the *Dallas Times Herald,* and the local radio and television stations have reports on plans for the visit: the arrival time at Dallas's Love Field airport, the motorcade route from the airport along Main Street downtown, the arrangements for the invitation-only luncheon for twenty-six hundred community leaders at the cavernous Dallas Trade Mart on Stemmons Freeway. Children with parental permission will be allowed out of school to watch the parade.

The news is full of stories about the reasons for JFK's visit to the Lone Star State: he is staking a claim on Texas for his 1964 reelection bid and trying to shore up a split between liberals and conservatives within the state Democratic party. Kennedy carried Texas in the 1960 election by a narrow margin. Liberal U.S. Senator Ralph Yarborough is barely speaking to LBJ. These Democratic squabbles are of less interest to you and most other Dallasites, who in 1960 handed Kennedy his worst defeat in any major American city.[2]

Your radio plays in the background. Local stations have pooled resources for live broadcasts from Love Field. It is a part of the saturation coverage planned for the visit.[3] Joe Long of station KLIF comes on the air:

> Radio: *A big city has been told to be on its good behavior today,* booms the voice of the announcer, *and we're it!*[4]

The president's trip includes all the major Texas cities in a brief two days: San Antonio and Houston on Thursday, with a late arrival in Fort Worth that night; Fort Worth and Dallas on Friday, ending up that evening with a big fundraising dinner in the capitol at Austin. The Kennedys will relax overnight at the Johnsons' ranch before they return to Washington on Saturday.

For your part, politics is probably less important than having a chance to see a charismatic president and his beautiful, stylish wife. The papers and magazines have been full of the Kennedys and their activities since 1960. You know that JFK has a bad back and that he was a hero in World War II. Poor Mrs. Kennedy has been out of the spotlight for a while during her last pregnancy, which ended with the tragic loss of the couple's infant son Patrick only three months before.

> Radio: *Right now, the eyes of Texas and the nation are focused on Dallas . . . and this is the heart of a real political tempest!*

Perusing *The Dallas Morning News,* the conservative morning paper, you note that the editorial extends a cautious welcome to the president from Massachusetts. We may not like your policies, it says, but we're glad to have you visit the city. Some of the previous editorials in the *News* have been less kind, calling the American Civil Liberties Union the "American Swivel Liberties Union" and referring to the Supreme Court as the "Judicial Kremlin."[5] Publisher Ted Dealey raised some eyebrows when, during a visit to the White House in 1961, he accused Kennedy of being a "weak sister."[6]

The morning edition of the *News* contains a full-page ad bearing the title "Welcome Mr. Kennedy" (Figure 1.1). Beneath the innocent headline is a list of grievances accusing the Democratic leader of being too soft on communism. The ad makes you ill at ease; it does not seem appropriate.

The name of the sponsor for the ad is listed as the "American Fact-Finding Committee." You assume it is another bizarre little group representative of the vocal right-wing fringe in the city. The John Birch Society, the Edwin Walker group, and the Indignant White Citizens' Council, to name a few, have been causing trouble for some time in Dallas without anyone taking strong action against their extremist views.[7]

> Radio: *Dallas Police Chief Jesse Curry has told the citizens and visitors that nothing must occur that will be disrespectful or degrading to the president.*

All big cities have their problems, you reason, and Dallas in 1963 is no exception. An affluent northern Texas metropolis with more than 600,000 citizens, the city is set amid a sprawling area populated by 1.5 million people. The radio announces the names of the official presidential welcoming committee. Many of them are elected officials, but they also represent some of the cream of the city's business community.

Dallas is the consummate corporate city. The economy is healthy; the average Dallasite makes a bit more than

WELCOME MR. KENNEDY

TO DALLAS...

...A CITY so disgraced by a recent Liberal smear attempt that its citizens have just elected two more Conservative Americans to public office.

...A CITY that is an economic "boom town," not because of Federal handouts, but through conservative economic and business practices.

...A CITY that will continue to grow and prosper despite efforts by you and your administration to penalize it for its non-conformity to "New Frontierism."

...A CITY that rejected your philosophy and policies in 1960 and will do so again in 1964—even more emphatically than before.

MR. KENNEDY, despite contentions on the part of your administration, the State Department, the Mayor of Dallas, the Dallas City Council, and members of your party, we free-thinking and America-thinking citizens of Dallas still have, through a Constitution largely ignored by you, the right to address our grievances, to question you, to disagree with you, and to criticize you.

In asserting this constitutional right, we wish to ask you publicly the following questions—indeed, questions of paramount importance and interest to all free peoples everywhere—which we trust you will answer . . . in public, without sophistry. These questions are:

WHY is Latin America turning either anti-American or Communistic, or both, despite increased U. S. foreign aid, State Department policy, and your own Ivy-Tower pronouncements?

WHY do you say we have built a "wall of freedom" around Cuba when there is no freedom in Cuba today? Because of your policy, thousands of Cubans have been imprisoned, are starving and being persecuted—with thousands already murdered and thousands more awaiting execution and, in addition, the entire population of almost 7,000,000 Cubans are living in slavery.

WHY have you approved the sale of wheat and corn to our enemies when you know the Communist soldiers "travel on their stomachs" just as ours do? Communist soldiers are daily wounding and or killing American soldiers in South Viet Nam.

WHY did you host, salute and entertain Tito — Moscow's Trojan Horse — just a short time after our sworn enemy, Khrushchev, embraced the Yugoslav dictator as a great hero and leader of Communism?

WHY have you urged greater aid, comfort, recognition, and understanding for Yugoslavia, Poland, Hungary, and other Communist countries, while turning your back on the pleas of Hungarian, East German, Cuban and other anti-Communist freedom fighters?

WHY did Cambodia kick the U.S. out of its country after we poured nearly 400 Million Dollars of aid into its ultra-leftist government?

WHY has Gus Hall, head of the U.S. Communist Party praised almost every one of your policies and announced that the party will endorse and support your re-election in 1964?

WHY have you banned the showing at U.S. military bases of the film "Operation Abolition"—the movie by the House Committee on Un-American Activities exposing Communism in America?

WHY have you ordered or permitted your brother Bobby, the Attorney General, to go soft on Communists, fellow-travelers, and ultra-leftists in America, while permitting him to persecute loyal Americans who criticize you, your administration, and your leadership?

WHY are you in favor of the U.S. continuing to give economic aid to Argentina, in spite of that fact that Argentina has just seized almost 400 Million Dollars of American private property?

WHY has the Foreign Policy of the United States degenerated to the point that the C.I.A. is arranging coups and having staunch Anti-Communist Allies of the U.S. bloodily exterminated.

WHY have you scrapped the Monroe Doctrine in favor of the "Spirit of Moscow"?

MR. KENNEDY, as citizens of these United States of America, we DEMAND answers to these questions, and we want them NOW.

THE AMERICAN FACT-FINDING COMMITTEE

"An unaffiliated and non-partisan group of citizens who wish truth"

BERNARD WEISSMAN,
Chairman

P.O. Box 1792 — Dallas 21, Texas

FIGURE 1.1
Advertisement that appeared in *The Dallas Morning News* on the morning of November 22, 1963, criticizing President Kennedy's policies. *Sixth Floor Museum Archives*

$6,000 a year, a respectable sum in 1963.[8] Dallas leaders believe in running the city like a business, and successful corporate executives are recruited to volunteer their time as elected officials. A group of men known as the Citizens' Charter Association exerts a strong influence on city government.[9]

The association was organized during the early 1930's to provide leadership for the town; it still proposes the candidates for city council and gets many of them elected. Another group, the Citizens' Council, was established during the mid-1930's to lend support to important civic projects. During the 1950's the Citizens' Council decided to integrate Dallas. Because of a concerted effort by both blacks and whites, the city was spared most of the unrest experienced during the era in cities such as Birmingham and Selma, Alabama.[10]

FIGURE 1.2

United Nations Ambassador Adlai Stevenson visited Dallas on October 24, 1963. After the ambassador was hit on the head with a placard during an appearance there, the city was criticized for allowing such actions by conservative radicals. *Courtesy, AP/Wide World Photos*

Radio reporter Joe Long states that there are nearly two thousand people waiting for the president at Love Field, many of them with signs. Most of the placards are supportive, but the announcer spots one large banner, made by a local student, saying "Help JFK Stamp Out Democracy."

Conservative Dallas voted heavily for Republican candidate Richard M. Nixon in the 1960 presidential election, despite the fact that Democratic vice presidential candidate Lyndon Johnson was a native Texan.[11] Now the town is showing strong signs of support for Republican Senator Barry Goldwater's campaign for the presidency in 1964. The ultraconservative groups that have sprung up in the city are few in number, but they are outspoken.

Admittedly, few of the radical right wing are leaders in Dallas, but the Citizens' Council has tended to ignore their reckless attacks against people they don't like, their hatred of the United Nations (UN), their condemnation of the federal government, their opposition to civil rights, and their absolutism. To these activists, anyone who is different from them is often labeled a communist.[12] Some well-to-do local women have become involved as volunteers with these organizations.[13]

> Radio: *Hundreds of additional police are on hand . . . it looks like a police convention. We have never seen as many Dallas police officers in one location.*

There have been some unpleasant incidents with visiting VIP's. Vice presidential candidate Lyndon Johnson and his wife came to Dallas early in November 1960, shortly before the presidential election. Their trip happened to coincide with Republican "tag day" in the city, when many Dallas women donned patriotic colors to distribute buttons and folders for their candidate, Richard Nixon.

The Johnsons were staying at the Baker Hotel downtown and experienced an ugly scene in the lobby there. The tag-day women, waving "Lyndon Go Home" signs, were joined by a group from a local "beer saloon"; the motives of this second group were less clear. While LBJ and Mrs. Johnson were walking across the street to a luncheon at the nearby Adolphus Hotel, conservative Republican Congressman Bruce Alger showed up, and the scene went from bad to worse. Mr. and Mrs. Johnson were spit on and

jostled by the crowd in what LBJ later described as "a mob scene that looked like some other country."[14]

But it was the recent Stevenson incident that caused most of the worry about security for President Kennedy's visit. On October 24, 1963, United Nations Ambassador Adlai Stevenson came to Dallas to give a speech commemorating the UN on its anniversary. Anti-UN forces, led by retired U.S. Army General Edwin Walker, staged a "United States Day" observance the day before Stevenson's speech. About twelve hundred people showed up at Walker's rally.[15]

Walker had gained national notoriety several years before when he was asked to resign his commission by President Kennedy for distributing right-wing literature to his troops. He went on to organize several demonstrations against communism and civil rights; Dallas became his base of operations.[16]

The city sent in additional police to protect the ambassador, but hecklers tried to disrupt his remarks, and dozens of picketers lay in wait outside the lecture hall. As Stevenson tried to reach his car, an irate woman hit him on the head with a placard; outside, a college student spit on him (Figure 1.2). The incident made the national news, and embarrassed city leaders quickly took action.

Few citizens ignored a concerted effort by the city fathers. During the month before President Kennedy's visit, cordiality became the order of the day. Dallas Mayor Earle Cabell fired the first salvo by denouncing the protestors as "radicals."[17] A few days after the Stevenson affair, the Dallas City Council adopted an antiharassment ordinance making it illegal to disrupt public or private assembly with "insulting, threatening or obscene language or intimidation."[18]

The Citizens' Council quickly offered to host a bipartisan luncheon for Kennedy. The two daily Dallas newspapers urged citizens to respect the president during his visit, and local clergy cautioned against incidents that might mar the political trip to Dallas.[19] The blitz was so intense that one newspaper ran an editorial cartoon in which a partially dressed Dallas citizen asked his wife, "Is my good behavior back from the cleaners yet?"[20]

You hope that nothing will disturb the president's trip. The locals have no real concern about Kennedy's safety, of course; Dallas is prepared for the visit with 365 police, 45 representatives from the Department of Public Safety, and 15 sheriff's deputies stationed along the motorcade route and at the Trade Mart.[21] They not only will protect the chief of state but also will prevent any demonstrations that might embarrass the president and the city.[22] The black-bordered ad in *The Dallas Morning News* was just such an embarrassment.

By 9:30 A.M. in Dallas, the rain has cleared off. The sun heralds a perfect Dallas Indian-summer day. You will be able to leave your raincoat at home.

> Radio: *And here comes Air Force number One, now touching down.*

The time is about 11:40 A.M.[23] The short hop by plane from Fort Worth, only thirty miles west of Dallas, must have taken only minutes. The announcer remarks on the tight security at the Trade Mart.

The highlight of the visit to Dallas will be President Kennedy's speech at the four-year-old Dallas Trade Mart. Tickets to that event have sold rapidly. It has been a problem to secure the building because of its open central atrium and its 450 showrooms.[24]

FIGURE 1.3
Aerial view of Dealey Plaza showing streets, landscape features,
and surrounding buildings as they appeared on November 23, 1963.
Squire Haskins, courtesy Squire Haskins Photography, Inc.

The mart's collection of forty free-flying parakeets, finches, and cockatiels will remain aloft; the head table has been located away from the area where they might be likely to "anoint" the chief of state. But organizers have admitted that a security advance man was "christened" during preparations for the visit.[25]

Radio: *And the crowd begins its cheer . . . and hundreds of tiny American flags are being waved toward the presidential jet.*

Parking may be a problem near the motorcade route, so you take a small transistor radio for the trip downtown. You may need it to find a good viewing spot. The car radio will provide updates on the progress of the parade and help you avoid traffic jams along the way.

Radio: *Every possible precaution has been taken . . . and here comes Mrs. Kennedy!*

Main Street is the center of the downtown business area, so you anticipate that crowds will be heaviest there. The car radio repeats the motorcade route:

Radio: *. . . west on Main to Houston, through the triple underpass to Stemmons Freeway, then on to the Trade Mart.*

You decide to go to the western end of the motorcade route, to the county complex at Dealey Plaza. Press reports indicate that the luncheon at the Trade Mart is due to begin at 12:30 P.M., so the motorcade should pass through the park about five to seven minutes earlier. The motorcade will have to get on Stemmons Freeway to reach the Trade Mart by the fastest route, which means that it will use the ramp at the end of Elm Street on the north side of the park. The ramp is located just west of Dealey Plaza.

Radio: *And here comes the president now. In fact he's not in his limousine; he's departed the limousine and he's walking . . . reaching across the fence and shaking hands.*

This is a change in the schedule. The announcer states that banners are being waved wildly, those supporting the president and those opposed to his policies. The motorcade will probably run late (see image opposite page one).

Radio: *He is seeing Dallas County politics at the height of a very boiling moment . . . this was one of those impromptu moments for which President Kennedy is so well known.*

The greeting at Love Field is positive, and at 11:50 A.M., you hear:

Radio: *The trip to downtown Dallas and the Trade Mart is under way.*

DEALEY PLAZA

Downtown, you find a space in a parking lot just south of Dealey Plaza. You walk over to Houston Street, which runs north-south, and head north toward the park (Figure 1.3). The parade will be almost over by the time it reaches this part of downtown, so it should be easy to find a good viewing spot.[26]

Dealey Plaza is not a huge park, about three acres, and was constructed in 1934–40 from several blocks that made up part of city founder John Neely Bryan's original town, which was laid out during the early 1840's.[27] The city acquired the old townsite during the 1930's to build a major new gateway from the west and to free up traffic along the railroad tracks that ran north-south along the western edge of the town. The construction of the park, substantially completed between 1934 and 1935, was hailed as an engineering marvel at the time (Figure 1.4).[28]

As you enter the park you notice that the plaza, although roughly rectangular in shape, is dominated by a large central triangle of streets with its wide base on the right along Houston Street. The point of the triangle is to your left to the west, where three major downtown streets slope down to converge into three lanes. These three streets—Elm to the north, Main in the center, and Commerce on the south—pass beneath a railroad bridge that connects the rail yards on the north side of the plaza to the railroad station several blocks to the south.[29] The entire structural arrangement—the three streets and the bridge itself—is known locally as the triple underpass (Figure 1.5).

FIGURE 1.4
Dealey Plaza under construction in 1934–35. The park was built over the site of the original town of Dallas, founded during the mid-nineteenth century.
DeGolyer Library, Southern Methodist University, P294.3.192

The names of the streets date back to Bryan's original survey of the town. All but two of the buildings around Dealey Plaza predate construction of the park (Figure 1.6).[30] The interior architectural features in the park were added as embellishments between 1938 and 1940 in the then-fashionable Art Moderne style.[31] The park was named for civic leader George Bannerman Dealey (1859–1946), general manager and later publisher of *The Dallas Morning News*. You walk past his statue, which was placed near Houston Street in 1949.[32] It faces the 1892 Old Red Courthouse, which occupies a block of land donated by Bryan in 1850.

At the north and south perimeters of the park are grassy, sloping gardens, each with a curved concrete pergola, or arcade, at the top of the rise. Broad concrete steps lead to each columned arcade. Landscaped areas beautify the edges of the park north of Elm and south of Commerce; the plantings are separated from adjacent properties by cedar fences about five feet tall.

The motorcade is passing along Main Street downtown (Figure 1.7).

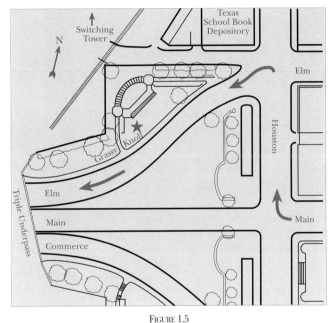

FIGURE 1.5
Map of Dealey Plaza showing the motorcade route and your location.
Map based on design courtesy R. B. Cutler, Cutler Designs

FIGURE 1.7
The presidential motorcade moving along Main Street in downtown Dallas. Crowds were thick and wildly enthusiastic.
William Beal/DALLAS TIMES HERALD Collection, Sixth Floor Museum Archives

FIGURE 1.6
Elevation of Dealey Plaza showing your location. From left: the triple underpass; interlocking railroad tower; grassy knoll; colonnade; Texas School Book Depository; Dal-Tex Building; County Records Building Annex; County Criminal Courts Building. *Stolly ©1988, Dallas County Historical Foundation*

Radio: *Here comes Jackie and Mr. Kennedy . . . they're driving at about five miles an hour.*[33]

You look at the big Hertz Rent-a-Car sign atop the Texas School Book Depository; its digital clock tells you that the time is 12:15 P.M. and the temperature is 65 degrees.[34] From the news reports, you know that the motorcade will enter Dealey Plaza on Main Street and then turn right, or north, for one block on Houston Street. At the corner of Elm and Houston it will make the 120-degree wide left turn onto Elm Street and then follow the sloping and curved road to go through the triple underpass. The ramp entry onto Stemmons is just past the underpass and on the right. A viewing spot along Houston or Elm would be the best place to see the president (see Figure 1.5).

Radio: KRLD's Bob Huffaker is on the air. *And what a crowd . . . this is a friendly crowd in downtown Dallas!*

In a glance you note that, along the right side of Houston Street, there are pedestrians in front of the Old Red Courthouse and the Criminal Courts Building; the latter has many sheriff's deputies standing in front. Similarly, the rest of Houston Street between Main and Elm is lined with people; in fact, the middle of Elm Street at Houston is blocked off by a motorcycle policeman, and crowds are standing in the street.[35]

Employees are pouring out of the Depository building to watch the parade. Houston Street on the Dealey Plaza side has many spectators standing along the curb and near the reflecting pools and colonnades. But to the west of the Depository, along the north side of Elm Street heading toward the triple underpass, the crowds are thinner.[36]

You head toward Elm Street, cross it, and turn left to walk west as the road curves toward the underpass. People have lined the curb all the way to the Stemmons Freeway sign on the grass, about a third of the way down from the corner of Elm and Houston; you keep on going.

Radio: *. . . not a placard in downtown Dallas . . . the crowd's closing in behind the motorcade!*

A stretch of grass that slopes up from the street to the curved concrete pergola on the north side of Elm is uncrowded. You see a middle-aged man and a young woman standing together on a four-foot plinth at the western edge of the two little steps that lead into the columned arcade; he has a movie camera.[37] If you stand in the grass you will be below him, not blocking his view.

The only people between you and the street are a young couple with two little boys who appear to be about two and four years old. They are standing directly at the curb on the sidewalk along Elm Street. Again, because the hill slopes down to the street, you will be above them, so they will not obstruct your view.[38] Satisfied with your position, you turn to face the street.

To your right, about forty feet away, are the garden steps that lead up from Elm into the pergola and rail yards west of the Depository; there are two men standing there.[39] Farther to your right, you see a few policemen and about a dozen men standing on the railroad bridge that covers the underpass (see Figure 1.6).[40]

Across Elm Street, scattered about in the small grassy triangle there, are more spectators. You see a kerchiefed lady holding a camera, and two other young women.[41] One of the women is wearing a bright red raincoat, and the other carries a Polaroid instant-photo camera, a relatively new invention that can produce a photograph in ten seconds.[42]

You turn left to look back at the roof of the Depository; the clock on the Hertz Rent-a-Car sign tells you the time is 12:29 P.M.

Radio: *People . . . are following the motorcade down towards Stemmons Freeway . . . the motorcade is just about to reach the location of the county courthouse.*

THE SHOOTING

Someone shouts, "Here they come!" Before you see anything, you can hear the cheers of the crowd on Main Street and the roar of the approaching lead motorcycle escorts.

Radio: Bob Huffaker is starting to wind up his coverage of the Main Street parade. *And any fears that might have existed in the minds of some about . . . the alleged small handful of people who might have launched severe demonstrations to mar the president's visit, these are apparently unjustified or at least taken care of in good order by the Dallas Police Department.*

The motorcycles make the turn onto Houston Street. You hear cheers, clapping, "Hey, Jack! Hello Jackie! Hi, Mr. President!"

The lead car appears, turning the corner from Main onto Houston. It is driven by Dallas Police Chief Jesse Curry and occupied by Secret Service men and Dallas County Sheriff Bill Decker.[43]

Radio: Huffaker concludes his broadcast. *There was no danger whatsoever and none in evidence of adverse reactions to the president's visit . . . a completely overwhelming welcome for the president!*

Here comes the big blue Lincoln convertible, American flags on the hood flapping in the strong breeze as it starts to turn onto Houston Street. Twin motorcycle escorts flank its rear, and a Secret Service car follows closely behind, agents standing on the running boards. Just as the Lincoln and the follow-up car make the turn onto Houston Street, you get a glimpse of the next vehicle, a convertible carrying the vice president, Mrs. Johnson, and Texas Senator Ralph Yarborough (Figure 1.8). From the news reports, you know that this vehicle is followed by another Secret Service car, the mayor's car, then press cars, automobiles carrying officials, buses, and a final follow-up car.

You focus on the limousine carrying the presidential party. In the front are two Secret Service agents, one of them driving. In the jump seat behind the driver is Nellie Connally, with the tall Texas Governor John Connally to her right. Jacqueline Kennedy sits in the rear seat behind Mrs. Connally. President Kennedy is seated to her right. Your location north of Elm means that you will get an excellent view of the president and Governor Connally.

The officials are waving to the enthusiastic crowd. President Kennedy is tanned; Jackie looks wonderful in a raspberry-pink Chanel suit with navy silk trim.[44] She sports a matching pink pillbox hat and is wearing white kid gloves. A gust of wind unsettles the pillbox; the first lady reaches up to secure it.[45]

The president's car is turning onto Elm (Figure 1.9). The big presidential car slows while making the wide turn and then settles into the center lane and accelerates, heading down toward your position.[46] At this point you notice that the motorcade is laid out like the letter Z, with one horizontal still on Main Street and the other turning onto Elm. The cross bar is moving along Houston Street.

FIGURE 1.8
The presidential limousine, flags waving from the hood, turning from Main Street onto Houston Street in Dealey Plaza. The arrow shows the location of the vice president. ©1964, 1978 Phil Willis. All rights reserved.

FIGURE 1.9
The limousine shown slowing to make the wide turn onto Elm Street. The Dal-Tex building is visible in the background. The time is 12:30 P.M. (CST). James M. Towner, courtesy Tina Towner

7

FIGURE 1.10
Frame 161 from Abraham Zapruder's 8mm film, capturing the presidential car moving down Elm Street after completing the turn. The occupants are shown waving to the crowds. ©1967 (Renewed 1995) LMH Co. All Rights Reserved

FIGURE 1.12
Frame 225 from Zapruder's film. As the limousine emerges from behind the sign, the president reacts to a wound. He clutches his neck. ©1967 (Renewed 1995) LMH Co. All Rights Reserved

"Hey Mr. President, look over here! We want to take your picture," shouts the woman in the bright red raincoat.[47]

You see photographers moving in and notice that a man carrying a little boy has moved near the location of the kerchiefed lady; other people in the crowd run along the curb on the south side of Elm Street, trying to keep up with the motorcade.[48] One little girl skips along in the grass.

Crack!

Abruptly, she stops (Figure 1.10).[49]

What's that? A backfire? A firecracker? Perhaps someone's playing a sick joke; it's not funny.[50]

The president's car has passed behind the Stemmons Freeway sign, temporarily blocking your view of JFK (Figure 1.11).

Another noise! Here he comes now. The president looks puzzled, his hands are moving up toward his neck (Figure 1.12).

Why is the limousine slowing down?

He's leaning toward Mrs. Kennedy. She has turned to look at him (Figure 1.13).

Governor Connally has turned to look at the president. Clapping, yelling, cheering. What was that?

Screams from the car: "Oh no, no, no!"[51] (Figure 1.14).

Mrs. Connally is pulling the governor into her lap.

FIGURE 1.11
Slide taken by military veteran Phil Willis just after he heard a shot ring out in Dealey Plaza. The limousine is about to pass in front of a Stemmons Freeway sign, blocking the view of Abraham Zapruder. Zapruder can be seen in the far background to the right and slightly above the level of the sign. The arrow points to President Kennedy's location. ©1964, 1978 Phil Willis. All rights reserved.

8

FIGURE 1.13
Frame 238, Zapruder film. Mrs. Kennedy, alarmed, is looking at her husband. Now Governor Connally also appears to have been wounded.
©1967 (Renewed 1995) LMH Co. All Rights Reserved

FIGURE 1.14
Frame 274, Zapruder film. Eyewitnesses in Dealey Plaza are aware that both President Kennedy and Governor Connally have been wounded by gunfire.
©1967 (Renewed 1995) LMH Co. All Rights Reserved

FIGURE 1.15
Frame 313, Zapruder film. The effect of another bullet is seen as the president's head explodes. *©1967 (Renewed 1995) LMH Co. All Rights Reserved*

FIGURE 1.16
Polaroid picture of the limousine a fraction of a second after the president is hit in the head.
Mary Moorman took the photograph as the car was passing the grassy knoll. *Mary Moorman, courtesy Mary Moorman Krahmer and AP/Wide World Photos*

FIGURE 1.17
Secret Service Agent Clint Hill racing toward the limousine. He reached it just as the car began to accelerate; Mrs. Kennedy is on the trunk, reaching for a piece of her husband's head. *Orville O. Nix film ©1963 and 1990, courtesy Gayle Nix Jackson*

Gunshots! Someone is shooting at the president!

A Secret Service man is sprinting toward the Lincoln from the follow-up car.

They're directly in front of you.

Don't slow down!

Another shot! President Kennedy's head explodes, throwing his entire body violently backward and to the left (Figures 1.15–1.16).

Oh my God! Pieces of skull, blue-white chunks of matter, blood, and water fly up into the air!

His ear! A large chunk of skull has fallen down over his right ear![52]

The young man in front of you shouts to his wife: "That's it! Hit the ground!"[53] They're falling down on top of those little boys, trying to shield them from the gunfire!

You're also in the open. Got to hide! No trees! No shelter!

Mrs. Kennedy is crawling on the trunk of the open limousine! She's trying to grab something in the air![54]

The Secret Service agent is reaching for the trunk of the car. Hurry! It's starting to accelerate! (Figure 1.17).

He leaps onto the trunk. Mrs. Kennedy slides back down into the seat.

The car speeds away through the triple underpass (Figure 1.18).

FIGURE 1.18
Agent Hill on the trunk as the car speeds toward the triple underpass. *James Altgens, courtesy AP/Wide World Photos*

The vice president's car follows.

They're gone!

Motorcycle sirens start to scream.

11

FIGURE 1.19
The scene immediately after the shooting. Motorcycle policeman
Clyde Haygood ran up the incline toward the railroad bridge and is seen here
scaling the triple underpass where it leads into a parking lot to the north.
*Harry Cabluck, FORT WORTH STAR-TELEGRAM Photographic Collection,
Special Collections Division, University of Texas at Arlington*

AFTERMATH

You are unhurt, lying flat on the ground. The rest of the motorcade continues to pass down Elm Street.

People are running. One of the motorcycle policemen curbs his bike and runs up the slope to your right toward the junction of the railroad bridge and the cedar fence.[55] He's searching in the rail yards! (Figure 1.19).

Other people are on the ground. Are they hurt? The rest of the motorcade drives by. Photographers are leaping from the press cars and buses to take pictures at the scene (Figure 1.20).[56]

The middle-aged man with the movie camera has left his perch and, after taking refuge in the pergola, is leaving the scene shouting, "They killed him, they killed him!" Tears stream down his face.[57]

Sheriff's deputies and policemen come running toward you from the direction of Houston Street. They too hurry up the slope to the area behind you (Figure 1.21).[58]

How much time has passed? The man across the street who was watching the parade with his son is sobbing. "His head exploded!"[59] The young couple near you continue to lie atop their sons, shielding them as long as possible from the horror of the moment.

Suddenly, spectators start to run up the garden steps toward the rail yards behind you (Figure 1.22).[60] You get up, grab your radio, and walk quickly away from Dealey Plaza toward your car, fiddling with the dial on the transistor, seeking some explanation of the shocking event that you have just witnessed.

Radio: Bob Welch of WBAP is talking. *It's not known for sure, but it is believed that President Kennedy has been shot. President Kennedy was in a motorcade en route to the Trade Mart . . . it has not been fully confirmed, but police radios are carrying that the president has been hit.*

Welch states that he is on his way to Parkland Hospital (Figure 1.23).

FIGURE 1.20
Photographers swarming into the area around the Newman family, who are shown lying on the grass.
AP photographer James Altgens is seen to the right, standing at the curb. *Clint Grant, courtesy THE DALLAS MORNING NEWS*

FIGURE 1.21
Officers and pedestrians racing toward the scene after the shooting. Mary Moorman and Jean Hill are shown seated on the grass south of Elm Street, just below the motorcycle policeman. To their left are the lady in the scarf and, behind her, Charles Brehm and his son Joe.
The Newmans appear to the north of Elm, lying on the grass near the curb. *Wilma Bond, courtesy the Estate of Wilma I. Bond*

FIGURE 1.22
Bystanders running up the garden steps leading from Dealey Plaza into the parking lot and rail yards. *Courtesy, F. M. Bell*

Radio: *This is Pierce Allman from the Texas School Book Depository Building for WFAA. Just a few minutes ago the president of the United States turned from Houston onto Elm Street . . . and as he went by the Texas School Book Depository on the way to the triple underpass, there were three loud reverberating explosions. . . . Officers . . . seemed to spring from everywhere at once. . . . There are two witnesses . . . who say that shots were fired, from which upper window we do not know. We do not and cannot confirm the reports at this time that the president has been shot.*

You finally reach your car and rapidly drive away from the scene, turning the dial on the car radio as you

FIGURE 1.23
The president's limousine shown racing toward Parkland Hospital at speeds in excess of 70 mph. A Secret Service agent in the follow-up car has drawn his weapons, and Clint Hill clings to the trunk of the car. *Al Volkland/DALLAS TIMES HERALD Collection, Sixth Floor Museum Archives*

head toward home. A United Press International (UPI) announcement comes over the radio:

Radio: *Three shots were fired at President Kennedy's motorcade today in downtown Dallas.*[61]

Then Ron Jenkins of local station KBOX comes on the air:

Radio: *The first unconfirmed reports say the president was hit in the head.*[62]

A station comes in with a bulletin from the Associated Press (AP):

Radio: *President Kennedy was shot today just as his motorcade left downtown Dallas. Mrs. Kennedy jumped up and grabbed Mr. Kennedy. She cried, 'Oh, no!' The motorcade sped on.*[63]

More from UPI:

Radio: *Kennedy seriously wounded. Perhaps seriously, perhaps fatally by assassin's bullet.*[64]

You hear that Vice President Johnson is injured or has had a heart attack. They say that a Secret Service man has been shot.[65]

At home, you turn on the television set, seeking further information about the horrible tragedy that you saw with your own eyes.

FIRST REPORTS

Had you stayed at the scene of the shooting, you might have been grabbed by a local reporter for an "eyewitness interview," thus becoming a part of the incredible barrage of press coverage that came out of Dallas over the weekend of November 22–25, 1963.

Local and national media had more than one hundred reporters and photographers stationed at the airport, along the motorcade route, and at the Trade Mart. There were sixty-eight reporters traveling with the president, fifty-eight from Washington. Most of the national group was riding in the two press buses far back in the motorcade procession. There were several press cars located behind the mayor's car; they contained representatives from the wire services and a pool of photographers and cameramen.[66]

The big wire-service reporting agencies, AP and UPI, were important to the dissemination of national news. The stories and photos were "wired" into bulky teletype machines that rang bells when a story came in and clattered out the news on a printed page. Journalists and businesses who subscribed to the services kept the machines nearby.

The reporters riding in the wire-service press vehicle immediately behind the mayor's car heard the shots and sprang into action. Merriman Smith, UPI's Washington correspondent, grabbed the car phone on the dashboard to report in. The wires were full of local farm and business reports, typical during the lunch hour, so the first transmission made at 12:34 P.M. from the motorcade was garbled. In many parts of the country it took more than five minutes for UPI wire-service subscribers to get a clear printout about the shooting.[67] It was Smith's UPI report from the motorcade that you heard on the car radio.

AP reporter Jack Bell was riding with Merriman Smith in the wire-service car, but Smith would not release the car phone so that Bell could report in. The car carrying the journalists followed the president's limousine to Parkland Hospital, screeching to a halt right behind the Lincoln convertible. Bell ran into the hospital and commandeered a phone from a clerk. Smith moved toward the Lincoln and asked Agent Clint Hill, who had ridden to Parkland on the trunk of the limousine, about the president's condition.

Hill: *He's dead.*[68]

One AP photographer, James "Ike" Altgens, had been standing across Elm Street from your location when the shots were fired. Earlier, he had stood near Main Street to take a picture of the limousine as it turned onto Houston, and he then ran across the grass to the south side of Elm in time to take two photos of the motorcade moving toward the triple underpass.

Altgens took a picture of the president's car just after it passed the Stemmons Freeway sign and another, showing Mrs. Kennedy on the trunk, as the car sped out of the plaza (see Figure 1.18). After the shooting he ran five blocks to a telephone to call his office. Altgens's story went out over the AP wires at 12:39 P.M., nine minutes after the shots were fired.[69] It was his AP bulletin that you heard on your radio too.

Walter Cronkite was standing over a teletype machine at the CBS studios in New York when the wire report about the shooting came through. He interrupted the soap opera *As the World Turns* at 1:40 (EST) with a voice-over announcement, the first network television report. Then he went on the air in his shirtsleeves, never thinking to don a jacket as the news continued to pour in during the long afternoon.[70]

Jay Watson, program director for the Dallas ABC affiliate, WFAA-TV, was standing on Houston Street and heard the shots; he sprinted back to the station and went live on the air about twelve to fifteen minutes after the shooting. The *Julie Benell Show* was in progress with a preview of women's winter fashions.

Shortly before you got home and turned on your television set, Watson had appeared, breathless, on camera, and read the first UPI and AP reports of the shooting.[71] By the time you tuned in, he was starting to interview some eyewitnesses to the shooting. You recognize the young couple who were standing in front of you and learn that their names are William and Gayle Newman. They sit with their little boys in their laps.

Bill Newman: *It was awful!*

Gayle Newman: *We wanted our children to see it.* Then, thinking back on what they had actually seen, Mrs. Newman becomes shaken. *It scared me and it was terrible!*

Quietly, she leaves the set.

Watson: *I'm so sorry you're so upset.*

Bill Newman remains for the rest of the interview and says he thought the shots came from behind where he—and you—had been standing, "back up on the, the uh, uh mall. I don't know what you call it." Soon the area where you had stood is being referred to as the "grassy knoll."

Jay Watson continues on the air, providing updates. The president is at Parkland; he is still alive. Transfusions have been ordered, and there has been a request for a priest.

Gayle Newman returns to the set and provides an eloquent account of the shooting:

Gayle Newman: *We were standing next to the curb so the children could see the president. . . . It all happened just right in front of us.*

She tells Watson that the couple's four-year-old is asking why anyone would shoot the president. No one has an answer.

WFAA's Jerry Haynes, star of a popular local morning children's show called *Mr. Peppermint*, offers a recap of the reports coming in over the wires and from the station's reporters in the field. Haynes had also heard the shooting from his position along the west side of Houston Street near Main. He and Jay Watson had turned to walk back to the station and did not see the shooting.

Haynes: *The motorcade for all practical purposes was finished.*

And finally, the announcement comes that President Kennedy is dead. WFAA switches to New York for remarks by network commentators Don Goddard and James Haggerty.

Then the station goes back to Dallas. Jay Watson and Bob Walker are in the studio and read a bulletin that a Secret Service agent and a Dallas policeman have been killed in separate incidents in the city.

The weapon used in President Kennedy's shooting was a high-powered rifle, they say. Shots came from the Texas School Book Depository.

TV: *Someone has been arrested in one of the downtown theaters!*

The newsmen speculate: is it the policeman's killer or the man who shot President Kennedy?

The television set shows film taken inside Sheriff Decker's office, where witnesses to the shooting are being interviewed; then the footage cuts to outside the Depository. Police Inspector Jay Sawyer reports that empty rifle shells have been found on the *fifth* floor of the building.

Sawyer: *There are witnesses who saw the man.*

The station goes back to the studio for another bulletin: a white man has been arrested in Fort Worth!

Then Watson extends an apology for the tragedy on behalf of the city of Dallas.

Next, you recognize the middle-aged man who was standing behind you on the pedestal taking movies. His name is Abraham Zapruder, president of Jennifer Juniors, an apparel firm located at the Dal-Tex building; the woman with him on the plinth was his receptionist, who climbed up to steady her wobbly boss. Mr. Zapruder tells Jay Watson that

he filmed the entire assassination with his camera. And his reaction?

Zapruder: *I'm just sick.*

They do not show the Zapruder film, but Watson announces that the station is processing film of the arrest of a suspect in a Dallas theater.

Then the station cuts back to New York. James Haggerty in ABC's New York studios reports that the rifle used in the president's shooting, a Mauser, has been found in the Depository building.

Haggerty: *[It] has to be a planned conspiracy.*

Feeling sick and frightened, you get up to turn off the TV.

Later, the Friday afternoon edition of the *Dallas Times Herald* arrives full of news of the shooting. One article identifies the woman with the Polaroid camera as Mary Moorman. She was watching the parade with her friend Jean Hill, the woman in the red raincoat. Mrs. Moorman said she took a picture of the president just as he was shot (see Figure 1.16).[72] The article also states that Mrs. Hill saw a man run up the hill (behind you) with someone else firing a gun at him. She says she heard six shots.[73]

Another article identifies one of the motorcycle policemen who were riding near the president's limousine (see Figure 1.16). B. W. Hargis has told the *Times Herald* that he was about two feet behind and to the left side of the presidential car when he heard two shots; after the second one, he was splattered with the president's blood and brains.[74]

Hargis thought shots might have come from "the trestle" (the triple underpass bridge). He did not find anything suspicious there or behind the cedar fence, so he moved beneath the underpass and then reported to the Texas School Book Depository. There, he learned that Bob Jackson, a photographer for the *Dallas Times Herald* who was riding in the photographers' pool car, had seen a rifle protruding from the sixth-floor window in the warehouse.[75]

EPILOGUE

Of course today is not 1963, and only a few people were actually there to see the terrible shooting of the president of the United States. But we have read about those who witnessed the assassination, or we have seen them on television. When you run across an account from that day so many years ago, keep in mind the confusion, the shock, and the tremendous fear that these people experienced. Close your eyes and count to six or eight. All the shots rang out in that short space of time. History changed in a matter of seconds.

CHAPTER 2
The Weekend

THE MEMORY

Learning that President Kennedy had been assassinated produced many individual images that remain vivid memories today. But it was the cumulative effect of events that took place during the entire weekend, from Friday afternoon through Monday afternoon, that generated the *collective* memory of John F. Kennedy's life and death.

Collective memory has been defined as "an image bequeathed to posterity."[1] It is shared memory, and it is important. Historians may question the accuracy of individual memory, but they often rely on collective memory when assessing the meaning of the past. This classification of memory begins as a mixture of both actual experiences and communicated information about experiences. As time goes by, the importance of firsthand experience lessens, and communicated information becomes dominant.[2]

Today's rememberers often speak about the shock of learning about the assassination in 1963 (a firsthand experience), but their memory embraces all of the major events of that incredible weekend in November (primarily communicated information). The collective memory of John F. Kennedy, alive or dead, also includes information that has come out since 1963.

One goal of this book is to help you to understand this memory, so a few warnings are in order. Events are one thing; individual memories *about them* are quite another. Events exist within a definite time frame, but personal memories lack clear boundaries, and they allow for new ideas to intrude.[3] This new input can influence, or even change, the original memory. Each of the rememberers has a personal memory of learning that the president had been shot; it is a unique recollection, not shared by many others. Chances are that the essence of that experience has remained relatively unaltered through time.

The big picture is there, but many of its individual elements are probably lost. Ask people where they were and what they were doing when they heard the news in 1963, and they can probably tell you. Ask them to describe the people who were around them at the time, what they had eaten for lunch, what they were wearing, or what they said in response to the news, and the memory is probably less clear.

My own memory is a good example. On Friday, November 22, I had just finished a "Great Books" class at Hampton High School in Virginia and was heading down a long hallway on the second floor toward the parking lot where our car pool had parked. Suddenly, I spied my classmate Prentis Gandy, who was clutching a transistor radio to his ear. "The president's been shot!" he shouted. The time was about 1:35 P.M. (EST).

At the time I was walking with a group of people. I cannot remember who they were. And the car pool? I remember only Bobby Soter, who wept during the drive to our neighborhood. People forget. In preparation for this book I called some of my old friends and asked them if they were with me when we heard the news. One of them, Sally Groome Powell, was in the same "Great Books" class, and we often carpooled together. She does not remember seeing Prentis but thinks that she may have been with me. Her memory focused on the hysterical reaction of another friend, Catherine Chapman. "Catherine may have been driving," said Sally. "I was afraid she would wreck the car."[4]

One study has shown that 100% of a group could remember an important event after two hours, but only 57% of them could do so after four months had passed.[5] Consider the recollections of witnesses to the assassination. The experience created a firsthand, personal memory of the shooting, but several factors influenced the witnesses' ability to remember the event, even at the very time it was taking place. First, the shooting was a major crime; witnesses were seeing someone murder the president of the United States. Second, the assassination was extremely violent. Witnesses tend to remember details of major crimes, but extreme violence diminishes their ability to retain information.[6]

Most witnesses to the assassination were in an exposed, open area at the time that gunshots were fired; they were probably more interested in finding shelter than they were in making mental notes about the exact time, the number of shots being fired, and the direction or timing of the shots.[7] Finally, people who left the scene without relating their initial memory to others were highly susceptible to outside influences from television, radio, newspaper accounts, and conversations with family or friends. Any of this input may have reshaped details of their first impressions, particularly those that were cloudy from the start. Overall, however, the memory of the *essence* of the event probably held its shape.[8]

Suppose that the witnesses to the assassination had all got together immediately after the shooting to compare memories. Bill Newman recalled seeing Kennedy stand up in the car after the first shot that hit him.[9] Charles Brehm, who stood almost directly across Elm Street from Newman with his five-year-old son Joe, said the first shot that hit the president caused Kennedy to "slump down" in the seat.[10] Newman thought that the fatal shot had blown off the president's ear. He also believed that a shot might have come from the area of the garden behind him.[11]

Abraham Zapruder, the man with the movie camera, could not recall the direction of the shots but clearly remembered seeing President Kennedy's hands move up to his face.[12] Newman, Brehm, and Zapruder all saw the president's head explode. Jean Hill, who was standing with her friend Mary Moorman almost directly across the street from the Newmans, heard five or six shots and did not remember seeing any blood at all.[13] Mary Moorman remembered taking several photos with her Polaroid camera but offered few recollections of the shooting itself.[14]

John Connally clearly remembered yelling, "Oh, no, no, no!" at the time he was shot.[15] Some nearby witnesses heard this exclamation, but others apparently did not hear Jacqueline Kennedy shout, "Oh my God, they have shot my husband!"[16] Jean Hill heard the first lady cry out, and so did the AP photographer James Altgens and Nellie Connally.[17] Secret Service Agent Roy Kellerman was sure that JFK said, "I am hit," after he received his first wound, but no one else in the limousine or nearby heard him utter a word.[18] The Newmans, Jean Hill, and Mary Moorman all fell to the ground in an effort to get out of the line of fire. James Altgens and several other witnesses who were only a few feet away remained standing.

Collectively, however, they all saw the president react to two wounds, and most of them realized that the shot to JFK's head was serious and probably fatal. Several got the strong impression that they were in the line of fire, so they tried to avoid being hit. The shooting left these people frightened and in shock. The number of shots, the direction from which they came, comments made by occupants of the limousine, and other details of the shooting registered quite differently with each witness. There was consensus about the major event, but the individual elements varied significantly.

During the rest of the weekend millions of Americans were eye- and earwitnesses to events *reported* to them by the media and other people. News reporters and commentators who talked about events associated with the assassination did not capture the intensity of the firsthand experience.[19] They were not there. Rememberers like me cannot possibly re-create from memory the actual sequence of events, nor can I recapture in words the emotion-charged atmosphere that prevailed.

It is important for you to try to understand the memory, because its impact on society has been profound. Public perceptions of John F. Kennedy's life were changed by it. The course of American history was altered by it. Finally, the collective grieving around the world created a feeling of global unity that many still yearn to recapture, even after all the years.

In all likelihood, the rememberers you know today were not in Dallas, and they did not see or hear the shooting in Dealey Plaza. Their memory was communicated to them at a distance from the scene of the crime. The collective memory of the weekend for Dallasites was heavily influenced by the presence of local media, who got the inside track on the investigation. Many details provided by these local reporters did not get aired on the networks. Today's rememberers stored information from a vast array of details and impressions that were presented to them over a period of four days. Still, Dallasites and others developed a shared collective memory of the assassination and of John F. Kennedy, a memory that is alive today.

Because the shooting occurred on a Friday, and Monday was declared an official national day of mourning, people had the entire weekend to focus on the death of the president. The collective memory took shape over an extended period of time. Events that provoke strong emotional reactions create the most powerful collective memories.[20] The weekend was the essence of high drama.

Similarly, events that are unique and those that require some form of psychological adaptation are the most memorable.[21] The assassination of President Kennedy was the first presidential murder in the United States in more than sixty years, since President William McKinley's death in 1901. Most people found it hard to believe that the president had been shot. Americans don't do that sort of thing, they said; the reports must be wrong.

The leadership of the country was forced to change, and the switch from Kennedy to Johnson required quite a bit of mental adjustment. One minute we had John Kennedy—charismatic, handsome, sophisticated, young, and vibrantly alive. Suddenly, we had Lyndon Johnson, an older man of infinitely different style, whose television persona was pale in comparison with that of JFK. LBJ himself would later comment on the awkwardness of the change in leadership. "I became president," he said, "but for millions of Americans I was still illegitimate, a naked man with no presidential covering . . . an illegal usurper."[22]

Later generations have grown up with violence and change; it spills into our homes daily via television and radio and is headlined everywhere in print media. My generation was appalled by the events of that weekend and by the feeling of upheaval that accompanied them. The Kennedy assassination was, for those four days in November, all-absorbing, all-powerful. The news came like a thunderbolt. It was totally unexpected, devastatingly shocking, ripe with the potential for dire consequence. Many people believed that the nation's future was at stake. The story that unfolded was more dramatic than any Hollywood script could have contrived—at once majestic then petty, provoking profound sadness, anger, frustration, and guilt.

THE NEWS IN DALLAS

Dallasites who did not witness the assassination learned about the event almost immediately after it occurred. Many of them were listening to accounts of the presidential visit when the first horrible reports came over the airwaves. In fact, local reporters were broadcasting the news before the first UPI wire bulletin, initially sent at 12:34 P.M., went clearly over the wires at around 12:39 P.M.

Two-thirds of the people in Dallas had heard of the attack by 12:45 P.M., only fifteen minutes after the shots were fired.[23] There was a tremendous immediacy to the reports; suddenly, news of international importance was happening at home, and the reports were being delivered by local journalists who were well-known and trusted. There was an intensely personal aspect to the story, like a real-life horror movie that starred your neighbors and was being filmed right next door.

NATIONAL NEWS

At the same time that Dallasites were learning of the shooting, the news spread to the rest of the country like wildfire. Nationwide, nine out of every ten Americans knew about it within the first hour, half of them within a quarter hour.[24] The wire-service reports from the motorcade and from Parkland did most of the initial work; within forty-five minutes of the shooting, the local affiliate TV stations were feeding reports live to the major networks.[25]

Some people did not learn of the shooting until after the 1:33 P.M. announcement that Kennedy was dead; yet one-third knew within fifteen minutes of that announcement, and 70% within forty-five minutes. They heard either by word of mouth or through the media.[26] By late afternoon on November 22, 1963, virtually everyone in the country who was capable of understanding knew that John F. Kennedy was dead.[27]

WORLD NEWS

Word spread rapidly outside the boundaries of the United States. Kennedy's program to set up a system of worldwide television communications satellites was tested with his death; the news swept around the world in a matter of minutes. Satellites beamed televised reports to Europe and to the Soviet Union; the Soviets then relayed the news to their Eastern Bloc nations.[28] By now we are all accustomed to instantaneous satellite communications and CNN; in 1963 the notion of a global village was in its infancy.

"The news traveled like some deadly contagion," wrote one reporter from London.[29] The sheer speed of its transmission produced shock. A Moscow TV announcer reportedly burst into tears on the air, and the anti-U.S. government of Yugoslavia was so shaken that it ordered its schools "to devote time to the study of Kennedy's politics."[30] Spending Friday afternoon at home watching television, I was surprised to realize that foreign nations were already aware of the American assassination. I was also amazed that other countries seemed to be genuinely upset about the death of our president.

Tokyo got the word of the *ansatsu* during the early hours of November 23; its satellite link went on-line only four hours after the shooting.[31] On Sunday a Catholic priest in Bogotá, Colómbia, was astonished to find national flags draped with black mourning bands in the primitive rural villages outside of the city.[32] People everywhere knew that the heartland of liberty had murdered its own chief.

On hearing the first reports, most people told someone else; only 2% reported talking to no one at all, while a third said they talked to fifteen or more people.[33] African Americans, as a group, took the news very badly; more than 50% did not even want to talk about the tragedy.[34] Telephone lines overloaded and became jammed in Washington and in Dallas.[35]

Typically, once people heard the news, they tuned into TV or radio to get confirmation that the report was true and then to obtain more information. Television news came of age during the weekend of November 22–25, 1963, and millions of Americans watched it happen. The average viewer watched thirty-two hours of television during the weekend.[36] People switched on their sets Friday afternoon and remained with the networks through the funeral on Monday; the average viewing time per household came to three ten-hour days. Of the nation's children, 98% reported watching more than their usual amount of television; even those between the ages of two to five logged in an average of more than eight hours each.[37]

The repetition set up a process of memorization that created a collective memory stronger than any that had preceded it. Television alone was not enough. People engaged in an orgy of information-seeking. They used radios in their cars and carried transistors along while walking down the street. The shooting took place midday on Friday, too late to make it into most afternoon papers. Saturday newspaper sales went up 17% as people scrambled for more details and keepsake editions.[38] Torn and yellowed papers with banner headlines proclaiming "KENNEDY DEAD / JOHNSON SWORN IN" can be found in countless American homes today.

The content of the printed page changed between Friday afternoon and Monday. Taking the weekend as a whole, roughly half the overall news in the nation's papers was devoted to the assassination—13% on Friday afternoon and 52% Saturday morning.[39] *The Dallas Times Herald* had reporters on the scene, so it was ahead of most other Friday afternoon newspapers, many of which were able to include only the first wire-service reports about the shooting. The papers devoted more space on Saturday and Sunday to "background" on JFK's life and career; outside of Dallas, the nation's Friday afternoon editions focused mainly on straight assassination coverage.[40]

The sheer volume of news was amazing. Network radio and television gathered a group of twenty-one hundred people to handle the coverage.[41] Today, we are accustomed to such massive broadcasting efforts; in 1963 we were astonished that the networks could garner the resources with such incredible speed. For the first time, network television canceled all commercial advertising and went full-time on the air with news; the estimated loss of revenue was $32–40 million.[42] NBC television and ABC radio topped the amount of broadcast time with more than seventy-two and sixty-eight hours, respectively.[43] NBC-TV news commentator David Brinkley later remarked: "The shocked and stunned nation was listening to six people at most, us commentators. It would have been so easy to start a phony rumor that would never die."[44]

Of course, the reportage was not without errors. Radio and television announcements immediately after the assassination provided a minute-by-minute, but jumbled, account of events. Years later, critics of the government findings on the assassination would cite these early published accounts in attempts to sway public opinion. As the weekend progressed, reports became more reliable and detailed. The style of all weekend reporting was dramatic and riveting.

People who heard the news absorbed it differently. Young Jim Anderson of Sheboygan, Wisconsin, returned from kindergarten to find his mother weeping at her sewing machine. He was only five at the time, but astute enough to realize that his mother's tears meant that something bad had happened. Once assured that the sad news did not involve his world, that of the Anderson family, he was relieved. Then, he recalled, "We all sat down and watched TV."[45]

Imagine spending an entire weekend in front of the television set with your family. In 1963 *couch potato* was an uncommon term; the average home set was turned on for six hours a day.[46] Between Friday and Monday there were no commercials, no detailed sports reports, few accounts of anything except events directly related to the life and death of John F. Kennedy. Aldous Huxley, author of *Brave New*

World, also died that weekend; ask your parents if they remember that fact. Televisions or radios blared in the background while families ate and while they performed their daily chores. Stores and restaurants played the news on the radio or on TV sets brought in to keep abreast of the latest happenings. It was impossible to miss many details because the networks kept repeating them, over and over again. One critical aspect of the weekend was the fact that certain news announcements and visuals were repeated so many times that they became ingrained in memory.

Here is what happened after the shooting.[47]

FRIDAY

In Dallas . . .

Security officials in the motorcade were slow to realize that a shooting had taken place. Dallas Police Chief Jesse Curry, driving the lead car, heard the shots, got confirmation that JFK was hit, and called in instructions to headquarters: "Go to the hospital . . . officers. Go to the hospital, Parkland Hospital. Have them stand by. . . . Get a man up on top of the triple underpass and see what happened up there. Go up to the overpass."[48]

The call came in to the dispatcher at the central police station at 12:30 P.M. (Figure 2.1).[49] Motorcycle police formed up around the limousine, which sped onto Stemmons Freeway and headed at top speed toward Parkland Hospital, about four miles away. Secret Service agent Clint Hill still clung to the trunk of the big blue Lincoln, beating it with his fists in anguished frustration.[50]

The president arrived at Parkland at 12:36 P.M. The car carrying Vice President Lyndon Johnson followed right behind. Secret Service Agent Rufus Youngblood was riding with the vice presidential party; when he heard shots, the security man whirled around to the backseat, screamed, "Get down!" and leaned over to cover Lyndon Johnson's body with his own.[51]

By this time people were just starting to hear reports about the shooting. The first wire-service bulletins and news reports contradicted themselves: announcements stated that there were six or seven people wounded, but witnesses said they had heard three shots; a Secret Service agent had been killed; LBJ had been shot, no, he had had a heart attack. People who listened to this early coverage obviously became quite nervous. There was no real sense of the number of people in Dealey Plaza who witnessed the assassination, and audiences began to realize that most people heard the shooting without actually seeing it. By the time cameramen arrived to take pictures and to film at the assassination site, audiences were doubly confused by the presence of thousands of people, who had converged on the park after the assassination. Police had to erect

FIGURE 2.1
Witnesses on the west side of the triple underpass. Unaware of the shooting, they continued to wave at the president's limousine as it sped toward the Stemmons Freeway ramp. *Courtesy, Mel McIntire*

barricades to secure the crime scene.[52] Television stations broadcast the first films of Dealey Plaza and the School Book Depository.

Dallas County Sheriff Bill Decker made calls from the lead motorcade car instructing all available personnel to search the railroad yards and nearby buildings.[53] Nearly one hundred police and sheriff's department officers showed up within minutes. Again, the first television footage showed Dealey Plaza literally crawling with officers. People assumed that they had been there all along and wondered why the officers had not provided better security for the motorcade.

These radio calls from Curry and Decker explained, in part, the initial attention given to the grassy knoll on the north side of Elm Street. Witnesses and the local investigators who ran into the rail yards north of Dealey Plaza found nothing except footprints and some cigarette butts behind the fence. Several witnesses told the authorities that they believed shots had been fired from that direction, and a few said that they had seen smoke or steam near the trees at the top of the knoll.[54] Some witnesses said that they encountered a policeman or a Secret Service agent in the rail yards, who told them to leave the area.[55] Later, officials stated that no Secret Service agents had been assigned to the park or the rail yards.

Television audiences who tuned in early got the news about the possibility of shots from the grassy knoll, but most Americans were like me and came into the story after the Depository was declared the sole location for a sniper. About a dozen witnesses who were standing near the corner of Elm and Houston Streets said they saw a gunman or at least a rifle protruding from an upper story in the Texas School Book Depository before or during the shooting. Others said they thought that shots came from that location.[56] The investigation immediately shifted to the old brick warehouse.

The shift in emphasis from the grassy knoll to the Depository took several minutes. Law enforcement personnel in Dealey Plaza immediately began to round up witnesses to take them to the nearby sheriff's office for formal affidavits. Calls flowed into police headquarters.

At 12:34 P.M., the same time that UPI correspondent Merriman Smith's first report on the shooting appeared, an officer in Dealey Plaza radioed the police dispatcher: "A passerby says Texas School Book Depository . . . the shots came from that building."[57] A similar report came in from another officer one minute later; a third report, offering up the fifth floor as the source, came in at 12:36, the same time that the president arrived at the emergency entrance at Parkland Hospital.[58]

One of these witnesses was a steam-pipe fitter named Howard Brennan, who had watched the motorcade while seated on the northeast wall of the reflecting pool near the corner of Elm and Houston Streets. He approached an officer shortly after the assassination and said he had seen a rifleman shooting from the sixth floor (Figure 2.2).[59]

At 12:45 P.M., fifteen minutes after the shooting, the police broadcast Brennan's description of the sniper: "The suspect in the shooting at Elm and Houston is supposed to be an unknown white male, approximately thirty, 165 pounds, slender build, height five feet ten, armed with what is thought to be a .30-caliber rifle."[60]

The local media was tuned into police radio channels and soon shared this information with the public. Actually,

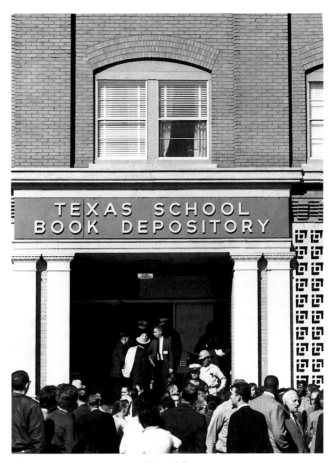

FIGURE 2.2
Witness Howard Brennan (wearing a hard hat), on the steps of the Depository. Brennan offered a description of the sniper only minutes after the shooting.
©*Jim Murray Film—all rights reserved*

it took about twenty minutes to seal off the Depository, occupied by publishers' representatives and a private company that stored and shipped textbooks to Texas schools. Investigators conducted a floor-by-floor search that lasted until 2:30 P.M. Reporters with cameras went inside about 2:45 P.M. Fire trucks with ladders were used in the search, and sheriff's deputies brought in spotlights to illuminate the dim interiors.[61] At first, many people believed that the sniper was still hiding in the building. Dallas ABC affiliate WFAA had two journalists inside the building before it was sealed. Pierce Allman called in reports by phone while reporter-cameraman Tom Alyea filmed the investigators searching for evidence.

Motorcycle policeman Marrion Baker had been riding in the motorcade behind the president. He heard shots and saw pigeons fly off the roof of the Depository building; the officer was riding along Houston Street toward the structure at the time. Baker parked his bike and ran into the warehouse, where he was joined by the building superintendent, Roy Truly.

The two men raced one hundred feet to the two freight elevators at the rear (north) of the building, only to find them inaccessible; they were stopped on upper floors. Turning to the left, the men ran up the staircase located in the far northwest corner of the first floor. The staircase was enclosed with wooden walls, affording no peripheral visibility between levels. As Baker ran out of the staircase into the open space on the second floor, seeking the door to the

FIGURE 2.3
The enclosed staircase on the second floor of the Depository.
The lunchroom was behind and to the left of this view.
Sixth Floor Museum Archives

FIGURE 2.4
Second-floor lunchroom at the Depository, where Lee Oswald was stopped
and released within two minutes of the shooting. *Sixth Floor Museum Archives*

enclosed stairs leading to the third, he spotted a man who had just entered a doorway to his right (Figure 2.3).

The officer followed, gun drawn, and confronted the man in an enclosed second-floor lunchroom. The time was between ninety seconds to two minutes after the shooting. Truly identified the man as Lee Oswald, a Depository company clerk, so Baker let him go and continued to race up the stairs toward the roof of the building (Figure 2.4).[62]

Shortly after 1:00 P.M., Roy Truly conducted a roll call of Depository employees. Oswald was among those who could not be located. At 1:12, less than forty-five minutes after the shots were fired, Deputy Sheriff Luke Mooney searched near the southeast corner windows on the sixth floor of the Depository, where he discovered boxes arranged like a sniper's nest and three spent bullet cartridges (Figure 2.5).[63]

At 1:22 P.M., roughly eleven minutes before the official announcement of President Kennedy's death, Deputy Sheriff Eugene Boone discovered a bolt-action rifle hidden among some boxes near the exit staircase diagonally across the sixth floor from the sniper's perch; the officer thought it was a Mauser.[64] By this time Dallas television broadcasts were being carried live on the national networks.

Earlier, at Parkland Hospital, stretchers had been brought out to transport President Kennedy and a wound-

ed Governor Connally. Spectators who arrived at the scene were appalled by the ruined condition of the president's head. Police Chief Curry ran up to the limousine; Mrs. Kennedy was leaning over JFK's body, "somehow hoping to heal it, like a little girl holds a doll."[65]

Agent Clint Hill realized that the first lady did not want anyone to see the president's wounds, so he removed his coat and she carefully wrapped it around Kennedy's head.[66] The president and governor were then rolled into the hospital and taken into two separate trauma rooms that faced each other on the hospital's first floor. Kennedy still had a pulse when he arrived at the hospital; technically and medically, he was still alive.[67]

Television audiences did not see any photographs or films of Kennedy or his wounds. There were scenes of the crowds awaiting word outside Parkland and panning shots showing the limousine. Most reports stated that the president was alive, and many people, far away from the scene, started to have hope for his recovery.

Bob Clark of ABC News saw Vice President Johnson rub his arm when he got out of the limousine, thus promoting the rumor that he had been shot or had had a heart attack.[68] He and his wife were sequestered in a small room near the emergency entrance, some distance from the trauma rooms (Figure 2.6). Signal Corps personnel scrambled to set up communications with the White House.[69]

Parkland in 1963 was Dallas's leading trauma center; an experienced team of doctors converged on Trauma Room #1 to try to revive the president of the United States. Kennedy was laid flat on his back; doctors observed a small gunshot wound in his neck, near the Adam's apple, and a gaping wound in his head. The remains of his brain were visible through the missing skull; in the rush of treatment, no one turned him over to search for additional wounds.[70] National audiences learned all of this later, after the official announcement of the president's death. During the waiting period, we received conflicting information: UPI quoted Secret Service Agent Clint Hill's comment that the president was dead, but other bulletins told us that JFK was alive and that blood transfusions had been ordered for his treatment.

FIGURE 2.5
The sniper's perch, found on the Depository's sixth floor and photographed on November 22, 1963. The original arrangement of boxes was disturbed by investigators; this view is one of the most accurate reconstructions recorded on that date. *Sixth Floor Museum Archives*

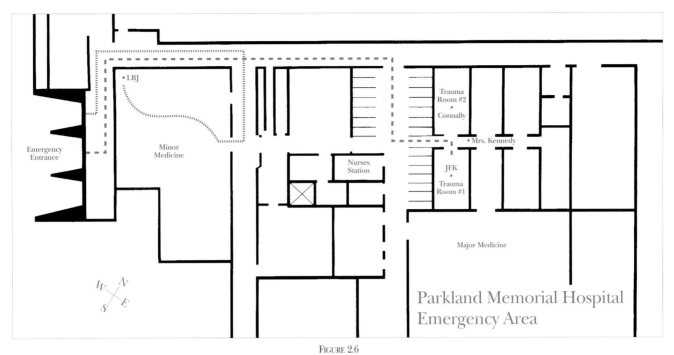

FIGURE 2.6
Map showing the location of the emergency entrance and Trauma Rooms #1 and #2 at Parkland Hospital.
President Johnson was sequestered in the section marked Minor Medicine. *Staples & Charles Ltd. and Tom Dawson Graphic Design, Sixth Floor Museum Archives*

The Parkland team knew that resuscitation efforts would be futile, but they automatically went though the trauma drill, opening airways through a tracheotomy through the neck wound and introducing saline solutions to reduce the risk of death by trauma shock. After all, JFK was the president of the United States. No efforts were wasted. They even tried closed-chest heart massage. Nothing worked.

Another team worked to save Governor Connally, who had bullet wounds in his back, chest, wrist, and thigh. The governor was rolled into surgery and underwent an operation that lasted several hours. It was midafternoon before we heard that he was likely to recover from the attack.

Mrs. Kennedy wandered in and out of Trauma Room #1 while emergency procedures were under way.[71] Television viewers were told that she was with the president; no cameras were allowed inside the hospital, so we did not see her suit and legs splattered with her husband's blood and brains.

Thirty minutes after the shooting there were still only a few dozen eyewitnesses who knew that Kennedy's head wound was probably fatal. The media had not reported that the president's head exploded in Dealey Plaza. Many people still clung to the hope that he might recover. Shortly before 1:00 P.M., two priests arrived at the hospital. News reporters told us that the priests had been called in at the request of White House officials to perform the last rites (Figure 2.7).

At home in Virginia we were dismayed to hear that priests had arrived at the hospital. Americans of all faiths knew

FIGURE 2.7
Father Oscar Huber, the priest who administered the last rites to President Kennedy at Parkland. *DALLAS TIMES HERALD Collection, Sixth Floor Museum Archives*

that the last rites of the Catholic Church were administered to the dying. Just before 1:20 P.M., the CBS radio network in New York carried a report from Dallas that JFK was dead, and at 1:32 P.M., UPI sent out a wire stating that one of the priests, on leaving the hospital, had confirmed that the president's wound had been fatal. One minute later the White House made it official: John F. Kennedy had died at 1:00 P.M.[72]

Johnson's Secret Service guard, fearing a widespread conspiracy, was desperate to get the new president to safety. In 1963 the Constitution did not have a provision for the appointment of a new vice president in cases of a presidential death; if Johnson died, the new president would be Speaker of the House John McCormack, then seventy-one years old.[73] McCormack in 1963 was not as vibrant as Ronald Reagan appeared to be at the same age two decades later; the Speaker was an old man.

LBJ was informed of Kennedy's death shortly after 1:00 P.M. and agreed to return to *Air Force One*, which provided better communications and less risk of attack. The new president and Mrs. Johnson were taken from the hospital and arrived at Love Field around 1:37 P.M., less than five minutes after the death announcement.[74] National audiences were told only that LBJ had left the hospital. We did not know where he was.

There was cause for alarm. Half the members of President Kennedy's cabinet were airborne over the Pacific, en route to a conference in Japan, when the teletype aboard the plane clattered the first news of the shooting. I remember feeling that no one was really in charge of the government in Washington. The cabinet plane turned around and headed toward Dallas, only to abandon that plan and continue toward Washington after the president's death was announced.[75] People feared that the assassination was part of a larger conspiracy.

In this atmosphere of anxiety some people were terrified that the assassination might give the Soviets an excuse to bomb the United States. Linda Carter, a sixteen-year-old high school junior from Davis, Oklahoma, was among this group. She and her family feared that Dallas would be a target for nuclear attack and wondered if the fallout from the mushroom cloud there would reach Davis, 142 miles away.[76]

Back at Parkland, the White House held a press conference at 1:30 p.m., during which Assistant Press Secretary Malcolm Kilduff made the announcement that President Kennedy was dead. The dreaded confirmation, anticipated by reports from CBS and UPI only minutes earlier, was broadcast at 1:35 P.M.[77] Many in the crowd of two hundred people outside the hospital wept openly. Several of the Parkland doctors then showed up in the press room to answer questions about the treatment they had provided.[78]

The doctors' comments were based on observations made during trauma procedures; they were not concerned with noting details of the nature of the wounds or the direction of the shots. The first press reports from this conference contained discrepancies; for example, one Dallas reporter wrote down in his notes that the president had a wound "in the lower portion of the neck and the right rear side of the head." The doctors could not say whether these two wounds were caused by one bullet or two. The journalist noted that the throat wound was an entrance wound and that the head wound "was either an exit or gangential [tangential] entrance wound."[79]

At the time of the announcement I assumed that the investigation into President Kennedy's death would be handled by the most powerful agencies in existence. But assassination of the president was not a federal crime in 1963, so jurisdiction for the investigation fell into local hands. The absence of federal authority would cause problems, since both the Secret Service and the FBI wanted to take part in the probe. Dallas Police Chief Curry would recall, much later, that the investigation "was a three-ring circus."[80] The FBI and the Secret Service sat in on the interrogations, although they initially lacked any official authority in the investigation.

Parkland Hospital required a release from the next of kin or another authorized person before a body in its possession could be removed from the premises. Jacqueline Kennedy duly signed the form. In cases of violent death, however, Texas law prohibited any body from being removed from the state without a separate authorization from the governor, lieutenant governor, attorney general, or a coroner's inquest (autopsy). Governor Connally was in surgery, and the other two officials were in Austin awaiting President Kennedy's arrival there.[81] While people outside Parkland wept over the news that the president was dead, nurses started to prepare Kennedy's body for the autopsy, which was to be performed by the Dallas County medical examiner. That is when things hit a snag.

The formal announcement of Kennedy's death led to heightened anxiety about the whereabouts of Lyndon Johnson and the status of his plans to take the oath of office. White House officials would not release any information, aside from the fact that Johnson was alive and well and elsewhere. For my part, I wanted him to get sworn in, and fast.

Johnson, safely aboard *Air Force One*, informed his security guards that he would not leave Mrs. Kennedy behind in Dallas, but Mrs. Kennedy refused to leave the city without her husband's body. Dallas County insisted on the right to perform the autopsy before releasing the body. There was a

standoff in the halls of the hospital involving county officials and Secret Service men, with the widow of the president looking on.[82]

The body was taken from Parkland, driven by hearse to the airport, and placed aboard *Air Force One* in an area near the rear of the plane. We were told that Jacqueline Kennedy rode in the rear of the hearse with her husband's coffin. Aboard *Air Force One*, seats were quickly removed to accommodate the heavy casket. Security at the airport was tight, and few cameras recorded the transfer of the coffin onto the plane. Later, we were told that JFK's body had arrived at 2:20 P.M.[83]

While awaiting Mrs. Kennedy and the body, Lyndon Johnson communicated from the plane with Attorney General Robert Kennedy about the requirements for the oath of office.[84] Johnson had already taken the basic oath when he was sworn in as vice president, but it was a custom to reaffirm the pledge when a second-in-command took over for a fallen president. On that Friday afternoon, the average American was not inclined to analyze legalities; Johnson had not taken the oath, and the minutes were turning into hours. No one had even told us he was aboard *Air Force One*.

In fact, we were unaware of the difficulties at Parkland. Reporters openly speculated about when and where the swearing-in would take place. Johnson decided to take the oath in Dallas. Federal District Judge Sarah Hughes, a Kennedy appointee, was summoned to the plane and delivered the oath at 2:38 P.M., approximately two hours after the assassination (Figure 2.8). Mrs. Kennedy attended the brief ceremony, then retired to the rear of the plane to sit near her husband's coffin. She refused to change her blood-spattered clothes. "Let them see what they've done," she said.[85] The new president's only comment after the swearing-in was, "Let's get this plane back to Washington." *Air Force One* took off at 2:47 P.M.[86]

Three members of the press were allowed to witness the administration of the oath; Sid Davis of Westinghouse Broadcasting remained behind in Dallas to brief the waiting press corps.[87] Television and radio stations quickly passed on the news that LBJ had taken the oath, thus allaying some of the widespread anxiety.

Meanwhile, investigators in Dallas were progressing in their efforts to find President Kennedy's assassin. At 1:18 P.M., between the time the sniper's perch was discovered and the rifle was found, a citizen using a police-car radio called central dispatch to report that a policeman had been shot in the Oak Cliff section of Dallas, south of downtown.[88] Journalists monitoring the police channel heard the report.

Police officers went to the scene on Tenth Street and found officer J. D. Tippit lying on the street near his squad car. He had been shot several times at close range. The officer was pronounced dead-on-arrival at Methodist Hospital. Bystanders at the crime scene reported either seeing the shooting or witnessing an assailant carrying a pistol and fleeing the scene on foot.[89]

At 1:24 P.M. the police broadcast the following description: "Wanted for investigation for assault to murder a police officer. A white male, approximately 30, 5 feet 8, slender build has black hair, a white jacket, a white shirt and dark trousers. The suspect last seen running west on Jefferson from 400 East Jefferson [Street]."[90] The similarity

FIGURE 2.8
Judge Sarah T. Hughes, left foreground, shown administering the oath of office to Lyndon Baines Johnson at 2:38 P.M. (CST) aboard *Air Force One*.
Mrs. Kennedy attended the ceremony and then retired to the rear of the plane to be near her husband's coffin.
Cecil W. Stoughton, courtesy Lyndon Baines Johnson Library

between this description and the one broadcast earlier for the sniper in the Kennedy shooting was not lost on the local police or the media. Later, the same description was broadcast on the news.

Witness reports on the location of the fleeing murderer of the Dallas policeman eventually led investigators to the Texas Theater, some distance from the scene where Officer Tippit had been shot. The featured movie was *War Is Hell*, starring Van Heflin. Police approached a man sitting in the lower rear section; he matched the description of a man who had acted suspiciously and then entered the theater without paying admission.[91] "It's all over now," he said and tried to shoot the arresting police officer, M. N. McDonald, with a pistol. There was a struggle, the gun misfired, minor injuries were sustained, and Lee Harvey Oswald was arrested for the murder of Officer Tippit. The time was shortly before 1:54 P.M.[92]

By this time Americans everywhere were abandoning their offices and going home to tune in to radio and television sets. Dallas and Fort Worth television audiences were told to stand by for WFAA film taken at the arrest of the suspect at the Texas Theater.

Oswald was taken to Dallas police headquarters, where officers realized that he was one of the employees who was missing from the Texas School Book Depository, already accepted as the prime site from which shots were fired at the

motorcade. Police began to interrogate the twenty-four-year-old suspect about both murders. Soon, Oswald became the focus of attention on the news.

The media reported his name and flashed his picture to viewers everywhere. Reporters finally discounted the earlier rumors that a Secret Service man had been killed. There were only two dead, they asserted, President Kennedy and Dallas police officer J. D. Tippit. From the onset, the media speculated that Lee Harvey Oswald might be connected to both slayings.[93]

Dallas's WFAA-TV cameraman Ron Reiland was on hand at the scene of the Tippit shooting, and he filmed inside the Texas Theater when police moved in. He hurried back to the station and went on the air with his own eyewitness account of the arrest. He also showed the footage taken at the theater.[94]

When Oswald arrived at police headquarters at 2:00 P.M. on Friday, there were a few journalists already present.[95] Within hours, approximately one hundred reporters and cameramen descended on the station, where they jammed the third-floor hallway and offices, the location of most of the homicide interrogations.

The hallway, measuring only about 7 by 140 feet, became congested with television cables, cameramen, and reporters, all thoroughly disruptive to the investigation. Oswald had to run a twenty-foot gauntlet of reporters whenever he was brought down for questioning from his jail cell on an upper floor. He made the trip down the hallway sixteen times between Friday afternoon and Sunday morning.[96]

IN WASHINGTON . . .

Audiences nationwide waited for *Air Force One* to return to the nation's capital with the two presidents. The trip seemed to take forever. Anyone who has lived through a family member's death that occurs away from home in a strange place knows the urge that many Americans felt during that flight: we wanted JFK and the new president back on the ground in Washington. In 1963 there was no TV show named *Dallas*, which later made the sites and accents of the city familiar to millions of Americans. The NFL Dallas Cowboys were not yet known as "America's Team." Certainly, we knew about "Big D" and Neiman-Marcus, but few of us had ever heard of Dealey Plaza or a triple underpass or Parkland Hospital. Washington was familiar turf, the seat of government and the base of national power.

The media promised that the plane would arrive at 6:05 P.M. (EST). News reporters told us that the government was keeping the flight plan secret in order to reduce the risk of attack. Millions were watching television when the presidential jet touched down at Andrews Air Force Base at 5:59 P.M. I remember being thankful that the arrival was early.

It was dark. We saw the big plane come to a halt, and we watched a giant contraption that looked like a catering truck—it was—roll up to the side door near the rear. A crowd of somber diplomats and government officials was waiting on the tarmac.

Everyone's attention was on the rear of the plane, where a military unit stood on the platform of the lift, waiting to unload President Kennedy's casket and place it into a waiting ambulance. JFK's main aides and security guards appeared in the doorway, brushed most of the soldiers aside, and carried the massive coffin. They struggled awkwardly with the heavy burden, but it was obvious that these faithful Kennedy cohorts were determined to lift him themselves.

We learned later that the idea had come from Jacqueline Kennedy, who had begun to exert a powerful influence over the manner in which her husband's death would be remembered. "I want his friends to carry him down," she told them.[97]

And there in the doorway behind the massive casket stood Mrs. Kennedy, still wearing the blood-stained suit. Yes, Americans had heard the report of the shooting; now we were seeing the reality of it for the first time. There was the naked casket, gleaming in the spotlights, and the grief-stricken widow, her suit darkened with awful stains. Audiences saw it in black and white, but the message was clear: *Look what they have done.*

Robert Kennedy was at her side. Unnoticed by many viewers, he had raced up the front steps of the plane and sought out his sister-in-law. He would remain near her for the rest of the weekend (Figure 2.9).

The truck lowered its platform, but the clumsy apparatus stopped above the tarmac. Men rushed to help the Kennedy aides off-load the casket. We knew by this time that Jacqueline Kennedy had remained constantly with her

FIGURE 2.9
The arrival of President Kennedy's casket in Washington, D.C. His widow, still wearing her blood-stained clothes, stands behind the coffin with Robert Kennedy. *Courtesy, AP/Wide World Photos*

husband since the shooting. She made a sudden move as if to jump down, but an aide quickly reached up and gently lifted her. The casket was loaded into the ambulance and Mrs. Kennedy, waving off a waiting limousine, moved to climb into the back of the ambulance for the ride to Bethesda Naval Hospital. The door was locked. It was a frustrating moment for everyone. It was also shocking because it was the first time that cameras showed her in full view, away from a protective crowd of agents or Kennedy staffers. From the waist down she was literally covered with gore; her legs were streaked with it. The door finally opened, and she climbed inside.[98]

After the ambulance pulled away, President Johnson and the new first lady deplaned and walked to a set of microphones set up nearby. The time was 6:14 P.M. The mood was somber. President Johnson's remarks were brief and ended simply: "I ask for your help, and God's."[99]

IN DALLAS . . .

At 7:10 P.M. Friday night, the Dallas police charged Lee Harvey Oswald with the murder of J. D. Tippit. The arraignment took place before the slain president's autopsy began at Bethesda Naval Hospital outside Washington, D.C.

By Friday afternoon, TV audiences knew that Oswald was an ex-Marine who had defected to the Soviet Union in 1959 and reentered the country in 1962 with a Russian wife, Marina. We knew that materials found in the temporary residence of his wife and children in the Dallas suburb of Irving tied him to pro-Cuban activist groups and that investigators had found Marxist literature among his meager possessions. We learned that police had also discovered an empty, rolled-up blanket that Marina Oswald said was used to store her husband's rifle.[100] As expected, Dallas Police Captain Will Fritz was placed in charge of the homicide investigation.

It may be difficult for nonrememberers to understand what the news of Oswald's communist leanings did to the average American. In 1963 the USSR was the enemy; contemporary analogies seem inadequate, but Russia was the equivalent of today's Middle Eastern madman with his finger on the detonator of a bomb. The USSR had many bombs. Only ten years earlier Americans had witnessed the persecution of its citizens by U.S. Senator Joseph McCarthy, whose investigative committee accused many people of being communists, destroying some careers and seriously damaging others. This wave of terror was past, but communism was still condemned in most American homes.

Cuba was another hot button. Cuban dictator Fidel Castro had come to power on the island in a coup in 1959 and then announced pro-communist leanings. Cuba's proximity to the United States caused fear of a Soviet-backed attack launched from the island, and in 1962 American intelligence agents confirmed those fears by discovering the installation of nuclear strike missiles there. The Cuban missile crisis occurred in October, only thirteen months before the assassination in Dallas. For days on end the country had waited anxiously and prayed that Kennedy and Nikita Khrushchev could avoid World War III. In the minds of many, Lee Harvey Oswald's connections were sinister.

The scenes in the hallway at Dallas Police headquarters were disconcerting. The press overwhelmed local police security. Reporters wanted to see Oswald to assure themselves that he had not been abused by his captors. Chief Curry bent to the media's demands for a Friday night "showing" of the suspect. The display lasted only about two minutes and took place shortly after midnight.[101] Oswald proclaimed his innocence in both murders and appeared surprised and sullen on camera. The media did little to discourage us from forming a negative image of the prime suspect. Reporters shouted questions and did not wait for him to answer. The place looked like a madhouse, and it was.[102] National law enforcement officials began to voice their fears that Oswald was being tried on television.[103]

By the time I went to bed, Oswald still did not have an attorney to represent him. The famous *Miranda* ruling, requiring investigators to inform suspects of their right to counsel, was still three years in the future. However, the police had already offered assistance, and the Dallas Bar Association sent its president to render aid to the suspect. Oswald insisted on one particular New York attorney, John Abt, known for his work with the American Civil Liberties Union, who subsequently declined to represent him.[104]

SATURDAY

When we tuned into the television early Saturday morning, reporters told us that Lee Harvey Oswald had been arraigned for the murder of the president of the United States.[105] Saturday's news shifted between the investigation at police headquarters in Dallas and the preparations for the fallen president's state funeral, scheduled to take place in Washington, D.C., on Monday.

President Johnson declared November 25 as a national day of mourning.

On Friday night the television networks had begun broadcasting highlights from Kennedy's life and career. By Saturday, there was more background on JFK. These documentaries were interspersed with updates from Dallas and Washington, creating a strong, new memory of Kennedy that effectively blended his life and his death. The biographical mood toward President Kennedy was kind and laudatory. Now was not the appropriate time to debunk him.

IN DALLAS . . .

Dallas authorities continued to gather a large body of evidence that seemed to link Lee Harvey Oswald to the murders of both Officer Tippit and President Kennedy. Witnesses identified Oswald in a Friday night line-up as the man they had seen at the site of Tippit's murder.[106] There were no witnesses who offered positive identification that Oswald had been the sniper firing from the Depository.

It seemed of little import. At the time of his arrest, Oswald was carrying different kinds of identification, some stating his name as Lee Harvey Oswald, some identifying him as A. Hidell or Alex Hidell (Figure 2.10). His boardinghouse landlady in Dallas said she knew him as O. H. Lee.[107] Why would an innocent man use so many aliases? we wondered at the time.

On the sixth floor of the Depository, officers had found Oswald's finger and palm prints on the boxes in the sniper's perch.[108] We knew by this time that the suspected assassin had been hired at the Depository on October 14 and regularly worked on the sixth floor filling orders, so the prints alone were not sufficient evidence. Although no prints were initially found on the rifle, the Dallas police said later that they lifted an Oswald palm print from beneath the stock of the weapon before it was shipped to the FBI lab in Washington.

Buell Wesley Frazier, a co-worker who drove Oswald to the Depository on November 22, said that the former Marine carried a brown paper package to work, which Oswald told him contained curtain rods. Although Frazier's estimate of the size of the bag varied from the size of the recovered evidence, officials concluded that this was the empty bag found in the sniper's perch and had actually

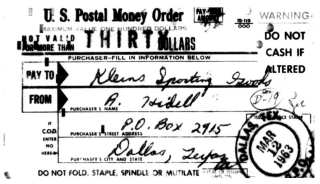

FIGURE 2.10
The postal money order sent by Oswald, using the alias A. Hidell,
to purchase the Mannlicher-Carcano rifle that was used in the assassination.
Warren Commission CE 788, National Archives

FIGURE 2.11
One of two photographs and two negatives that local officials discovered among Oswald's personal possessions. The images show him holding the weapons used in the shootings of JFK and Officer Tippit. Oswald said, "This picture is a fake." *Warren Commission CE 133A, National Archives*

been used to carry in the murder weapon.[109] On Friday, the media made much of the fact that officers had found another bag, containing the remains of a lunch partially eaten by another Depository employee, near the sniper's perch; at first we imagined the assassin calmly munching on fried chicken while waiting for the presidential limousine to arrive in Dealey Plaza.[110]

On Saturday we also learned that the Dallas investigators had searched Oswald's residence in Irving and discovered photos of the suspect holding the rifle that was found on the sixth floor and the pistol that he was carrying when he was arrested in the Texas Theater (Figure 2.11). Oswald was uncooperative with police investigators, telling them the photos were fakes. "I'm just a patsy," he insisted to reporters.[111]

Early Saturday morning the FBI traced ownership of the rifle to one A. Hidell, an alias for Lee Harvey Oswald, and investigators confirmed that the weapon was not a Mauser but a 1940 Italian-made Mannlicher-Carcano, which had been mounted with a telescopic sight.[112] On Friday, police had performed nitrate tests on the suspect's hands and cheek to determine if there were signs that he had fired weapons. Saturday morning Chief Curry told reporters that he believed that both tests had been positive; his account was in error about the cheek test, but national audiences did not know it at the time.[113]

IN WASHINGTON . . .

News from Washington revealed details of the plans for a state funeral, modeled after the one held for Abraham Lincoln nearly a century earlier. The media made frequent comparisons between the martyrdom of Lincoln in 1865 and the death of John F. Kennedy. Images associating the two men would stick in many minds.

The autopsy was complete by early Saturday morning, and the president's body was carried to the White House. Many viewers saw this predawn film footage in one of the endless replays that television provided. Military units stationed at the portico received the casket at about 4:22 A.M. (EST) and transported it to the center of the East Room, which had been draped in black in the manner of the Lincoln funeral (Figure 2.12). A solemn crowd had assembled in the dark outside the White House gates, waiting for the hearse to arrive with the body. Mrs. Kennedy, still dressed in the pink suit, followed close to the casket. Inside the East Room, military guards were stationed at each of four corners of the bier; priests rotated every two hours intoning prayers for the soul of John F. Kennedy.[114]

Saturday in Washington dawned rainy, blustery, and glum, befitting the nation's mood. The family held a private mass in the morning, but viewers got a peek at the faces of the former presidents and other officials who showed up at the White House to pay their respects. The visitors streamed through all day.[115] I was relieved that former President Dwight Eisenhower was meeting with Lyndon Johnson. Eisenhower had been the first president that I remembered clearly from my childhood; I believed that he was fatherly and wise, a military general who would help Johnson get the nation under control again.

Other details were dutifully reported during the day. The slain president's mother, the devout Rose Kennedy, had attended mass at 8:00 A.M. in Massachusetts. Family members had finally informed Joseph Kennedy, already seriously ill and partially paralyzed from a stroke, about the loss of his second son. The former ambassador, largely mute and confined to a wheelchair, had managed to withstand the traumatic news.[116]

Reports focused lavish attention on Jacqueline Kennedy, although we did not see her. TV recounted the story of one of Mrs. Kennedy's final acts at Parkland Hospital the day before: she had placed her wedding band on her husband's finger.[117] Everyone was worried about the

FIGURE 2.12
The East Room of the White House, shown draped in mourning. President Kennedy's casket was displayed here on Saturday. The decorations were based on the materials used for the Lincoln funeral a century earlier. *Abby Rowe, National Archives, 79-AR-8255-M*

28

Kennedy children. We learned that they had been told about their father's death, but it was doubtful that little John understood the news. He would celebrate his third birthday on Monday, the day of the funeral.

During the afternoon we were told that John Kennedy would be buried with full military honors at Arlington National Cemetery. Mrs. Kennedy was reported to have visited the site herself.[118] World leaders were telegramming their intentions to attend the funeral in Washington. LBJ, firmly in charge, called his first cabinet meeting.[119] The images switched to those of happier days, of Jack and Jackie's wedding, of vacations with the children at the family compound at Hyannis Port, Massachusetts, of the inauguration and the receptions that followed it. The coverage was endless.

IN DALLAS . . .

The scene at police headquarters in Dallas continued to be chaotic, with reporters grabbing anyone who entered the third floor for interviews. During the morning the press leaped on police to get information about another man who had been brought in for questioning. Was he another suspect, they asked, referring to Depository worker Joe Molina, who had volunteered to come to headquarters?

Dallas police had searched Molina's house earlier and found nothing. Investigators told the press he was involved in subversive activities. Actually, Molina was a member of the American G.I. Forum, a veteran's group for Mexican-Americans.[120] Finally, the hapless Molina dropped out of the story.

Dallas Police Captain Fritz told reporters and viewing audiences that Oswald's case was "cinched." Officials determined that criminal prosecution for the murder of President Kennedy fell under the jurisdiction of Dallas County, so District Attorney Henry Wade was interviewed about his plans to try Oswald. Wade firmly announced that he would win the case against the accused assassin. According to established procedure, the prisoner would be transferred to the county jail in the Criminal Courts Building on Houston Street in Dealey Plaza.

Reporters kept pushing Police Chief Curry to tell them the time that Oswald would be moved on Sunday. At 8:00 P.M. on Saturday night, he told them that if they arrived by 10:00 A.M. the next morning, they would not miss the transfer.[121]

SUNDAY

IN WASHINGTON . . .

Sunday began with news recaps of the previous day, and much attention was given to the first major public mourning ceremony, a congressional tribute at the Capitol rotunda scheduled to begin at noon. Many people went to church; by this time audiences were familiar with the television style of reporting and knew they would be able to see replays of the coverage later. TV cameras lined up outside the north portico of the White House to await the appearance of the widowed first lady.

By 12:20 P.M. (EST) a large crowd of mourners had assembled outside. Suddenly, a buzzing went through the crowd. *Oswald's been shot!*[122] Back in Dallas, yet another murder in forty-eight hours had just taken place.

Viewers who were already tuned in to NBC television actually saw the murder. The network had switched from Washington to Dallas to provide live coverage of Oswald's transfer from the city to the county jail.

IN DALLAS . . .

The transfer was running about an hour late. Oswald came down by elevator to the basement, where a group of about seventy-five reporters and an equal number of armed policemen waited. There had been threats against Oswald's life, so security was tight.[123] The suspect, escorted by two Dallas policemen, was handcuffed to Officer James Leavelle, who wore a white suit and Stetson hat. When Oswald, dressed in a dark sweater and slacks, came into view, radio reporter Ike Pappas was nearby. He shouted, "Do you have anything to say in your defense?"[124] The time was 11:21 A.M.

Suddenly, a man streaked past the reporter, lunged at Oswald, and shot him in the abdomen at point-blank range (Figure 2.13). Oswald fell to the ground, his handcuffed arm pulling the astonished Officer Leavelle down with him. Policemen jumped on the assailant, wrestling for his pistol. One reporter shoved an officer who was inadvertently blocking the NBC camera lens. Pandemonium broke out.

"He's shot! Oswald's been shot!" exclaimed Pappas as reporters ducked for cover and police waved their guns in fury.

NBC's camera stayed on; it was the first such live broadcast on television. Other networks hastened to switch to

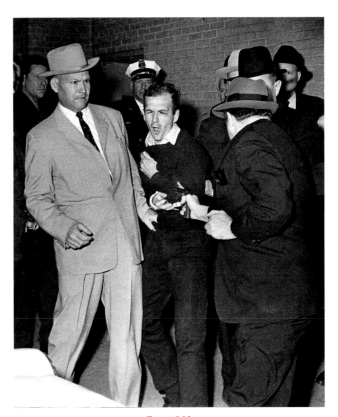

FIGURE 2.13
Jack Ruby, shown shooting Lee Oswald at 11:21 A.M. Ruby had entered the basement at Dallas police headquarters on November 24, during the accused assassin's transfer from the city to the county jail. Oswald died at 1:07 P.M. during surgery at Parkland Hospital. °*1963 Bob Jackson*

Dallas, and eventually all television stations were showing the same incredible event.[125]

Viewers sat frozen and open-mouthed in front of television sets. We quickly learned that the shooter was a Dallas nightclub operator and police groupie named Jack Ruby (formerly Rubenstein). "One more awful thing," observed Jackie Kennedy, when she was told later about the shooting of the prime suspect in her husband's murder.[126] The attack on Oswald opened a door for the federal government to enter the case.

IN WASHINGTON . . .

The scene on television shifted from chaos to dignity. Jacqueline Kennedy had appeared on the steps of the White House, dressed in black. It was her first public appearance since she returned from the autopsy. She had Caroline and John, Jr., with her, one standing on each side and holding on to a gloved hand. The two children were nattily outfitted in little short coats and looked oblivious to the meaning of the ceremony (see image opposite page 17).

The procession to the Capitol left at 1:08 P.M. (EST), marching slowly to the beat of muffled drums.[127] The drums made an eerie sound, not hollow but dull. Somehow, their rhythm was relentless. It was a formal parade, the procession moving at one hundred steps per minute. Marching units included the U.S. Marines, Army, Coast Guard, and Air Force. The Joint Chiefs of Staff were present. It was a grand military affair for a fallen commander-in-chief. Although the news said that such trappings were customary for a deceased head of state, the ceremony gave me the

impression that Kennedy had fallen on the field of battle and not in an open limousine riding through a Dallas park (Figure 2.14). It was symbolism of the highest order.

Six handsome gray horses pulled a black-draped caisson, the same one, we learned, that had carried President Franklin Roosevelt's casket in 1945. A riderless horse followed, symbolizing the death of a leader. The boots in the stirrups were reversed, another symbol of loss. Television dutifully reported the name of the horse, Black Jack; the animal was skittish, not liking his role at all (Figure 2.15). The *clop, clop, clop* of his hooves on the street created another powerful sound that I have always associated with that weekend.

The parade moved down Pennsylvania Avenue toward the Capitol. Thousands of people, most of them young, lined the streets. Once the procession had passed, a crowd of one hundred thousand mourners broke through a police barricade and quietly joined in the march on foot. At the end of the parade, the cameras switched to the base of the Capitol, where the family waited. We heard a twenty-one-gun salute from cannons. Beneath this booming noise came "Hail to the Chief," played slowly as a dirge. It was usually played at a lively pace; for me, it had always been the president's cue to enter a room. On Sunday it became a sound of farewell. I finally accepted the fact that John Kennedy was not coming back.

Next, the strains of the "Naval Hymn" slowly wafted through the crowd. The sounds brought back recollections that JFK had been a naval hero in World War II. Military escorts hauled the heavy casket up the thirty-six steps into the rotunda. The family followed behind. It was devastatingly sad.

FIGURE 2.14
Flags from the fifty states dipping in homage as the funeral cortege begins its march from the White House to the Capitol rotunda on Sunday. *UPI/Corbis-Bettmann*

FIGURE 2.15
Black Jack, shown in the Sunday procession honoring the memory of John F. Kennedy. In military funeral parades, a riderless horse symbolizes the loss of a leader. *Courtesy, AP/Wide World Photos*

Cameras took us inside the vast dome of the rotunda, and we watched John F. Kennedy's casket as it was placed upon the same catafalque that had once held the coffin of Abraham Lincoln. Short tributes were read. One of them,

by Senator Mike Mansfield, had a particularly poignant refrain: "And so she took a ring from her finger and placed it in his hands."[128] Mansfield repeated it over and over again.

Mrs. Kennedy remained calm. Following the speeches, President Johnson delivered a huge wreath to the bier, and the ceremony was over, or so we thought. Heads turned toward the widow, waiting for her to leave. Instead, she and her daughter walked over to the flag-draped casket, where they both knelt. Jacqueline Kennedy briefly kissed the coffin; Caroline reached beneath the flag and touched it (Figure 2.16). The moment became one of the most powerful icons of that terrible weekend.[129]

After the ceremonies ended at 2:19 P.M., the doors of the Capitol were thrown open to the public. The fallen president, we learned, would lie in state for the rest of the afternoon, until 9:00 P.M. that evening.[130] Officials soon realized that they would have to extend their deadline. Cameras stationed in the rotunda showed the lines of mourners who walked past the bier. TV captured their solemn faces and their tears.

IN DALLAS . . .

Oswald had been taken to Parkland Hospital by ambulance, where some of the same doctors who had worked on President Kennedy and Governor Connally tried feverishly

FIGURE 2.16
Mrs. Kennedy and Caroline kneeling at President Kennedy's bier at the conclusion of the memorial service in the rotunda of the Capitol. *Courtesy, AP/Wide World Photos*

31

to save his life. The single gunshot had caused massive internal wounds, however, and Oswald died at 1:07 P.M. during surgery. He never regained consciousness.[131] Parkland Hospital announced the death of Lee Harvey Oswald at 1:25 P.M., six minutes after the ceremony at the rotunda in Washington had concluded.

Local reporters were already at Parkland to cover a press conference given earlier by Texas First Lady Nellie Connally. When Oswald's ambulance had arrived at the emergency entrance to the hospital, the waiting reporters had surged through the doors with the attendants and the wounded suspect. Eventually, Parkland officials restored order and put the media in the same room where the announcement of JFK's death had been made. Once again the doctors answered questions about their unsuccessful treatment of the patient.[132]

People everywhere were speechless. It didn't "take an expert to suspect that something of gigantic proportions was going on," thought assassination witness Howard Brennan at the time.[133] The notion of conspiracy flared in the public mind.

FIGURE 2.17
Some of the 250,000 people who came to view President Kennedy's bier. Even though government officials extended the viewing hours at the rotunda, many people were turned away. *UPI/Corbis-Bettmann*

MONDAY

IN WASHINGTON . . .

Monday was the official day of mourning, so most U.S. businesses and schools were closed. It was also the day of John F. Kennedy's burial. The state funeral was a grand affair, involving more than 7,000 members of the military. Officials had postponed their plans to close the rotunda to mourners on Sunday night and kept the bier on view until Monday morning. Early on Monday the line of mourners outside the Capitol was three miles long. By the time the rotunda closed its doors shortly before the funeral, 250,000 people had walked quietly past the body (Figure 2.17).[134]

My brother Billy, age twenty, and some members of his fraternity left East Carolina University in North Carolina around 11:00 P.M. (EST) on Sunday night and drove to Washington to view the coffin. "I couldn't believe any of this was real," he recalled. "These things only happened on TV."[135] The line at the Capitol was too long, so they decided to find a place along the funeral route to watch the procession.

Shortly after 10:50 A.M., the caisson carrying John F. Kennedy's coffin left the Capitol. The route called for the procession to return to the White House, then proceed to St. Matthew's Cathedral for a requiem mass before the final trip to Arlington National Cemetery. The entire distance was more than six miles. One million people lined the route.[136]

Exhausted, we television viewers tuned in to watch the president's funeral. Weekend news accounts had revealed that Mrs. Kennedy had decided to walk behind the caisson from the White House to the cathedral, about eight blocks away. More than one hundred foreign heads of state or official representatives had descended on Washington to participate in the ceremonies. When they learned that Mrs. Kennedy planned to march on foot, they insisted on accompanying her. Security agents were aghast but unable to coax the world leaders into their limousines. As one observer reported, "People were scared to death."[137]

Jacqueline Kennedy's family and aides tried to talk her into riding to the church. Some of the visiting dignitaries were too old to march, they warned. The aged president of Turkey had been a major when Dwight Eisenhower had been a young cadet at West Point, they said. *He* could ride, stated the widow. *She* would walk.[138]

The procession to St. Matthew's Cathedral formed up at 11:30 A.M. outside the White House. Mrs. Kennedy returned with the caisson from the Capitol, got out of the limousine and then, flanked by Robert and Edward Kennedy, she squared her shoulders and began the march. She was followed by members of the family and by President and Mrs. Lyndon Johnson. Leaders from most of the nations followed them, walking abreast in a ragtag line through the crowds lining the streets of Washington. For long, anxious minutes, people watched and prayed that no more shots would ring out.

It was an unforgettable sight. There was tall French President Charles de Gaulle, a repeated target of assassins, striding with diminutive Ethiopian Emperor Haile Selassie, whose military sword nearly dragged on the street. Queen Frederika of Greece marched. British Prince Philip marched. Prime ministers, ambassadors, African chiefs, Arabian sheiks, and third-world dictators marched (Figure 2.18).[139]

Church bells in the federal city tolled mournfully, and the procession kept time to the doleful sounds of bagpipes played by the Scottish Black Watch. Jacqueline Kennedy's face was covered by a mantilla, but her stride was purposeful (Figure 2.19). She became "a symbol of national catharsis."[140]

My brother and his friends stood curbside on Connecticut Avenue along the route. They had staked out a claim very early in the morning, so the crowds formed behind them eighteen people deep. No one shoved, no one pushed. There was little talking at all, and that was carried on in hushed tones. A television crew was stationed in an upper window in the building behind them. When the

FIGURE 2.18
Dignitaries marching in President Kennedy's state funeral in Washington on November 25. The tall man seen to the left of center is
French President Charles de Gaulle; Ethiopian Emperor Haile Selassie is to the right. Mrs. Kennedy insisted on marching to the cathedral mass on foot,
so the world's leaders, from one hundred nations, followed her. *Robert Knudsen, courtesy John F. Kennedy Library*

FIGURE 2.19
The Kennedys, leading the march to St. Matthew's Cathedral; from left, Robert, Jacqueline, and Edward Kennedy. *Robert Knudsen, courtesy John F. Kennedy Library*

reporters started to chat among themselves, a burly man in the crowd wheeled around and warned them to show some respect to the memory of the fallen president. They too fell silent.

Charles de Gaulle passed within thirty feet of Billy's location. My brother does not remember the church bells or the bagpipes. Instead, he recalls the sound of footsteps and the clatter of Black Jack's hooves. "I have never been in a place that was that quiet," he recalled. "There was a huge number of people and no sound."

Television viewers missed this dimension of the ceremony. My brother and his friends were not worried about assassins. They were attending the nation's funeral while standing on the street. The media was unable to convey some other important elements of the real ceremony. "All of these people you had seen on TV were not the same size," said Billy. De Gaulle was a giant, and Jacqueline Kennedy appeared much smaller than he had imagined. The caisson carrying the dead president was "an itty-bitty thing." Did his expectations match the experience itself? "It was a huge reality check."[141]

At the entrance to the cathedral, Catholic Cardinal John Cushing came outside to meet the caisson. Mrs. Kennedy knelt to kiss his ring, and he blessed the casket. Then, at 12:10 P.M., the procession moved inside for the mass. At every seat was a pew card printed with a memorial inscription penned by Jacqueline Kennedy: "Dear God please take care of your servant John Fitzgerald Kennedy."[142]

The ceremony was all pomp and poignancy. Prayers were read, along with excerpts from John Kennedy's writ-

FIGURE 2.20

John F. Kennedy, Jr., age three, offering a salute to his father's caisson from the steps of the cathedral after the funeral mass. *UPI/Corbis-Bettmann*

FIGURE 2.21

JFK's caisson, shown crossing Memorial Bridge heading toward the interment at Arlington National Cemetery. One million people lined the funeral route on November 25. *UPI/Corbis-Bettmann*

34

FIGURE 2.22
Jacqueline Kennedy, lighting an eternal flame to mark her husband's grave.
Abby Rowe, National Archives #79-AR-8255-3L

At the cemetery a band played the "Star-Spangled Banner," and air force bagpipes played "Mist-Covered Mountain." Soldiers hauled the casket up a hill to the grave, located in a line between the Custis-Lee Mansion above and the Lincoln Memorial below. At 2:54 P.M. fifty military jets, flying in a V-formation, staged a flyby. One plane was left out—again, a symbol of the fallen leader. *Air Force One*, right behind them, came in low at five hundred feet and slowly dipped its wings in tribute. "He loved that plane," said JFK aide Dave Powers.[145]

The Irish Black Watch performed a silent drill. Then the commitment service prayers were said. Cannons fired one last twenty-one-gun salute, and soldiers fired rifles: three volleys each.

At 3:07 P.M., a bugler began "Taps." One note came out high. No one cared except the bugler, who had been deafened by the sound of the rifle fire. The band played the "Naval Hymn" again, and the flag draping the coffin was folded with precision and presented to the widow. Finally, clutching the flag to her chest, Jacqueline Kennedy moved toward the casket. She grasped a lighted taper and leaned over to ignite a flame that would burn forever at her husband's grave. She had learned of the symbolic gesture while on a trip to France and felt it would be appropriate (Figure 2.22).[146]

At 3:15 P.M. it was all over. With Gallic assurance, Charles de Gaulle later remarked of Mrs. Kennedy: "She gave an example to the whole world of how to behave."[147]

After the service, the family and visiting dignitaries left Arlington to return to the White House for a formal reception. Members of the Kennedy family took turns receiving the illustrious guests. Later, Mrs. Kennedy herself appeared to extend personal thanks. At the same time President Johnson hosted a separate reception at the State Department.[148]

Television cameras lingered at the grave site, panning the surrounding hills covered with floral tributes. It seemed that no one wanted to say a final goodbye. The superintendent of Arlington National Cemetery thought otherwise. He did not want audiences to witness the final descent of the casket into the ground, so he pulled the plug on the electricity to the cameras. At last we were disconnected from the events of the weekend. The time was 3:34 P.M.[149]

IN DALLAS . . .

Many people have forgotten about two more funerals that took place that day, both of them in Texas. The service for slain Dallas police officer J. D. Tippit began in Dallas at 2:00 P.M. and was televised locally. City officials, private citizens, and seven hundred police officers attended.[150] In Fort Worth, plans for the funeral of Lee Harvey Oswald went awry. Determined to let Oswald be buried in peace, local officials called for tight security at Rose Hill Cemetery. Arrangements for a minister were made in advance, but the signals got confused.

When the Oswald family arrived for the service, there was no preacher. Louis Saunders of the Fort Worth Council of Churches finally performed the brief ceremony at 4:00 P.M. The widowed Marina Oswald was there with her two young daughters. Marguerite and Robert Oswald, mother and brother of the slain suspect, also attended.[151] At the conclusion of the service, organizers realized there were

ings and speeches. Many Americans did not watch the entire funeral service, delivered in Latin, and went instead to services organized at local churches and synagogues to coincide with the official mass. I went to early services and was back in front of the television before the closing of the service at St. Matthew's. At the end, Cardinal Cushing, who had officiated at the marriage of John and Jacqueline Kennedy ten years before, switched from Latin to English for his final blessing and said, "May the angels, dear Jack, lead you into Paradise."[143]

Outside, the caisson procession formed up again, and the widow and her children appeared on the steps of the cathedral to hear "Hail to the Chief" one more time. As the casket moved past, young John F. Kennedy, Jr., urged by his mother, stepped forward and offered a handsome salute (Figure 2.20).[144] Many of us saw it from a distance on television. There was the little soldier, standing in his short coat with his knees exposed. It was the close-up photographs that ran in newspapers and magazines later that truly cemented that image in the minds of millions.

The final procession left the church at 1:30 P.M. This time the officials rode to the grave site, but it was more than an hour before the long line of limousines arrived at Arlington National Cemetery. Along the route stood people, one million people, silent and weeping. Television cameras made it seem as if we were with them (Figure 2.21).

FIGURE 2.23
Reporters, pressed into service to act as pallbearers at the funeral of Lee Harvey Oswald. The service was held in Fort Worth on Monday, November 25.
Courtesy, Gene Gordon

no pallbearers to attend to the coffin. Reporters pitched in to carry Lee Harvey Oswald to his final resting place (Figure 2.23).[152]

IN WASHINGTON . . .

At 6:00 P.M. (EST) on Monday night, the Kennedy family held a birthday party for John F. Kennedy, Jr., at the White House. He was three years old.

THE REACTION

On November 22, the initial reaction to news of the Kennedy shooting was disbelief. One college student who listened to the radio continuously on Friday night stated the reason: "If we listened to it long enough, we'd believe it."[153] This sense of denial stayed with my brother and his friends throughout the weekend; acceptance did not set in until they saw the caisson in Washington during their "reality check." After the initial disbelief came acceptance and then suffering. More than two-thirds of the American people reported symptoms of physical illness—nausea, headaches, depression, bouts of crying—during the weekend after the assassination. A majority reported that they had never felt a comparable emotion; those who could recall a similar feeling likened it to the loss of a family member or other loved one.[154] I went through periods of nausea and depression and wept during the more poignant moments of the weekend television coverage. The sense of loss of a close friend was strong and unrelenting.

Why did we experience this sense of personal loss? After all, most Americans did not really know John Kennedy, and many, including my parents, had not even voted for him. A part of the answer lies in the qualities of the man, and the rest can be ascribed to the close ties that most Americans felt to the office of the presidency. In addition, Kennedy was too young to die. That was one of the dominant thoughts of the weekend. He was born in *our* century, the youngest president, at forty-two, elected to the office.[155] Everyone was wounded by the sense of waste associated with the death of such a young and vibrant leader.

In a sense, his death did not fit the pattern of leadership that many Americans had come to expect. Two earlier American presidents, Lincoln and Roosevelt, had led the nation to success during terrible wars; they died victorious. Kennedy "died not at the moment of triumph but in the middle of battle."[156] For many rememberers, the cold war was a very *real* war.

We were deeply affected by the repeated, televised images of his young and beautiful widow and of Caroline and little John. Polls showed that more than 90% of the nation felt keen sympathy for Mrs. Kennedy and the children; it was the most deeply felt emotion at the time.[157] People had been fascinated by all of the Kennedy activities, from the touch football games to the White House nursery that Mrs. Kennedy had set up for Caroline and some of her acquaintances.

The repeated flashbacks on television to JFK as a young man, as a naval officer, and as a politician reminded audiences of his charm, his good looks, his wit, and the now-famous Kennedy style. All told, he was an exceedingly attractive man with a beautiful wife and children. Their wealth was a plus with many; we believed that a little royalty and class could only help the United States in its global efforts.

The events of the weekend also created an emotional bond with the rest of the Kennedy family. Robert Kennedy, clearly suffering, resolutely remained near his sister-in-law throughout the public weekend ceremonies; other members of the clan were frequently on view. The media provided detailed information about the reaction of each family member to the loss of their son or brother. We were constantly reminded of the earlier deaths of Joe Kennedy, Jr., of JFK's sister Kathleen, and of two of the president's children, a stillborn girl and little Patrick. News reporters remarked on the curse of the family—illness and death. The Kennedys shared their pain publicly with millions of people, and millions adopted the family as their own. The new generation can make a clear separation between JFK and the rest of his clan; for my generation, they all blended into the collective memory.

The image of the presidency in 1963 was also important in the American mind.[158] At the time of President Kennedy's death, the office was held in high regard. Although my parents had not voted for John Kennedy in 1960, there was deep respect for him, as president, in our household. During the early 1960's, seven out of every ten Americans expressed faith that the government would generally do right by its people; by 1992 only 29% felt the same way.[159]

The president was the first political figure known to children, who traditionally looked on him as both important and benign. I never looked on JFK as a father figure, although he was the same age as some of the parents of my friends. My first memories were of Truman and Eisenhower, and compared with those presidents, Kennedy was young. Many little boys of my era wanted to grow up to be president of the United States; in those days it was a noble ambition.

People identified personally with the president; he was a vicarious outlet that allowed them to participate in powerful decisions. JFK's style enhanced this tendency to associate the presidency with power, the personification of government, leading the charge against communism and other evils of the day. This personal sense of identification also explained the intense interest that we all had in what the Kennedys wore, what they ate, and whom they entertained at the White House.

Finally, the president served as a symbol of national unity and stability. The assassination made me feel like a part of my foundation had collapsed. JFK symbolized many of the characteristics of the United States after World War II: young, rich, powerful, and dedicated to the ideals of freedom and equality. With Kennedy gone, I wanted someone to restore order and to get the nation under control.

Television coverage during the weekend took viewers on an emotional roller-coaster ride. Scenes shifted rapidly from the chaos at the Dallas police station to the sheer majesty of the military funeral rites, from the surliness of Lee Oswald to the quiet dignity and grief of the widowed first lady. On Friday, the shock of learning that the president had been assassinated was bad enough, but half the nation also heard the unsettling rumors that LBJ, Mrs. Kennedy, or a Secret Serviceman had been shot.[160] The murder of Oswald on Sunday was almost too much to bear.

Some viewers came to feel that the unrelenting focus on Mrs. Kennedy was an invasion of her privacy; still others questioned the role that reporters might have played in prejudicing Lee Harvey Oswald's chance of a fair and impartial trial.[161] By and large, however, two-thirds of the nation felt that the television coverage of the weekend was impartial. Those who sensed bias expressed belief that the material was too favorably slanted toward John F. Kennedy; only 14% said the media was prejudiced against Lee Harvey Oswald.[162]

The extensive coverage had other, psychological, effects on its audiences. It helped to create a positive bond between the people and the new president.[163] Television repeatedly assured the nation's people that Lyndon Johnson was strong and in charge of the government. Shortly after viewers learned that President Kennedy was dead, an ABC News commentator in New York observed that Johnson was "the best-informed vice president in history," tacitly ignoring predecessors such as John Adams and Thomas Jefferson.[164] The stock market plunged twenty-two points before regulators shut it down on Friday afternoon; restoring the people's confidence in the nation became the order of the day.[165]

Throughout the weekend Johnson was shown looking presidential. These reassurances relieved anxiety about the stability of the United States.[166] By Monday, few questioned that the nation would move forward under LBJ's stewardship.

Watching television or listening to radio also produced something of a narcotic reaction. On the one hand it helped people accept the incredible news and also served as a safe haven in the storm. At the same time the endless repeating of powerful images was repelling; we turned off the set, only to return to it again and again, like addicts.[167]

News reports shaped American opinion about the investigation into the crime. By the end of the weekend, 72% of adults and 75% of children believed that Lee Harvey Oswald had killed JFK; in terms of motive, 62% of the adults and 96% of the children said they thought he was part of a conspiracy.[168] These feelings have dominated public opinion about the assassination ever since.

I was among the many people who assumed that the assassin was crazy.[169] Although there was a general sense of conspiracy, few actually believed that Oswald had been acting directly as an agent for the communists or any other major enemy of that era.[170] In fact, people expressed no strong desire to track down the conspirators, if they existed.[171] This hint of apathy remained with many of the rememberers in the years that followed.

The majority of Americans rued the death of Lee Harvey Oswald; only 10% expressed any desire for vengeance against him. Although Jack Ruby became a figure of almost universal scorn, most people expressed hope that he would get a fair trial.[172]

The funeral service for the dead has served for centuries to provide resolution and release for the anguish suffered by family and friends. The Kennedy state funeral was no exception. The funeral was portrayed by the media as the great catharsis; it drew the largest weekend viewing audience—excluding the church service itself—and promoted a feeling of rededication to the basic values of American society.[173] Many people felt better after the ceremony; the memory of Kennedy the man and Kennedy the symbol had been honored, and national order under a new president had been restored.

People in other nations shared the grief of the American people over the death of John F. Kennedy. It was the depth and breadth of foreign suffering that came as such a surprise. European correspondents reported that the overall reaction was unparalleled for a foreign head of state. Britain's Parliament heard the news, rose to give tributes, and then adjourned, an honor normally reserved for the monarch or the prime minister.[174]

After word reached West Berlin on Friday night, one hundred students from the Technical University staged an impromptu torch parade toward the city plaza where Kennedy had given his famous "Ich bin ein Berliner" speech.[175] In thirteen minutes the crowd had swelled to three thousand, and it continued to grow until sixty thousand people finally spilled into the square (Figure 2.24). We Americans heard of these tributes and felt a new sense of brotherhood with strangers in other lands.[176]

FIGURE 2.24

An impromptu torchlight parade in West Berlin. Shortly after news of the shooting reached Germany on Friday, students paid tribute to the memory of John F. Kennedy. *UPI/Corbis-Bettmann*

FIGURE 2.25
Young Argentineans at the American embassy in Buenos Aires, bearing a floral tribute in memory of JFK. *National Archives*

American embassies and consulates in other countries were jammed with visitors who arrived to sign the books of condolence there. One of the surprises of the weekend was the news that Soviet Premier Nikita Khrushchev had gone to the American Embassy in Moscow on Saturday morning to personally sign the register. Argentinean schoolchildren appeared at the embassy in Buenos Aires carrying huge sprays of flowers (Figure 2.25). Bulletins were posted in foreign consuls so that citizens could keep up with the news.

In the African Congo a council of Bantu chiefs and their wives went to the consulate there to commiserate over "the passing of a great chief," and the then-ruling military junta in the Dominican Republic—not even recognized by the United States—declared nine days of mourning for John F. Kennedy. On Saturday, the bell at Westminster Abbey in London tolled each minute from 11:00 A.M. until noon; it was another tribute normally reserved for British monarchs or political leaders.

When Charles de Gaulle arrived in Washington for the state funeral, he announced grandly, "I represent the French people; they sent me here."[177] De Gaulle, an obstacle to the movement toward the economic unification of Europe, had caused JFK much discomfort. His appearance on American soil was frankly shocking to many Americans. Max Lerner, writing in the *New Statesman*, summed up the events of the weekend as "the most dramatic happening in modern world history."[178] This may sound like hyperbole to readers today, but in 1963 Americans received a clear message from abroad: JFK had been Europe's promise for the future and its protector against nuclear annihilation.[179] His symbolism was very real to many people in foreign lands.

Other people joined Americans in attending President Kennedy's state funeral. Television made this possible by broadcasting the ceremonies. In addition, many religious groups in other nations scheduled memorial services to coincide with the mass at St. Matthew's in Washington. A series of global tributes were launched at the same time that mourners were scheduled to enter the portals of the cathedral in Washington.

Some tributes lasted only seconds, others for up to five minutes. Salutes were fired at U.S. military bases around the world, and ships tossed wreaths into the sea. The Panama Canal closed. In Greece, police stopped all rush-hour traffic for a few moments of silent tribute. Cab drivers in New York City abandoned their vehicles and stood outside their cabs, heads bowed, while "Taps" was broadcast in Times Square. Trucks pulled over to the sides of the nation's roadways, and airplanes delayed departures. For the only time in its history, the Associated Press wires fell silent.[180]

This sense of global unity made a strong impression on people everywhere. The cold war was at its height when Kennedy was slain. For several days, at least, warring nations stopped fighting. At home, liberals and conservatives, blacks and whites, poor and rich, men and women, came together with a single agenda: to grieve together over the loss of an American president. The yearning for collective harmony became a part of the memory.

By the end of the weekend, Kennedy, the slain president, had been transformed into John F. Kennedy, the legend. The myth of JFK had been born. Dallasite Larry Wright would recall, "Kennedy . . . became my hero, more in death than in life."[181] Polls taken shortly after the assassination showed a change in attitude toward the man who had won the 1960 presidential election by a mere 120,000 votes. Nearly 80% of Americans said he had been a great or "better than average" president; college students called him a "hero" and a role model.[182] Before his death, 42.5% of the people of Poland credited JFK with responsibility for the preservation of world peace; the number rose to 83.3% after the assassination.[183] The mythology of Kennedy became integral to the collective memory.

One other major component in the memory took shape during that weekend in 1963. Many Americans, and millions abroad, decried the forces of hatred that were alive in the nation. No one man could strike down the leader of the free world, they reasoned; something bigger must have done it. Journalists, politicians, and preachers across the United States made hurried pronouncements condemning the existence of a spirit of hatred that would allow an assassination to occur.

Chief Justice Earl Warren, one of the speakers at the ceremony at the Capitol on Sunday, used the forces of hatred as the theme for his remarks. Hatred was the force that had killed the president of the United States, he said. Since most human beings had experienced the emotion of hatred, no one felt entirely innocent of the crime.

Europeans took one look at the three Dallas murders and announced that the deaths confirmed the existence of an undercurrent of violence that ran through the American soul; after Oswald's death, the French jumped on the idea of conspiracy, with only 18% crediting Oswald as the sole perpetrator of the crime.[184] Diplomats and residents abroad sent dire warnings for the United States to solve the murders, and fast. From Rome: "The promptest possible exposure of everything involved in the tragic events seems very important for the image of the United States."[185] This pressure would have an impact on the investigation into the crime.

Non-Texas journalists, recalling many B-grade Cowboy-and-Indian movies, likened white-collar Dallas to the Wild West. The *New Statesman* warned that Oswald had "acted in accord with a dreadful American tradition . . . in the end, Mr. Kennedy perished under the savage code of the old frontier." The *New York Times* proclaimed on November 25 that Dallas was "not too far removed from the vigilante traditions of the old frontier."[186] Blaming the entire nation for the death of the president did not make too much sense, so Dallas became the symbol of the forces of hatred in the United States.

Dallas's reaction to the assassination itself was traumatic. The city closed down. When locals heard the news of the shooting, 58% of them completely stopped what they were doing; 86% reported feeling shame that the event had occurred in their city.[187] A spokesman for the AFL-CIO intoned: "The president would probably have been safer in Berlin or Moscow than he was in Dallas . . . we must take a long, hard look at our city."[188] Dallas citizens began to send flowers to Dealey Plaza, where they were placed on the grassy knoll. Thousands of people showed up at the park to walk past the display; honor guards were stationed at the site (Figure 2.26).[189] The gesture marked the initial transformation of Dealey Plaza into a memorial to President Kennedy.

"Terrible history has been made in Dallas," said the *Times Herald*, "and the magnitude of our city's sorrow can only be measured against the enormity of the deed."[190] Offices were emptied, concerts canceled, schools let out, and stores closed.[191] People prayed for their own and for the city's soul. Other American cities reacted in the same way, postponing or canceling events and shutting down offices. But in Dallas, people felt a need to hide. Dallas's reputation as a haven for right-wing extremists led many at first to assume that the shooting had been the work of the ultras. The arrest of Oswald, a confessed left-winger, seemed to negate this assumption. Anxious for damage control, the city fathers were quick to place the blame on Oswald.[192]

Perhaps no one had anticipated how strongly Americans would grieve over the loss of the president. But anger is a natural stage of the grieving process, and 73% of American adults expressed anger over President Kennedy's death.[193] After the murder of Oswald, many focused their ire against the city where the shootings occurred.

National journalists joined in the tirade. The press put a spin on events, roundly condemning Dallas's atmosphere of hatred. It did not matter that the prime suspect was a left-wing radical working in a profoundly conservative city; hatred did it, they said. Dallas did it. There was a tidal wave of abuse. Mayor Earle Cabell received death threats and had to hire security guards to protect himself and his family for several weeks after the shooting.[194] Telegrams poured into the city manager's office; one repeated the word "shame" fifty-one times while others compared the Dallas Police Department to the Keystone Kops or the Girl Scouts of America.[195]

There were a thousand slights. When UPI journalist Merriman Smith was packing up to leave the city, he turned to reporters in the offices of *The Dallas Morning News* and said, "Big D is little D now."[196] The *New York Times*'s editorial for November 25 called the botched transfer—in which the paper admitted its own employees had participated—"an outrageous breach of police responsibility."[197]

Aided by a negative media, Dallas suddenly became the city of hate. Although countless people had felt better after the cathartic effect of the state funeral, Dallas continued to suffer. "How can anybody blame a million people for the action of one?" asked one local newspaper writer a week after the slayings.[198]

Long after the shooting, Dallas residents were subject to abuse from other Americans: operators disconnected long-distance calls; attendants refused service at restaurants and gas stations; cars were pelted with rocks; drivers threw passengers out of their taxicabs. Decades after 1963, one foreigner was introduced to a Dallas woman and commented, "Oh yes, that's where you kill presidents."[199]

What effect did this added legacy of pain have on the witnesses to the assassination? Studies have clearly shown that victims of trauma, such as those who witnessed the shooting, needed release through communication. But there they were in Dallas, a town collectively traumatized in another way, a town that never encouraged them to talk about their trauma lest it remind the city of its own. After those painful days in November, some witnesses freely told their story, primarily to outsiders. Some would speak about the event, but they skimmed over the details, offering no invitation to delve into the emotional intensity of the memory. Some witnesses simply disappeared and never came forward; they are known only by the films and photographs taken by the men and women with cameras at the scene.

Myth, martyrdom, mourning, majesty, and mystery—this, then, was the collective memory of John F. Kennedy that emerged after those four long days in November 1963. Like all other things American, the memory today is uneven. The adults of 1963 remember mourning a man and a president; Jim Anderson remembers his childish concern over his mother's tears. For some, images from the weekend—little John saluting his father's caisson, the riderless horse, the flag-draped casket—still take them back decades in time. The details have blurred, but the memory lives on.

FIGURE 2.26
Dealey Plaza, after the assassination. Grieving Dallasites placed hundreds of flowers here in memory of the slain American leader.
Bill Winfrey, courtesy THE DALLAS MORNING NEWS

CHAPTER 3

JFK as Man and Myth

THE KENNEDY YEARS
1960–1963

On January 20, 1993, thirty-two years after the inauguration of John F. Kennedy as the thirty-fifth president of the United States, I watched another swearing-in on television, just as I had in 1961. This time, William Jefferson Clinton, forty-six, was taking the oath of office as the third-youngest president.[1] Clinton and I were born in the same year. For better or worse, the boomers had come of age. Clinton had campaigned hard using the memory of the promise of John F. Kennedy, so comparisons between the two were inevitable.

When JFK was inaugurated in January 1961, Bill Clinton and I were only fourteen, still seven years too young to vote. Thinking back to my own feelings when Kennedy was sworn in, I remembered being curious to hear what he had to say to me, the "new generation" that he had so arduously courted during his difficult campaign.

As Clinton repeated the words of the oath, I was transported back in time and mentally saw John F. Kennedy speaking the same words (see image on opposite page). The day was bitterly cold, brilliantly sunny. Jackie wore a buff-colored ensemble. The poet Robert Frost, old and so famous that we already studied his work in school, had written a dedication honoring JFK for the well-known poem "The Gift Outright," but the sun blinded him and the wind scattered his script. LBJ gallantly stepped forward and offered his hat to shade Frost's eyes. It was an awkward moment until the old wordsmith abandoned his prepared text and recited the poem from memory.

Changing the format came as no surprise. The nation had just elected the first Catholic president in American history; no one really expected to follow an established script. Kennedy, hatless as always, stood to take the oath from Chief Justice Earl Warren. His speech was full of rhetoric, full of promise, and full of conviction. JFK made every issue sound as if the future of the planet was at stake. "We will pay any price, bear any burden, meet any hardship, support any friend, oppose any foe," he pledged, "to assure the survival and success of liberty." At the end, he challenged the nation to "ask not what your country can do for you, ask what you can do for your country."[2]

Thirty-two years . . . such a long time. Clinton launched into his speech. It was good, very good. Even George Bush, the defeated opponent, said it was a good speech. However, it lacked the power of Kennedy's words. Gone was the cold war rhetoric of 1961. Gone was the exuberant sense of confidence that Americans, working together, could accomplish virtually anything. Gone was the focus on America as a leader for the cause of freedom throughout the world. The new president promised to get America moving again, just as JFK had done in 1961. But this time I had the fleeting mental image of a nation hooked up to jumper cables, waiting for Clinton, or someone else, to fire up the tired battery. Even worse, I felt the chilling conviction that we were sending the man from Hope, Arkansas, into a lion's den of deficit spending, special-interest favoritism, entrenched bureaucratic control, and partisan gridlock.

What a difference three decades make. In 1961 I was inspired to do something for my country. In 1993 I said aloud, "Good luck, Bill, you're in it now," and privately bemoaned the fact that Americans, whatever their cynicism about government, still expect too much from their president.

The episode reminded me of a book, *The Past Is a Foreign Country*, whose title was taken from the following quotation: "The past is a foreign country, they do things differently there."[3] JFK would probably not have run for the office of president in 1992; he existed within the context of his time, and reliance on context is a cardinal rule of historic interpretation. JFK lived in an era of progressive liberalism, of cold war, of belief in the boundless promise of science and technology. It was a period when the United States was, indisputably, the richest and post powerful nation on earth. Since his death, Kennedy has come to symbolize many of the characteristics of that era, with the additional protection afforded by his martyrdom. Former LBJ aide and journalist Bill Moyers summed up the spirit of the age: "Those of us who lived through the period remember the Sixties as a time when we believed individuals could demand that government do good and government could ensure individuals the chance to do their best."[4]

Moyers's description of the spirit of the early Sixties rings true to me, but it may sound foreign to others. The early 1960's *was* an exciting era when people *could* make a difference. Author David Halberstam described it as a "glittering time," when the "best and the brightest" of the nation's intelligentsia entered politics to join JFK in his mission to "get America moving again."[5] The America of the Sixties had lost no international wars and had experienced no Watergate or Iran-Contra; it had no failing public education system, no overburdened entitlement programs, no huge deficits. People believed that government worked for the people and not vice versa.

During the early 1960's the economy was booming, our technology produced new goods for consumption, and Americans and their children had the money to buy them. Soldiers who had returned from service after World War II had married and moved into comfortable homes in the suburbs, where they sired that huge generation that came to be known as the baby boomers. It was a time of ranch-style

OPPOSITE PAGE:
John F. Kennedy being sworn in as the thirty-fifth president of the United States on January 20, 1961.
His inaugural address challenged Americans to get involved with their country.
Cecil W. Stoughton, courtesy John F. Kennedy Library

41

FIGURE 3.1

The Kennedy family in England. From left: Rose, Ted, Rosemary, Joe, Jr., Ambassador Joseph Kennedy, Eunice, Jean, John, Robert, Patricia, and Kathleen.
Courtesy, Gilbert Adams/Camera Press/Retna Ltd.

houses, two-car families, and the promise of college for unprecedented numbers of American youths.

In 1960 the nation had a population of about 177 million people. The decade began with the development of the laser and digital displays and the organization of the American Football League. John Wayne starred as Davy Crockett in the blockbuster film *The Alamo*, and Alfred Hitchcock presented his classic thriller *Psycho*. The decade was only two days old when John F. Kennedy announced his bid for the presidency.

THE MAN FROM MASSACHUSETTS

John Fitzgerald Kennedy was the second of nine children born to Joseph P. and Rose Fitzgerald Kennedy.[6] His parents' forebears had immigrated to Boston from Ireland during the nineteenth century, and both families were well-established, financially successful, and active in Democratic politics when JFK appeared on the scene. His maternal grandfather, John F. "Honey Fitz" Fitzgerald, served in Congress and as mayor of Boston. JFK's father, Joseph Kennedy, was a tough, successful businessman who served as ambassador to the Court of St. James in London from 1938 to 1940 (Figure 3.1). "Big Joe" initially groomed his eldest

son, Joe, Jr., for a career in politics, but Joe was killed in 1944 while flying a mission in Europe during World War II.

JFK grew up rich and privileged. Some contemporary writers have made a fuss about discrimination against the Irish-Catholic Kennedys by the entrenched old-guard Protestant Boston elite, long dominated by names like Cabot and Lowell. Admittedly, the Kennedys were denied admission to some country clubs and social soirees, but none of them failed to find employment or missed a meal due to the color of their skin or their religious heritage.

Young Jack Kennedy was educated at Choate and Harvard. He spent time in England during his father's stint as ambassador and later wrote his Harvard thesis about England's late entry into the war. It was published as the book *Why England Slept* in 1940, thus launching his literary career. Kennedy then served in the navy during World War II. After rescuing several of his crewmen when his PT boat #109 was rammed and sunk near the Solomon Islands, JFK was decorated for heroism (Figure 3.2). This and other exploits of the Kennedy family were prominently featured in the nation's papers and magazines of the day. Joe Kennedy was ambitious, wanted fame for his family, and made sure that the Kennedy name was splashed across the headlines. One friend commented, "You had to be rather a

FIGURE 3.2
Naval Lt. Jack Kennedy, shown in his PT boat #109, in 1943. JFK was decorated for heroism after he rescued several crewmen when his boat was rammed and sunk in the Solomon Islands. *Courtesy, John F. Kennedy Library*

stupid person by 1945 not to have heard of the Kennedy family."[7]

Thanks to the efforts of his family, JFK was able to run for Congress in 1946 and to win the election. His career in the House was relatively undistinguished, but he made a successful run for the Senate in 1952, where he served for a little more than one full term.

In 1953, a year after his election to the Senate, the well-known bachelor married Newport socialite Jacqueline Bouvier, another Catholic (Figure 3.3). The couple later had a stillborn child, in 1956. Daughter Caroline was born in 1957, and John, Jr., arrived in 1960, shortly after his father's election to the presidency. Another son, Patrick Bouvier Kennedy, was born in 1963 and died of a respiratory ailment only a few days later. The infant was buried about three months before JFK was assassinated in Dallas.

The future politician was plagued by illness throughout his youth, and he developed a serious back complaint that was aggravated by the PT-109 ramming during the war. Writers later concluded that JFK's poor health, which was kept secret, was the result of Addison's disease, a glandular disorder. The back injury was well-known. JFK underwent several surgeries for the back ailment, none of them entirely successful. A major operation in 1954 nearly killed him, and he used the period of his lengthy convalescence to organize his most famous book, *Profiles in Courage*, which was published in 1956 and won the Pulitzer Prize.

The Kennedy forces made an unsuccessful bid for the vice presidential nomination during the Democratic National Convention in 1956 and then organized themselves for a presidential race in 1960. When Kennedy launched his campaign on January 2, he was forty-two years

FIGURE 3.3
Senator John Kennedy and former debutante Jacqueline Bouvier at their society wedding in Newport, Rhode Island, in 1953. *UPI/Corbis-Bettmann*

old, running under a program of progressive liberalism called the New Frontier. Central to this ideology was the belief that the distribution of wealth in the nation was unequal and that social reform could balance the scales and create a truly equal social structure. Although America was supposed to be a classless society, progressive liberalism professed a goal of achieving a true "middle."

THE 1960 CAMPAIGN

"The world is changing. The old era is ending. The old ways will not do," said the candidate, and the message for positive change caught on with the populace. It did not seem to matter that the twenty-one-year-old age requirement would prevent me from voting for JFK either in 1960 or in 1964. Many in my age group listened to what he had to say. In 1960 half the American population, swelled by the baby boom, was under the age of twenty-five.[8] Kennedy's youth, his family, his charismatic style, and his energy all helped him on the campaign trail.

The New Frontier, patterned on Franklin Roosevelt's New Deal and Harry Truman's Fair Deal, called for major new social and economic programs. This time, however, the programs would be taken abroad. Progressive liberalism had evolved earlier in the century; JFK's platform carried it forward. Conservatives were not impressed with the young liberal and professed worry about Kennedy's youth and inexperience. They also fretted that his programs would be inflationary. Finally, they wondered if he would be able to

deal effectively with the threat of communist domination.

Communism and the threat of nuclear war were powerful issues in 1960. I grew up with an almost palpable fear of the "Reds." Senator Joseph McCarthy had launched his anticommunist witch-hunt against American citizens less than seven years before the 1960 campaign, and thousands of Americans had constructed bomb shelters, a naive protection against nuclear attack, during the administration of Dwight Eisenhower. Nikita Khrushchev's "We will bury you" speech at the United Nations in 1960 was ringing in the nation's ears (Figure 3.4). The cold war made the World War II weapons industry a permanent fixture in the American economy, and most people felt it was needed.

The Supreme Court had moved toward liberal reform during the 1950's. The landmark school-desegregation ruling, *Brown v. Board of Education*, had come out of the Court in 1954, and in 1956–57 the justices had handed down a series of rulings upholding the rights of communists. Yet the *Brown* ruling had not caused much positive change, particularly in the South. In 1957 the Reverend Martin Luther King, Jr., and others formed the Southern Christian Leadership Conference, and King led a more active effort toward the removal of racial barriers. His philosophy of nonviolence dominated the early years of the Sixties. Change was in the air.

During the campaign primaries, Senators Hubert Humphrey and Lyndon Johnson were Kennedy's main Democratic opponents.[9] Kennedy's Catholicism was a major issue in the campaign, with Protestant detractors insisting that Rome would end up running the country. Although this issue may seem ludicrous today, one must recall that many of the original thirteen colonies were founded on strong Protestant principles; some colonies enacted laws prohibiting Catholics from holding office. This stigma lingered in the American mind. JFK eventually made a speech in Houston clarifying his relationship to the church and his responsibilities to the office of president. As a result, some concerns about his religion were allayed. When the ballots were cast in November, Kennedy garnered 78% of the Catholic vote as opposed to 38% from the Protestants.[10]

Kennedy won the party's nomination at the convention in July and then faced Republican Vice President Richard M. Nixon in the November election. JFK chose Senate Majority Leader Lyndon Johnson as his vice presidential running mate. His brother Robert Kennedy served as campaign manager. The Kennedy and Nixon platforms were similar, but Kennedy used the relatively new medium of television to advantage with the voters. The presidential debates of September 1960, the first in history to be televised, showed Nixon with a dark five-o'clock shadow and showed Kennedy looking very presidential (Figure 3.5). An estimated seventy-five million viewers, the largest television audience to date, tuned into the programs.

During the debates, JFK charged that there was a missile gap between the United States and the Soviet Union. Although his charges were exaggerated, he played on the nation's fear of communism and nuclear war. His rhetoric had an urgency about the need to maintain American power and leadership at home and abroad. Viewers heard him caution that only action would prevent historians from writing that the 1960's were the decade when "time ran out on the United States."[11]

FIGURE 3.4
Soviet Premier Nikita Khrushchev shown pounding his fist during an appearance at the United Nations in 1960. U.S.-Soviet relations were strained during the early 1960's. *Courtesy, AP/Wide World Photos*

44

FIGURE 3.5
Presidential candidates John F. Kennedy and Richard Nixon in the first televised debates in 1960. Kennedy's poise in front of the cameras helped him win the election. *UPI/Corbis-Bettmann*

On election night in November the vote was so close that the Democratic candidate went to bed without knowing the outcome. The final returns gave him the presidency by less than 120,000 votes out of a total of sixty-nine million cast. Kennedy had won the election without a clear mandate, and the sheer closeness of the race would produce some of the caution that characterized the early years of the New Frontier administration. Accusations of voting irregularities surfaced immediately after the vote, but Richard Nixon bowed out gracefully, refusing to ask for a recount.[12]

THE KENNEDY WHITE HOUSE

John F. Kennedy's inaugural ranked among the most festive celebrations that Washington had seen in decades. The inaugural address was an appeal to public commitment, particularly by the young. He drew in top talent from both parties. Ford Motor Company chief Robert McNamara was named to head the Department of Defense,

and Rockefeller Foundation President Dean Rusk took over the Department of State. JFK's selection of his brother Robert as attorney general caused alarmed cries of nepotism, but the new president relied on his famous wit to quell the storm. He said he wanted to "give Bobby a little experience" before his brother went out to practice law.[13]

Kennedy also brought in academics, businessmen, economists, and political theorists to prepare reports on policies and programs. Historian Arthur Schlesinger was installed as informal historian-in-residence, a clear sign that Jack Kennedy planned for his administration to be memorable. The "eggheads," as they were known, were joined at the White House by the members of Kennedy's inner circle of political advisers, called the "Irish Mafia," which included Lawrence O'Brien, Kenneth O'Donnell, Dave Powers, and Theodore Sorensen, with Pierre Salinger acting as press spokesman.

Kennedy's style was a critical element in his presidency, and he came to personify the "imperial presidency," following in the tradition of FDR. This sense of personalizing the office was enhanced by his new approach toward television. JFK launched a practice of regular press conferences, averaging one meeting for every seventeen days that he spent in office. During the Kennedy administration there were no brief comments offered under the roar of helicopter blades. People felt a closeness to the power of the office, an intimacy not felt before or since. Government was less complicated during the early 1960's, and the media was less antagonistic in the days before Watergate. The televised appearances were perfect platforms for displays of the Kennedy charisma, the Kennedy rhetoric, and the lively Kennedy sense of humor.

The Kennedys allowed the people into the White House. Regardless of political leanings, Americans were fascinated with the activities of this young and handsome family. No children had resided in the White House for nearly half a century. Jackie Kennedy promptly set up a White House nursery, and photojournalists were given ample opportunity to capture scenes of the two Kennedy children playing with their father in the Oval Office (Figure 3.6). The first lady launched a private campaign to restore

FIGURE 3.6
Caroline and John, Jr., shown with their father in the Oval Office. *Cecil W. Stoughton, courtesy John F. Kennedy Library*

FIGURE 3.7

A dinner honoring the nation's Nobel laureates in 1962. The first lady is shown speaking with poet Robert Frost; the president converses with novelist Pearl Buck. The Kennedys regularly brought leading artists to the White House. *Robert Knudsen, courtesy John F. Kennedy Library*

historic furnishings to the mansion, and she led the nation on a televised White House tour through the refurbished apartments in the public rooms in 1962.

In a country created with the prime goal of eschewing monarchy and its traditions, the Kennedys became the unofficial American royal family. The more recent fascination with the British royals is similar to the curiosity about the Kennedys. Americans wanted to know what they ate, what they wore, and how they played. Mrs. Kennedy wore high fashion and brought in a French chef. In addition, she promoted the arts, setting a trend that became an important part of her legacy. Jackie induced the internationally known cellist Pablo Casals to perform after a presidential banquet. When the Kennedys hosted a dinner for American Nobel prizewinners, JFK introduced the group as "the most extraordinary collection of talent, of human knowledge, that has ever been gathered together at the White House with the possible exception of when Thomas Jefferson dined alone" (Figure 3.7).[14] The Kennedys continued earlier administrative efforts to create a national cultural center in Washington, Jackie promoted youth performances at the executive mansion, and JFK planted the seeds for both the National Endowment for the Arts and the National Endowment for the Humanities.

ADMINISTRATIVE AFFAIRS

JFK's economic program was similar to the later plan of President Ronald Reagan, calling for induced federal budget deficits to encourage spending during periods of economic growth. In 1961 it was a radical departure from the balanced-budget formula of the earlier Eisenhower administration, and it generated some public outcries. The deficit was tiny by today's standards. Kennedy's economists moved against a threat of recession in 1961 by introducing the first significant minimum-wage law since 1938. The program added coverage to retail, service, and construction fields and called for raising the basic wage from $1.00 to $1.25 within four years.[15] The 1962 Trade Expansion Act was designed to increase exports and boost the economy.

American business did not look on Kennedy's programs with favor, although the administration did little to hinder economic growth in the nation. JFK felt angry and betrayed in 1962 when the U.S. steel industry announced a price increase, a move that Kennedy believed was inflationary. By directing that the government purchase only from companies who held to lower prices, by calling for an antitrust investigation into the industry, and by personally appealing to those companies that had not already announced a hike in their prices, the president exerted tremendous political pressure on the industry to rescind the increase. The move caused an uproar, but the big steel companies repealed the increase.

Kennedy had campaigned on a platform of new social programs at home and abroad, and he proposed a wide variety of them during his first year in office. Many of his bills stalled in Congress. On the foreign front, one of the first was his plan for volunteer training in underdeveloped nations, a program he called the Peace Corps.[16] The name and much of the idea came from Congressman Henry Reuss and Senator Hubert Humphrey, but JFK formally launched the project and got it moving. He tested the idea shortly before the 1960 election at a speech on November 2 at the Cow Palace in San Francisco. After the election he got the Peace Corps Act passed and placed his brother-in-law Sargent Shriver in charge; soon, the program was under way. By 1986 the Peace Corps could boast 120,000 alumni, including five congressmen and former U.S. Senator Paul Tsongas (Figure 3.8).[17]

JFK's Alliance for Progress, described as a "10-Year Marshall Plan to Build Up Latin America," was launched in 1961 and called for massive aid to developing countries in the southern half of the Americas. The program never reached its potential for either economic or social restructuring in the Latin American nations.[18]

The cold war dominated the Kennedy years, centering on efforts to control the spread of communism and maintain a balance of power between the two nuclear giants, the United States and the Soviet Union. JFK's administration launched the largest peacetime defense buildup then on record, which was devoted to halting the spread of communism, particularly among emerging nations. The first test was in Laos, where JFK decided to maintain the status quo. Communist-controlled Cuba was another matter. Shortly after assuming power in 1959, Fidel Castro had declared himself a Marxist and turned toward the USSR for support.

U.S. claims of a vested interest in the affairs of its southern neighbors dated to the Monroe Doctrine of 1823.

FIGURE 3.9
JFK at the Berlin Wall before addressing a huge crowd of German citizens in 1963. Erected during the summer of 1961, the wall was torn down in 1989. *National Archives #63-3346*

Cuba's fall into communism caused widespread alarm. JFK inherited a plan, formulated during the Eisenhower administration, that called for a U.S.-backed invasion of the island by Cuban exiles; the strategy was to encourage the residents to revolt against the Castro regime. The CIA was behind the plan, and Kennedy approved the invasion, which took place in April 1961. Cuban refugees landed on the island at the Bay of Pigs, but Kennedy refused to send in air cover, the plotters were arrested, and the invasion failed miserably. Admitting that "victory has a hundred fathers and defeat is an orphan," JFK accepted full responsibility for the foreign policy fiasco, but he was furious with the leadership of the CIA and later replaced some of its administrative personnel.[19] Many America-based Cuban groups felt betrayed by the Democratic administration.

In 1961 Kennedy went abroad. First, he had an unpleasant meeting with French President Charles de Gaulle in Paris; Kennedy backed the idea of forming a European Common Market, and de Gaulle rigorously opposed it. Then the president held a tense conference with Soviet Premier Nikita Khrushchev in Vienna. The communist chief threatened to sign a peace treaty with Soviet-controlled East Germany. At one point the new president, frustrated by the Soviet hard line, turned to a companion and asked, "Is it *always* like this?"[20]

The carving up of Europe that followed World War II split the city of Berlin, which was located within the eastern bloc. Khrushchev's plan would have eliminated access to democratic West Berlin. Kennedy insisted on maintaining access, and the Soviets responded by building a wall dividing the city into two zones. The wall went up late in the summer of 1961; thousands of Germans fled into West Berlin before the final barrier was in place. Television and magazine pictures showed the refugees trying to scramble under barbed-wire fences in last-minute efforts to find freedom in the West. Threats were exchanged, and troops squared off at the wall, but no hostile actions were taken. Kennedy allowed the wall to remain, and Khrushchev postponed signing the treaty. When JFK visited West Berlin in 1963 and delivered his "Ich bin ein Berliner" speech, he was given a hero's welcome (Figure 3.9).

The Cuban missile crisis in 1962 terrified the nation and the world. For thirteen days during October of that year

FIGURE 3.8
Delores Tadlock, a volunteer with the Peace Corps in India. JFK launched the program at the beginning of his term in 1961. *Courtesy, The Peace Corps*

we prepared for nuclear war. American intelligence services discovered that the Soviet Union was constructing offensive missile sites on Cuba, located only ninety miles off the southern tip of the Florida coast. The proximity placed the missiles within striking distance of most major eastern and southern U.S. bases. Kennedy angrily demanded that the missiles be removed; the Soviets refused. Finally, JFK ordered a naval blockade against vessels carrying equipment to the island and went on television to advise the American people of the plan.

It was hard-line rhetoric, in which he appealed to Khrushchev to "abandon this course of world domination and to join in an historic effort to end the perilous arms race and to transform the history of man."[21] The Soviets tested the U.S. president by sending a ship into the blockade. There was a tense standoff on the high seas, and Khrushchev finally backed down by ordering the ship to turn back. JFK opted for a flexible settlement of the affair. The Soviets promised to dismantle the missile sites if the United States pledged not to invade Cuba. Kennedy's avoidance of nuclear war earned him a rise in popularity at home, but conservatives, chagrined by his earlier allowance of the Berlin Wall, again charged him with being overly accommodating to the communists.

During 1963 JFK made further attempts to ease U.S.-Soviet relations. Kennedy viewed the Nuclear Test Ban Treaty, signed that summer, as his greatest achievement. The famous "hot line" telephone connecting Moscow and Washington was also set up. These moves toward peaceful coexistence, now known as *détente*, worried hard-line conservatives at home.

The U.S. presence in Vietnam, which predated the Kennedy administration, was another example of American attempts after World War II to stem the spread of communism to underdeveloped nations. American policy was based on the domino theory, which maintained that when one nation fell to communism, others around it were likely to follow. When JFK took office, the United States had support personnel in South Vietnam, a free nation trying to stave off advances from communist-controlled North Vietnam. During 1961 JFK dispatched the first "advisers," who served to train native fighters and to provide technical support. Kennedy created the elite Marine Special Forces, or Green Berets, who were sent to teach guerrilla warfare and other tactics to the South Vietnamese. This strategy toward counterinsurgency was a hallmark of Kennedy's policy in Southeast Asia. During his three years in office, JFK increased the number of advisers and support personnel there from roughly 5,000 to 17,000. Shortly before his assassination, the White House issued a press release reporting Defense Secretary Robert McNamara's belief that the major part of America's task in defending South Vietnam could be completed by the end of 1963, possibly allowing the withdrawal of 1,000 American military personnel.

But throughout the Kennedy administration, the United States provided direct financial aid to South Vietnam and went so far as to allow the use of helicopters and defoliants. American soldiers were permitted to defend themselves from attack, but no combat troops were on the ground. The administration backed the resident, corrupt government of President Ngo Dinh Diem, a Catholic aristocrat trying to rule a peasant, mainly Buddhist country.

The war was not a major public issue when Kennedy was president. In December 1962, *Newsweek* informed its readers that the United States had 11,000 troops in Southeast Asia, with fewer than 50 casualties. "All the communists have is dedication," an American captain told a reporter with confidence. The South Vietnamese, we were told, had 300,000 armed troops and 175,000 regulars, whereas the communist-backed Viet Cong were manned by only 22,000 guerrillas.[22]

One month later *Life* magazine quoted JFK's opinion on Vietnam: "We don't see the end of the tunnel."[23] At virtually the same time, *U.S. News & World Report* cautioned its readers that U.S. troop strength had risen to 12,000 and that the war was costing the country a million dollars a day.[24] At the time, most Americans did not sense that the United States was losing the war, which was, of course, limited warfare using conventional weapons. This was the standard formula for fighting after the United States dropped the bomb on Hiroshima.

The "space race" was also an extension of the cold war during the Kennedy era. It was provoked by the successful Soviet launch of *Sputnik I* in 1957. This was threatening news because the launch clearly showed that the communists were getting ahead of the United States in technology. The conventional wisdom of the era reasoned that dominance in space could lead to unprecedented military power. In April 1961, the Russians launched cosmonaut Yuri Gagarin into orbit, further solidifying their position as leaders in the race for the conquest of the last frontier. At that time U.S. rockets were blowing up on the launchpads. JFK lent his support to the U.S. space program in May 1961, delivering a special address to Congress under the "freedom doctrine." He called for funds to put an American on the moon before 1970.[25]

American astronaut Alan Shepard went up in 1961, and in February 1962 John Glenn successfully orbited the earth, thereby narrowing the space gap (Figure 3.10). Kennedy heralded the success of the Glenn flight. "This is a new ocean, and I believe that the U.S. must sail on it," he said.[26] Like so much of his rhetoric, these were heady words. The final moon landing took place on schedule, in July 1969, nearly six years after JFK's death. Like many other Americans, I watched the unbelievable scientific achievement on television, swelled with pride, and regretted the fact that John Kennedy had missed seeing his technological dream come true.

Echo I, the first U.S. communications satellite, had been launched in 1960. The Satellite Communications Act was made law in 1962, and in July of that year the first *Telstar* satellite began to relay television programs between the United States and Europe. The system gave the United States superiority in TV and radio communications, a role that it has enjoyed since the Kennedy era. Developments from the space program have been successfully applied to electronics, medicine, metal fabrication, and weapons research.

The civil rights movement was already under way when JFK took the oath of office in 1961. Restaurant sit-ins in the South and freedom rides in Alabama produced violence during 1960 and 1961, and civil rights leaders urged the president to introduce legislation to end discrimination against Negroes, as African Americans were then called. Kennedy did not approach Congress with a bill, opting

FIGURE 3.10
The president, the first lady, and LBJ watching the launch of American astronaut Alan Shepard into space in 1961. Kennedy's goals for the space program called for putting a man on the moon by 1970; the mission was completed in July 1969. *Cecil W. Stoughton, courtesy John F. Kennedy Library*

instead to use his executive powers to enforce court-ordered desegregation, to push for the elimination of discriminatory poll taxes, and to appoint blacks to more government jobs. He also created the Committee on Equal Employment Opportunity, later known as the Equal Employment Opportunity Commission (EEOC). Many civil rights leaders believed he was dragging his feet.

In 1962 and 1963 the Kennedy administration sent in federal troops to force integration at the University of Mississippi and the University of Alabama. In 1963 most Americans were appalled to see photographs and television footage of police brutality against passive African-American demonstrators in Birmingham, Alabama. The marchers were flattened by torrents of water from fire hoses and were viciously attacked by police dogs and cattle prods. Public demand for legislation to end discrimination grew (Figure 3.11).

Finally, on June 19, 1963, JFK submitted a huge civil rights bill, the largest since Reconstruction, to Congress. The bill called for the creation of a Community Relations Service to assist local communities seeking progress in integration, new programs for job training, authority to withhold federal funding from any activity practicing racial discrimination, a ban on discrimination in public accommodations, authority to the attorney general to seek desegregation of public education on behalf of others, and an expansion of jurisdiction and authority for the EEOC. On August 28, a crowd of more than two hundred thousand people, led by the Reverend Martin Luther King, Jr., held a

FIGURE 3.11
Photograph showing peaceful civil rights marchers in Birmingham, Alabama, being sprayed with fire hoses. Kennedy proposed a massive civil rights bill later in 1963. *UPI/Corbis-Bettmann*

49

FIGURE 3.12
Crowds at the Lincoln Memorial, where the Reverend Martin Luther King, Jr., gave his famous "I have a dream" address. On August 28, 1963, Dr. King led more than two hundred thousand civil rights activists in a peaceful demonstration in the nation's capital. *Courtesy, AP/Wide World Photos*

peaceful demonstration in Washington, D.C. King made his famous "I have a dream" speech at the Lincoln Memorial, and Kennedy agreed to meet with the leaders of the march at the White House (Figure 3.12). Kennedy's civil rights bill was unpopular with many Americans, particularly whites in the South. After he proposed the legislation, JFK's popularity rating fell to 59%, his lowest in office.

Kennedy made other progressive moves during his tenure in the White House. In 1961 he appointed a committee to study the status of women. His Wilderness Act bill called for protection of the nation's natural resources; it was passed during LBJ's administration. Meanwhile, American extremist groups cried out against Kennedy programs. Right-wing ultras hated Kennedy's flexible approach toward U.S.-Soviet relations and labeled him a pawn for the Reds. Left-wing radicals, including the pro-Castro factions, cried that the president was a warmonger, begging for military confrontations at every turn. Robert Kennedy's Justice Department, backed by the president, launched an aggressive war against organized crime. The government probed the activities of suspected racketeers and labor leaders, prosecuting some prominent figures. The crackdown infuriated the mob.

Most Americans viewed the constant bickering about Kennedy as American politics as usual, but JFK in action was great fun to watch. He actually seemed to enjoy being president, keeping the witticisms flowing at a steady pace. He did not age noticeably during his three years in office, and he commented about the job, "The pay is good and I can walk to work." Americans were treated to photos of the rambunctious Kennedys playing touch football at Hyannis Port,

the family beach retreat on Cape Cod. Scenes of the kids in the Oval Office and of the kids seeing him off or welcoming him back gave a homey, softening touch to the awesome work of the presidency (see frontispiece).

There was something very right about seeing the beautiful Jacqueline Kennedy charm old Charles de Gaulle when the American president and the first lady visited France during the spring of 1961. JFK and his elegant wife looked at home at the state dinner at Versailles. Their elegance made Americans feel less awkward, more cultured, and somehow more comfortable with their postwar role as the guardians of freedom around the world. The Kennedys looked like royalty and acted like royalty, and some critics expressed fears that the Kennedys were launching a new American political dynasty; after JFK, they cautioned, we would inherit Robert Kennedy and then Edward "Teddy" Kennedy, the youngest brother, who was elected to the U.S. Senate in 1962.

Kennedy professed himself confident that many of his programs, then being held up in Congress, would be passed during his second term. The economy was healthy. On November 2, 1963, South Vietnamese President Diem was assassinated, forecasting a change in the U.S. approach toward the war in Southeast Asia. Less than three weeks later, John F. Kennedy was dead.

For a time after Kennedy's funeral, his detractors had the grace to remain silent while the nation recovered from the tragedy. Lyndon Johnson sensed a favorable political wind and went to Congress to call for passage of the Kennedy programs as a memorial to the fallen leader.[27] It was a brilliant move. In less than a year after the shots were fired in Dallas, Johnson had his way. *Look* magazine was able to report, "What Congress did not give [Kennedy] while he lived, it gave him as he lay dead."[28] The Kennedy package sailed through Congress. "It is now widely expected," continued *Look*, "that the groundwork he laid will be the foundation . . . for the first big social advance in a quarter of a century: general tax-financed medical and hospital care."[29] The federal Medicare bill became law in 1965, with a Medicaid rider that provided health services to the poor.

LBJ's "War on Poverty" and "Great Society" programs embraced the fifty-odd pending bills proposed by his predecessor; Johnson saw the Kennedy program through and was able to obtain passage of an additional two hundred bills of his own. Congress also cleaned up some legislative loopholes that were exposed by the assassination of the young American leader. The Twenty-fifth Amendment to the Constitution was passed in 1967, establishing clear laws relating to presidential succession and calling for the appointment of a new vice president when that office is vacated.[30] Assassination of the president became a federal crime, but it was not until after the assassination of Robert Kennedy in 1968 that Congress offered security protection to presidential candidates.

THE ORIGINS OF THE KENNEDY IMAGE 1963–1969

What happened to America and to the memory of JFK after his death? Nationally, only ten years after 1963, the *New York Times* remarked that the assassination "marked the beginning of the end of an era filled with the ebullient optimism and confidence identified throughout the world with the spirit of America."[31] We discovered that the nation had limits to its power, to its ability to grow economically, and to its natural resources. Public attitudes shifted. And the JFK image was created.

TRANSITION AND TRENDS IN SOCIETY

According to social scientist Tom Schachtman, the assassination of JFK set up a dual path of public thought: some people became "searchers," seeking the cause of this terrible threat to the American system, while others became "preservers," dedicated to salvaging the core values of society. The author notes that the public has tended to react to the shocks in the years that followed by dividing into camps that fall along these same lines.[32] Although various other writers have also struggled to name this trend toward divided thought in the American people since 1963, the Schachtman model of "searchers" and "preservers" is as useful as any of them.

Looking back on the decade of the 1960's, many writers take the position that the period now known as the Sixties really began with the death of John Kennedy in 1963 and continued through Watergate and the resignation of Richard Nixon in 1974. In terms of trends in society and overall public attitudes, this uneven division makes sense. Trends continued from one decade to the next, almost seamlessly. My age group of early boomers shared much with the youths of the "silent generation" of the 1950's, and we also participated with the all-out rebels who dominated the news during the late 1960's and early 1970's.

Radical change did not happen overnight. The first three years of the decade laid the groundwork for much of the turmoil that followed. Kennedy-Johnson insider Harris Wofford would later recall that it "was one of those times in our society when it looks as though everything is going to come into focus, when there will be common goals and people will be galvanized as a country to work for those goals."[33] The public actions by civil rights leaders fostered a spirit of change that caught on with the young, and the quest for equality soon spread to other groups that believed they lacked fair representation in the American system.

In 1960 the U.S. Food and Drug Administration had approved the release of birth control pills, thus creating a new sense of freedom for millions of American women. In 1963 Betty Friedan published *The Feminine Mystique*, an important early feminist manifesto. In 1962 the Supreme Court banned prayer in the nation's public schools, sowing a seed for discontent among Americans who cherished this traditional link between church and state. Rachel Carson's *Silent Spring* appeared on my family's bookshelf in the same year; it was an early call to think carefully about preserving the environment, warning that American businesses were poisoning the atmosphere around us. In 1964 we got discos with go-go dancers, and the government introduced zip codes to expedite the mail system.

The changes during the 1960's were all set to music.[34] Yes, we had Elvis during the 1950's, but the Beatles did not make their appearance in the United States until 1964, after Kennedy's death. Jimi Hendrix and the Doors were typical of the violent period of the late 1960's. The dominant trends in music during the Kennedy administration were Tin Pan Alley, the choice of my parents and the older youths of the Fifties, and dance-style rock and roll. Albums by Frank Sinatra and Johnny Mathis topped the charts while JFK was in the White House; it was Sinatra who performed "High Hopes," the Kennedy campaign song. The Beach Boys' surfing style was coming into its own the year that JFK was shot. Chubby Checker's "Twist" was the rage in 1962, the same year that Bob Dylan released his classic soft protest song "Blowin' in the Wind."[35]

Much has been made of the sexual revolution that occurred during the 1960's. True, women had more sexual freedom after the introduction of the pill, but new trends were slow to catch on with large numbers of the young. The boomers began to experiment openly with sex and alternate lifestyles during the era, partly to show rebellion against tradition and partly to prove their own individuality in American society. But in *Tom Jones*, the Academy Award winner for best picture in 1963, the sexiest scene involved the lovers eating oysters lasciviously. High school friends and I watched the *Dick Van Dyke Show* on television; Mary Tyler Moore was a pretty housewife, and Dick brought home the money for their blissfully happy family.

It all changed later in the Sixties, of course. It changed even more during the 1970's and 1980's. Let's compare some popular television comedies. *Father Knows Best* topped the charts in the year that JFK was elected to the presidency. The show was the embodiment of the Fifties: father worked, mother ran the home, and the well-adjusted children got into minor skirmishes during their teenage years. There were no drugs, no teen demonstrations, no unplanned pregnancies, no gangs. The cast was white, and no one talked back to dad Robert Young. They were middle class, the embodiment of the ideal American family during that era.

During the 1970's came *All in the Family*, featuring daddy as a proverbial jerk. *The Mary Tyler Moore Show* brought back Dick Van Dyke's earlier wife as a single career woman on the pill. *The Cosby Show* dealt with an upper-middle-class African-American family with two working professional parents, a handful of precocious, outspoken children, and clear references to the problems of parenting in modern society. The family sitcom evolved into the 1990's family of *Roseanne*, with two parents struggling to survive, the old middle-class American dream of the early 1960's in shambles.

The stability of the early 1960's gave way to the rapidly changing late 1960's, which saw rapid business expansion and mergers. By the end of the decade two hundred corporations controlled 58% of all manufacturing assets in the nation. Technological improvements gave us new products, and by 1968 the manufacture of synthetics had surpassed natural fibers. The decade saw the beginning of the credit-card boom and found drug and grocery stores adding six thousand new products per year. Computer fraud was born.[36] By 1965 color television had become the preferred visual equipment. In 1966 and 1967 scientists unraveled the mysteries of DNA and RNA. An African doctor performed the first heart transplant in the latter year. The Super Bowl was born in 1966.

Some of the contradictions of the decade were expressed through two events of 1965: the *Sound of Music* was the most popular film; and the Grateful Dead held its first major concert. The growing power of broadcast news was confirmed by the premier of *60 Minutes* in 1968. The nation's increasing awareness of the fragility of the environment led to a ban on the use of DDT as a pesticide. Stanley Kubrick's beautiful space odyssey *2001* gave people hope that there were still frontiers to conquer.

American society during the late Sixties was dominated by violence, the war in Vietnam, and the youth movement. Passage of Kennedy's Civil Rights Act meant that private businesses serving the public had to abandon racial discrimination. Meanwhile, the black power movement, characterized by a spirit of intense nationalism and separatism, began to gather force. Removing barriers to participation was not enough, said the new leaders; we want total equality, the equality guaranteed under the Constitution. Anti–civil rights forces were active in the nation throughout this period. Southern conservative Alabama Governor George Wallace ran for the presidency in 1964, and both he and Republican candidate Senator Barry Goldwater went on record against the Civil Rights bill. Johnson won the election by a wide margin, however, and moved ahead with the Civil Rights Act, his War on Poverty, and his Great Society plans. The Johnson social programs designed to combat poverty followed in the tradition of progressive liberalism.

The promise of economic equality was there, but change did not come fast enough. The Great Society programs did not equalize the status of the economically disadvantaged, particularly those in the inner cities, and LBJ's escalation of the war in Vietnam drafted many of the poor, including a substantial percentage of African Americans. Resentment and despair reached the boiling point. In August 1965, the Watts section of Los Angeles exploded in violence. There were murders in Selma, Alabama, in the same year. Johnson won passage of the Voting Rights Act, encouraging fair practices in voter registration for African Americans, but the aggressive phase of the civil rights movement continued to gather force.

During 1966 the Black Panthers appeared on the scene, and there were Black Power riots in Chicago and Cleveland. Worse rampages were recorded the following year in both Detroit and Newark. The early 1960's dream of common cooperation divided along lines of black and white. Nonviolence as a means to achieve change was replaced by a trend toward destruction. People became frightened.

As the Sixties progressed, Martin Luther King's philosophy of nonviolence no longer dominated. Early in April 1968, the Reverend Dr. King went to Memphis to support a strike by the city's sanitation workers. "We, as a people, will get to the promised land," he predicted in a speech.[37] While standing on the balcony of the Lorraine Hotel in the city, he was assassinated by James Earl Ray, a white extremist. Riots and arson fires erupted in 125 American cities; the nation's capital was seriously damaged (Figure 3.13). The 1968 Civil Rights Act, guaranteeing fair housing to minorities, marked another benchmark in direct government efforts to remove racial barriers. When LBJ signed the act, he commented: "The proudest moments of my presidency have been such times as this when I have signed into law the promises of a century."[38]

Vietnam rose to the forefront as a public issue during the administration of Lyndon Johnson.[39] During the winter of 1964–65, communist Viet Cong attacked naval vessels in the Gulf of Tonkin, and LBJ asked Congress for funds to

FIGURE 3.13
Fires and destruction in Washington, D.C., in April 1968. The assassination of Dr. Martin Luther King, Jr., set off riots in more than 125 American cities.
UPI/Corbis-Bettmann

support aggressive air strikes against North Vietnam. The Gulf of Tonkin Resolution gave Johnson, as president, tremendous power to order attacks to counter communist advances. The president began to escalate American involvement in Southeast Asia early in 1965 and launched sustained bombing of North Vietnam in February. By spring, U.S. troops were actively engaged in open combat.

These actions were followed by search-and-destroy missions, extensive use of defoliants, a strategic hamlets program, and finally, an effort to improve "kill ratios." Guerrilla warfare did not produce major organized battles leaving slain soldiers on the field. Troop levels, sustained by the draft, rose from 150,000 in February 1966 to 550,000 in 1969. Throughout the escalation the government continued to assure the American people that the war was being won.

The war and the civil rights movement both fueled the youth rebellion of the late 1960's, and the huge number of baby boomers gave the movement force. As one boomer recalled, "We expected to have everything—idealism, fulfillment, and money, too."[40] Dustin Hoffman in *The Graduate* (1967) conveyed some of the self-importance that characterized many in my age group at that time. The main character returns home after graduating from college, floats in the family pool, has an affair with an older woman, and waits to find himself. "There's a great future in plastics," advises a male member of the materialistic establishment, "think about it." Hoffman looks on the world of adults and their traditions with a hint of scorn while treating his comfortable surroundings as a birthright.[41]

On June 23, 1968, the Vietnam War became the longest American conflict on record, having lasted 2,376 days at a cost of 25,068 lives; the American Revolution fell into second place, having taken 2,375 days and resulting in a loss of 4,435 colonial lives.[42] The 1968 figure for American casualties was only half the number of dead that would eventually be inscribed on the wall of the Vietnam War Memorial in Washington, D.C. The war was a continuum, a "scarlet thread" that ran through the protest years and cannot be separated from the youth movement.[43] Sixties campus radical Jerry Rubin summed it up well. "If there hadn't been a Vietnam War," he said, "we would have had to invent one."[44]

When students at Berkeley started the "don't trust anyone over thirty" Free Speech movement during the early part of the war, reporters asked them if communists were behind the effort.[45] Experimentation in changing traditional rules became the order of the day. Harvard professor Timothy Leary promoted the use of LSD as a means to heightened spiritual awareness—"Turn on, Tune in, Drop out" was the slogan—and many young people tried it, along with marijuana and other mind-altering drugs. California launched the hippie trend toward "flower children," who staged Be-ins and preached a message of love and peace. Yippies, who combined hippiness with a political agenda, were active toward the end of the decade.

Some of the boomers cast off adherence to the U.S. domino theory and also openly questioned the war on moral grounds, asking if it was right for the United States to dictate the future of another country. Craig McNamara, son of Robert McNamara, JFK's secretary of defense, joined this group. "You know," he said, "things were so split in the Sixties. You were either for the war or against it."[46] Students began with teach-ins about the war and then advanced to active demonstrations against it. Lacking the power of the vote, and encouraged by their own strength of numbers, they took on *the system.*

In October 1967 protestors staged a massive demonstration in Washington, including an advance on the Pentagon to "exorcise it."[47] Johnson, constantly heckled by demonstrators outside the gates to the White House, became a virtual prisoner in office. "Hey, hey, LBJ, how many kids did you kill today?" was a popular taunt at the time. Much of the rest of the populace split into camps; those in support of the war were labeled hawks, those against, doves.

In January 1968, the North Vietnamese launched the Tet offensive, attacking major cities in South Vietnam. The communists were advancing aggressively. Suddenly, millions of people sensed that the long-promised victory in Vietnam had been an illusion. It was an election year, and LBJ was facing competition. Eugene McCarthy of Minnesota announced for the presidency on November 30, 1967, and Robert Kennedy formally entered the race on March 16, 1968. McCarthy, a dove, did well in the New Hampshire primary.

I was sitting at Eddie Price's, a campus bar and restaurant near the Tulane campus, on the evening of March 31, 1968, when LBJ came on television to give an address to his "fellow Americans." He looked terrible, old and beaten. To the amazement of the students in the cafe, he announced a halt to the bombing of North Vietnam and then added, "I shall not seek, and will not accept, the nomination of my party for another term as your president."[48] LBJ's withdrawal from the competition came two weeks before my twenty-second birthday; the 1968 election marked my official passport into the presidential voting booth.

Robert Kennedy came out against the war; McCarthy was already against it, and Republican candidate Richard Nixon—JFK's old opponent—pledged that he too would end the fiasco that American involvement in Vietnam had become. In early June, RFK won the California democratic primary. Then, after his victory speech, RFK was assassinated by Sirhan B. Sirhan in Los Angeles. The death of Robert Kennedy left the nation with a choice between Vice President Hubert Humphrey, who took the Democratic nomination, and Nixon. I opted to vote for Nixon. Unfortunately, he did not hurry to get us out of the war.

The military targeted my age group for the draft, and for that reason alone Vietnam was destined to become a major issue. During the Sixties many of the male baby boomers engaged in a variety of activities to avoid going to Southeast Asia. Until the initiation of the lottery in 1969 there were deferments for continuing education, so countless men of my generation stayed in school. Half of all Ph.D.'s awarded in the United States between 1861 and 1970 were given out during the 1960's.[49] There were medical deferments; men starved themselves, induced sickness, and otherwise became too permanently ill to pass the medical tests at the induction centers. Hawks called them "draft dodgers," but many of them believed that the war was illegal and that dodging was preferable to a death sentence.

There were some deferments for married men with children; too many people marched down the aisle only to end up in divorce court later. Once the draft lottery was enacted, it became something of a game of chance, but there were certain types of alternate service for conscientious objectors, who eventually numbered more than 170,000.[50] According to fellow Tulanian Larry Wright, who ended up teaching English in Cairo to avoid service in Vietnam, the entire movement to avoid the draft was "keeping white men safe in America."[51]

The war caused terrible divisions in American society. Some men of my generation felt targeted for execution in a war that was not even official, since Congress had never passed a war act. We could not vote, thus enhancing the sense of impotence. The draft was particularly hard on some Americans, especially African Americans who could not afford expensive higher education or other ploys that would keep their boys at home. Since many white youths joined in the civil rights movement, there was considerable resentment all around. Fathers who had served in the military in World War II or Korea argued in frustration with their draft-resisting sons. Mothers raised to always support the war effort bickered with their rebellious daughters. People talked openly about the "generation gap."

When I applied to graduate school in 1969, the draft worked to my advantage; few men of my age were around to compete. Although our class ended up with seven women and two men, one member of the selection committee later confided to me that the admissions officers were afraid the class of 1971 would be an "all-girl band."[52] Meanwhile, student groups across the nation were disrupting the campuses.

When my age group entered college, students had little voice in academic or operational affairs. Many of the nation's youths embraced the idea of gaining more influence in the way that colleges were run and the types of courses that were taught. Student rights became a major theme during the youth movement of the late 1960's. However, the movement was relatively short-lived and did not engage the active participation of a majority of my generation. I sympathized with some of the basic ideas of the movement, but I did not join a sit-in or march. There was a spirit of high idealism and a general antibusiness, antiestablishment attitude. Yet one of the most commonly shared characteristics of the boomers was our respect for another's individual right to "do your own thing."

The year 1968 was the first in the trend toward campus takeovers, when students forced themselves into university buildings and held the structures pending negotiations for new student rights. As one administrator recalled, "The students wanted to bring down society, to change society fundamentally, and the university was the closest thing they could get hold of."[53] Students demanded a more active voice in university decisions, including alterations to the curriculum. The armed takeover at Cornell University by African-American students hinged on the curriculum issue.

Many men of my generation believed strongly in the war and willingly went to Vietnam, enlisting and then signing on for additional tours of duty. And many who philosophically opposed the war nevertheless supported the men who fought there. The spirit of nonconformity, allowing people to express their individuality, carried the day. Therefore, hawks in my generation were free to express themselves, and few of us felt the need to join in their fight. The same applied to the doves. A large field called the quad in the middle of the Tulane campus became the stage for pro- and antiwar activities during my final year in undergraduate school. The ROTC drilled there, preparing young men for military service. The doves protested there, yelling slogans; some of them chained themselves to fire hydrants. They did not attack each other, as I recall, but used the quad at different times of the day, as if by reservation. The rest of us walked past these two groups to class, barely noticing the opposing camps that they represented in a very divided generation.

I was home in Virginia during the summer of 1968 and remember watching the demonstrations and violence that took place during the Democratic National Convention in Chicago during August of that year (Figure 3.14). This was the demonstration planned by Jerry Rubin and the Yippies, and it took youth protest to a level of violence that terrified, and subsequently alienated, a large segment of society. Chicago police retaliated against the students with clubs and tear gas. The atmosphere was chaotic. The stress was palpable among the reporters who provided television coverage of political events. There was a strong sense that society was swirling out of control. King and RFK had been killed that year, political commentators called each other names on TV, and it all seemed like madness.

FIGURE 3.14
Riots at the Democratic National Convention in 1968, after antiwar youth protestors staged demonstrations in Chicago. *UPI/Corbis-Bettmann*

Americans, appalled by radical elements in the youth and civil rights movements, began to realize that the price of change was perhaps too high. In 1968 the American political scene began dividing into camps, usually dubbed the "new left" and the "new right." Many Democrats abandoned the party and recast themselves as "neo-conservatives," joining in league with the new right to defend familiar traditions. The new right branded the left as the radical, antiestablishment element in society while proclaiming adherence to norms: conformity, respect for authority, love of family and the *American way.*[54] These accusations would characterize political discussions for the next two decades.

Overall, 1968 was a terrible year. First there was the Tet offensive, then came the assassinations of Martin Luther King, Jr., and Robert Kennedy and the violence of the black riots and student protests. Jacqueline Kennedy married Greek shipping magnate Aristotle Onassis, a surprise occurrence that millions of Americans greeted with dismay. *Time* magazine called the union "The End of Camelot."[55]

CAMELOT

There is a fashion in journalistic circles to imply that the death of President Kennedy opened up some sort of Pandora's box, letting out the race riots, Watergate, and all the other evils in American society. As CBS anchorman Dan Rather put it: "And really, wasn't this when all the craziness started? Dallas, Oswald, Ruby, Watts, Manson, Ray, Sirhan, Bremer, Vietnam, Watergate, FBI, CIA, Squeaky Fromme, Sara Moore . . . the endless lunatic newsreel?"[56] This is not historical analysis. Certainly the assassination has, *after the fact*, been viewed by the rememberers as a benchmark for change. But was it a trigger? The seeds for explosive change were already present in society; gunfire in Dallas did not necessarily detonate the charge.

Historian Thomas Brown, author of *JFK: History of an Image*, does not accept the view that the assassination was a catalyst for change. He instead asserts, "Kennedy's murder has taken on retrospective significance because of the period of war, political scandal, and domestic turmoil that followed it."[57] In this view, the collective memory of JFK was itself *changed* by other events; the memory was mentally reassessed in different ways by both searchers and preservers. It was in the looking back that the rememberers have assigned such great importance to that tragic day in Dallas.

Writers took a divided track in discussing the slain president, some assessing his life and career and others focusing on an analysis of his death. Brown has argued that it was the assassination, and not the accomplishments of Kennedy's life, that "elevated him to a primary place in the political consciousness of America."[58] The funeral, notes the author, "reinforced the sense that Kennedy's death was a national catastrophe . . . [that weekend] . . . humanized him, yet elevated him above the ordinary mass of politicians and public figures."[59] Brown here encapsulates not only the *image* of John F. Kennedy that came out of the 1960's but also the essence of the *myth* of JFK. The flattering literature of the 1960's set up the foundation for the ongoing arguments about the importance of JFK's accomplishments.

The legacy of John F. Kennedy from 1963 to 1969 took shape as an extended eulogy. "Camelot," the term often used to describe the Kennedy years, was handed to the American people, courtesy of *Life* magazine, by Jacqueline

Kennedy late in 1963.[60] The idea came from the legends of the court of King Arthur, as presented in a popular Broadway musical of the time. Millions adopted this idealized version of the Kennedy years, and Camelot became one of JFK's widow's most lasting contributions to his legacy.

During the months after the assassination, most of the photo-magazines prepared special memorial editions devoted to the memory of JFK, and every politico who had not extolled the president's virtues during the funeral weekend came forth to offer him posthumous praise. Both wire-services agencies rushed into print with photo essays about the assassination weekend. UPI's *Four Days*, issued in cooperation with *American Heritage* magazine in 1964, became a top seller.[61]

The card catalogue at the Dallas Public Library, a typical big-city repository, lists eleven titles on Kennedy that were published between 1960 and 1963; in the year of his death thirteen more were released. In 1964, however, thirty-six new titles entered the stacks, the single largest number of titles devoted to the late president in any year through 1992.[62]

In the immediate aftermath of the shooting in Dallas, books on Kennedy took a positive tone. Victor Lasky's critical *JFK: The Man and the Myth* was on the bestseller list in 1963 at the time of the assassination. The author immediately halted publication of the book and canceled all of his speaking engagements. "As far as I'm concerned," said Lasky, "Kennedy is no longer subject to criticism on my part."[63]

The first crop of posthumous JFK books was penned by prominent journalists and members of the Kennedy inner circle. These were *not* historical biographies but personal remembrances. Since they were written by JFK insiders, they tended toward positive analysis of Kennedy as a man and political leader.

The positive image of JFK that was laid down during the weekend of his death solidified in print. Many people embraced it as a permanent part of their memory. Jim Bishop's *Day in the Life of President Kennedy* was nearing completion when the president was assassinated, so the book came out as a living memorial in 1964.[64] Volumes by admiring journalists in the same year included friend Benjamin Bradlee's *That Special Grace* and Hugh Sidey's *JFK Presidency*, as well as *Kennedy Years*, published by the *New York Times*.[65] Administration insiders Ted Sorensen, Paul "Red" Fay, and Pierre Salinger wrote books during the 1960's, along with White House historian Arthur Schlesinger, whose *Thousand Days* sold heavily in 1965–66, winning the Pulitzer Prize.[66]

Historian Thomas Brown asserts that the "main shapers of the JFK image have been the members of the Kennedy family themselves."[67] Certainly this is true. Brown notes that the Kennedys exerted powerful control over writers during the formative years after John F. Kennedy's death, trying to block release of Maude Shaw's remembrance, *White House Nannie*, because Shaw admitted in the book that she, and not Jacqueline Kennedy, had to tell Caroline the news of her father's death.[68]

JFK's old friend Red Fay angered the Kennedys with his book, *The Pleasure of His Company*; the clan demanded major revisions to the manuscript and then refused to accept his contribution to the Kennedy Library after he failed to make them all.[69] The worst confrontation came with William

Manchester's *Death of a President*, long considered the authoritative account of the weekend from the standpoint of the mourning; the book was commissioned by the family, who then tried to cancel the project in 1967. Manchester was worshipful of JFK's memory, but the family insisted on some major changes that the historian resisted. Jacqueline Kennedy finally took Manchester to court. "*I* will decide when it should be published," she insisted.[70] So loud was the controversy over the official assassination book that it spawned the publication of *The Manchester Affair*, which detailed the historian-author's painful negotiations with the Kennedys.[71]

Another author, Jim Bishop, went public in 1966 with assertions that Jacqueline Kennedy had written to ask him to cease his efforts to write *The Day Kennedy Was Shot* and that she then took action to silence his sources and even intervened with the publisher when her entreaties failed.[72] Bishop accused the former first lady of trying to "stand in the doorway to history."[73]

The family's attitude toward the death of the president helped shape his popular image. The Kennedys have been on record for years that they prefer to celebrate the legacy of Kennedy's *life* and not dwell on the horror of his death. They realized that there would have to be some official history of the assassination, so they selected William Manchester to write it. His book, and the official Warren *Report*, were supposed to record the events of the weekend and settle the question of how JFK had died, so that history could then focus on the way that Kennedy had lived. Bishop's earlier book on JFK, *A Day in the Life of President Kennedy*, was released posthumously, but it followed the Kennedys' desire to focus on the living man. Bishop crossed over into foreign territory when he tried to write about the assassination. This leaves the question of the Kennedys' right to try to influence the written record. Within the context of the latter part of the Sixties, however, the family had little reason to suspect that the Warren *Report* would be subject to so much criticism.

It is easy in hindsight to blame the family for overt manipulation of the Kennedy legend. The Kennedys may have led the march toward adulation of the slain leader, but there were plenty of musicians who volunteered to play loudly in the band. Prominent journalists heaped praise on the dead president. The Democrats promoted his image, LBJ deliberately blended his programs with Kennedy's, African Americans adopted him as their second Lincoln, and Catholics extolled the virtues of the first man from their faith to win the White House.[74]

The writers of the Kennedy court made much of JFK's successes in foreign policy, using his cool but flexible handling of the Cuban missile crisis as the obvious pinnacle. The books written by members of the inner circle came out while the war in Vietnam was escalating, so Kennedy's defenders concentrated on two major themes: JFK as a leader who tried to prevent the spread of communism in Southeast Asia, and JFK as a leader who wanted to avoid "large scale commitment of American land troops" there.[75] Kennedy's flexibility, they said, kept him balanced between the demands of the hawks and the doves.

These early collective efforts on JFK *the man* created JFK *the image* in the public mind. The transitory love for the slain martyr that many felt during the weekend of his death was made permanent in these published memoirs. Brown summarizes the main elements of the Kennedy image that came out of these books:

1. A *man of reason* who was a *victim of hate*

2. A symbol of the *new political stylist,* who used the media to take his message directly to the people

3. A *mysterious, suffering (ill) inner man with infinite promise*

4. A *young idealist who was anti-bureaucracy*

5. A man who was *growing* at the time of his death, a *symbol of thwarted promise*

6. A man who was *better than LBJ: Robert Kennedy as heir* to his brother

7. A man of achievement in foreign policy, a *flexible leader*[76]

This model of Kennedy entered into the collective memory during the decade of the Sixties and gained a sizable following. Millions of Americans bought and read these early books on Kennedy's legacy. The image became the standard against which disclosures and assessments would be measured in the decades that followed his death.

No one could tell during the years immediately after the assassination of Kennedy what kind of long-term image he might have. Historians, who had not yet penned biographies about the thirty-fifth president, expressed some skepticism that an administration lasting only one thousand days could produce much of a record of achievement.

JFK AS HISTORY
1969–1994

The collective memory of JFK as a man and politician changed dramatically after the 1960's, but his stature as a legend survived nearly intact. This created a legacy of seeming contradictions about the man and his accomplishments, further complicated by an enduring controversy surrounding the cause of his death, a subject treated in Chapter 4.

Events in the nation since the late 1960's had an effect on how the rememberers viewed JFK, alive and dead. Trends in society altered the memory of the president. It is impossible to understand the meaning of John F. Kennedy without some examination of the context of the times and the shifting attitudes of the people.

SOCIETY, 1969–1994

The election of Richard Nixon in 1968 put the Republicans in the White House. Older voters and the newly enfranchised boomers chose a seasoned, if somewhat scarred politician to take on the nation's growing crises. The approach toward Nixon was far from idealistic; we wanted someone to get the job done. As one boomer recalled, somewhat nostalgically: "Kennedy was the existential goal, the American dream personified. . . . In Nixon we saw ourselves."[77]

More campus takeovers occurred in 1969. Widespread demonstrations in October led Vice President Spiro Agnew to denounce the youthful rebels as an "effete corps of impudent snobs."[78] The summer of 1969 gave us the musical festival Woodstock, and by the end of the decade it was obvious that the voting age should be lowered to eighteen. The Twenty-sixth Amendment to the Constitution, ratified during the early 1970's, was the most important accomplishment that the young rebels could claim.

President Richard Nixon went on television on November 3, 1969, to outline his plan for getting the United States out of the war. Instead of withdrawal, however, he asked the "silent majority" of Americans to go along with the war until the United States could negotiate a "peace with honor." About 75% of the nation supported him. Not everyone was happy with the delay, however, and 250,000 protestors marched in Washington on November 15. For my part, belief in an honorable end to the conflict seemed worth the wait, at least for a while.

If the Tet offensive showed us that the American effort to halt the spread of communism did not seem to be working, the Soviet Union's invasion of Czechoslovakia that same year proved it. The incursion crushed that nation's brief flirtation with reform.[79] By the 1970's it had become obvious that American power was resented, that American expertise could not keep the world safe, and that the nation's ability to grow and prosper forever had definite limits.

The Seventies had a significant impact on the legacy of JFK. In 1973, ten years after the assassination, a reporter asked a college student what he thought about JFK: "What did it all mean besides glamour, Jackie and football at Hyannis Port?"[80] In ten short years, Kennedy's halo had slipped. Suddenly, he was a "hawk, cold warrior, liberal imperialist" who never had the right to commit the nation to its disastrous course as a dictator in world affairs.[81] The debunking had begun.

Negativism was a watchword for the Seventies. During this decade, society was hit by a new wave of baby boomers born after 1950 and a series of political blasts whose fallout had a tremendous impact on the American psyche. Escape and experimentation ruled the era. The Fifties and early Sixties were recast as nostalgia of a better, bygone day. George Lucas's 1973 film *American Graffiti* was an attempt to recapture the innocence of youth "before Da Nang and Dealey Plaza."[82] The term "nostalgia trip" became a household word.[83] A rock-and-roll revival provided new audiences for older singers like Fats Domino, Chuck Berry, and Elvis Presley. Marilyn Monroe, who had died in 1962, became a star again, along with Humphrey Bogart and other former giants of the silver screen. Meanwhile the first group of the nation's boomers, those born between 1946 and 1950, entered the work force in large numbers.

The 1970's events that had the strongest impact on the memory of JFK were the Vietnam War, Watergate and later high-level government scandals, an inflationary economy, and a loss of confidence at home about the nation and its position in the world. These events caused a shift in American confidence in the presidency, the government, and its agencies.

The first years of the decade were schizophrenic in dress, a polyester wonderland full of weird-looking people decked out in hot pants, peasant dresses, bell-bottoms, minis, maxis, and wobbly platform shoes. Hairstyles changed almost as fast. The early part of the Seventies called for long locks on men and women and for afros on African Americans, who were continuing their move toward equality.

The Seventies began with Earth Day, a warning to pay attention to ecology, even at the price of unlimited growth. Later years saw the birth of the health food craze, the passage of the Clean Air Act, and the growth of the Environmental Protection Agency. The early part of the decade was dominated by the emerging women's movement, part of the general trend toward equality that continued the efforts launched by blacks during the 1950's and 1960's. In 1970 New York and Hawaii passed laws to allow abortion; *Roe v. Wade*, the Supreme Court ruling guaranteeing women the right to choose an abortion, followed in 1973, a year after Gloria Steinem founded *Ms* magazine. The National Organization for Women became an active voice for the leading edge of women's rights during the era. Helen Reddy's song "I am Woman" was adopted as the anthem of the movement.

The sexual revolution of the Sixties paled in comparison with the move toward the overt "kiss-and-tell" sexuality that took hold during the 1970's and 1980's.[84] Women on the pill assumed an aggressive approach toward sexual fulfillment. Suddenly there were singles bars, waterbeds, singles "pads," coed dormitories at U.S. colleges, open cohabitation, and a trend toward full disclosure of every sexual peccadillo ever practiced by every politician since George Washington. Traditional marriage was put off or abandoned entirely as young people adopted alternate lifestyles. One boomer recalled, "Our generation was on the road to individual freedom, and marriage was a perverse detour . . . a cop-out in an age when all options should remain open."[85] The sexy oyster-eating scene from *Tom Jones* in 1963 was replaced ten years later by the carnal matings in *Last Tango in Paris*.

The gay rights movement sprang out of New York and San Francisco, spreading nationally. Earlier, gays had given disco to the popular scene, and during the 1970's the dance craze was immortalized by the music of the Bee Gees and the devotion to the disco culture depicted by John Travolta in the 1977 film *Saturday Night Fever*. Drug use spread to a broader proportion of society; drugs were, in the words of one writer, "the perfect consumer item for a culture dominated by teens and adolescents."[86]

The questioning of all things traditional continued. New spiritual groups sprang up in what one writer calls a "salad bar" of Moonies, Krishnas, and Scientologists, fully launching the new age. The 1978 mass suicides at Jonestown in Guyana became the "hippie ethos gone haywire."[87] Werner Erhard's "est" movement preached total self-reliance as a means to independence from everything.[88] The rock opera *Jesus Christ, Superstar* played on Broadway. The Age of Aquarius had begun.

In music, the 1970's began with the breakup of the Beatles. Radio, struggling against the growth of television among consumers, increased its restyling into niche markets; the decade saw the rise in FM culture. Major music was made by the Rolling Stones, the Who, Jefferson Airplane, and the new "heavy metal" sound of Led Zeppelin. In African-American music Motown, which had started at the beginning of the 1960's, continued in the 1970's with the additional voices of Marvin Gaye and Stevie Wonder. Ray Charles was already an American icon. By late in the decade, youth audiences were tuned into Elton John, Bruce Springsteen, and the rising punk sound of the Sex Pistols.[89]

The movies offered clear insights into the confusion that dominated thinking during the period. The Beatles' last song recorded together, "I, Me, Mine," could be used to describe the sense of separateness, self-consciousness, and alienation that dominated films during the late 1960's and early 1970's—*Easy Rider, Five Easy Pieces, Midnight Cowboy*, and the first *Dirty Harry* movie. Filmmakers decided to appeal directly to the youth audience during the early part of the 1970's, and relevance was the dominant theme. The height of the trend toward antiheroes came with *The Godfather* and its sequel, described by one writer as "an inversion of the Kennedys" and an exposé of the inherent evils of capitalism.[90]

The violence of the late 1960's was memorialized in *A Clockwork Orange*, a film that inspired Arthur Bremer to shoot presidential candidate George Wallace in 1972.[91] *One Flew over the Cuckoo's Nest* (1975) and *Network* (1976) paid homage to the counterculture. Howard Beale's famous line in *Network*—"I'm mad as hell and I'm not going to take it anymore"—fairly summarized the youth attitude of the period from 1968 to about 1975.

The Seventies was the decade of disaster movies—the *Airport* series, *Poseidon Adventure*, *Towering Inferno*, and *Earthquake*—and, finally, escapism. In 1975 American filmmakers abandoned the theme of relevance with *Jaws*, followed by the epic *Star Wars* two years later, which "summed up all the comic-book mysticism of the emerging new age."[92] Boomers Steven Spielberg and George Lucas began the trend toward escapist movies that paid less attention to content than to special effects and cinematography. One writer described them as "children's movies for grown-ups."[93] Political events launched a fad in conspiracy movies. Alan Pakula's *The Parallax View* and the sinister movie *Executive Action* were both based on the Kennedy assassination; later, Watergate spawned *All the President's Men*, based on a popular book of the same title.

Television during the 1970's gave us *Monday Night Football*, the miniseries, and PBS. By 1975 TV followed film and fled into nostalgia and escapism.[94] *All in the Family* opened the decade, and *Mork and Mindy* closed it. The Seventies saw the death of the traditional western; in 1975 both *Gunsmoke* and *Bonanza* went off the air. They were replaced by urban cop shows that constantly reminded the nation of the growing problem of crime in the streets. The 1976 series *Charlie's Angels*, described as a "male fantasy coated with a veneer of women's liberation," summarized society's lack of unanimity over the feminist movement.[95] The premiere of *Saturday Night Live* in 1975 showed that Americans, whatever their malaise, were still willing to laugh at themselves.

Ethnic films and television series began to appear during the 1970's, proof of the institutionalization of the civil rights movement. The "Shaft" series and films like *Blacula* were in high contrast to the lighter-fare television provided by *Sanford and Son, Good Times*, and *The Jeffersons*. Whereas Redd Fox was the junk dealer of the early part of the decade, the ambitious Jeffersons kept right on "movin' on up" until they were replaced during the 1980's by the wealthy Cosby family. In 1977 television gave America its first miniseries, *Roots*. Based on Alex Haley's novel, the series drew audiences from all races and economic levels and proved that television, at its best, could effectively combine education with entertainment.

The decade produced hand calculators and hot tubs, streaking, mood rings, and pet rocks. It launched the PC revolution and the popularity of the VCR. The psychology of Jung took over from Freud, running became an exercise fixation, and Citibank introduced automatic teller machines. In automobiles, there was a vogue for vans— two million were on the roads by 1977—many equipped with CB radios, the mid-Seventies manifestation of the antiestablishment movement.[96]

Then came the Eighties, which began with the fifty-ninth day of the Iran hostage crisis and finished with the collapse of the Soviet Union, thus ending the cold war. When the Berlin Wall went down in 1989, I was having dinner with a small group of friends, all boomers. We shared our memories of the anxiety we had felt when the wall was first erected back in 1961, and then one of the guests turned to me and asked, "Did you ever dream that we would live long enough to see it fall?" Frankly, the cold war had been such a constant symbol in my life that I had always assumed that it would go on forever.

The decade began with a growing awareness of AIDS as a new threat to society. Records show there were 163 deaths in 1981; by 1989 the total had climbed to more than 83,000.[97] A confused young man named John Hinckley tried to shoot Ronald Reagan in 1981; fortunately, he failed. The disclosure that the assassination attempt was motivated to gain the attention of teenage actress Jodie Foster struck me as more bizarre than any of the Kennedy assassination theories that had ever been proposed. Debate about gun control continued through the rest of the decade, with few concrete results. The antiweapon Brady Bill, named for James Brady, the main shooting victim in the Reagan assassination attempt, was passed during the early 1990's, but in 1996 Texas, one of several states with this provision, reinstituted the right for individuals to carry concealed weapons.

Computers became popular fixtures in American homes in the Eighties. The right of a woman to choose an abortion became a key political issue and remained one. During the 1980's the antiabortion movement began to swing into violence, thus repeating the earlier trends in the civil rights movement and the youth rebellion. The American people united on three major occasions in 1986: they joined "hands across America"; they celebrated the rededication of the refurbished Statue of Liberty; and they denounced the "New" Coca-Cola, a brief attempt by America's leading soft-drink maker to change the formula of a beverage that had become a staple in the nation's lifestyle.

In 1986 the Iran-Contra scandal broke, followed by an official probe during 1987. Investigators disclosed that the government had clandestinely backed illegal arms sales to Iran, the nation that had held American soldiers hostage during the presidency of Jimmy Carter. As had happened with Watergate, everyone asked what President Reagan might have known about the affair and when he might have known it. Reagan said he didn't remember much, and nothing much was done about the illegal trading in arms. The key figure in the affair, Colonel Oliver North, went on to run as a Republican for the U.S. Senate seat from Virginia in 1994; he lost. The stock market crashed in 1987, but no one threw themselves from office buildings, as they reportedly had after the great crash in 1929.

We discovered a hole in the ozone layer, were angered over the Exxon-Valdez oil-tanker spill, and otherwise became more active in efforts to recycle in order to protect the environment from ourselves. We even staged another Earth Day. We fought a little war in Grenada during the 1980's and an impressive one in the Middle East during the early 1990's. We won them both.

Nixon, Vietnam, and Watergate

Nixon's pledge to get us out of Vietnam with honor took a long time to carry out. He authorized troop withdrawals, but the war ground on relentlessly. Death tolls continued to mount. There were years of negotiations and promises. It took weeks for the parties to agree on the shape of the negotiating table. Yes, in 1969 the earlier deferments gave way to a draft lottery, but there was an attitude of "hell no, we won't go" about the continuing effort to make Vietnam into a war that it never was. In 1969 Nixon ordered the bombing of Cambodia, and there were massive antiwar demonstrations across the country.

In 1971 Daniel Ellsberg leaked an internal Pentagon history of the U.S. involvement in Vietnam, which was published by the *New York Times*. The conclusion: the military had been lying to the people about the war.[98] Many Americans began to be skeptical about government. Earlier books about the Kennedy assassination, implying a government cover-up, suddenly seemed to make more sense.

On April 30, 1970, President Nixon announced on television that the United States was sending in troops to invade Cambodia. In my view, invading yet another country did not fall into the category of a negotiated peace with honor. At home on a break from graduate school that weekend, I turned to my father in amazement. "He can't do that," I said. By Monday afternoon, four students had been killed at Kent State University; more than four hundred American colleges had to cancel classes before the end of the term (Figure 3.15). On January 27, 1973, the agreement to end the war in Vietnam was signed, and many of the prisoners of war came home. That summer Congress passed the War Powers Act, prohibiting any American president from deploying U.S. forces without informing Congress within forty-eight hours. In April 1975, Saigon fell to the North Vietnamese. The American effort to contain the spread of communism had failed, costing the nation more than fifty-five thousand lives.

Vietnam had a profound effect on the American people. Historian Henry Steele Commager wrote that it caused "a loss of faith in the integrity of our government, loss of confidence in the ability of the press and television to retain their independence . . . [and showed] denial of that access to information which the Founding Fathers deemed essential."[99] Later baby boomers, those who never had to serve in large numbers in Southeast Asia, split off from the older part of their generation. Referring to my age group, one younger boomer wrote: "Vietnam seems to have broken them."[100] It did indeed dampen some of our high idealism, but it did not kill our ideals. Besides, the early boomers were not the only ones to grow skeptical about the effectiveness of government and the media.[101]

The boomers entered the job market at a time when the economy had been overstrained by the cost of the war. Preoccupation with Southeast Asia also eroded American strength with the Atlantic Alliance and warped our overall foreign policy.[102] In the two decades between 1950 and 1970 only North Vietnam and Cuba, and possibly Tibet, went

FIGURE 3.15

Ohio's Kent State University, where on May 4, 1970, National Guardsmen fired on students during a protest against the U.S. invasion of Cambodia. Four people were killed, and nine others were wounded. *UPI/Corbis-Bettmann*

communist; during the 1970's an average of one nation per year fell to Marxism.[103] This was difficult for Americans to accept; we had been dedicated to the role of preserving freedom everywhere, and it became obvious that our plan was not working. Suddenly, we were losing our position as the richest and most powerful country on earth.

The financial burden that the war placed on the budget led to inflation and recession, two factors that dominated the economics of the 1970's. When veterans returned from the battlefields during the early part of the decade, few received the traditional heroes' welcome; they were viewed as competitors for jobs in a tightening market, and many had a hard time finding employment. Also, many veterans were derided by the former doves for their military service.

Watergate occurred within this general atmosphere of malaise. On June 17, 1972, burglars were arrested during a break-in at the Democratic National Committee Headquarters in the Watergate Hotel complex in Washington, D.C. Nixon, campaigning for another term as president, was reelected by a large margin in the following November. A month after the election the White House confirmed the existence of an internal "plumbers' unit," set up after the "Pentagon Papers" scandal to track down the source of the leak that had disclosed the truth about the abortive war. The Watergate burglars and the plumbers were related.

Americans started paying attention to Watergate articles in the press early in 1973, at about the same time that the treaty to end the war in Vietnam was signed. The following June, White House attorney John Dean began testifying before Sam Ervin's Senate Select Committee on Watergate, and Americans heard a litany of horrors that included "subversion of the Constitution, wiretapping, espionage, sabotage, extortion, blackmail, forgery, burglary, perjury, bribery, obstruction of justice, [and] illegal offers of executive clemency."[104] Dean testified that the White House had actively covered up the facts of the Watergate break-in and that Nixon knew about it.[105]

By the summer of 1973 I had worked for two years for a Virginia historic preservation organization headquartered in Richmond. One day when I was at lunch with my boss, Angus Murdock, the Watergate hearings before the Ervin committee were being aired on a television nearby. When Alexander Butterfield admitted to the committee that the Oval Office had tapes of its internal conversations, every head in the restaurant suddenly turned upward toward the television screen. We were all stunned.

The widespread concern over Watergate, just like the reaction to a presidential assassination, was caused by the fact that the office of the presidency was involved. "The presidency," says one author, "magnetizes events as nothing else in our civic life can."[106] The idea that a bunch of incompetent burglars tried to rifle the files of the Democratic National Committee Headquarters never mattered much to me; it was the idea that Nixon might have been behind it that was totally unacceptable. "People want to be able to trust, most of all in the presidency," and we found that we could not.[107] Our closest personal link to government was breaking.

The period between July 1973 and August 1974 was horrible for many people. Nixon took shelter behind the tremendous power of his presidency, staving off repeated attempts to get at the tapes. In October, Vice President Spiro Agnew pleaded no contest to accusations of illegal financial dealings and resigned from office. Republican Congressman Gerald Ford was appointed to replace him. Ten days later, Nixon engineered the "Saturday Night Massacre," firing Archibald Cox, the White House special prosecutor in charge of the Watergate investigation; top-level government officials resigned in protest to the dismissal.

By the next summer more than three dozen men affiliated with the Nixon presidency had been indicted in the Watergate scandal. In June 1974, a District of Columbia grand jury named Nixon as an unindicted coconspirator, and a month later, the House Judiciary Committee began voting on Articles of Impeachment. No one came forward to claim responsibility or to apologize to the American people. I felt that the Watergate conspirators believed they were no longer accountable to the public they had pledged to serve.

I was working in Washington when the final act of the Watergate drama took place. As the Nixon tapes were released the contents were published, with the result that the American people had a clear view of the pettiness and paranoia inside the Oval Office. A batch of tapes revealing the president's role in a cover-up of the Watergate break-in was released in July 1974, and most people realized that the Nixon presidency was doomed.

On August 9, 1974, news reporters wandered in and out of the White House gates, looking self-important. The atmosphere was tense and sad, as if we were awaiting word that the chief executive inside had died after a long illness. That night Nixon went on television and announced his

FIGURE 3.16
Richard M. Nixon, leaving Washington in August 1974. The Watergate scandal led to the first resignation of an American president. *UPI/Corbis-Bettmann*

resignation. The next day he was gone (Figure 3.16). Many of my age group were elated; my saddened father predicted that the fall of Nixon was a devastating blow to the country. He was right.

Watergate made a monster of the media. The *Washington Post* duo of Bob Woodward and Carl Bernstein gained a Pulitzer Prize and fame for their dogged coverage of the Watergate scandal, later immortalized in the book and film *All the President's Men*. But authors have pointed out that the press did not uncover the story without the assistance of quite a few administration insiders, notably the unidentified "Deep Throat."[108] Watergate launched a trend in journalism to be hostile toward the presidency and to report on every seedy aspect of the private lives of political officials.[109] This trend has continued without abatement to the present day (Figure 3.17).

Among the people, Watergate further shattered the public's faith in government and at the same time generated a surge of morality, which showed up in the form of idealistic expectations about the proper behavior for elected officials.[110] The media's new "no-holds-barred" approach toward officeholders and office-seekers ran afoul of this new puritan strain among the populace. Qualified people with all-too-human weaknesses began to shy away from politics.

Gerald Ford

The Gerald Ford years, 1974–77, have been remembered as the "time for healing."[111] The term is an epitaph for the brief tenancy of the only president ever appointed to office. Ford's unconditional pardon of Nixon hurt his chances for election on his own in 1976. Some of my friends were furious about the pardon, believing that Nixon should have been put on trial. On the issue of the pardon, I took the stand of preserver; I was relieved that Watergate was over.

Ford suffered from the new style of journalism. Collectively, the press created an image of an uncoordinated, if not bumbling, chief of state. Texans still talk about the tamale-eating fiasco, when the northern president gamely tried to eat the Mexican delicacy without removing the corn-husk cover first. Inflation and recession dogged the Ford administration, which finally issued WIN (Whip Inflation Now) buttons to an electorate suffering from unemployment rates that rose to 12–13%. Like later presidents, the Republican leader also had problems with a Democratic-controlled Congress that blocked passage of many of his bills. Furthermore, Ford was attacked twice, within a matter of days, by armed assassins; both were women, and both failed.[112]

It was President Ford who revealed that the CIA and earlier presidents had been involved in assassination plots against foreign leaders, and much of his term was dominated by the unsettling disclosures that came out of two government probes. In mid-September 1974, journalist Seymour Hersh began to run a series of stories about the CIA in which he alleged that the intelligence agency had been involved in a plot to overthrow Chilean leader Salvador Allende; in December he revealed information that the agency had spied on domestic protestors and left-wing activists during the 1960's.[113] These revelations were followed by the identification of CIA operative Howard Hunt as a tie to the 1973 break-in of the office of psychiatrist Daniel Ellsberg, the man who had leaked the Pentagon papers.

FIGURE 3.17
"Outland" cartoon. Since the mid-1970's the media has disclosed sordid details about the private lives of national heroes;
Americans complain about the practice but follow the accounts closely. ©*Berkeley Breathed*

In 1975 Ford appointed Vice President Nelson Rockefeller to head a formal investigation of the Central Intelligence Agency. The president confided that the CIA might have been involved in assassination attempts against other foreign leaders, and journalist Daniel Schorr broke the story on CBS news. The issue of assassination was added to the responsibilities of the Rockefeller Commission, but it proved too volatile for the panel.[114] The commission released its report in April 1975, passing on the other questions about assassinations to the Church Committee.[115]

The Senate Select Committee to Study Government Operations with Respect to Intelligence Activities, chaired by Senator Frank Church, looked further into the CIA-assassination issue.[116] The committee issued its *Report* in 1976 and found no evidence of CIA complicity in the Kennedy assassination.[117] But it revealed that the CIA had enlisted the help of the Mafia in plots to assassinate Fidel Castro during JFK's term in office and that the agency, along with the FBI and the Secret Service, had withheld this information, which "might have substantially affected the course of the investigation," from the Warren Commission, which had been appointed in 1963 to investigate the JFK assassination (Figure 3.18). The disclosures from these two intelligence investigations further eroded the people's trust in government.

The Church Committee's findings also dealt another blow to the prestige of the office of the presidency. The committee discovered that there had been U.S. assassination plots against foreign leaders and that these had involved every American president from Eisenhower through Nixon. The negativism about Nixon began to ooze over the memory of the earlier leaders. We learned that the plots against Castro—they all failed—had involved the use of cigars infused with poison, laced drinks, and even a diseased fungus introduced into a scuba wetsuit.[118] Apparently

'Let's see . . . Warren Commission . . . contribution by C.I.A. and F.B.I. . . . '

FIGURE 3.18
Warren Commission cartoon. A Senate follow-up probe about U.S. intelligence agencies in 1976 found that the FBI, the Secret Service, and the CIA had withheld information that might have led the Warren Commission to further investigate the issue of conspiracy.
Tony Auth, in the PHILADELPHIA INQUIRER

the CIA had not always kept President Kennedy informed of its diverse alliances with assorted criminal elements in the U.S. underworld.

I found a perverse fascination in these disclosures about the misbehavior of government agencies. We learned that both the CIA and the FBI had opened individuals' mail illegally and that CIA scientists had developed special secret poisons. The FBI had eavesdropped for presidents from 1939 forward. This was not government of or for the people; this was a police state financed by American taxpayers.

The Carter Years

The 1970's were characterized by institutionalization of civil rights into the bureaucracy, with a strong movement toward affirmative action. The presidential election of 1976 caused avid debate among the members of my age group. The nonforgivers went with Georgia "outsider" Jimmy Carter, but others believed that the Democratic candidate and former Georgia governor did not have the insider's experience to handle either the office or the ballooning bureaucracy in Washington. Carter the outsider, untainted by Washington or Watergate, won the election. Some changes in election laws, which allowed for the formation of Political Action Committees (PACs) gave him support that had earlier come only from the established political guard.[119]

The Jimmy Carter years, 1977–81, marked the end of the Seventies. The Georgian had trouble gaining support from the special-interest groups that had gained a major hold on Congress. He launched a human-rights approach to American foreign policy in an effort to reduce U.S. support for tyrants abroad, an attempt, as one author put it, to "look at the world as something other than a field of operations for American interests."[120] But many voters viewed the effort as a bitter confirmation of the decline of American world influence. When Nicaragua and Iran staged uprisings, the United States did not intervene to support their leaders.

Finally, the fanatical Ayatollah Khomeini returned from exile to Iran and set up a militantly anti-American regime; late in 1979 students seized the U.S. Embassy in Teheran and held sixty Americans hostage, demanding the return of the deposed shah, who was sheltered in the United States (Figure 3.19). The hostages remained in captivity throughout the remainder of Carter's term.

In 1977 the Panama Canal Zone was eliminated after thirteen years of talks. Carter showed real leadership in effecting a treaty between Israel and Egypt with the Camp David Accords in 1978, and on January 1, 1979, the United States formalized relations with the People's Republic of China (Red China), an alliance initiated earlier by Richard Nixon. When, in December 1979, the USSR invaded Afghanistan, the United States made no military move, deciding to institute sanctions instead. The latter included a boycott of the 1980 summer Moscow Olympics.

The American mood after Vietnam did not welcome war, but many people saw Carter's foreign policy approach as weakness, and they looked back nostalgically to the years of "give-em-hell" Harry Truman and John F. Kennedy, who had pledged that we would "support any friend, oppose any foe, to assure the survival and success of liberty."[121] Few liked to accept the idea that America had lost its strength. After

FIGURE 3.19
Hostages during the 1979–80 Iran hostage crisis, which showed a loss of American influence abroad and contributed to a growing spirit of disillusionment at home. *UPI/Corbis-Bettmann*

the capture of the U.S. Embassy in Iran, American allies did not offer assistance. The United States felt alone.

Despite the attacks from the media, both Ford and Carter helped restore some respect for the office of the presidency. Carter's high moral tone and genuine Christian faith were refreshing to a nation starved for decency in government. So disillusioned had we become that one boomer, who attended the Carter inaugural, was startled to see the new president and Mrs. Carter leave their limousine to walk among the people during the parade down Pennsylvania Avenue. "He was trusting us not to kill him," he thought at the time (Figure 3.20).[122]

The equality movement gained full steam with the addition of women and gays to the voices demanding that they receive equal treatment under the Constitution.[123] But economic opportunities for improvement had diminished, at least by the standards of the earlier postwar era. The economy remained bad, and jobs were tight. Furthermore, many whites lost their earlier sense of direct participation in fostering the movement toward racial equality. As Congress passed more and more regulations during the 1970's, some people came to feel that equality was being dictated by government bureaucrats; no one was asking whites to help anymore.[124]

Between 1973 and 1986 the wages earned by young white men declined 18% while earnings of male high school dropouts plummeted 42%.[125] The maturing of the baby boomers further burdened the job market. Between the late 1960's and mid-1970's more than seventy-eight million young people entered the labor pool; only 5% of them would earn more than $30,000 a year, thus qualifying for the designation of Yuppie.[126] The high idealism of the Sixties, based on a foundation of wealth, began to wane in the harsh light of the marketplace. As the well-educated boomers pressed for jobs, corporations cut back and replaced people with machines. Japanese products began to predominate, and the sophisticated culture of consumers in the United States bought them because they worked better than our own. Americans stuck in the lower economic brackets found themselves squeezed out of the market by educated youths who took lower-paying jobs.

The shock of losing South Vietnam in 1975 was accompanied by the growing realization that an ever-increasing use of science and technology had "an effect of diminishing returns."[127] If America was supposedly the most advanced nation on earth, then why did its technology fail to help win the war in Southeast Asia? During the mid-1960's a large section of the United States experienced an electrical blackout caused by a power failure, affecting more than thirty million people. The conventional wisdom for energy supplies articulated for the 1970's called for nuclear reactors to provide the juice for the ever-increasing use of power. But the Three Mile Island near-meltdown, films like *China Syndrome*, and media disclosures of towns dangerously contaminated by corporate nuclear waste products showed the American people that nuclear energy had a strong negative side. By the late 1970's an antinuclear movement was in full swing.

Faith in the world importance of the United States and our own belief in our ability to keep on growing took another downturn when the Arab nations launched their oil embargo in 1973. The message was clear: small nations could have a serious effect on the lifestyles of Americans.[128] Progress through improved technology, a concept that had long been central to the American dream, proved to have a limited future. Americans began to understand that unlimited growth might destroy the planet; the age of ecology was born.[129]

The Great Society programs in education launched during the Sixties had produced a basic change in the way subjects were taught. There were new programs—new math, new English—and a new reliance on social sciences that promoted personal evaluation over the traditional three "R's." By the early 1980's potential employers were complaining that young applicants were scientifically literate but could not write English and knew practically nothing about the humanities.

Educators came to realize that many of their experimental programs had not worked. The influx of baby boomers had created a behemoth, the educational bureaucracy; the public education system in the country declined.[130] In 1955, 27% of the nation's youths had continued on to college; by 1965 the percentage had risen to 40%.[131] Yet educated Americans simply could not find jobs.

FIGURE 3.20

President Jimmy Carter in 1977. Security for elected officials and major candidates was strengthened as a result of the Kennedy assassination; here, in a clear departure from security procedures, newly inaugurated President Carter and his wife walk down Pennsylvania Avenue. *Courtesy, Jimmy Carter Library*

In my youth, higher education was considered a privilege; during the 1970's, people began to speak of it as a right. An educational report released in 1993 showed that half the adult population in the United States was unable to read or write in accordance with contemporary standards of literacy.[132] The report blamed declining standards in elementary and secondary schools and a tendency to promote students without sufficient merit, partially as a means to separate failing adults from younger learners.

Public policy during the decade favored a continuation of the "downward distribution of wealth."[133] The middle class, once the American dream of equality, declined during the 1970's; by 1984, statistical pie charts showed that 40% of the families in the nation owned more than two-thirds of the wealth, and the middle class was left with only 17% of the total.[134] America had begun to shift into a two-tier society of rich and poor.

Only 30% of the women in my mother's generation had worked, but 70% of women in my age group entered the work force; meanwhile nearly one-quarter of all the new jobs created between 1963 and 1978 were either at or near the poverty level.[135] My father had spent 14% of his income on housing when I was growing up; by the mid-1980's I would have to spend nearly 44% of mine.[136] Overall economic growth declined during the 1970's, with less productivity and a 14% inflation rate that rose to 20% by 1980.[137] Many of the new poor were divorced women. Americans began to suspect that the welfare system did not work. The sense of promise that we had felt during the early 1960's drifted away.

The entry of the boomers into a competitive labor market caused them to change their behavior. By the mid-1970's America saw the beginning of what author Tom Wolfe called the "Me Decade." The new laborers abandoned their polyester bell-bottoms for conservative designer clothes and shifted their focus from "doing your own thing" to making a living or, in many cases, struggling to survive. Sales of suits went up 40% in 1976 alone.[138]

Women postponed marriage and tried to move up the ladder of success, and young marrieds formed working households in order to pay the mortgage. The American dream of home ownership became a challenge to attain. Radical Yippie Jerry Rubin changed his philosophy during the late 1970's and eagerly joined the establishment. He married, set up a successful business organizing networking parties for well-heeled singles in New York City, and started drinking Perrier. "I had come to the decision that the way to change America is by amassing as much power, financial or otherwise, as one could, and *then* to create a new establishment," he later reasoned. "America is not going to be changed from below. . . . In America you've got to follow the dollar, right?"[139] Many boomers nostalgically yearned for a return to the Kennedy era, when people had asked what they could do for their country.

During the 1970's a new movement to turn back the long tide of progressive liberalism gained momentum. The new right developed an effective political organization and grew powerful, aided by the neo-conservatives and the religious right, two groups that expressed a desire to return to "traditional values"—their term—eschewing violence and "irrational ideas."[140]

Evangelism came out of fractures that developed within major churches during the 1960's, and by late in the

Seventies there were fourteen hundred radio stations and thirty television outlets specializing in religious broadcasts.[141] Evangelists like Pat Robertson and Jerry Falwell became political, and Falwell's Moral Majority allied with the new right, urging a return to the sanctity of the American family.[142] Moral character became an issue of great concern to this group. The new right attacked affirmative action, accusing "reverse discrimination" against qualified whites. Liberalism, they said, meant nothing more than more bureaucracy and taxes. Liberals, on the other hand, warned against the shortsighted abandonment of principles developed over decades.

The Reagan Revolution

During the 1980 presidential campaign, Ronald Reagan came in with a promise to improve the economy *and* return America to world power *and* reaffirm traditional American values. Reagan was the antithesis of the "liberal ideal" that the right wing insisted prevailed in government, universities, and foundations; liberalism was blamed for the loss of American power abroad, for inflation, and for the growing influence of the media in shaping society.[143] Liberalism was symbolized by the Democratic party, which had fallen to pieces.

By 1980 the machine politics of the 1950's had given way to election by the "image makers," a California invention of the 1930's that came to dominate the way that candidates for office packaged and sold themselves to the voters.[144] John Kennedy had popularized the notion on a national scale; Reagan perfected it. Reagan became the greatest communicator since Kennedy, and people listened to what he had to say.

During the liberal years, including Nixon's terms, government seemed to some people to have grown out of all proportion; federal courts increased their influence on the operation of schools, on police departments, on civil servants, on the unions, and on business.[145] The postwar era had seen the birth of class-action lawsuits, the swelling of a bureaucracy added to oversee laws passed by a nearsighted Congress, and a flourishing of regulatory agencies.[146] Law schools graduated attorneys by the thousands; the nation became a country of lawsuits for petty grievances and every type of personal injury. Crime rose; people began to feel that criminals had more rights than law-abiding citizens did.

The efforts of the 1960's and 1970's toward true equality had resulted in entitlements and a splintering of society into warring factions.[147] Reagan said he would recapture the American dream, and the baby boomers and the under-thirty age group voted for him in droves.[148] One-fourth of the Democrats switched parties, accepting Reagan's promise to reverse the terrible slow death of American optimism. One thing was certain: the election of Reagan to the White House marked the end of the long period of progressive liberalism.

Like Kennedy before him, Reagan called for increased defense, took a hard stand against the USSR, cut taxes, and tried to cure federal deficits through growth. "It is spring time for America once again" became the motto signifying the Reagan philosophy.[149] He worked to dismantle the systems that government had put in place to effect forced equality. Many Americans were convinced these systems did not work, so they supported the actions that he took.

Russian dissident Alexander Solzhenitsyn had forecast the backlash against entitlements, welfare, and civil liberties during a speech in 1978 at Harvard. "The defense of individual rights has reached such extremes," he said, "as to make society as a whole defenseless against certain individuals. It is time in the West to defend not so much human rights as human obligations."[150] Author Theodore White declared that by the dawn of the Reagan era, America "was officially, in many jurisdictions a racist society." White added, "In trying to eradicate racism, the politics of the Sixties and Seventies had institutionalized it."[151]

Geraldine Ferraro, the first woman to run for the vice presidency, lost the election in 1984 on Walter Mondale's presidential ticket, and during the 1980's the feminist movement, at least on the surface, seemed to slow down. The Equal Rights Amendment, calling for a Constitutional amendment to guarantee equal rights for women, was formally defeated in 1982, but working women continued their advances within the marketplace. Reagan appointed Sandra Day O'Connor as the first female member of the Supreme Court in 1981. Bill Clinton appointed the second female to the court in 1993.

Women continued to demand change in their domestic relationships.[152] The 1990's has seen large numbers of women openly express their anger against the actions of some men in the workplace and at home. The Supreme Court confirmation hearings of Clarence Thomas were one example of this trend. Senate insiders leaked a private FBI clearance interview in which former Thomas employee Anita Hill described incidences of sexual harassment by the nominee. The issue was presented in public hearings before the Senate Judiciary Committee, promoting a "he did it, she lied" gender debate between many Americans.

Thomas was confirmed by the all-male Senate committee, thus angering many women. The gender debate was rekindled in the national media when beautician Lorena Bobbit of northern Virginia dismembered her ex-Marine husband, John Wayne Bobbit, in 1993 in a protest against his alleged sexual abuse. At the ensuing trial, neither party was jailed.

The 1980's was the probusiness decade. In 1973 only one-seventh of the nation's college students opted for a corporate career; by 1983 one out of four graduates had business degrees.[153] In 1968 fully 85% of the nation's young believed that college would help them "develop a philosophy of life"; by 1984, according to one disgruntled author, there had been "almost a 50% decline in idealism and a 100% increase in venality."[154]

The trend toward a two-tier society increased; the economic shift to a service economy eliminated more than eleven million jobs between 1979 and 1986, and the affluent political leadership made drastic cuts in public spending.[155] Reagan instituted the first upward trend toward the distribution of wealth since World War II.[156] The poor got poorer and the rich got richer. Enrollments at African-American colleges peaked in 1986 and then began to fall.[157] Reagan tried to reduce the size of government, but the Democratically controlled Congress balked.

Reaganomics was a return to JFK's tactic of inducing deficits during a time of economic growth, but it worked out quite differently during the 1980's. Reagan and his successor, George Bush, maintained spending and allowed the deficit to balloon to a level approaching $4 trillion. But the lobbyists and even the traditionally Democratic special-interest groups clamored for their share of the public pie; for a long time no one seemed too concerned about the future. It was during the 1980's that people overtly voted by economic class and not by party.[158]

The Eighties and early Nineties were marked by expensive consumerism, with middle-class goods at Sears taking a backseat to more conspicuously costly wares offered by specialty shops such as Nordstrom's and Neiman-Marcus.[159] During the 1980's the threat of disease turned many away from sex and created, some argue, a new focus on foods—ethnic foods, low-cholesterol foods, new American, new Southwest, and low-fat foods. Exercise became "the Yuppie version of bulimia."[160] Upscale consumers threw out their polyester from the 1970's and swathed themselves in natural fibers. Drugs continued in the culture, but pot and other recreational substances gave way to cocaine, "the missing link between the self-conscious Seventies and the materialistic Eighties."[161] The poor turned to crack, a cheap version of cocaine that was just as deadly.

Liberals issued warnings during the 1980's. "There is something wrong with a culture that values Wall Street sharks above social workers, armament manufacturers above artists," noted one author, but Reagan's thinking prevailed.[162] The boomers, by no means united in their attitudes, showed a tendency to remain socially liberal and economically conservative.[163] Given the overall election trends of the era, they voted for their economic interests.

The 1992 Election

The election of 1992 showed another major shift in the attitudes of American voters, who cried out for political, governmental, and economic reform. Independent candidate Ross Perot gained a large following by calling for a reduction in the deficit and the elimination of government waste being generated within the Washington beltway. Again, the campaign provoked a major debate within my generation, a debate this time focused along the lines of economics versus a desire to return to the social moral values of the 1960's. Like Jerry Rubin, many who had chased and found the dollar said they would vote Republican, not only to preserve their place in the economic hierarchy but also to avoid a return to flagrant social giveaway programs that they believed would not work. Perot had appeal for many in my age group because he harked back to the old credo that government should belong to the people and "not to the highest bidder."[164]

Despite cries from detractors that he was a "tax and spend" liberal, candidate Bill Clinton took a central approach within a newly unified Democratic party. Questions about his morality on the issues of marital fidelity and avoidance of service in Vietnam failed to deter voters at the polls. Clinton's pledge for economic reform and a return to social consciousness appealed to enough Americans to give him the election. However, the public staged a political revolution in the fall elections of 1994 by sending a majority of Republicans to both the Senate and the House of Representatives; these politicians pledged massive reform in a new "Contract with America."

The Nineties have combined some of the violence of the Sixties with the confusion of the Seventies. As a rememberer, I find myself hoping that America will use this decade to find a way to pull itself together as a nation so that it can be productive in the next century. The media tells me that the new generation has little optimism about the future, that you have not embraced the culture of hope that runs like a binding cord through the history of the nation. "All American kids should have to make a trip to a foreign country," philosophized an Iranian cabdriver to me last year in Dallas, "then they'll appreciate what it means to be an American." Cabdrivers gave me the same advice thirty years ago.

BOOKS ON KENNEDY, 1969–1994

"Awareness of history," according to one historian, "enhances communal and national identity, legitimizing a people in their own eyes."[165] Yet in 1969, the American public was abandoning the printed historical word in record numbers. During the 1960's the social sciences had begun an upsurge, and professional historians participated in the search for a scientific basis for the past.[166] Academic historians, facing tons of new data to process and evaluate, moved into narrow fields of specialization, with the unfortunate result that they "denuded history of both its synthetic power and its diverse audiences."[167] The Seventies simply magnified the pluralism of society. History divorced itself from the humanities and fractured into many different subjects—black history, women's history, civil war history, eighteenth-century legal history. Student audiences turned away from the formal study of the subject. BA degrees in history declined 60% between 1970 and 1982.[168] Students moved over into the social sciences; between 1960 and 1980 the number of psychological therapists in the United States rose from 370 to nearly 2,000.[169] By the early 1990's a prominent sociologist admitted that scholars "had unwisely turned their collective backs on history."[170]

People were thus aware of specialized chunks of history, but the big picture had disappeared. Meanwhile, television's influence had increased. As one writer mournfully remarked, television "transformed the American people into root vegetables."[171] The average person just did not read as much anymore.

Nevertheless, writers continued to produce books. JFK first began to interest historians as a subject for study during the late 1960's, after his papers at the Kennedy Library became available for study. Journalists and political scientists also focused attention on John F. Kennedy's life and career. Not all of them adopted the Kennedy image developed during the 1960's; uniform admiration for any individual is impossible in our pluralistic society, particularly at a time when large numbers of people still remember him. There are quite a few Americans alive today who dislike Kennedy's memory as much as they disliked his policies when he lived. And some have passed these feelings on to their offspring. Abraham Lincoln was not uniformly admired after his death either. Franklin Roosevelt's big-government policies caused discomfort to quite a few of your grandparents' generation. Although both political parties called up the forceful spirit of Harry Truman to support their platforms during the 1992 presidential campaign, there was a time in my youth when some could only blame Truman for the moral horror of Hiroshima and Nagasaki.

Toward the end of the 1960's, critics of JFK began to speak out from both the left and the right wing. Leftists accused him of having failed to lead Congress, claiming that he had heightened the tensions of the cold war by creating crises.[172] The right said Kennedy was "killed because he failed to fulfill Moscow's designs quickly enough" or that he was too soft on the communists, that his economics were heresy, and that he pandered to the extreme elements of the civil rights movement.[173] Neither side could tolerate the sheen of JFK's image and attacked the "canonization of JFK and his family [as] symptomatic of the moral corruption and decadence of American society."[174]

The period of revisionism by academic historians set in during the late 1960's, at the same time that society began to doubt the effectiveness of the strategy to contain communism and realized its growing unhappiness with welfare and other elements of domestic policy, all linchpins of the progressive liberal philosophy.[175] The debunkers condemned Kennedy's increase in the American presence in Vietnam and sneered at his flexible approach toward the cold war. His personal style in the White House earned him the post-Watergate title of "imperial president," to which LBJ and Nixon were the heirs. Kennedy was a cold warrior, had caused the arms race, and had promoted racial unrest at home by being too slow to propose legislation. The space race was merely a manifestation of his "obsession" with beating the Russians at whatever cost. Critics dismissed the Peace Corps as a "public relations device," and some accused JFK of using ghostwriters to pen *Profiles in Courage*, his most famous book.[176]

The revisionists dismissed or made light of one of Kennedy's greatest strengths in our television society—his inspirational style—and they attacked the political legacy of JFK with as much fervor as displayed by the nation's youths of the late 1960's in attacking the establishment. In many other respects the debunkers mirrored trends in society between the late 1960's and the mid-1970's. Nancy Clinch's *The Kennedy Neurosis* embraced the rising interest in psychology and claimed that JFK's "drive to power and dominance of others" was neurotic. Henry Fairlee's book, *The Kennedy Promise*, asserted that Kennedy's strong style led the masses to expect too much; government would disappoint, and Kennedy was no exception.[177]

As historian Thomas Brown points out in *JFK: History of an Image*, the revisionists removed JFK from his context, the era of the Sixties, and placed him within the context of the Seventies; the antiwar attitudes during and after the collapse of South Vietnam were at a far remove from the strong anticommunist feelings of the early 1960's. Yet the revisionists' prose did not make much of an impact on society. Brown notes that the influence of the revisionists was confined to "certain liberal and academic circles."[178]

Besides, a 1973 national poll showed that a majority of Americans still awarded Kennedy the vote as the "most popular" president in history. Many people bought *Johnny, We Hardly Knew Ye*, a 1972 volume of remembrances by Kennedy aides Kenneth O'Donnell and Dave Powers and left the revisionists in the ivied halls of the academy to argue among themselves.[179]

The counterattack by Kennedy supporters began after Watergate, with writers making much of JFK's style and inspirational manner of leadership. In 1975 the Kennedy Library in Boston published *JFK: A Reading List*, which listed recommended books and excluded some of the more revisionist volumes.[180] But Watergate cheapened the image of the American presidency and made the holders of the office, alive or dead, open to unlimited scrutiny. The post-

Watergate era saw the first real disclosures about Kennedy's private life, particularly his reputed relationships with other women. One former congressman remarked to me that Kennedy "was a man's man."[181] By 1974 Americans began to hear allegations that he had also been a lady's man.

The "exposing" of JFK was a side effect of the CIA investigations during the mid-1970's; it was also a reflection of the media trend to open all doors and "consumerize" the presidency by encouraging Americans to view their vote as an act of "self definition in which one selects an image supposedly emblematic of one's taste and lifestyle."[182] Finally, one must recall that the press works in a highly competitive marketplace supported by sponsorship and audience participation; sex, the great American neurosis, sells well in the United States. By paying attention to the rumors and innuendos about the private lives of American leaders, alive or dead, the American people have actively participated in the cheapening of the institution of public service.

But *lifestyle* was a major buzzword during the 1970's, part of the drive toward a new kind of individual identification. The notion of presidential image, which Kennedy helped to launch, became ingrained as an accepted fact in society. How ironic that JFK's own legacy came under fire as a part of the new consumer attitude toward the presidency.

The tragic 1969 drowning death of former Robert Kennedy aide Mary Jo Kopechne at Chappaquiddick, Massachusetts, while riding with Senator Ted Kennedy, led many Americans into a renewed discussion of the Kennedys. The opening of JFK's papers in the same year provided a new window into many of the details of his life.

In 1974 author Norman Mailer and gossip columnist Earl Wilson followed the then-current Marilyn Monroe revival and hinted that the Kennedy brothers may have been involved with the famous actress.[183] Rumors about JFK and Marilyn Monroe had circulated during his presidency. Many people saw the New York television broadcast in May 1962, when she showed up sewed into a sequined dress at Madison Square Garden and sang a version of "Happy, Birthday, Dear Mr. President" that was so seductive it should have melted the candles on the cake. The president was handsome, the actress had made a career of being sexy, and it was logical for a few tongues to wag.

It was the 1975 disclosure of the Judith Campbell Exner liaison that legitimized disclosures about the private life of John F. Kennedy. The Church Committee investigation in that year revealed a tie between the Hollywood starlet and JFK and also showed that she was involved with two mafiosos, Sam Giancana and his lieutenant Johnny Roselli. Giancana was the head of the Chicago mob, and both men, we soon learned, had "participated in CIA plots to kill Castro."[184] The committee took her testimony in private in September, but her name leaked to the media, and the *Washington Post* broke the story in November 1975.[185]

Exner herself came forward in mid-December and admitted she had been "close to Kennedy" while he was president but denied any knowledge of assassination plots. Her book claiming that they had had an affair came out in 1977, and she also revealed that JFK had relied on injections from Dr. Max Jacobson, also known as Dr. Feelgood.[186] Frank Sinatra apparently made all of the introductions: JFK and Campbell, Campbell and Giancana.[187] Exner later asserted that she had met with JFK "about twenty times in the White House"; the White House phone logs for the period from 1961 through the end of the summer of 1962 indicated more than seventy calls to her.[188] Exner also later stated that she had been asked by Kennedy to serve as a courier to take messages to Giancana after the Bay of Pigs disaster.[189]

The Church Committee itself was unable to prove that JFK had actually known about the CIA-Mafia plots against Castro.[190] The Exner disclosures had an effect on the media, which began to give prominent coverage to other allegations of possible JFK liaisons, to atone for its earlier "indulgence" of the popular president.[191] So Americans only had to wait for the press to tell them virtually every rumor that surfaced. At first the major news organizations treated the subject with care. Soon, the Kennedy sexual rumors became regulation sidebars in countless media stories and began to appear in the mainstream literature devoted to a serious analysis of the thirty-fifth president. Since the mid-1970's, everyone's knowledge of JFK has been liberally salted with these tales, as if they ranked equally with his handling of the Cuban missile crisis and the movement toward détente with the Soviets. At an informal lecture in Dallas in 1995, *Time* presidential columnist Hugh Sidey reminisced about the Kennedy years, which he had followed from the campaign onward. He acknowledged JFK's sexual liberality but characterized it as a cultural trait. "I never saw it interfere with his presidency," Sidey concluded.[192]

On the matter of a JFK affair with Marilyn Monroe, the evidence is hardly conclusive. Accounts vary, but Monroe and John Kennedy met sometime between 1954 and 1957, using Kennedy brother-in-law Peter Lawford as the contact.[193] There is no doubt that Monroe and the president were friendly and were seen together on a number of occasions. But was there more to it?

For now, the public tends to believe the rumors. If Kennedy had a liaison with Monroe or anyone else, he did so with the confidence that the media would not disclose it. We live in a different world today. Kennedy was not serving as president at a time of post-Watergate morality, when Americans seem to demand perfection from their leaders, knowing that they will not get it.

In the case of the Exner relationship, there is a valid question of possible involvement between the president of the United States and organized crime. Certainly, we can accept the argument, put forth with regularity, that the peccadillos offer insights into Kennedy's character; but does our moral code today really equate to the moral code of another era? History taken out of context can be distorted beyond all value. Had the image-makers *after* JFK not transformed presidential elections into consumer events, we might not be exposed to so much information about sexual escapades.

Historical scholarship during the latter part of the 1970's once more reflected society's main concerns: the limits of power and a rising awareness that the "optimism and confidence . . . that had once characterized liberalism no longer seemed sustainable against a backdrop of shrinking resources, blows to American prestige abroad, and the mushrooming of federal entitlement programs with little demonstrable social impact."[194] Appropriately, Kennedy emerged in this period of writing less as a man in charge of the nation's future than as a product of the social forces that drove his times.[195]

The writers of the later 1970's and 1980's borrowed a little from the harsh assessments of revisionists in order to tone down the earlier adulation and came up with an adjusted JFK image that was neither great nor awful but somewhere in between. Image historian Brown thought the balanced view of JFK might come to dominate the academy but warned, "Its insights are too complex and refined for mass consumption."[196]

Herbert Parmet's two-volume biography of Kennedy, drafted during this period, reflected the trend toward balance. In Parmet's hands, JFK came across as something of a cold warrior but fully within the demands of his times. Yes, he was slow to push for legislation for civil rights, but he was working toward it.[197] Kennedy was a politician and did not want to throw away his reelection chances by losing the southern vote.

Gary Wills's 1982 book *The Kennedy Imprisonment* cast JFK as a victim, "trapped" by the web woven by his father, Joe, and by the wealth, image, and greed of the Kennedy family.[198] This is science in search of a formula to explain all human behavior. One is reminded of psychology books written for lay audiences since the 1960's, in which human failings are attributed to codependency, alcoholic parents, and poor potty training.

The mid-1970's privacy scandals eroded Kennedy's image further. "Camelot," says historian Brown, "could never appear to be the pristine place its celebrants had claimed—there were simply too many Mafia dons and party girls dwelling within its precincts."[199] However, the myth of JFK, which was composed of elements from his earlier image, survived the onslaught intact. A Gallup poll conducted in November 1975 asked Americans to identify the greatest president, and the people awarded the honor to JFK, by 52% to Lincoln's 49%. College graduates, presumably better-read, favored Lincoln, but the youths of America gave the edge to John F. Kennedy; Americans between the ages of nineteen and twenty-nine liked him best, and they barely remembered him.

During the 1980's Camelot enjoyed a resurgence. Publishers reissued some of the early books about Kennedy, works purely adulatory in tone, and added a few more for memorial bookshelves. In 1983 the twentieth anniversary of the assassination saw a wave of such publications. Simon and Schuster reissued *Four Days*, the old UPI-*American Heritage* photo-essay of the assassination weekend. Jacques Lowe, who had served as photojournalist to document JFK's 1960 run for the White House, came out with *Kennedy: A Time Remembered*.[200] *One Brief Shining Moment* by William Manchester carried an inscription from *Le Morte d'Arthur*.[201] These books sold well, as have later volumes that celebrate the promise of a bygone era.

The 1980's witnessed more efforts to see Kennedy within the context not only of his presidency but also of his family. In 1984 John Davis, a relative of Jacqueline Kennedy's, came out with the epic *The Kennedys: Dynasty and Disaster*, which traced the highs and lows of the entire family from the early days of immigration from Ireland to the present day.[202] In 1987 Doris Kearns Goodwin published *The Fitzgeralds and the Kennedys*, an American version of royal history.[203]

The thirtieth anniversary of the Kennedy assassination in 1993 generated another spate of books about JFK, some produced in the tradition of Camelot and others leaning toward a more critical review of the legacy of the thirty-fifth president. Journalist and political scientist Richard Reeves wrote *President Kennedy*, an examination into the inner workings of the politics of the Kennedy administration.[204] The media lauded the book, a product of a member of their own fraternity. Reeves's work is a microscopic analysis of Kennedy as a politician and alleges that he lacked a moral commitment, except to anticommunism. The author examines only the political figure, so beware the lack of broader cultural context in this well-written work.

During the decade of the 1980's it became obvious that the public still did not seem to care overly much about the informed opinions of the academic community. A poll taken in 1985 showed that Americans continued to believe JFK was the greatest president that ever lived; he even came in second with Republicans. Reagan was in office at the time. A 1993 CNN poll named Kennedy as the greatest president on record by a margin of 20%. Image historian Brown attributes the enduring popularity of JFK, at least in part, to "Americans' appalling ignorance of their country's history."[205] Although Brown may have a good point, I submit that Americans may be tired of the barrage of facts that are unveiled in modern publications and broadcasts on JFK. Perhaps both a cultural predisposition to admire individuality and a skepticism of authority have led millions to *decide* to adopt JFK as a hero. Perhaps he is a tie, however fragile, that binds the people to their nationhood.

KENNEDY AS MYTH

When my younger nephew Steven was a little boy, he asked me if Kennedy and Lincoln had known each other. "Not while they were both alive," I ventured, reminded of the incredible telescoping effect of history, where centuries merge effortlessly into a seamless past. Steven knew of both former presidents as heroes. His knowledge of these men lacked any contextual anchor of time or place. They were simply a part of his world, a positive presence, and in that sense they were alive. As he understood it, both men had tried to do good things and had gotten killed. Like all children, he was shaky on the details. In his young mind, the importance of both men lay in the positive works of their lives and not in the mysteries surrounding their deaths. Steven had adopted the myth of JFK.

The transference of mythology by word of mouth from adult to child is one proof of lasting heroism. Details of political failures or other elements of firsthand memory rarely make the trip from one generation to the next. Kennedy transferred as a positive, inspirational force in society, a symbol of endless promise, cruelly thwarted.

Historians and social scientists worry about myth; it is so *unscientific* and resists documentation. Myth transfers orally. Scholars think nervously of the primitive days when man's understanding of his universe came from folklore told to the members of the tribe around the village fire. Give credence to myth, they fear, and the storytelling will revert to the shaman, leaving no role for themselves. What the revisionists and sexual whistle-blowers of the 1970's and later have discovered is the disconcerting fact that the American public has found something to admire in Kennedy, something that is beyond their ability to challenge.

Anyone who has studied history soon discovers that few political leaders led completely exemplary lives. Believers in myth tend to "read into" the literature in search of confirmation of the values to which they adhere. Americans angered by affirmative action could look back on Kennedy and authoritatively state that he never proposed such programs. Americans in favor of affirmative action could

look back and say that Kennedy's civil rights bill paved the way for the later trend toward attempts by government to aggressively ensure equality.

Nostalgists of all persuasions could recall the Kennedy era as a time when America was a great nation, full of the promise of growth and wealth. Because growth and promise were central to the Kennedy image, it was easy to blame his political failures on his untimely death. Had he only lived, said the mythologists, he would have done it all. The rich could claim him as one of their own, and the poor could accept his wealth because he suffered and he worked on their behalf. His flaws somehow make him more human, just like ourselves.

What is the difference between *myth* and *image?* Image, says one authority, is deliberately "created and cultivated for mass consumption."[206] People *buy* into image, they consume it. Consumer tastes change, so some images might fall out of fashion. The early works of the Kennedy court created a powerful image of JFK the man and the president. This image was tarnished by disclosures made during the Seventies and later.

Myth, however, is not for sale. It is available to anyone who chooses to believe in it.[207] If one is a matter of taste, the other is a matter of faith. Unlike image, myth is not within the realm of scientific analysis, so it resists definition and change.[208] Myths date to the origins of human civilization. They have been out of vogue during much of our scientifically driven century, but we still believe in them. They are an integral part of the glue that binds us together as Americans. We need them.

Consider the American heroes who have endured as positive symbols of America. George Washington survives on this plane, as do many of the other Founding Fathers. Lincoln also shares the upper levels of American faith. The images of these heroes have had their ups and downs at the hands of historians over the years because "Americans have sought a middle way between proper regard and highfalutin' gush . . . demigods not being allowed for in the Constitution."[209] Kennedy revisionists have been practicing a time-honored tradition by trying to bring the legend back down to earth.

Many other world cultures are homogeneous, sharing a common spiritual heritage complete with ancient myths and their accompanying taboos. The Norwegians have their Trolls, the British their Druids. Our American culture is highly diverse, however, and includes a spiritual melting pot. The Constitution was drafted by men who adhered to the scientific tenets of the Age of Reason. Indeed, there was no room in the plan for demigods. Americans have awkwardly made room for them anyway.

Washington, Lincoln, Benjamin Franklin, Thomas Jefferson, and FDR have survived as real heroes, not gods certainly but demigods who hover above the fray of ordinary mortals. Few contemporary writers make serious attempts to debunk them entirely. Flaws can influence image, but they can no longer rattle the solidity of heroic stature in the popular mind. Somehow, the very idea of muckraking becomes taboo. Our heroes are all above politics.

How would these heroes survive in the hands of the post-Watergate White House press corps? Would Washington, with his ill-fitting false teeth and aristocratic demeanor, come across well on the campaign trail? Fortunately, his exalted status precludes the thought. Victorian novelist Nathaniel Hawthorne, when asked to consider the possibility of a nude heroic statue of Washington, remarked, "He had no nakedness, but I imagine was born with his clothes on and his hair powdered."[210] *That* is myth.

Lincoln's unruly hair would make the modern presidential image-makers nervous, but they will never get their hands on it. What a roadblock to election Jefferson's slaves would be, but he will never run for office again. Today's stern guardians of American morality would probably love to condemn some of the peculiar actions of many an early American hero, but no one asks for their opinion.

Instead, these heroes survive as symbols of the American civil religion, defined as "a set of beliefs, symbols, and rituals with respect to sacred things that Americans share without sharing a formal religion."[211] They are symbols of *ideal* traits that Americans imagine we share as a people. They are as sacred as the flag, Fourth of July fireworks, cowboys, and the bald eagle. They are also a part of the way that we learn to be Americans, the tools we use to acquire our peculiarly distinct culture. They give us our national identity.[212]

Former President Richard Nixon's funeral in April 1994 was an exercise in the practice of our civil religion; it honored the office of the presidency. My young colleagues were amazed by the accolades offered by the media and many world leaders. Virtually overnight, Nixon, the perpetrator of Watergate, became Nixon, the politician who dominated the second half of the twentieth century. It was quite a change. Every living American president attended Nixon's funeral. The ceremony was dignified and quite moving.

The public reaction to the death of former first lady Jacqueline Kennedy Onassis less than a month later was another example of national unity in action, practiced by the rememberers. Women were particularly affected by her passing. The news coverage virtually ignored her second husband, Greek shipping magnate Aristotle Onassis, whose name was seldom mentioned during the private funeral ceremony. Her long relationship with Maurice Tempelsman was reported on gently, as if the media sensed that the nation was determined to remember her *its way*, as a heroic model of courage during a time of tremendous personal pain, as a symbol of the style and elegance of a past time, as a mythmaker who created Camelot to describe her era, and as an outstanding mother who overcame impossible odds to raise her children normally, despite "the glare of a million lights."[213]

To many of your age group she was a mystery, avoiding publicity as much as possible. My women friends agreed with me that she had earned her privacy during that bleak weekend in November 1963 and that the marriage to Onassis gave her the money to protect herself and her children. We were proud that she chose to die in the same way that she had found a way to live in peace after 1963, "in her own time and on her own terms."[214] Her death gave closure to the Camelot of the Kennedys, and this was fitting, since she had named the era herself.

Despite our devotion to reason and the egalitarian principles of the Constitution, our mythical practices and heroes fit perfectly into the nebulous "culture of hope" that binds our diverse society together. Author James Robertson, in *American Myth, American Reality*, noted that myths serve the valuable function of helping people deal with the ambivalence between "what Americans profess and what they do."[215] We profess to be a peace-loving society, yet we shoot each other with apparent abandon; we espouse equality for all, but we practice racism. Robertson identifies a

cosmos of myth in America but notes that individuals pick differently from the extensive menu. This is to be expected in a nation composed of multiple cultures.

Our mythical heroes all have qualities that symbolize positive aspects of the times in which they lived. Our culture applauds efforts to tame wilderness, we admire rugged individualism, and we celebrate the "pursuit of happiness."[216] George Washington symbolizes the era of the founding, of independence itself. Lincoln is the symbol of the transition between an agrarian and an industrial society.[217] Franklin Roosevelt embodies the myth of the "creator of big government and a consumer society."[218]

During my lifetime there have been few individuals who conveyed the timeless qualities of a Washington or a Lincoln. Somehow, we seem to have confused heroism with celebrity. Mythical heroes endure from one century to the next, not from one decade to another. Their fame lasts longer than fifteen minutes. And the absence of mythical heroes can cause problems. Our society's downgrading of the validity of myth may have had a negative effect on its people. As one author has cautioned, the removal of traditional mythological taboos from society has led to a "rising incidence of vice and crime, mental disorders, suicides and dope addictions, shattered homes, impudent children, violence, murder and despair."[219] Since World War II, says Robertson, Americans have been looking for a new type of hero, one "who can show us how to continue to be Americans—frontiersmen, pioneers, successful, independent, pathfinders, idealists, innocents—in the modern, scientific, urban, industrial, bureaucratic, and anonymous, consuming world we have made for ourselves."[220]

Will Kennedy endure as a myth? After all, he has been dead for only a few decades. Robertson's model for the postwar American mythical hero calls for a person who came from origins that were either poor or deprived, who overcame some handicap if he was aristocratic, who worked hard, and who had training and achieved the high level of education needed to handle the complex issues that confront society.[221]

Many of the elements of the Kennedy image as defined during the 1960's seem to apply. JFK was never poor, but later writers have noted the deprivation he suffered due to persistent illness. His back pain also offsets his aristocratic upbringing. Kennedy's energy as president was legendary, and Harvard gave him a good education. He was a speed-reader who wrote books and was applauded as a "practical" intellect in the tradition of Benjamin Franklin.[222] JFK's frontier, a wilderness to be tamed, was space, and he pledged to develop marvelous technology to make it happen. Access to heroic stature, according to Robertson, now comes from the mass media, and JFK's success with television certainly follows the formula.[223]

It was the mythical Kennedy that Oliver Stone extolled in his 1991 film *JFK*. Actor Kevin Costner, cast as Jim Garrison, acknowledged *Hamlet* in the teary but fictitious finale to the dramatic recap of the late 1960's Clay Shaw conspiracy trial.[224] Kennedy, said Stone, "was the godfather of my generation," too old to be a brother but loving and helpful in setting us on the right pathway in life.[225]

National polls show that the new generation has adopted this purified version of JFK, yet it is still too early to tell whether future generations will accept Kennedy's qualifications to remain in the American mythological cosmos.

317
HOMICIDE & ROBBERY

CHAPTER 4

The Endless Trial of Lee Harvey Oswald

Two weeks after the Kennedy assassination, the *Dallas Times Herald* offered an editorial on the challenges that faced the newly formed Warren Commission. The presidential panel, chaired by Chief Justice Earl Warren, was charged with the official examination into President Kennedy's death. "The investigation of the assassination," it said, "will undoubtedly be the most thorough job of research in modern history. If the nation cannot believe the findings of this investigation, then there is little it can believe."[1] Less than four years later, *The Dallas Morning News* ran another editorial assessing the work of the presidential panel. "If the Warren Commission saw its task as a laying [to] rest of suspicions," commented the paper, "it failed."[2]

Today, more than thirty years after the tragedy in Dallas, most Americans still harbor doubts about the Warren Commission's central conclusions that Lee Harvey Oswald, acting alone, fired three shots, wounding Governor John Connally and killing President John F. Kennedy.

What happened? The problem lay in the details, and that is where it has remained. The details spawned a half-dozen more government-sponsored probes between 1966 and 1982. Most of them involved efforts to eliminate confusion about the medical evidence associated with the crime. All told, the *official* effort, spanning a period of nearly two decades, consisted of the following:

1. The FBI Investigation—a four-volume report submitted to the Warren Commission in December 1963, with a one-volume supplement in January 1964[3]

2. The Secret Service Investigation, 1963, which included more than fifteen hundred interviews[4]

3. The Texas Attorney General Investigation, 1964[5]

4. The Warren Commission Investigation, 1964— a one-volume report with twenty-six additional volumes of hearings and exhibits

5. The Ramsey Clark medical panel reviews, 1966, 1968

6. The Rockefeller Commission Investigation on CIA Activities, 1975

7. The Senate "Church" Committee Investigation on Intelligence Activities, 1976

8. The House Select Committee on Assassinations, 1979—a one-volume report and twelve additional volumes of hearings and exhibits on the JFK murder

9. The National Research Council Report on Ballistics Acoustics, 1982 report

FIGURE 4.1
A small sampling of JFK books from a large private collection. The controversy over Kennedy's assassination has spawned thousands of books on the subject of the president's death.
Andy Reisberg, courtesy Mary Ferrell, photo Sixth Floor Museum Archives

Cumulatively these reports asserted that Governor Connally was injured and President Kennedy was killed by Lee Harvey Oswald, who fired three shots from the sixth-floor southeast corner window of the Texas School Book Depository.

The same details generated a body of literature critical of the federal findings. An assassination bibliography published in 1980, more than fifteen years ago, listed over five thousand books and articles (Figure 4.1).[6] One writer in 1993 estimated the total number of *books* at more than two thousand.[7] The Kennedy assassination debate, led by preservers and searchers and bolstered by timely updates from the media, has, in the words of author Norman Mailer, left the American people "marooned in one of two equally intolerable spiritual states, apathy or paranoia."[8]

The Kennedy assassination debate was set up, at least in concept, by the manner in which the Warren Commission conducted its investigation and presented its findings. The panel relied on existing government investigative agencies to handle much of the legwork; it then interviewed ninety-four people at its hearings, which were held in Washington during the winter, spring, and summer of 1964.[9] The questioning did not follow the adversarial format common to criminal trials.[10] The *Report*, as published, presented a strong argument for the prosecution. Years later, Tom Wicker of the *New York Times* confirmed this view of how the commission worked: "In every crime . . . the prosecution (in this case the Warren Commission) examines available evidence and presents a theory of what might have happened. The defense presents an opposing theory. Neither theory is likely to be airtight, without flaws or questionable assertions.... But in the end, a jury usually believes one theory or the other, and convicts or acquits on that basis."[11] No strong voice for Oswald's defense was presented in the investigation, and the thousands of pages of depositions and exhibits included in the supplementary volumes included information that seemed to contradict the findings of the *Report* itself. The commission had acted as the jury, deciding which evidence was compelling enough to accept.

Despite our everyday bickering about the weaknesses of the American criminal justice system, Americans believe in trial by jury and the concept of innocence until proven guilty. The initial group of searchers became convinced that Oswald had not received an adequate defense, and they collectively embarked on an effort to give him one after the Warren Commission had finished its work.

Admission to the ranks of assassination researchers has never required a law degree or a license to practice medicine. People from all walks of life became interested in the "case," and the debate took shape as one that pitted the government against the people in the trial of Lee Harvey Oswald. The trial has lasted for more than three decades. The case for the prosecution has been argued in one set of books, articles, and film specials and the case for the defense in another.

Literary argument has a long history in America, but as one author cautions, "We no longer debate on the high plane of the *Federalist* Papers."[12] The official investigations, taken as a whole, presented a strong case against Oswald as the assassin who caused all the wounds to the occupants of the limousine; only one investigation, the House Select Committee, made any serious inquiries into the issue of conspiracy. The literature of the searchers evolved as a series of questions or disclaimers about perceived flaws in the official investigations. Collectively, both sides have presented an enormous amount of conflicting information to the public. The data includes a great deal of trivia. Little of the complex material in this literature can be compressed into two-minute summaries on the evening news or two-column-inch recaps in *People* magazine. The new generation has matured during the debate without the benefit of guidelines showing what is old and what is new in the matter of the death of the president.

The searchers have far outweighed the preservers in the number of books published. Their literature has become a genre borrowing certain practices from historiography. Writers are expected to thoroughly document all sources through citations to printed material or actual interviews; references to scientific tests are couched in technical jargon. Critical books abound in footnotes. The searchers are expected to know the official literature and return to *primary* documents rather than rely on the summary presentations listed in official reports. Searchers are subject to critical review not only from the preserver camp but also from their own peers within the assassination-research community. Handling the review process often falls to the media, which has traditionally sided with the preservers.

The overall literature of persuasion on the assassination is highly specialized. The first wave of questioners set up a trend in sharing information among themselves. Many researchers came to the aid of Jim Garrison during his New Orleans investigation during the latter part of the 1960's. After passage of the Freedom of Information Act (FOIA) in

1967, Harold Weisberg and other researchers filed FOIA requests and in some cases instituted suits for release of classified documents. When the searchers obtained the release of documents, they shared the materials with their colleagues, a practice that continues today.[13] *The Fourth Decade*, a leading researchers' newsletter, and other publications and computer network bulletin boards provide updates on information.[14]

Harold Weisberg's private collection of documents, many of them obtained through FOIA requests, includes hundreds of thousands of pages. Many documents are available for study at the Assassination Archives and Research Center in Washington, which is located near the FBI Building and is currently directed by attorney Jim Lesar, who has worked pro bono on many FOIA requests. The Sprague photographic collection at Western New England College in Massachusetts contains hundreds of visuals associated with the assassination; other researchers have amassed notable collections of photographs and films that have yet to make their way into the public domain.

Researcher Mary Ferrell has another huge collection of material. Mrs. Ferrell's database of names contains forty thousand entries, which she uses to assist official investigators and searchers alike. Cumulatively the data available for study of the assassination represents millions of pages of information, much of it concerned with details. The searchers continue their quest to find connecting pieces in a giant puzzle that *might* be assembled into a clear picture of the killing. Many of the preservers have not read much of this material.

Conspiracy has become big business; many New York publishing houses no longer shy away from printing the work of the questioners. Some publications have been condemned by preservers and searchers alike, and serious questions have been posed about the responsibilities of publishers to check on the accuracy of material before it goes into print.[15]

Preservers have long accused the searchers, as a group, of writing their books for material gain. Some of these books have sold well, but most have not. Given the large body of material produced, there have probably been some writers who did it for the money, but it would be patently unfair to dismiss all such efforts as commercial ventures. Some people look on the searchers as crusaders who have committed themselves to keeping the government straight with its people on the matter of JFK's death—a role that was once given to the media.

Historian and social analyst Christopher Lasch has asserted that the media's overconcentration on the forces of hatred in society as a cause for the assassination turned people away from a focus on Oswald as the potential assassin and led instead to years of collective "soul searching." "This pseudo-introspection," he says, "did not address the still unanswered questions about the number and location of shots... nature of... wounds, or the specific circumstances that might have led to the shooting."[16]

WHO KILLED JFK? 1964–1969

Within a week of the slaying in Dallas, President Lyndon B. Johnson established the Warren Commission.[17]

FIGURE 4.2
Members of the Warren Commission, shown presenting the official *Report* to President Johnson in September 1964.
From left: John J. McCloy, Chief Counsel J. Lee Rankin, Sen. Richard B. Russell, Rep. Gerald Ford, Chief Justice Earl Warren, former CIA Director Allen W. Dulles, Sen. John Sherman Cooper, and Rep. Hale Boggs. The work of the commission later came under harsh attack. *Courtesy, Lyndon Baines Johnson Library*

Historical context is critical in assessing how the president's assassination came to be investigated in 1963–64. The members of the commission were prominent leaders, all of them highly respected by the populace at the time. The panel hired a staff of attorneys and set out to determine who murdered John F. Kennedy. The Warren Commission relied on the FBI, the CIA, and the Secret Service to perform the legwork in the case. *Life* magazine and the *New York Times* conducted their own private investigations; other media agencies followed the federal probe closely. Basically, the press decided early that the Warren Commission was progressing well in its probe. The *Times* closed its investigation in January 1964, and everyone waited for the final *Report*, a weighty 888-page tome that was delivered to President Johnson in September 1964, only ten months after the shooting (Figure 4.2).[18]

Two months later the commission published an additional twenty-six volumes of transcripts from testimony, affidavits, or depositions taken from more than 550 individuals and reams of exhibits that were entered into the record. There was no complete index to the twenty-six volumes. Earlier presidents had formed specially appointed panels to study major issues, but it was somewhat unusual to follow this format for a presidential assassination. The idea of publishing the volumes was presumably to bring the facts before the people.

The Warren Commission worked with the full knowledge that the American people had serious doubts about the Dallas murders; a Gallup poll taken within days of the shooting found that 29% believed that Lee Harvey Oswald was solely responsible for the shooting, another 52% feared a plot, and 19% did not know exactly what to make of the bizarre weekend. Foreign governments strongly hinted that the United States needed to get its affairs in order if it wanted to maintain its position of leadership around the globe.

Release of the one-volume Warren *Report* was lauded by the media, which promised that the remaining unanswered questions about the assassination would cause niggling among historians without generating widespread civic anxiety. Still, Harrison Salisbury of the *New York Times* issued a prophetic warning in 1964 when he wrote, "The year 2,000 will see men still arguing about the president's death."[19]

The *Report*'s central conclusions were that Lee Oswald, acting alone, had fired three shots that hit the occupants of the presidential limousine; one shot missed, one shot wounded both President Kennedy and Governor Connally, and one shot hit Kennedy in the head and killed him. The theory—it was presented as a theory at the time—that a "single bullet" had passed through Kennedy and caused wounds to Governor Connally later proved to be hard for the public to digest.

Ownership of the rifle and partial fingerprints and palm prints at the scene tied Oswald to the crime, and the recovered bullet fragments and a nearly whole bullet found at Parkland Hospital had definitely been fired from the rifle, said the *Report*. Oswald had also killed officer J. D. Tippit. An implied reason for the killing: the assassin was a disgruntled, maladjusted loner looking for a moment of fame. He was the personification of the forces of hatred that lived just beneath the surface in America. The *New York Times* cooperated with the government and arranged a special, fast-printed edition of seven hundred thousand copies of the official *Report*.[20] Shortly after publication of the findings, Louis Harris, a former Kennedy pollster, reported that 69% of people surveyed believed the lone assassin theory; this was the high point of public confidence in the investigation.[21]

The honeymoon between the Warren *Report* and the rest of the country lasted for about two years, until 1966.[22] During the interim, few journalists and only a handful of Americans bothered to pore over the twenty-six volumes of supporting material from the Warren investigation. Altogether, the government sold 2,650 sets—at $76.00 each—before it ran out of copies of these volumes in June 1972.[23] Most of us knew only the summary findings printed in the *Report*. But some readers found discrepancies between the summary and the backup volumes, and they began to write questioning articles that appeared in print.

A Gallup poll conducted in 1966 showed that only 39% of the public still believed that Oswald, acting alone, had killed the president; adherents to the notion of a plot and the undecided made up the remaining 61%. Much of this shift in opinion can be traced to the work of the critics of the Warren *Report*. Writers who questioned the government's investigation were getting their work printed before the Warren panel had even completed its work.[24] Thomas Buchanan's *Who Killed Kennedy?*, based largely on news reports, came out during this period.[25]

The Warren *Report* did not include any illustrations of President Kennedy's wounds, but the volumes of exhibits showed an artist's renderings of both injuries (Figures 4.3–4.4). Visually, the drawings did not match either the witness descriptions or the testimony from the Parkland doctors, both of which versions had circulated widely in the press immediately after the shooting.

The year 1966 might be called "the year of the buffs" because books about major problems with the Warren *Report* began to appear in large numbers.[26] The Supreme Court issued its famous *Miranda* decision, requiring that defendants be read their rights and afforded access to legal counsel to assist them. Some later books argued that Oswald should have had counsel before he died, claiming that this would have influenced the outcome of a trial. Such assertions take the events out of their context.[27]

Political scientist Edward Jay Epstein wrote his Cornell master's thesis on the inner workings of the Warren Commission and published the thesis in 1966 as *Inquest*, a lucid and well-documented argument that the busy commission members were less interested in solving the crime than in finding a "political" truth for the assassination in order to dispel international anxiety about the U.S. government.[28] Epstein's work has been called "the high-water mark of an intellectual assault on the unwisdom of establishing a blue-ribbon commission to look into the death of a president."[29]

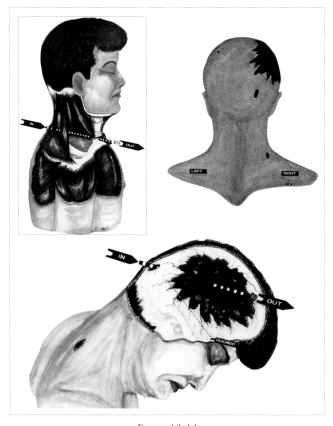

FIGURES 4.3–4.4
The Warren Commission's published drawings of the president's injuries. These depictions caused many people to question the accuracy of the commission's conclusions. Later medical panels determined that both drawings were in error on the location of wounds.
Warren Commission CE 385, 386 and 388, National Archives

Texas journalist Penn Jones of the *Midlothian Mirror* lived close to many original sources in the Dallas area, and he published his first book in a series entitled *Forgive My Grief*, pointing out flaws in the government's probe.[30] The book had a small circulation, but Jones influenced many other critical writers by introducing the notion that there were an unusually high number of deaths among people associated with the crime. Richard Popkin's *The Second Oswald* was another book with this same specialized sphere of influence, presenting the theory that an Oswald "double" had performed the murder.[31] Leo Sauvage, U.S. correspondent for the French newspaper *Le Figaro*, offered up his *Oswald Affair: An Examination of the Contradictions and Omissions of the Warren Report*, which gave low marks to the FBI and Dallas police while asserting that the Warren Commission had not proved its case against Oswald beyond a reasonable doubt.[32] Harold Weisberg's first volume in his *Whitewash* series was published in 1966; he later gained national fame for his successful Freedom of Information Act suits to declassify sealed documents.[33] These attacks were directed largely against the commission, the way it conducted its work, and the validity of its conclusions.

It was Mark Lane's *Rush to Judgment*, also released in 1966, that became the first major critical best-seller the following year. The controversial author toured the college lecture circuit at the very time that the major student protest movement was gaining force.[34] Lane was already relatively well-known when his book came out. The former New York assemblyman and attorney, who had campaigned for JFK, was retained by Oswald's mother, Marguerite, to defend her son before the Warren Commission. After the commission refused his brief, Lane put it into print. The author alleged major mistakes and omissions in the official *Report*, cast doubts on the credibility of witnesses who had supported the government's case, and launched an all-out attack on the single-bullet theory.[35] These early books seriously undermined public confidence in the commission's performance and the validity of the single-bullet theory; the missile was renamed the "magic" bullet.

One of the best-written critical books to come out during the early years was the 1967 *Six Seconds in Dallas* by Haverford College philosophy professor Josiah Thompson.[36] Thompson joined in the general denunciation of the work of the commission but turned his attention to a study of Dealey Plaza and an analysis of trajectories and other physical aspects of the murder. He asserted that three snipers had fired on the presidential limousine and that Governor Connally had been injured by a shot fired after President Kennedy had already been hit in the back. The notions of cross fire and a later shot that wounded Connally became popular critical themes in later books. Connally himself always stated his belief that he and Kennedy had been hit by separate bullets, so this important witness was frequently cited as being one reason to disbelieve the government's conclusion.

Actually, Connally said that he supported the conclusions of the Warren Commission, except on this issue of the single bullet.[37] Sylvia Meagher, a career United Nations employee, made credible contributions to the literature in 1966 and 1967 with two books: *Subject Index to the Warren Report and Hearings and Exhibits* and *Accessories after the Fact*.[38] The index, later updated to embrace the House Committee investigation data, became the key to accessing information in the commission's follow-up volumes, whereas *Accessories* provided a step-by-step series of arguments about problems with the government's case. Publication of the index showed that there was considerable interest in the subject among a growing number of Americans.

It would be impossible to find a common motive among these writers for their attacks on the Warren *Report*, aside from the obvious one that they did not believe the government had done a very good job investigating the death of the president. They came from diverse fields and were of differing ages at the time their books were published. What they shared were roles as "searchers," dedicated to finding the root cause of this terrible tragedy. Others would follow their lead.

By late in 1966 and 1967, some of the nation's major news organizations dropped their strong adherence to the Warren *Report* and began to call for another probe into the Kennedy assassination; in 1966 *Life* called for a new investigation.[39] The magazine had purchased the original Zapruder film shortly after the assassination, providing copies for the government to use in its investigation. Assassination researcher Thompson served as a consultant to *Life*, and he informed the magazine and the public that the copy of the film used by the Warren Commission was less clear than the original copy that *Life* kept locked in a vault.[40] The magazine had shown stills from the film but kept it off television. *Life* brought in Governor John Connally to view the Zapruder film, and the Texan was more convinced than ever that he had been shot by a

separate bullet.[41] CBS performed its own investigation in 1967, which supported the Warren investigation findings. But *The Dallas Morning News* editorialized on November 21, 1967, "The *News* speaks for a great reservoir of national opinion in concern that too many loose ends remain untied."[42]

The apparent discrepancies in the medical evidence were a major public concern. The government felt the pressure to explain why the drawings of the president's wounds in the supporting volumes of the Warren investigation did not seem to match the Parkland doctors' testimony in the *Report*, so in 1966 and 1968 Attorney General Ramsey Clark convened two panels to review the original medical evidence gathered during the autopsy at Bethesda Naval Hospital. By this time the public knew that the entire Warren Commission had not seen the medical evidence (X-rays and photographs taken at the autopsy) during its investigation. The Clark panels agreed with the Warren Commission that the president was hit by two bullets, both fired from above and behind him, but stated that the president's head wound had entered his skull at a location *four inches higher* than shown in the Warren documents.[43] No new drawings were published with their report.

Following standard procedure, the Warren Commission sealed the unpublished documents from its investigation in the National Archives for a period of seventy-five years. Passage of the Freedom of Information Act in 1967 changed the way that such records were handled, allowing for review of a classified document and its release if no clear threat to national security or personal privacy was involved.[44] The critics began asking for release of many of the sealed papers.

New Orleans District Attorney Jim Garrison launched a criminal investigation into the Kennedy assassination in 1966, which culminated in an abortive trial against local businessman Clay Shaw early in 1969. Garrison had charged Shaw as a conspirator in a plot to assassinate JFK. During the investigation, however, the district attorney garnered headlines about a possible conspiracy, thus fueling public doubts about the lone-assassin conclusion of the Warren Commission investigators.[45]

I was a senior at Tulane during the trial in 1969 and watched some of Garrison's comments to the press on the local evening news. I was generally satisfied with the findings of the Warren Commission, not having read any of the critical literature except the articles in the popular magazines. Clay Shaw was head of the International Trade Mart in New Orleans and a highly respected local citizen. Garrison came across as a politician with a weak case, and I was not surprised to hear that Shaw had been acquitted after less than an hour of jury deliberations. The collapse of the Garrison probe halted media demands for a new federal-level investigation.

Nevertheless, the doubts crept back in over time. Many of the rememberers today are satisfied with the basic conclusion that Oswald, alone, killed President Kennedy. Some believed this conclusion and later changed their minds. Others never accepted the lone-assassin ruling. But ever since the first pollster asked the first question during the assassination weekend in 1963, there has long been a distinction between the commission's conclusions and the general public attitude.

The issue of Oswald as the assassin who fired the shots that wounded and then killed the president and the shot that wounded Governor Connally is separate from the one about conspiracy. Within days of the shooting, 72% of the public said it believed that Oswald was the shooter.[46] On the issue of conspiracy, however, the public never completely supported the government's argument that Oswald performed the assassination without outside assistance. The work of the early critics reinforced an existing attitude of doubt. Today's authors and polls often state that the public has "doubts" about the conclusions of the Warren Commission, without differentiation. Many people believe that the investigation left unanswered questions about details of the crime, but they embrace the central Oswald-did-it thesis.

The Sixties period of admiration for the slain president conformed to American traditions to honor the dead who have been killed in office. Seen through the longer lens of American presidential assassination history, the adulation of JFK and the resistance to accept Oswald as the lone assassin have been branded as "typical, not exceptional."[47] Lincoln, Garfield, McKinley, and Kennedy were all deeply mourned by the people in the years following their deaths. Garfield and McKinley did not survive in the long term as legends in the popular mind, but Lincoln's legacy of greatness is alive and thriving in the late twentieth century.

The point is this: within the context of the Sixties, the government had no real reason to suspect that the public was reacting any differently than it had in 1865, or 1881, or even 1901. Every earlier assassination had spurred wide-spread public belief in the notion that "something big and terrible" was plotting to undermine the American system of laws.[48] That something "big and terrible" became manifest in ideas of massive plots. Historically too, the government reaction had been to soothe these concerns and to show, as soon as possible, that the killing had been the "work of a psychotic or a small group of isolated conspirators."[49]

During the 1960's, officials and social scientists told the rememberers that American presidential assassinations were the work of loners or small groups of loners.[50] Other countries have murdered their despotic leaders in coups, said the officials; America is a democracy. The political murders during the latter part of the decade made people wonder. In 1969 the government released the report of the National Commission on the Causes and Prevention of Violence, which told us that belief in conspiracy was a form of fantasy.[51] The implication was clear: it was wrong to think that we lived in some kind of banana republic.

LINCOLN AND KENNEDY: A COMPARISON

Some comparisons of public reaction in the Lincoln and Kennedy assassinations may be helpful. Abraham Lincoln was the first American president to die by assassination. We have all read literature that aligns JFK and Lincoln; aside from the manner of their deaths, their activities in civil rights made a logical tie-in, along with the less important fact that they were both elected to the presidency in a year ending in "60," exactly a century apart.

Abraham Lincoln was shot less than a week after the final surrender in the Civil War while attending a performance of *Our American Cousin* at Ford's Theater in Washington, D.C. The date was April 14, 1865, the Friday

FIGURE 4.5
Engraving of the Lincoln assassination.
On April 14, 1865, the actor John Wilkes Booth shot President Abraham Lincoln in the head during a performance at Ford's Theater in Washington, D.C.; Lincoln died the following day. *From FRANK LESLIE'S ILLUSTRATED NEWSPAPER, April 29, 1865, courtesy National Park Service*

before Easter. American actor John Wilkes Booth entered the president's box and shot him in the head at close range with a pistol. Booth then jumped to the stage and fled (Figure 4.5). Hundreds of stunned theatergoers saw him; since he was already a well-known actor, hundreds could identify him. Booth apparently shouted "Sic Semper Tyrannis" (Down with Tyrants) from the stage before he escaped.

Since this was the motto of Virginia, late capital of the Confederacy, many people asserted that the president's death had been planned by the South. Lincoln was carried to a bed in a home across the street and died the following morning. Booth remained at large until April 26, when he was reportedly trapped and killed in a burning barn in Virginia.[52]

Lincoln's death set off an orgy of mourning. American clergymen used the date of Good Friday, the day of his assassination, to establish a trend of comparison between the slain war president and the martyrdom of Christ.[53] Lincoln, said the preachers, led the Union to safety, just as Moses had led the children of Israel to the promised land.

Authorities identified Booth, a Southern sympathizer, as part of a plot to assassinate several upper-level government officials, including Lincoln, Secretary of State William Seward, and Vice President Andrew Johnson, a southerner. Seward was attacked and wounded, but Johnson's assassin did not complete his mission, and the vice president was left unharmed. The sermons delivered between April and June 1865 showed that the clergy did not accept the theory that a little band of conspirators had planned the murders; instead they cast a wider net of blame for the assassination. The top leadership of the Confederate States of America was drawn into the net, along with officials from the American Copperheads, the name used to describe northerners who sympathized with the Southern cause.[54] This tendency to seek out a larger group of assassins was similar to the impulse, a century later, to blame Kennedy's murder on the forces of "hatred" and then on specific conspiratorial groups.

Like the Kennedy funeral later, the Lincoln funeral began with a viewing in the East Room at the White House before the body was taken to the Capitol to lie in state. There was no television in 1865, and the body lay in state for a week. Then Lincoln's coffin was loaded on a funeral train bound for Springfield, Illinois.[55] The trip took two weeks with intermittent stops for public viewing, attracting more than seven million people along the route.[56] After the interment, rumors spread that the tomb was empty. The custodian at the grave site had to reassure visitors constantly that Lincoln's body was actually there.[57]

The same thing happened a century later with JFK. During the late 1960's, American tabloids began circulating stories that Kennedy was still alive. In 1969 readers were told that Kennedy was "alive and in a vegetable state," in Athens, Greece.[58] Later stories placed JFK, usually in a severe state of debilitation, at Parkland Hospital, at Camp David, at a retreat in the Swiss Alps, or even, in better physical shape, at the grave site of his widow, Jacqueline, at Arlington National Cemetery; tales of reincarnation have also found their way into the popular news features.[59] The idea of the spiritually wandering hero ("Elvis lives") is as old as myth itself.

Meanwhile, conspiracy theories after the death of Lincoln became, in the words of one writer, "a hearty perennial displaying many varieties."[60] The first trial of the alleged conspirators was conducted by a military tribunal, not a court of law. According to the tribunal, the plotters had participated in a huge Confederate conspiracy that led back to rebel President Jefferson Davis.[61] Four alleged conspirators, including one woman, were convicted and hanged on

July 19, 1865, and three others received life sentences (Figure 4.6). One accused conspirator, John Surratt, fled the country and was not captured until November 1866; he was acquitted at a regular criminal trial a year later, after the jury failed to reach a verdict.

The Lincoln military tribunal can be compared to the Warren Commission a century later. Regardless of the actual quality of the work performed, there was public doubt about the *structure* of the inquiries. In Victorian times critics lambasted the idea of a military rather than a regular criminal trial; during the 1960's critics clamored against the notion of a presidential commission that did not use the adversarial format employed in criminal procedures.

Booth, like Oswald, never went to trial, and rumors circulated that the actor had escaped the burning barn and was still at large. The *New York Times* added to the rumor in 1867 by printing an article stating that Booth was reputedly hiding in Ceylon.[62] Historians later attributed this myth to the Christian notions of Judas and other more ancient folklore, in which "the slayer of a hero was never allowed to rest in peace in his grave, but was believed to be wandering the world, friendless and granted with infamy."[63] Writings about an Oswald "double" bear some resemblance to this example.

Lincoln assassination historian William Hanchett blames much of the innuendo about Booth on the fact that "popularizers" dominated the literature until 1982.[64] Noting that "the history of Lincoln's assassination is full of lunacies," Hanchett cites one murder buff who found evidence

FIGURE 4.6

The hanging of Mary E. Surratt, Lewis T. Payne, David E. Herold, and George A. Atzerodt, as conspirators in the assassination of Abraham Lincoln. After a military trial, other conspirators were given jail sentences; one suspect was later acquitted in a civil trial. *U.S. Signal Corps photo, Brady Collection 111-BA-2034, National Archives*

of seventeen different John Wilkes Booths and "knew of someone who had information on twenty-two."[65]

The professional field of history, as we know it, did not exist in the Victorian period, and many documents associated with Lincoln's assassination were not available for study until the 1930's.[66] It was virtually impossible for historians of the Lincoln era to meet the demands of modern historiography. Similarly, few professional historians have delved into the mysteries of the Kennedy assassination because important documents deemed essential for adequate historical analysis have remained sealed in government archives.[67]

Lincoln's death fed conspiracy theories because, in the words of one author, he "was the object of far more hatred than love" at the time of his death.[68] At least Booth's ties to the South were valid; some accusations that the Marxist Oswald was somehow tied to the conservative, anticommunist elements in Dallas have been strained to the point of incredulity.

Lincoln conspiracy theorists alleged that some of the convicted plotters were simply pawns who took the blame for government leaders or that Vice President Andrew Johnson himself had been behind the scheme.[69] The idea that the Kennedy killing was part of an internal government plot that led to the top later found thin soil. Oliver Stone's 1991 film *JFK* suggested this scenario but did not try to prove it.

For thirty years after the assassination of Lincoln, the issue of blame fell along partisan political lines.[70] Republicans said the Democrats were behind it and vice versa. Here the Kennedy death legacy veers off, if only because the Lincoln assassination was clearly recognized as a conspiracy, and the issue of *possible* conspiracy in the JFK murder remains the key element in the debate. Politicians as a group have aligned themselves with the current government view that Kennedy's death was *not* the result of a plot, so neither party can cast blame on the other for something that officially did not happen.

By the 1890's, writers had decided that the military tribunal that had tried the Lincoln conspirators had been "organized to convict."[71] The Warren Commission, deemed to have followed a similar path, was labeled "the case for the prosecution of Lee Harvey Oswald." Within three decades of Lincoln's death the idea of a grand Southern scheme had slimmed down to a simpler scenario.[72] Arguments about the Kennedy assassination have also fallen into a semblance of order, with the boldest hypotheses now focused in the area of conspiracy.

Most of the conspiracy books about Lincoln were written during the first three decades after his death. Yet in 1937, writer Otto Eisenschiml wrote a book called *Why Was Lincoln Murdered?*, which put conspiracy theories about Lincoln back into the limelight. Eisenschiml was a chemist and a businessman from Chicago who said his theory would pass the most stringent tests of modern science. The theory stated that the *real* culprit behind the Lincoln assassination had been Secretary of War Edwin M. Stanton. Earlier writings were by that time gathering dust in libraries, so the theorist gained an avid following among nonrememberers. "It was Eisenschiml's example," notes one later historian, "that encouraged writers to shape evidence into grotesque preconceived patterns and to look for depraved explanations for routine events."[73] Some of the Kennedy assassination researchers have followed in the Eisenschiml tradition,

FIGURE 4.7
Rockefeller Commission cartoon.
The 1975 Rockefeller Commission investigation into the activities of the CIA raised allegations that the agency had cooperated with the Mafia in plots to assassinate Fidel Castro during the Kennedy administration.
Ed Gamble, original in the Gerald R. Ford Presidential Library

seeing ominous patterns in everything associated with the 1963 crime.

THE CRITICS HAVE THEIR DAY, 1970–1994

Had the critics of the Warren Commission written a script for the Seventies to force another official investigation into the Kennedy assassination, then they might have come up with Vietnam, Watergate, and the official probes into the activities of U.S. intelligence agencies. The loss of American prestige abroad, the decline in faith in the concept of unlimited progress through technology, and frustration with the effectiveness of progressive liberalism to obtain true equality added to the atmosphere of distrust about government.

Release of the Pentagon papers in 1971 showed that the military had lied to the American people about Vietnam. Many citizens now asked themselves if the government-sponsored Warren Commission had been totally honest. Watergate revealed corruption within the nation's most trusted office, the presidency, and Americans wondered if such corruption had been there all along. Disclosures that the CIA and the Mafia had been in partnership to kill Fidel Castro during the early 1960's and that the CIA, the Secret Service, and the FBI had deliberately withheld information from the Warren Commission led people to ask if Castro had plotted to kill Kennedy in retaliation (Figure 4.7).

As for the Warren Commission, critics' earlier accusations that it had not adequately proven its case made a great deal more sense when one knew for a fact that the commissioners' own intelligence agencies had willfully withheld information from them. In 1975 the public learned that a Dallas FBI agent, James Hosty, had received a note from Oswald before the assassination, warning the agent not to harass his Soviet-born wife, Marina. Shortly after Oswald's death, Gordon Shanklin, the FBI agent's boss, told Hosty to destroy the note, which he did.[74] The coup de grâce came in the early spring of that year, when Geraldo Rivera did a feature on the assassination and showed the Zapruder film on network television for the first time. Twenty-five members of Congress who saw the show immediately endorsed a move to reopen the investigation into the Kennedy shooting.[75] "People have lost faith in the credibility of their government," said one official, "and that's a very dangerous situation in a democracy."[76]

Americans who watched the airing of the Zapruder film on *Good Night America* on ABC were shocked to finally see the movie, which had been enhanced by Kennedy researcher Robert Groden to clarify the images.[77] It *appeared* as if Connally had been shot by a different bullet from the one that injured JFK in the back, and it *seemed* that the fatal head shot drove Kennedy's head backward, as if he had been shot from the *front*, from the area of the grassy knoll or the railroad bridge.

A Gallup poll taken in mid-December 1976 revealed that only 11% of the nation still believed that Oswald, acting alone, had killed the president; another 81% expressed the feeling that there had been more people involved in the shooting. High schoolers, none of whom remembered the assassination, were remarkably skeptical, indicating an 85% rating for conspiracy. Young Americans between the ages of eighteen and twenty-four voted 88% in favor of a plot, and the twenty-five to twenty-nine age group ranked conspiracy as the more likely scenario by 89%. Even among Americans over the age of fifty, those most likely to be "preservers" and not "searchers," 73% feared that the president had died as a result of a larger plan.

On the question of *who* these mysterious conspirators might have been, predictably the Cubans topped the list at 15%, with U.S. politicians placing second with 7%. Suddenly, our own elected officials outranked the Soviet Union on the list of most likely suspects. During the 1960's the critics had theorized a CIA involvement in a conspiracy to kill President Kennedy; the revelations of the mid-1970's seemed to support their claims, and more books came out pointing fingers toward the CIA in a possible plot.[78]

District Attorney Jim Garrison's case, which suggested a CIA link in a conspiracy based in New Orleans, was demolished at the 1969 Clay Shaw trial, but no one knew at that time about the CIA-Mafia plots against Castro or the deliberate withholding of this and other evidence from the Warren Commission. Furthermore, the Church Committee probe later showed that the CIA had used the media in an attempt to undermine Garrison's credibility in the New Orleans investigation.

The Church Committee *Report* was released in April 1976; five months later the House of Representatives voted to conduct another official investigation into the assassinations of both John F. Kennedy and civil rights leader Dr. Martin Luther King, Jr. The House Select Committee on Assassinations was born.[79] The committee started badly. Although Virginia Democratic Congressman Thomas S. Downing, who was scheduled to retire early in 1977, chaired the committee ably during the remainder of 1976, he was then replaced by Texas Democrat Henry Gonzalez, who sparred with the chief counsel and staff director, Richard Sprague. Within months Gonzalez himself stepped down as chair, giving the post to Ohio Congressman Louis Stokes; then Sprague resigned. Attorney G. Robert Blakey came on board as new chief counsel in June 1977.[80] The committee

spent $5.5 million in thirty months, about half of what the Warren Commission had spent in only ten months.[81]

The committee's work was published in 1979 in a summary *Report*, followed by twelve volumes of hearings and exhibits devoted to the Kennedy probe. Blakey placed a high priority on scientific testing of the original evidence, including acoustical analysis of a Dallas Police Department Dictabelt recording that might have contained sounds of the gunfire during the assassination. Special panels of experts reviewed the medical and photographic evidence.

In many respects the House Committee's conclusions agreed with the central findings of the Warren Commission: the committee stated that Oswald was the assassin, firing three shots from the sixth-floor corner window of the Depository building. Whereas the Warren panel was vague about which shot had missed, the House Committee said that Oswald's first shot missed the limousine entirely, his second shot hit the president in the back and went on to cause all of Governor Connally's wounds, and his third shot hit Kennedy in the back of the head and killed him.

The committee discounted the Warren Commission conclusion that Oswald had been the lone assassin and voted by a majority that the assassination had been the result of a conspiracy by persons unnamed. The investigation was nearly over when the committee received the final results of a scientific analysis of the police recording. The analysis led scientists to conclude that, by "a probability of 95% or better," a fourth shot (the third in the sequence) was fired from behind the cedar fence on the grassy knoll; according to the House panel, this shot missed. Possible conspirators included unnamed individuals from the mob or disgruntled Cubans. The committee criticized the effectiveness of the work provided to the Warren Commission by the FBI, the Secret Service, and the CIA but cleared all three agencies from any direct involvement in the plot. The House asked the Justice Department to perform further acoustic analysis and to scientifically examine some photographic evidence from the crime scene.

The House Committee blamed Oswald for the murder but assuaged public sentiment that someone else had plotted the president's death. The committee's use of new and improved scientific tests to evaluate the original evidence was an important contribution to solving the crime, but much of this work was lost in the media reportage about the findings of the acoustic analysis.

In 1980 the Justice Department asked the National Academy of Science to convene a special panel to take another look at the acoustics analysis developed for the House Committee.[82] Two years later its National Research Council issued a report that concluded that the House Committee analysis did not show that a shot had been fired from the grassy knoll; the report argued that cross talk on the tape proved that the recording had been made about one minute after the assassination, perhaps outside Dealey Plaza.[83] After several years of silence, in 1988 the Justice Department formally closed the investigation into the Kennedy assassination, stating that there was "no persuasive evidence" of conspiracy. Officially, at least, the government had gone full circle.

The searchers seem to have created a niche for themselves among Americans who are distrustful of government and want to stage minor protests against it, if only in the form of refusing to believe that Oswald, acting alone, killed

John F. Kennedy. Some support for this notion came from the television series *On Trial: Lee Harvey Oswald*, originally produced by London Weekend Television-Showtime in 1986 and then reaired by Tribune Entertainment in 1988 under the auspices of Geraldo Rivera.[84]

The five-part program used real attorneys and an actual judge and jury. The trial took testimony from original witnesses, and a Dallas panel decided the verdict. The jury convicted Oswald by a majority vote, but the producers of the 1988 broadcast then took the issue to the audience by encouraging calls to a special 900 number. The announcer asked the question: is Oswald guilty of firing the shot that killed the president? No specific question about other plotters was asked. The callers acquitted. In the 1986 airing of the show, the number who voted "not guilty" was more than 80%.

This call-in vote for acquittal did not match results from contemporary national polls on the issue of Oswald's guilt or innocence; most Americans surveyed during the 1980's stated a belief that Oswald was the assassin, but they did not believe that he acted alone. The call-in showed how public opinion about conspiracy can flourish outside the controlled environment of a courtroom. The endless trial of Lee Harvey Oswald has become an issue of "what if?" and not one of "what happened?"

The televised trial was helpful in offering audiences arguments for both the prosecution and the defense in one presentation. The literature on the assassination does not. To properly assess the guilt or innocence of Oswald or the validity of a conspiracy theory, we must refer to books from both the preservers and the searchers. The books that I have cited in this volume have been selected as much for their ready availability and their *influence* on public opinion as for their accuracy. I do not endorse any of them.

The House Committee investigation opened new avenues of research for conspiracy theorists who produced new books during the 1980's and 1990's. During this period the voice of the preservers dimmed. British journalist Anthony Summers's *Conspiracy* appeared in 1980 as a continuation of the Cuban, Mafia-CIA scenario.[85] Although the committee medical panel had fully examined the original autopsy materials stored in the National Archives, some authors were not convinced. A notably controversial addition during the 1980's was David Lifton's *Best Evidence*, which alleged that the president's wounds were altered after the assassination to disguise evidence of shots from the front.[86] Robert Groden and Harrison Livingston's *High Treason* questioned the authenticity of the medical X-rays and photographs.[87]

Two other popular books of the Eighties were Jim Garrison's *On the Trail of the Assassins*, a memoir of his New Orleans investigation during the late 1960's, and Texas journalist Jim Marrs's *Crossfire*, a lengthy compendium of nearly all the theories that have ever been put forth about the crime of the century.[88] These two books were important published sources for Oliver Stone's 1991 blockbuster film *JFK*. As a result of the movie's popularity, both volumes became best-sellers.

The controversy over the movie encouraged other assassination writers to ride the crest of interest with new titles and some old ones. Mark Lane's *Rush to Judgment* was reissued in 1992. Stone's notion of Vietnam as a motive for murder came from researcher Dr. Peter Dale Scott, a professor at the University of California at Berkeley.[89] But new,

detailed research on the issue of JFK and the war came from University of Maryland academic John M. Newman, whose dissertation, *JFK and Vietnam*, was published with Stone's help in 1992.[90] There are other scholars who continue to argue that JFK had not made a firm commitment to withdraw from Southeast Asia at the time of his death.

After the death of FBI Director J. Edgar Hoover in 1973, the former intelligence chief's image began to tarnish. As the lead agency gathering materials for the Warren Commission, the FBI suffered during the Church probe in 1976, which disclosed irregularities among the nation's intelligence services. Apparently, few were willing to take on the powerful and ruthless FBI chief while he was alive, but in 1991 some writers began to try to link him to a plot to kill John F. Kennedy. Mark North's *Act of Treason: The Role of J. Edgar Hoover and the Assassination of President Kennedy* came out in that year; Anthony Summers's exposé on Hoover appeared on the stands in 1993.[91]

Summers's book adds to the weight of argument that the bureau engaged in a cover-up of the actual facts of the assassination. The idea gained credence in conjunction with Watergate and never lost any of its appeal for many critics. In discussing the FBI's approach toward the Warren Commission investigation, Summers asserted, "Edgar's priority from the start was to protect himself and the Bureau and to insist that Oswald was the lone assassin."[92] Summers cites former Kennedy aide Kenny O'Donnell, who believed that a shot had come from the grassy knoll. "I told the FBI what I had heard," said O'Donnell, "but they said it couldn't have happened that way. . . . So I testified the way they wanted me to."[93]

Conspiracists came out with some new entries in 1993, during the thirtieth anniversary of the assassination. Gaeton Fonzi, who had worked for the Church investigation and the House Select Committee, published *The Last Investigation* which chronicles his work with the House probe and provides information about his research into the actions of Maurice Bishop, a rogue CIA agent.[94] If lay audiences wanted *Cliffs Notes* to the various theories, Bob Callahan's *Who Shot JFK?* came out in 1993 as a readable, witty, and heavily illustrated guide to the subject.[95]

David Belin, a former staffer on the Warren Commission and the director of the Rockefeller Commission probe, published *Final Disclosure* in 1988, which tried to stem the conspiracy tide. Jim Moore's 1990 pro-lone-gunman book, *Conspiracy of One*, differed from the Warren Commission's findings on several major issues.[96] The importance of faith in American institutions was central to both books. Said Moore, "If as a people, we don't choose to believe the Warren Commission got it right, then we choose not to believe our government as well."[97]

Gerald Posner's 1993 hardback volume *Case Closed* also made an attempt to breathe new life into the official conclusion that Oswald, acting alone, had killed President Kennedy. Posner differed significantly from the Warren Commission's conclusions on the sequencing of shots, but he offered a summary of all the official investigations.[98] Posner's book passed lightly over the work of the House Committee, except to condemn its acoustic analysis. The author also attacked several of the major searchers and their writings on the assassination. *Case Closed* launched a series of counterattacks from the community of searchers.

Gerald Posner provided a public service by discounting some of the older and unlikely assertions of the searchers, but in other areas of his research he tended to overstate his case against a plot by simply ignoring data or greatly simplifying material that might weaken his thesis. Posner's book will probably become the yardstick against which conspiracy literature is compared during the remainder of the 1990's.

We rememberers are accustomed to these shifts in the debate. Since all the major preservers and searchers return to the scene of the crime, Dallasites are particularly jaded about the endless twists and turns involved in the analysis of the event. In 1988 one local writer admitted that every time he drove past the Texas School Book Depository he would look up at the sixth-floor window, hoping to find "a group of guys in black sniper's caps waving at me to come up and take their confessions."[99] A *Dallas Morning News* columnist suggested some appropriate titles for the rejoinders destined to follow Posner's book: "Case Reopened"; "Case Closed by Conspiracy"; "Case Cloaked"; and "Just in Case."[100]

Television produced a considerable number of specials on JFK's life and death, particularly in 1983, 1988, and 1993, all major anniversary years of the assassination.[101] Following in the tradition of CBS from the 1960's, *NOVA* in 1988 conducted its own probe into the controversy surrounding JFK's death, again backing the Oswald-as-assassin conclusion but using some interesting computer animation in the broadcast.[102] This program has been shown on PBS, off and on, ever since.

In response to the preservers' persistent demands that the critics "name names" of potential conspirators, British film producer Nigel Turner produced *The Men Who Killed Kennedy* in 1988, which attracted a large viewing audience in England and Europe.[103] American networks refused to air the show; it finally appeared on the cable Arts & Entertainment network in 1991 and later. The first part of the film focused on visual and witness evidence that indicated a shot was fired from the grassy knoll. The second part of the film, which named several European conspiracists as shooters, was later found to have several major flaws.

Searchers and preservers will continue to have their say because the Warren Commission is forever tainted by the knowledge that it conducted its investigation without complete information and because the House Select Committee's conclusions were shadowed by the sensational aspects of its acoustics analysis. But perhaps the most telling result of all the paper that has been devoted to efforts to prove a point of view in the matter of the president's disturbing death has been found in national polls that asked the following question: should there be another investigation into the Kennedy assassination? Levels of interest have varied over the years, but in 1983 nearly seven out of ten Americans answered with a resounding "No!"[104] A 1988 poll showed that 55% of the nation still opposed another official investigation into the crime.[105] In 1996, 75% of the public continue to profess doubts about the official findings into the Kennedy assassination. Perhaps the American people have lost confidence in the government's ability to solve the murder.

KEY ELEMENTS IN THE ASSASSINATION DEBATE

The following brief overview does not attempt to solve the crime to the satisfaction of the new generation; I doubt that anyone could. The history of the Lincoln assassination controversy provides valuable insights. History does not repeat itself, but we have seen that Lincoln's murder sparked a thirty-year quest among searchers who wanted to find a larger, more compelling reason than a rather simple conspiracy for the death of the great emancipator. The first wave of detectives were rememberers. Next, the myth of Lincoln kept alive the searching urge among subsequent generations who did not remember him at all. In the case of the death of the Civil War president, the issue of conspiracy was an accepted fact; the search reflected a compulsion to find a bigger and more powerful force behind the plot.

JFK's assassination differs significantly from Lincoln's in the important matter of conspiracy. The official government opinion since 1988 has reverted to the earlier Warren Commission finding that there is "no persuasive evidence" of conspiracy. Searchers keep trying to convince us that there *is* persuasive evidence. We must allow for the lingering emotional attitudes of writers who experienced the events of 1963. "In our culture," says psychologist James Pennebaker, "the major key to understanding is learning what causes what."[106] We seek meaning, or a value system, for those things that cause us suffering. Pennebaker cites written communications and "retellings" as two effective means to work through trauma and achieve understanding about upsetting events.[107]

The large number of books, articles, movies, and television presentations on JFK and the public adherence to notions of conspiracy suggest unresolved feelings about the murder. There remains an urge to assign a value system to explain the tragedy. For my part, the seemingly endless official and critical investigations and the media retellings over the years keep churning up the painful memories of the weekend itself. "Time heals all wounds," they say, but *when* has there been time to reflect and resolve the trauma of the president's death? During the thirtieth anniversary of the JFK assassination in 1993, the news reported that there were enough Kennedy documentaries, movies, and memorial features to stock a separate cable channel.[108]

The decade of the 1990's finds us at a point where we can take stock of the debate. The quest among the searchers has divided into three phases. The first, launched during the 1960's, presented the argument that the Warren Commission was inadequate in its efforts to prove conclusively that Oswald, acting alone, had killed the president. The investigation was flawed, but its central conclusion that Oswald was the assassin was reaffirmed in later probes. The second phase focused attention on efforts to prove that the crime *was* a conspiracy. Since the House Committee investigation, the searchers have entered their third phase, continuing their research to prove *what kind* of plot was behind the killing. Except for a brief flurry of trust between 1964 and 1966, the majority of the public, for a variety of reasons perhaps totally unrelated to the facts of the crime, has supported the idea of conspiracy.

The linchpin in the assassination debate has always been *who shot* the president. The government said Oswald did it, but some of the searchers insisted that the accused assassin was exactly what he said he was, a patsy. The searchers' argument for Oswald's acquittal never met with much agreement from the rememberers. Many of us had developed a negative impression of Oswald before he was killed. Ask a rememberer to describe his or her reaction to the way that Oswald smirked in front of the TV cameras; many of us have never forgotten it. Then the Warren *Report*

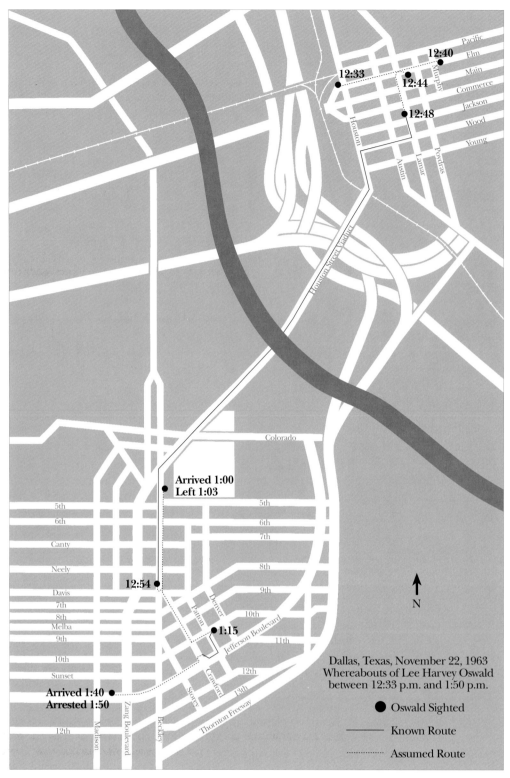

FIGURE 4.8

The Warren Commission's version of Oswald's route between the time of the Kennedy assassination and his arrest in the Texas Theater for the murder of Officer Tippit. *Staples & Charles Ltd. and Tom Dawson Graphic Design. Research by Gary Mack, based on Warren Commission CE 1119A, Sixth Floor Museum Archives*

devoted considerable space to a compelling analysis of Oswald's life and character in order to prove that he was indeed a disgruntled misfit who was capable of killing the president of the United States.[109] The attitude of an assassin must remain a key element in any effort to understand presidential murder.[110] Our criminal system searches for motive behind such an act of violence. Finally, we knew how to separate the major evidence from the details; during the Sixties Oswald was always at the center of the drama.

Gerald Posner's 1993 portrait of Oswald clearly resembled the government's original image of a loner, dissatisfied

with the system, who wanted his moment of fame.[111] Oswald grew up the product of an unhappy childhood, spoiled by his self-centered mother, shuffled from one school to another, and was increasingly frustrated by people and institutions that did not treat him as the special person he believed himself to be. Posner's account may be harsh, but it is a timely reminder that murder is committed by people and not by sinister forces at large in society.

Much of the critical literature before the 1990's shied away from a presentation of Oswald's biography, except to assert that he was someone else than who the government purported him to be.[112] As the searchers moved into highly specialized areas of conspiracy research, Oswald emerged as a minor player, a pawn for the Russians, the CIA, the FBI, the mob, the Cubans, or whatever group was presented as the *real* reason for the assassination. In certain books Oswald was the antihero, a character type popular with film audiences during the late 1960's and early 1970's—a loner, of course, but ultimately a victim of the evil system that brought him down.[113]

The government's case for motive lay in Oswald's capacity to commit violence. The murder of Dallas Police Officer J. D. Tippit was essential in this regard. The Warren Commission presented a plausible explanation of Oswald's activities after he was seen in the second-floor lunchroom at the School Book Depository (Figure 4.8).[114] He left the building by the front door (no one remembered seeing him leave), walked east, and boarded a bus (the bus driver and a passenger remembered him); the bus got stuck in traffic, so he got a transfer ticket (it was found on him), exited the bus, walked several blocks south to a bus station, and hailed a cab, which took him several blocks from his boardinghouse at 1026 North Beckley Street in Oak Cliff. The cabdriver remembered him.[115] Oswald entered his boardinghouse around 1:00 P.M., was seen by the landlady there, put on a jacket, and left by about 1:03 P.M.

He walked about nine-tenths of a mile (unseen en route) and then encountered Officer Tippit at 10th and Patton Streets (Figure 4.9). One witness saw Oswald shoot the policeman with a revolver at point-blank range; others saw him empty the cartridges from the pistol and/or flee the scene on foot. He was apprehended in the Texas Theater, and *all* of the officers who later testified said that he resisted arrest.

The House Committee investigation spent little time revisiting the Tippit murder, with the result that its analysis of motive was presented only briefly in its *Report.* Furthermore, the committee performed scientific analyses of the evidence associated with this crime and determined that the spent bullet cartridges found at the scene came from the revolver that Oswald was carrying at the time of his arrest. The bullets found in Tippit's body could not be traced to the gun because of a modification in the weapon that allowed it to fire different types of ammunition not specified by the manufacturer. Oswald owned the revolver, so the House panel reaffirmed the Warren Commission's original conclusion that Oswald was the murderer of J. D. Tippit.[116]

Some researchers still work hard trying to acquit Oswald of the Tippit murder to weaken the government's case that this shooting proved his capability to assassinate the president. The searchers have tried to discredit individual witnesses to the Tippit slaying and hint that there were two gunmen, based on the word of some people who were near the scene. They have cast doubts on the testimony of arresting officers, questioned Oswald's ownership of a jacket discarded near the scene, tried to dismiss the authenticity of the cartridges found near the murder site, and wondered why the Dallas Police Department did not send all the ballistics evidence at once to the FBI. The government's inability to ballistically link the bullets to the gun has encouraged some searchers to argue that the gun used to shoot Tippit was not the gun Oswald was carrying at the time of his arrest.[117]

FIGURE 4.9
Officer J. D. Tippit's squad car. Tippit had left his car and was walking around the front when he was shot down on November 22, 1963.
Darryl Heikes/DALLAS TIMES HERALD Collection, Sixth Floor Museum Archives

Finally, the searchers have used a stopwatch technique to assert that Oswald could not have made the long walk from his boardinghouse to the location of the murder in time to shoot Tippit. The call about the shooting came into police headquarters at 1:18 P.M. None of these arguments have disproved the facts that there were eyewitnesses who saw Oswald shoot the officer and that cartridges from Oswald's revolver were found scattered on the ground nearby. Nevertheless, many of the searchers speculate that the murder took place several minutes before the time the dispatcher received the report, thus further reducing the amount of time that Oswald would have had to reach the crime scene from his boardinghouse.

The Warren Commission backed up its claims that Oswald was capable of violence by concluding that he had tried to kill the ultraconservative General Edwin Walker in April 1963.[118] On the night of April 10 someone shot through a window at Walker's Dallas residence while he was working in his study; the general was unharmed. Investigators found photographs of Walker's house among the Oswald family's possessions, and Marina Oswald testified that her husband admitted to her that he had tried to murder the conservative activist. Searchers have tried to discount this evidence by questioning the reliability of Marina Oswald's testimony—highly contradictory on some issues—and by asserting that two men were involved in the attack.[119]

The assassination literature of the 1990's shows a trend toward a closer study of Oswald as a person. PBS's 1993 documentary on the assassination, aired in November on *Frontline,* offered a balanced presentation of the alleged assassin.[120] The film included commentary from Oswald's brother, Robert, who stated that although the searchers have questioned many aspects of the government's case against Lee Harvey Oswald, they have been unable to discount *enough* of the evidence to acquit him of involvement in the JFK murder.

For a time some of the searchers focused on trying to prove that Oswald's odd behavior was caused by various "doubles" or by his being a government plant for the

Russians.[121] The defector was not procommunist, said Jim Garrison in *On the Trail of the Assassins*. Garrison simply did not believe that Oswald was the assassin, and he came up with witnesses to support his claim.[122] But remember, the government had produced witnesses for *its* case also.

Some searchers have argued that Oswald liked President Kennedy and thus would not have shot him.[123] This train of thought discounts Kennedy's important presidential role as the personification of government; officials, supported by social scientists, argue that an assassin could have loved Kennedy as a man and still fired shots to kill the *system* that Kennedy symbolized.[124] Some authors have argued that Oswald was the shooter but that he was aiming at Governor Connally.[125]

One of the critics' most persistent arguments has been that the government's case against Oswald was a fabrication. Casting doubt on our faith in government brings up memories of Vietnam, Watergate, and other instances in which the government has been dishonest with the people. The most paranoid view in the assassination debate calls for a conclusion that JFK was killed in a government-planned coup.

Oliver Stone's *JFK* film offered a menu of possible conspiracies, most of them leading to the highest levels of American officialdom. This case for a coup d'état was rejected by many rememberers, who did not accept the thesis that multiple agencies of the United States, working with local Dallas officials, could have *collectively* planned and executed the killing. Such a hypothesis remains unsupported by hard evidence, runs afoul of the foundations of the American myth, our civil religion, and strains common sense. Some searchers have made inroads in showing that various agencies of government tried to hide information or conceal mistakes—the FBI letter from Oswald is one example—but they have not proven advance planning with the intent to commit murder.[126] The notion of a coup d'état was popular for a while with the Lincoln searchers also, but it eventually died down.

Belief in the infallibility of science influences our acceptance of the evidence that has been brought forth in the assassination debate. Americans are culturally predisposed to place their faith in science, but Newtonian laws calling for absolutes in "space, time, and measurement" were radically undermined by twentieth-century physics with its theories of relativity and quantum mechanics.[127] The years since 1963 have seen dramatic changes in science; *whose* science, as applied to the Kennedy assassination, are we going to believe, and *what* new approaches might be developed in the future? Much of the official and the critical literature lapses into scientific jargon, with the result that lay readers find it difficult to comprehend the analyses at all.

Officials have argued that some of the critics have misread scientific data; critics seek their own scientists to counter the claims put forth by the official specialists.[128] One is reminded of the use of experts in mental-competency trials: one doctor says the defendant is insane, the other disputes it. Psychiatrists are not engaged in *pure* science, you may say, but what is "pure science" these days? Scientific differences lie at the heart of the House Committee's acoustic analysis. The committee used qualified acoustic scientists to perform the work, and another group of scientists reached a conflicting conclusion about the data.[129] Two respected groups of scientists produced two different interpretations. Perhaps there is a need for a third analysis to settle the matter.

Attorneys familiar with criminal procedures and how they have changed since 1963 have a good foundation for evaluating some of the literature on the Kennedy assassination, assuming that the case ever came to trial. Without such specialized knowledge, it is difficult to assess *what* information presented, pro or con, has legal pertinence to the issue of Oswald's guilt or innocence. The media is unable to sort things out for us, since most reporters cannot claim expertise in matters of criminal law or procedure. Indeed, many of today's journalists are too young to remember the assassination and have no idea if the news they are presenting is "new" or old.

THE EVIDENCE

WITNESS TESTIMONY

In the first chapter you became a witness to the assassination from a vantage point on the grassy knoll. There were only a few other pedestrians around you at the time, and you went home without offering any statements to investigators at the scene. After 1963 a remarkable number of people came forward to state that they had been with you on the knoll.[130] In fact, the little hillock became so crowded with late-arriving witnesses that longtime researcher Mary Ferrell was moved to remark that there was no room left for a sniper there (Figure 4.10).

Earlier, we saw that eyewitness memory relating to traumatic events can be highly unreliable. It also fades or distorts over time. When a book mentions testimony from a witness who remained unknown for more than a day or two after the shooting, we must ask ourselves how much that person could have been influenced by press reports that aired during the assassination weekend. When a witness comes forward after five or more years of silence, we should allow for the influence of public opinion about the assassination on that person's memory.

Nevertheless, attorneys use witnesses to support their arguments during trials, and juries tend either to believe or to disbelieve them. These trials usually take place within weeks or months of a crime, when the memory is fresh. After decades, the preservers and the searchers are still using witness testimony, old and new, to support their arguments about the assassination. Many witnesses who were in the park on November 22, 1963, have lived to see their original statements used freely in the debate.

No one has ever come up with an acceptable head count for the number of people who saw the assassination, much less for the number who heard it. The Warren Commission took testimony from 190 witnesses; later searchers have located additional people who said they were present and saw or heard the shooting. Josiah Thompson listed 268 on a master list he compiled in 1967; other witnesses have come to light since then.[131] Estimates on the number of shots varied from one to eight, but a majority seemed to agree on three. Estimates on the direction varied widely, as did estimates on timing. One expert on eyewitness memory cautions that these two elements—direction and timing—are among the most unreliable aspects of testimony in shooting crimes.[132]

FIGURE 4.10
Grassy knoll cartoon. In the decades since 1963, the popularity of conspiracy
theories has led many people to come forward and claim that they were
present on the grassy knoll at the time of the assassination.
Jim Borgman. Reprinted with special permission of King Features Syndicate

The witness statements included in the supporting volumes of the Warren Commission are a hodgepodge of conflicting opinion. Some of the depositions were not taken until months after the shooting, leaving ample time for press accounts or other influences to reshape original memories. Some witnesses, angered by having their accounts used freely without their permission in the assassination debate, have subtly shifted their statements over the years since 1963.[133] Some people have come forward very late and claimed to have been present, despite available photographic evidence to the contrary. Some unidentified witnesses who were recorded in photographs taken at the scene have never been found.[134]

It is helpful to note *when* witnesses gave testimony and to seek some visual confirmation of their presence in the park.[135] Witnesses divided into loose groups based on their testimony that shots came either from the Depository or from the direction of the knoll or rail yards. The testimony itself sometimes makes it difficult to distinguish between the knoll or the general area running along the top of the cedar fence on the north side of Elm Street. Preservers and searchers who try to come up with reliable percentages are taking great liberties with the actual data.[136]

The Warren Commission slanted its report to include testimony from witnesses who supported its conclusion that shots came from the Texas School Book Depository. It did not adequately explain the other, smaller pattern of testimony that indicated a shot having come from the vicinity of the grassy knoll or the north side of the hill. For example, S. M. Holland, who was standing on the railroad bridge, with a clear view of the shooting, provided statements on November 22, 1963, and again on April 8, 1964; he said he heard a shot from the grassy knoll and saw a puff of smoke beneath the trees near the cedar fence.[137] The House Committee used witness statements to support its own case that shots came from both locations. However, officials have not relied heavily on witness accounts *unless* there was additional hard physical evidence to back it up. Investigators who ran up the knoll after the shooting to look behind the picket fence found no hard evidence there.

Thompson and other early searchers stressed the accounts of the witnesses who said that they had heard shots fired from another direction besides the Depository.[138]

During the years before the House Committee investigation concurred with the idea of a shot having been fired from the grassy knoll, it was the *cause célèbre* of the searchers, whose literature made one argument after another—heavily weighted with witness statements—that someone had fired from beneath the trees or behind the cedar fence. Although the government has discounted the House Committee's acoustic results, the searchers still claim the knoll as their preferred location for the source of the head shot that killed JFK. They say that the Zapruder film and reports from most of the Parkland doctors back up their assertions.[139]

BALLISTICS EVIDENCE AND BALLISTICS DISCLAIMERS

Officials said that evidence found on the sixth floor of the Depository included a 1940, bolt-action 6.5mm Mannlicher-Carcano rifle containing one live shell, three empty cartridge cases, a brown paper bag, and fingerprints and palm prints of Lee Oswald. Other ballistics evidence included the nearly whole bullet discovered on a stretcher at Parkland Hospital, bullet fragments found in the presidential limousine and the victims, a cracked windshield in the car, a dent in the window trim of the limousine, and a chipped curbstone removed from Main Street near the triple underpass; the curb mark was near the location of witness James Tague, who received a minor cheek wound, presumably from a ricochet.[140]

Ballistics experiments with the rifle showed that it was operable and capable of causing the wounds to the occupants of the limousine. On the afternoon of the assassination, investigators went to the residence of Marina Oswald and were told by the suspect's wife that Oswald owned a rifle, which he kept stored in a blanket in the garage. The blanket was empty, but fibers from it were consistent with fibers found in the paper bag in the sniper's perch. The FBI traced ownership of the surplus Italian military rifle to Oswald, who had ordered the weapon by mail on March 12, 1963. Ballistics tests showed that the cartridges had been fired from the rifle, to the exclusion of all other rifles. Later scientific tests conducted on the bullet fragments found in the limousine and on the nearly whole bullet showed that they were fired from the Oswald gun.

Neutron Activation Analysis (NAA) performed on two of the bullet fragments from the limousine proved conclusively that they came from Carcano ammunition. NAA is considered an extremely reliable test. The small bullet fragments removed from Governor Connally's wrist during surgery were tested in 1977 and were linked to the near-pristine bullet found on the stretcher at Parkland Hospital. The cracked windshield and the dent in the window trim were both on the inside, consistent with a shot having been fired from behind the presidential limousine.[141]

Buell Wesley Frazier, who gave Oswald a ride to work on the morning of November 22, later testified that the suspect carried a paper package, which Oswald told him contained curtain rods. Frazier's sister also saw the package. Officials concluded that Oswald used a paper bag to carry the disassembled rifle into the Depository on the morning of the assassination. In a departure from his usual custom, Oswald had visited his wife in Irving on the evening of Thursday, November 21, and investigators assumed that he had retrieved the rifle at that time.

Oswald was seen by coworkers on the sixth floor during the morning of November 22; the last sighting in that location occurred approximately thirty-five minutes before the shooting. Between ninety seconds and two minutes after the assassination, Dallas Police motorcycle officer Marrion Baker stopped Oswald in the second-floor lunchroom in the building. Oswald was seen immediately thereafter walking toward the south side of the second floor. A roll call of employees taken at 1:03 P.M. revealed that he was no longer in the building. Oswald had been hired at the warehouse in mid-October 1963, several weeks before the final route for the presidential motorcade was determined.[142]

Three warehouse workmen watched the motorcade from the fifth floor of the Depository from a location immediately below the sniper's perch. Although their statements were not taken until March 1964, two testified that shots were fired from above them. Harold Norman said, "I could also hear something [that] sounded like the shells hitting the floor and the ejecting of the rifle." Another worker had debris fall on his head as a result of the activity on the floor above.[143]

Several witnesses standing in Dealey Plaza saw a rifle protruding from an upper-story window at the Depository; some said they saw one gunman; others saw two. *Dallas Times Herald* photographer Bob Jackson said: "Then after the last shot . . . I just looked straight up . . . at the School Book Depository and I noticed two negro men in a window . . . and my eyes followed right on up to the window above them and I saw the rifle or what looked like a rifle."[144] There was confusion as to which floor the witnesses identified, but authorities relied on the eyewitnesses to show that someone was firing from an upper window in the warehouse.

Only one witness, Howard Brennan, offered a detailed description of the gunman to investigators; this was the description broadcast on police channels at 12:45 P.M., fifteen minutes after the shooting. The description closely matched the description of Oswald. Brennan was asked to attend a lineup on Friday night, at which time he stated that he was unable to offer a positive identification of Oswald as the sniper. When Brennan later testified before the Warren Commission, in March 1964, he offered positive identification of Oswald as the man he had seen shooting from the sixth floor at the motorcade.[145]

In terms of the physical evidence, critics have argued that proper procedures were not uniformly followed by investigators at the scene, which might have influenced their ability to introduce the material at a trial. No official photographs were taken of the sniper's perch before the boxes were disturbed by the investigators. Witness testimony about the paper bag was challenged on the basis that both Frazier and his sister estimated that the length of the bag was about twenty-seven to twenty-eight inches, considerably shorter than the thirty-five inches required for the disassembled rifle.[146] Critics also questioned the fact that the bag was not photographed in place before it was removed from the crime scene (Figures 4.11 and 4.12).

Photographs taken of the spent-bullet cartridges showed that they fell scattered near the wall; one critic has argued that the ejected cartridges were originally found in neat rows and that they were moved or even planted before the photos were taken (Figure 4.13).[147] Critics claimed that the Oswald fingerprints and palm prints on the book cartons were meaningless, since he worked on the sixth

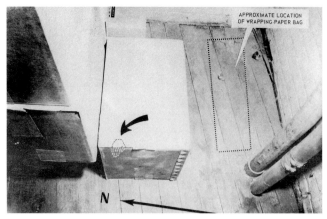

FIGURE 4.11
Government photograph showing the presumed location of the paper bag and of Oswald's palm print at the sniper's perch. The bag was not photographed before it was removed from the scene. Oswald normally handled boxes as a part of his duties.
Warren Commission Studebaker Exhibit F, National Archives

floor frequently. The initial identification of the rifle as a .30-30 or a Mauser led early detractors to argue that the original rifle found at the scene was substituted for Oswald's or that more than one rifle was found.[148]

The nearly whole bullet found at Parkland has been a target for the critics, who cite its poor chain of possession as

FIGURE 4.12
Dallas policemen removing the paper bag from the Depository on November 22, 1963. The Warren Commission concluded that Oswald had used the bag to carry the rifle into the building on the morning of the shooting.
William Allen/DALLAS TIMES HERALD Collection, Sixth Floor Museum Archives

86

one complaint and its high state of preservation as another. The stretcher on which the missile was found was left unattended for a lengthy time, making it possible for someone, said the detractors, to have planted the bullet there.[149] Government authorities have based much of the single-bullet theory on the assumption that the stretcher was used to transport Governor Connally, but searchers insist there was no proof for this claim (Figure 4.14).[150]

Paraffin tests performed on Oswald's cheek after his arrest did not reveal traces of nitrates, evidence that he had fired a rifle-type weapon. FBI officials insisted the tests were unreliable and that, with the Carcano rifle, nitrates would not necessarily have shown up on the suspect's cheek anyway. The critics argued that the negative results proved that Oswald did not fire the weapon at all.[151] Critics also pointed out that other Depository employees were missing at the 1:03 P.M. roll call and that reports singling out Oswald as the lone deserter were incorrect.[152] They insisted that there was ample time for another, unnamed, assassin to have left the building after the shooting, since the front door of the warehouse was not secured until nearly twenty minutes after the murder.[153]

Brennan's change in testimony has been used by the searchers as reason to discount his witness testimony entirely; critics have argued that he was unduly influenced by federal investigators to change his story. Others have accused Brennan of poor eyesight, even though his eye problems postdated 1963.[154] The literature has made much of the testimony of other eyewitnesses who said they saw two

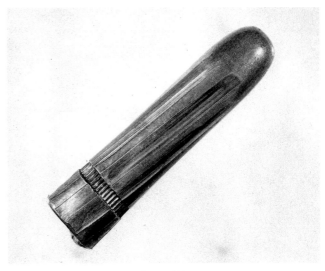

FIGURE 4.14
The near-pristine bullet found on a stretcher at Parkland Hospital about seventy-five minutes after the assassination. Two government probes have concluded that this bullet, fired from Oswald's gun, caused wounds to both President Kennedy and Governor Connally. Searchers have asked how a bullet could break bones and retain so much of its shape. They have also questioned the government's conclusions about the alignment of the men in the car at the time the bullet struck. Neutron Activation Analysis tests performed in 1977 proved that the bullet fragments taken from Connally's wrist came from this bullet, but the searchers questioned the authenticity of the fragments themselves. *Warren Commission CE 399, National Archives*

FIGURE 4.13
Official photograph showing the arrangement of the spent-bullet cartridges—from Oswald's Mannlicher-Carcano rifle—on the floor in the sniper perch. Critics asserted that the cartridges were planted there. *Sixth Floor Museum Archives*

men with a gun on the same floor of the Depository where the evidence was found.[155] The searchers have brought in statements from warehouse co-workers who used the staircase shortly after the shooting, noting that none of them recalled meeting or hearing the alleged assassin during his descent.[156]

Fifteen years after the shooting, former Depository employee Carolyn Arnold told researchers that she had seen Oswald in the second-floor lunchroom of the warehouse shortly after 12:15 P.M., about the same time that another witness outside the building had seen a gunman and a second man on the sixth floor. Arnold's earlier statements, given to the FBI in 1963 and 1964, did not mention the sighting, and she has asserted that the FBI reported her original observations inaccurately.[157]

The searchers have argued that Oswald could not have fired the shots and run down four flight of stairs in the ninety seconds to two minutes that elapsed before Officer Baker approached him in the second-floor lunchroom. However, government reenactments and tests performed by some of the searchers themselves clearly showed that the journey down four flights of stairs could be made within the time frame allotted. One researcher has written that it was a five-story descent, a clear distortion of the architectural layout of the warehouse.[158] Much has been made of an account that Oswald had a Coke in his hand at the time he was seen by Officer Baker; researchers have maintained that the alleged assassin would not have had the presence of mind or sufficient time to make the descent *and* buy a Coke before Baker's arrival on the scene.[159]

Oswald himself apparently told authorities that he was having lunch in the first-floor breakroom at the time the shots were fired and that he left by the front door within a few minutes of the shooting.[160] Researchers have used Oswald's testimony to assert that *another* sniper, using Oswald's rifle, must have been on the sixth floor at 12:30 P.M.

The mark on the curbstone has led critics to accuse the FBI of a failure to properly investigate the evidence. Although local news photographers took pictures of the mark on the curb the day following the assassination, the FBI did not examine the curb until repeated requests from the media and the Warren Commission forced it to do so. After several months of street-cleaning and rains, the FBI said that the visual mark had disappeared. The curb, with the mark still visible, was finally removed by the FBI and taken to Washington in August 1964, nine months after the assassination, where tests showed traces of lead, consistent with a mark from a bullet or bullet fragment that had lost its copper jacket.[161]

Researchers have questioned the chain of possession of the bullet fragments recovered from the limousine, noting that the car was exposed to possible plants while in Washington.[162] Neutron Activation Analysis was possible on the larger fragments found in the limousine but not on the smaller ones. On the NAA tests done during the House Committee investigation on some of the fragments from Connally's wrist, a few critics have argued that although the bullet fragments examined obviously came from the Oswald-related bullet, the chain of possession on the *fragments themselves* did not show that they were the fragments actually removed from Connally during surgery.[163]

AUTOPSY EVIDENCE AND AUTOPSY DISCLAIMERS

Discrepancies in the medical reporting have led to some of the most bitter arguments in the assassination controversy. Parkland doctors focused on life-saving measures and never turned Kennedy over to see the bullet hole in his back and the one in his skull. The tracheotomy enlarged the small frontal wound in his neck below the Adam's apple. The physicians' comments at the press conference after Kennedy's body left Parkland were widely circulated in accounts that asserted JFK had been shot in the neck from the front and that his head wound had come from a shot to the temple. The question immediately became: how could the president have been hit in the front with bullets fired from behind him?

Bethesda Naval Hospital doctors who performed the autopsy on the body on Friday night conducted the procedure in an amphitheater crowded with top military officials and intelligence agents. The three operating physicians were not experts in forensic pathology relating to bullet wounds. The Kennedy family, waiting on an upper floor for

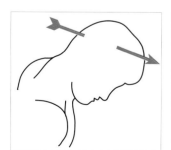 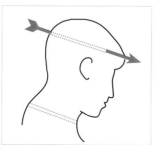

FIGURES 4.15–4.16
Sketches of the president's head wound. Compare the different government conclusions about the nature of this wound. Figure 4.15, prepared for the Warren Commission, suggests that the bullet entered low on the rear of Kennedy's head. Figure 4.16, produced for the House Committee, shows the bullet having entered his head four inches higher.
Based on Warren Commission CE 388; HSCA F-65, National Archives

the procedure to be completed, instructed the medical team to hurry and to bypass some normal autopsy procedures; this pressure may have influenced the doctors. The internal organs were not examined, and the doctors eliminated the customary procedure of tracking the path of bullets, through the back and the brain. Finally, Commander James Humes, who was in charge of the autopsy, did not call the Dallas doctors before the autopsy to check on the treatment that the president had received at Parkland, so he was unaware of the pretracheotomy neck wound. Bethesda doctors examined the president's back wound with a finger and a metal probe but did not find the path of exit, presumably obscured by the tracheotomy.[164]

Photographs and X-rays of the president were taken at the time of the Bethesda autopsy, but Humes did not refer to them in preparing his final report. In fact the Bethesda doctors did not see those materials at all until 1966. Humes checked with a Parkland doctor on Saturday and corrected his report to indicate that the bullet that hit the president in the back exited through the neck. The naval commander burned his original medical notes, later testifying to the Warren Commission that they were splattered with blood and that he had feared they would end up as a gruesome curiosity in a museum.

The Warren Commission as a whole did not examine the original photographs or X-rays of the president, but it asked a medical artist to prepare sketches of the wounds for publication in the final volumes of exhibits; the three drawings were based on verbal descriptions provided by the Bethesda doctors. As a result, the drawings were later found to be incorrect in the placement of the wounds. These errors cast additional doubt on the validity of the trajectory analysis. Investigators and a bystander found three pieces of the president's skull in Dealey Plaza, consistent with the hole in Kennedy's head that was observed by doctors both at Parkland and at Bethesda (Figures 4.15–4.16).

The government turned over the medical evidence to the Kennedy family, which deposited it in the National Archives in 1966 with a proviso that it remain sealed to outside review until 1971. Two medical panels convened by Attorney General Ramsey Clark in 1966 and 1968 were permitted to examine this evidence, and both concluded that the president had been shot twice from behind him. The panels relocated the head wound entry point four inches *higher* than the place shown on the Warren Commission illustration. The Clark panels did not publish any exhibits with their findings.[165]

When the Rockefeller Commission became involved in the Kennedy assassination it empaneled another group of medical experts to review the medical evidence; the panel supported the Warren Commission conclusions that the president had been shot twice from behind. Again, no exhibits were included in the final report.[166]

The House Select Committee convened a large medical panel during its 1976–78 investigation, which published its findings in a separate volume of exhibits. The panel, as a majority, concurred that both wounds had come from shots fired from the rear, but the panel relocated the Warren Commission's point of entry for the neck wound several inches *lower* on the president's back. The panel's report published photographs of the X-rays and close-up drawings of the entry wounds, based on autopsy photographs (Figures 4.17–4.18).

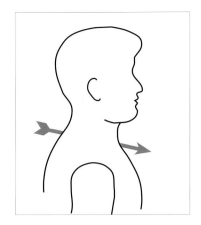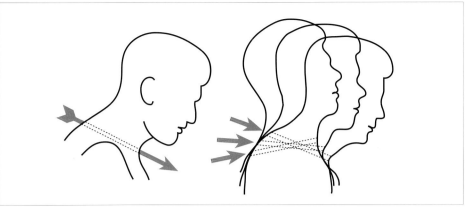

FIGURES 4.17–4.18

Sketches of the president's back wound. The Warren Commission drawing of the president's wound, Figure 4.17, showed the bullet entering at the back of the neck. A detail from the House Committee drawing, Figure 4.18, shows the entry location of the wound on the back, approximately five inches lower than the placement in the Warren Commission drawing. Five medical panels convened between 1966 and 1978 agreed, as a group, that all wounds to the president were fired from behind and above. *Based on Warren Commission CE 385 and HSCA F-46, National Archives*

Critics attacked the accuracy of the Bethesda autopsy and questioned the incorrect drawings published in the Warren Commission exhibits. Indeed, it was their accusations that led the government to perform later examinations of the original X-rays and photographs in an effort to determine just where the bullets entered the president and just how many wounds there were. The Warren, Clark, and Rockefeller panels did not publish photographs based on drawings of the original materials, and the withholding of the original medical evidence kept the debate alive.

The Kennedy family retains ownership of the materials. The critics, in their self-appointed role of defense attorneys, have demanded to see the original evidence so that they can decide its accuracy for themselves. This distrust of government investigations influences the continuing controversy.

The House Committee did publish some photos of the X-rays and the above-mentioned details from some of the autopsy photos. During its investigation the original materials were made available to the medical panel. A Secret Service agent had made copies of the medical evidence during the 1960's, and prints of the autopsy photos began to circulate among the critics during the Eighties. David Lifton published the photographs in 1988; Oliver Stone used photos and a re-creation of the autopsy scene in his movie *JFK*. One of the photographs showed up in the 1993 Clint Eastwood film *In the Line of Fire*.

One vocal and highly qualified critic of the medical findings has been Dr. Cyril Wecht, the former medical examiner for Allegheny County, Pennsylvania, and an acknowledged expert on forensic science related to bullet wounds. Wecht obtained permission to examine the medical evidence in the National Archives in 1972 and published a paper asserting that some of the evidence did not match the Warren Commission's findings.[167] Wecht also sat on the House Committee's medical panel, where he cast the lone dissenting vote about the group's conclusion that two shots were fired from the rear, causing all the wounds to the occupants of the limousine.[168]

A part of Dr. Wecht's difficulties with the evidence related to the manner in which the original autopsy was conducted—"incomplete, superficial," he said—and to the absence of some of the original evidence from the National Archives. As stated earlier, the Bethesda doctors did not section the president's brain to determine the bullet path. When the collection of medical material was finally transferred to the National Archives in 1966, the president's brain was missing.[169] Other tissue samples and slides were found to be missing as well.

Since 1979 some writers, along with two of the original Bethesda autopsy and photo technicians, have argued that the 1963 medical photographs and X-rays have been doctored to disguise the real nature of Kennedy's wounds— a shot from the grassy knoll. Others have kept up the older tradition that shots were fired from the rear but from another location, not from the sixth-floor corner window. David Lifton's 1980 hardcover book *Best Evidence* presented the theory that the president's body was surgically altered between the time it left Parkland and the time the Bethesda doctors performed the autopsy, during a small window of opportunity.

Lifton's thesis was supported by reports from some technical personnel at Bethesda who recalled different wounds, who said they received a different casket, and who stated that the corpse arrived in a body bag and not in the coverings used at Parkland. Lifton based his case for surgery in part on a 1963 report filed by two FBI agents who attended the autopsy; this report stated that when the body was unwrapped at Bethesda, "it was also apparent that a tracheotomy had been performed as well as surgery of the head area, namely, in the top of the skull."[170] Robert Groden and Harrison Livingston took a somewhat different medical tack; in their 1989 volume *High Treason*, they asserted that the medical evidence in the National Archives had been faked.[171]

The 1992 book *JFK: Conspiracy of Silence*, by Dr. Charles Crenshaw, supported the searchers' claims that the problems with the medical evidence have not been totally laid to rest. Crenshaw was a surgical resident at Parkland in 1963 and was present during the treatment of the president and Oswald. His subsequent career in medicine was a distinguished one. His book stated that he believed that President Kennedy was struck by two bullets fired from the front; when shown some of the critics' copies of the Bethesda autopsy photos, he said the wounds had been changed.[172]

We know, however, that the Parkland doctors did only a brief examination of the president's wounds at best and did not turn the body over to assess the presence of possible entry wounds in the rear. We also know that several different medical panels, convened to review the medical evidence, disagreed with Crenshaw's recollections.[173] We have a debate within the medical community.

In recent years there has been a quiet movement among some of the critics to seek an exhumation of the president's body from his grave at Arlington National Cemetery. The issue of exhumation falls into the contemporary scientific realm known as bioethics.[174] Support for exhumation arises from the critics' sense of ownership of the crime, from the incomplete autopsy, and from their success in forcing the exhumation of Lee Harvey Oswald in 1981.

The Oswald "double" theory, espoused by Leo Sauvage in Europe and popularized in this country by Richard Popkin during the 1960's, gained some supporters over the years. Several Dallas witnesses testified that they saw Oswald, or someone who looked exactly like Oswald, at times when the alleged assassin was known to be somewhere else.[175] Some of these witnesses have been extremely difficult to dismiss out of hand, although many officials have tried to do just that.[176] Several researchers thus have argued that Oswald was replaced in Russia or elsewhere by another person.[177]

British attorney Michael Eddowes became an ardent advocate of the exhumation movement, which resulted in a formal request from Marina Oswald to dig up the body.[178] The procedure was carried out in 1981, when a team of forensic experts checked the remains against dental records. The conclusion: the body buried in Rose Hill cemetery was definitely that of Oswald (Figure 4.19).[179] Still, some searchers maintain that the original body of the "double" was taken out of the grave sometime between 1963 and 1981 and the body of the real Oswald was then placed inside the coffin.[180]

Former President Zachary Taylor's body was exhumed early in the 1990's in an attempt to determine if he had died of arsenic poisoning. The test results showed no arsenic. There is an important ethical consideration in the scientific argument about Kennedy's body; the president's children are still alive, and the family usually must give permission for an exhumation. Based on the black market for the 1963 autopsy photographs, there is little reason to believe that materials from an exhumation would be handled with respect for privacy.

TRAJECTORIES, TIMING OF SHOTS, AND DISCLAIMERS

Government agencies used different methods in their analysis of bullet trajectories. The Warren Commission restaged the assassination and measured the angles from the sixth floor down to a limousine that was positioned at different locations on the street (Figure 4.20).[181] The angles were compared with individual frames from the Zapruder film and other photographic evidence that showed the occupants of the car reacting to the shots. The House Committee used another approach. It relied on photographic evidence to line up the occupants in the car, then used the medical evidence of points of entry to draw a line back to the point of origin. The Depository sixth-floor window was in the trajectory projection for both shots (Figures 4.21–4.22).[182]

The Zapruder film has been the official "clock" for the assassination, used by both the officials and the searchers in their arguments about angles and timing. Analysis showed that the 8mm movie ran at an average speed of 18.3 frames

FIGURE 4.19
The exhumation of Lee Harvey Oswald's body in 1981.
Some searchers, attempting to acquit Oswald of the murder,
have argued that a "double" was acting in his place during the shooting.
Oswald's body was exhumed to settle the dispute. The corpse in the grave
was identified as that of Lee Harvey Oswald. *Courtesy, AP/Wide World Photos*

per second, so this breakdown was used by investigators to determine the timing of the shots and the trajectories for the wounds. Individual frames of the film were assigned numbers; the fatal shot, for example, became Z-frame #313. The two major federal inquiries agreed on the trajectories for the shots, but they did not agree on the timing.[183]

To a lay observer who has seen the film in motion, it appears that the hard backward and left movement of the president's head after the fatal shot was caused by a bullet fired from in front or to the side and not from the rear as the Warren Commission and later medical panels had claimed. But the scientifically enhanced, slow-motion versions of the film clearly show that the president's head

FIGURE 4.20
A marksman on the sixth floor of the Depository during the Warren
Commission investigation. The commission determined trajectories for the
wounds to the occupants of the limousine by stationing a marksman and
measuring down to a limousine that was moved to different locations
on the street. *Warren Commission CE 877, National Archives*

moved rapidly forward for a brief fraction of a second (Zapruder frames 312–313) and then slammed back toward the rear (frames 313–314).

Furthermore, it appears from the film that Kennedy reacted to his first injury significantly before Governor Connally showed signs of distress, suggesting that two separate shots may have struck the occupants of the limousine. The FBI tested the rifle using expert marksmen and deter-

mined that it took a minimum of 2.25 to 2.3 seconds to refire the Carcano.[184] This time frame for refiring was used by the Warren panel, which concluded that the actual time between JFK's and Connally's reactions to bullets was only 1.5 seconds, lending support to the single-bullet theory. Overall, the Warren investigators estimated that the elapsed time for the assassination was 5.6 seconds, whereas the House Committee—largely based on the acoustic analysis—

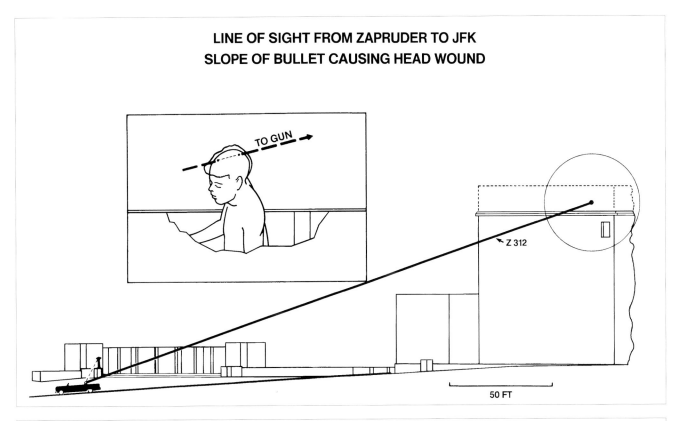

LINE OF SIGHT FROM ZAPRUDER TO JFK
SLOPE OF BULLET CAUSING HEAD WOUND

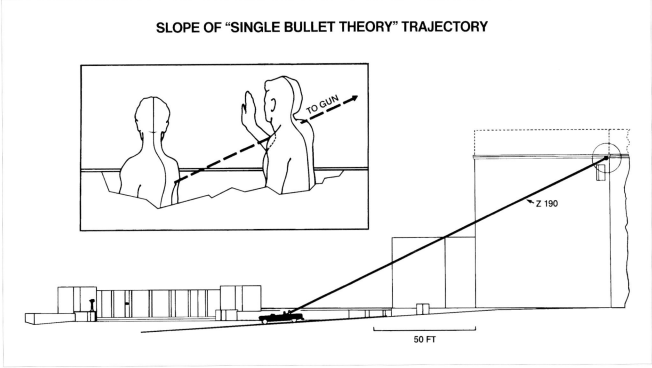

SLOPE OF "SINGLE BULLET THEORY" TRAJECTORY

FIGURES 4.21–4.22
The House Committee trajectory analysis. Trajectories were determined by analyzing medical and visual evidence to determine alignments and then measuring angles back from the limousine. The Depository fit into the trajectories for all wounds. *HSCA F-145 and F-139, National Archives*

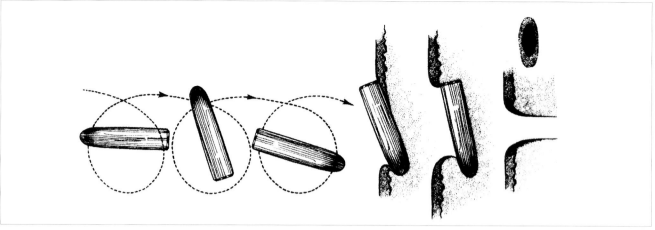

FIGURE 4.23
The path of the near-pristine bullet. Medical specialists have suggested that the bullet tumbled when it exited President Kennedy's throat, entered Connally's back at an angle, then exited bottom first and hit his wrist, breaking it. The bottom of the bullet is deformed. They reasoned that the governor's broken rib was caused by a "slap fracture," resulting from the proximity of the high-speed projectile as it traveled down the bone. These opinions helped to explain, in part, the near-pristine state of the missile. *HSCA VII, Figure 46, National Archives*

estimated 8.3 seconds. The issue of the total time of the assassination was secondary to that of the amount of time it took to refire the old Italian, bolt-action weapon. The House Committee tested a similar rifle (not the original) and determined that a marksman could refire in less than 1.66 seconds if he did not use the telescopic sight.[185]

Investigators examined the line of sight from the sixth-floor corner window down into the street and determined that the branches of an oak tree blocked the sniper's view from frame Z-166 until 210, with a little opening in the leaves around frames 186.[186] The view of the president in the Zapruder film disappeared at frame 207, when the car passed behind a freeway sign, obscuring the cameraman's view. By the time Kennedy reappeared in view at frame 225, he had clearly been shot.

The Warren Commission was unable to determine which of the three shots had missed the limousine, but it concluded that the first shot to hit President Kennedy had made contact between frame 210 and 224. The House Committee said that Oswald's first shot missed and was fired at frame 161. (They did this sequencing by lining up the acoustic impulses with the Zapruder film.) The committee timed his second shot at frame 191, an elapsed time of 1.64 seconds.[187] This shot, said the House panel, passed through Kennedy and wounded Connally, who did not show any reaction until frame 224, about 1.8 seconds later. (Some critics assert that he did not show any reaction until frame 234 or later.)

The idea of the missed first shot supported Governor Connally's testimony; he always maintained that he was hit *after* he heard the initial rifle report. This still left the matter of his delayed reaction. The two major official investigations agreed that Connally did have a delayed reaction to his wounds after he was hit. The panels also concurred that the last shot from the sixth floor was fired at Zapruder frame 312, hitting the president in the head at frame 313. The House Committee said a third shot came from the grassy knoll and was fired at Z-frame 295 but did not hit the limousine or its occupants.[188]

The Warren Commission came up with the single-bullet theory because it realized there was no other way to explain the wounds, based on the number of shots that it determined had been fired from the sixth floor. The assumption, of course, was that *all* shots came from the sixth floor. The rifle, three spent bullet cartridges, eyewitnesses who had seen a rifle, and other hard evidence suggested there had been three shots and one assassin firing. All the identifiable bullet fragments and the near-pristine bullet came from the rifle found on the sixth floor, so the Warren Commission members asked themselves what had caused all the wounds to Governor Connally. They also had to account for the wound to the observer James Tague, and it was doubtful that one of the bullets that had struck Kennedy had continued on down the street for hundreds of feet to hit the curb near the triple underpass.

The FBI investigation, conducted before the Warren Commission really got down to work, was somewhat problematical, since it had concluded that Oswald fired three shots and that all of them had hit the occupants of the limousine—the first hit Kennedy in the back and did not exit, the second wounded Connally, and the third killed the president. This did not allow for the wound to Tague.

Commission attorney Arlen Specter, later a U.S. senator from Pennsylvania, offered the hypothesis that since the bullet that exited Kennedy's neck had to go somewhere, it could have gone into Connally, who was sitting a short distance in front of the president. Further examinations of the photographic evidence and the nature of the wounds made the idea seem plausible, but the alignment of the two men in the car was crucial to the theory. The Warren Commission adopted the single-bullet theory by a split vote of 6–3, and the idea was offered to the public as a *theory*. Later media reports and many of the critics have implied that the commission voted unanimously to adopt the single-bullet idea, but this was not the case.[189]

Eventually, the official medical panels gave an opinion on the single-bullet theory: the near-pristine bullet entered Connally's back below the shoulder blade, traveled along one of his ribs and fractured it, exited his chest, entered the top of his wrist and fractured the radial bones, and then exited again and finally lodged in the muscle beneath the skin of his left thigh.[190] The track of the bullet along the rib actually caused it to veer off course. The rib fracture punctured one of the governor's lungs. This was the bullet that the government said ended up on the stretcher at Parkland, where it was discovered at between 1:45 and 1:50 P.M. on the afternoon of the shooting.

The House Committee accepted the single-bullet theory based on scientific reexamination of the medical evidence—wounds of entry from the rear—and on the ballistic and trajectory tests. Remember, the committee measured the trajectories from the limousine backward, not from the sixth floor downward. The House Committee scientists decided that the bullet tumbled as it exited the president's neck, entered Connally's back at an angle, and came out bottom first. They concluded that the thick lead bottom, which is deformed, hit the governor in the wrist, breaking it (Figure 4.23).[191]

The Parkland doctors, as a group, have never seen the official medical evidence, although four of them viewed the material in Washington in preparation for a *NOVA* television special that aired in 1988.[192] New York urologist John Lattimer became interested in the wound ballistics and forensics of the assassination during the 1960's; he and his sons performed a large number of experiments on cadavers in his backyard. Lattimer also viewed the original medical evidence in 1972 and concurred with the government conclusion that the shots were fired from the rear and that the single-bullet theory was conceivable. His work was published in an interesting volume that compared the wounds inflicted on Kennedy and Lincoln.[193]

Searchers have criticized all the science that was used by the government in tests conducted to determine trajectories. They have complained that the FBI used fixed targets to perform its rifle refiring tests for the Warren Commission; the House Committee marksmen were chided for using another Mannlicher-Carcano and not the original gun. (The committee determined that Oswald's rifle was too worn to be usable.)[194] The issue of Oswald's proficiency with a rifle became a major theme, with the government stating his ranking as a sharpshooter in the Marines and with the searchers producing records and witnesses from his military days attesting that before his discharge his shooting skills had deteriorated considerably. For its 1967 examination into the assassination, CBS used marksmen to try to approximate the original sequence of shots.[195] All failed. Whereas most official testing showed that the sequence of events was *possible*, the critics have never abandoned their assertion that it was *implausible*.

The plausibility of the single-bullet theory has been seriously attacked by virtually all of the searchers, and many people share their skepticism.[196] Detractors have argued that there were more fragments left in Governor Connally than were missing from the bullet.[197] Not all bullets weigh the same amount, however, so the debate about the missing pieces has some room to play.

Early critics came up with a drawing that showed the "magic" bullet darting left and right, in and out, between the bodies of the president and the governor. It is this weaving image that caught the popular imagination and became a metaphor for all of the public's doubts about the assassination itself. "There's no way that bullet could have zigged and zagged the way the government says it did," remarked Rodney Mills, a Dallas resident, "and you can't tell me that hours after Parkland was crawling with FBI, Secret Service,

and police some orderly just walked up and said, 'excuse me, look what I found.'"[198]

On the matter of trajectories and timing, the searchers have used the Zapruder film to support arguments that Connally's delayed reaction was proof of another gunman firing from the rear. The old Dal-Tex building fits into the trajectory range for some theorists, as do other locations within the Depository. No evidence was found in the Dal-Tex building, but it was never searched after the shooting. Josiah Thompson claimed during the 1960's that there were three shooters—at the Depository, at the knoll, and at either the Dal-Tex or the Records Building—and some other writers have fallen into a camp that holds out for a triangulation of fire, more in keeping with the style of hired assassins in a coup d'état.[199]

Arguments about the fatal shot that hit the president in the head have fallen into two distinct arenas. The official science holds that the head shot entered President Kennedy's skull from the rear and that the speed of its transit through the enclosed brain cavity caused such pressure that it blew out the right side of his head when it exited the cranium. The violent movement backward and to the left was caused by a huge neuromuscular reaction in which the powerful back muscles all tensed at once, effectively pulling the body with them. The process was aided by Kennedy's back brace, which tended to keep his body stiff.[200]

Searchers have sworn that the violent backward, left motion, as seen in the Zapruder film, was the result of a shot from the front striking the president's head and driving it farther back in the direction of the bullet's path; they have also relied on the Parkland doctors' accounts that Kennedy had a large hole in the *back* of his head.[201] They used witness testimony attesting to a shot from the front and have often cited the fact that motorcycle policemen, riding adjacent and to the rear of the limousine, were splattered with blood and brains. Preservers counter that the motorcycles were moving forward and simply passed into the cloud of bloody tissue.[202]

PHOTOGRAPHIC AND ACOUSTIC EVIDENCE

The Warren Commission used some enhancement techniques to examine the photographic evidence from the scene of the crime, but scientific advances after 1964 allowed the House Committee to employ new technology in evaluating visual materials associated with the murder.[203] Another look was needed because the critical community had examined dozens of photos taken at the scene and claimed to spot snipers hiding in the bushes. The committee also analyzed a Dictabelt tape that recorded sounds transmitted from a policeman's motorcycle and that might have included the sounds of gunfire.

The Warren investigation examined about 510 visuals; the House Committee checked this body of material, plus the autopsy photographs and X-rays and some additional assassination photographs not made public in 1963–64. The House also had the benefit of independent scientific work that had been done over the years by private researcher Robert Groden to clarify the images in the Zapruder film. The photographic specialists empaneled by the House used new chemical processes and photographic digitization to "read" the visual record.[204]

Since amateur photographers took most of the visuals that recorded the assassination and its environment,

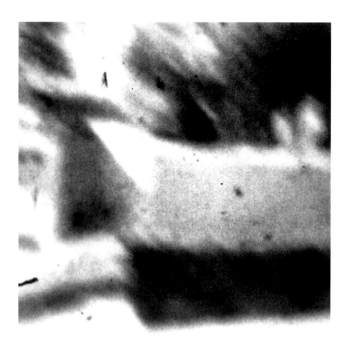

FIGURE 4.24
A detail from a slide taken by Phil Willis. Searchers, examining photos taken by witnesses, thought they saw gunmen in the background. The House Committee, using a panel of photographic experts to perform detailed tests on these visuals, concluded that this slide *did* show a human form in the background. *HSCA F-134, National Archives*

scientists working for the House Committee had to enhance image contrast, remove blur, and otherwise try to clean up the images. They looked for gunmen in the windows of the sixth floor and in the bushes at the grassy knoll. Critical claims that the three photos of Oswald holding his weapons were faked led the committee scientists to check an original negative and six prints, plus the camera that took the pictures.[205] The panel concluded that the Oswald images were genuine, an opinion still debated by some of the searchers.[206]

Researchers had claimed that the backgrounds of several photos taken by witnesses showed additional assassins. The House Committee enhanced a slide taken by witness Phil Willis at the scene and determined that there was an unidentified human form in the area on the grassy knoll behind the retaining wall (Figure 4.24). The House recommended that the Justice Department try to enhance the badly deteriorated Polaroid photo taken by Mary Moorman, but Justice failed to act.[207] None of the House Committee's tests showed additional snipers on the sixth floor, but the committee recommended that the Justice Department take another look at a film taken by witness Charles Bronson; again, Justice did not perform the tests.[208] The committee scientists also relied on the photographic evidence to pinpoint the location of occupants of the limousine at the time shots were fired.

The acoustic analysis dominated news accounts of the House investigation. Researcher Mary Ferrell attended a meeting with the committee in Washington in 1977 and told Bob Blakey about an old police Dictabelt recording, citing some work that had been done by Fort Worth researcher Gary Mack. Mack believed that the recording might have preserved sounds of the assassination. Ferrell had a clearer copy of the Dictabelt recording, which had originated with the Dallas Police Department.[209]

The House Committee tracked down the original Dictabelt in the possession of a retired Dallas police officer and contracted with Bolt, Beranek & Newman (BBN) to analyze its sounds. BBN was the firm that had performed the analysis of recordings of the Kent State University shooting and the examination of the missing eighteen and one-half minutes on the Nixon White House tapes.[210] Dr. James Barger, in charge of the investigation, initially filtered out engine noise and other repetitive sounds in the tape. His report showed that there were five or six noise patterns, or impulses, that *might* have the characteristics of gunfire. These were matched with test recordings in Dealey Plaza taken in August 1978, which involved firing shots from both the Depository sixth-floor window and the grassy knoll (Figure 4.25). The sound patterns on the tape and the test recordings showed a correlation suggesting a fifty-fifty chance that a shot had been fired from the grassy knoll.

The House and Dr. Barger asked a team at Queens College to perform additional refinements using physics and geometry, and the scientists reported that there was "a probability of 95% or better" that a shot had been fired from the grassy knoll. They said that the physical layout of Dealey Plaza created a measurable environment for sound waves, which created a "sound fingerprint" unique to the site and the assassination itself (Figure 4.26). Gunshots could be confirmed because rifle fire is preceded by a shock wave, which also appeared on the tape. This acoustical analysis was the deciding factor in the committee's majority vote in favor of conspiracy.

In 1982 the National Academy of Sciences (NAS) acoustics panel, convened at the request of the Justice Department in 1980 and chaired by Professor Norman Ramsey, issued a report on its reexamination of the House Committee's work. The NAS report noted the appearance of cross-talk on the recording, statements that were known to have been picked up by the police dispatcher about one minute after the assassination, when the motorcade was en route to the hospital. The NAS panel concluded that the sounds on the tape were recorded *after* the shooting and perhaps away from Dealey Plaza.[211] Yet defenders of the House Committee analysis have asked how the NAS panel could discount the shock waves and the sound fingerprint in Dealey Plaza, so the debate goes on.[212]

CONSPIRACY

The Warren Commission did not find any evidence leading to a conclusion of conspiracy in the assassination, but it was later determined that the main investigative agencies for the commission had withheld information that might have led the panel to look in the direction of a plot.[213] The House Committee paid a great deal more attention to the issue of conspiracy, although it was put on the trail fifteen years later. Witnesses had died, and some official records had been destroyed. The time period in which the House Committee performed its fieldwork was extremely short—about six months. Blakey, the staff director, was a noted specialist on the workings of organized crime, and the conclusions of the probe showed the influence of his expertise in this area.

The committee's investigation revealed several connections between the principals in the assassination and possi-

FIGURE 4.25

Microphones used during the 1978 acoustic analysis performed for the House Select Committee. Committee scientists performed a test in Dealey Plaza and later arrived at the conclusion that there was a probability of 95% or better that someone fired at the limousine from behind the cedar fence on the grassy knoll. *Courtesy, THE DALLAS MORNING NEWS*

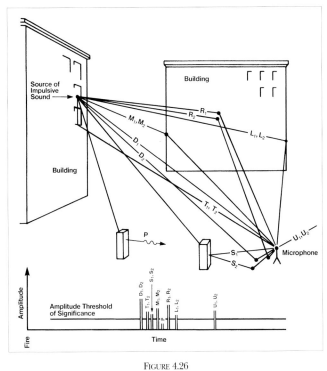

FIGURE 4.26

A schematic showing how sound waves bouncing off hard surfaces generate a measurable pattern. Acoustic scientists determined that Dealey Plaza had a measurable "sound fingerprint" unique to that environment. *HSCA F-334, National Archives*

ble conspirators. Overall, the investigation ruled that no agent of the U.S. government had actively plotted the murder of the president. The committee stated that the Soviet Union, as a government, was innocent of any plot, as was organized crime as a group and Cuba as a government. The committee pointed to individuals within the mob or to anti-Castro Cuban activists as potential conspirators but could not name any names.[214] Blakey and former *Life* magazine reporter Richard Billings later wrote a book, *The Plot to Kill the President*, which offered a Mafia scenario for the killing.[215]

During the early years after the assassination, the searchers presented a wide variety of theories relating to conspiracy. Some went relatively far afield, casting blame everywhere. Two articles in *Esquire* magazine in 1966–67 listed more than fifty possible conspiracies, ranging from the mob to the mysterious actions of the "umbrella man."[216] The umbrella man was alternately credited with the role of signaler or of firer of poison fléchettes (darts) during the assassination. The man was tracked down by a researcher and testified to the House Committee, where he said that his actions were a simple protest, with no malicious intentions against the president.[217]

With the exception of the House investigation, the field of conspiracy belongs almost entirely to the searchers, who have probed deeper and longer than anyone else. To a certain extent the theories of the searchers have followed general attitudes in society. Nearly all the theories were presented during the 1960's, but some have gained prominence since then, during periods when related events made the theories more plausible.

When the Russians were the enemy during the cold war, for instance, there were many theories that the assassination could be traced to agents for the Soviet Union. During the 1970's the revelations about illegal activities of the CIA and a trend for spy novels led to more active speculation that Oswald had ties to the agency. Searchers' claims that Oswald was linked to the FBI date back to the first wave of books, but the FBI and military intelligence have become popular in recent years as potential employers of Oswald. Lyndon Johnson speculated during his presidency that the searchers would one day try to link him to Kennedy's murder, and they have done so, waiting until after his death to make their most vocal attacks.[218] What follows is the briefest of summaries of the most enduring conspiracy ideas that the searchers have presented about the crime.

JACK RUBY

Jack Ruby's shooting of Oswald led many people to believe that the nightclub owner might have been hired to silence the prime suspect in the president's death. Before his 1964 trial, Ruby's presumed motive was distress over the assassination and a desire to spare Mrs. Kennedy and her children the ordeal of a trial. Ruby told Warren Commission members that he acted alone in shooting Oswald, but he made comments that his life was in danger

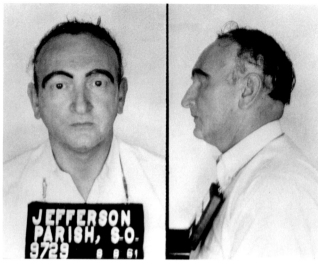

FIGURE 4.27

David Ferrie. The House Committee investigation and the searchers both looked into the activities in New Orleans of Ferrie, who had ties to anti-Castro elements, the mob, and former FBI agent Guy Bannister. Ferrie had been a target in Jim Garrison's conspiracy probe in 1967–69, but he died before he could be brought to trial. *Courtesy, AP/Wide World Photos*

in Dallas. The commission found no ties between Ruby and organized crime and no role for him in any conspiracy scenario.[219]

The House Committee looked hard at the mob and found that Ruby had ties with associates of Mafia chieftains Carlos Marcello and Santos Trafficante. The committee determined that Ruby had stalked Oswald for more than a

FIGURE 4.28

House Committee cartoon. The committee probe and many books by critics have found connections that suggest that members of organized crime may have been involved in a plot to kill President Kennedy. The mob hated the Kennedy administration's policy toward its operations and the growth of détente with Cuba, where they had profitable casino operations. *Pat Oliphant, Sixth Floor Museum Archives*

day before he shot him, and it likened the basement murder to a Mafia "hit." Although unable to prove its theory, the House Committee suggested that Ruby's financial difficulties may have led him to accept a contract from the mob to murder Oswald.[220]

Critics, angered that the Ruby trial did not look into the issue of conspiracy, took the lead from Ruby's oblique statements and searched for further connections between the Chicago-born hustler, Oswald, the Mafia, and anyone else. The searchers have expanded this base to link Ruby to Jimmy Hoffa and have explored ties that lead further into a Cuban connection.[221]

ORGANIZED CRIME

The Warren Commission examined organized crime only as it related to Jack Ruby. The early searchers looked more deeply into the matter. The mid-1970's disclosures about a CIA-Mafia plot to kill Castro, combined with the mob's hatred of the Kennedy brothers for their efforts to shut down Mafia operations, led the House Committee to look into the subject. Staff director Blakey had specialization in this field, so some leads in this direction were to be expected.

The committee linked Oswald to associates of New Orleans chieftain Carlos Marcello, whose territory extended as far as Dallas. John Davis and other conspiracists have examined the possible involvement of Marcello or his lieutenants in a plot.[222] Ties included anti-Castroites David Ferrie and former FBI agent Guy Bannister (Figure 4.27). Bannister worked as a detective and had an office at 544 Camp Street, on the corner of Camp and Magazine Streets, in New Orleans. The House Committee said Oswald probably knew them both, a claim long asserted by the searchers. The 1993 *Frontline* TV special showed a photograph, presumably genuine, of Oswald and Ferrie with a group of men. One connection between the two men was the building at 544 Camp Street; Oswald used the Magazine Street entry into the same building as an address for his "Fair Play for Cuba" literature. The government also ruled that Oswald's uncle, Dutz Murret, and his mother, Marguerite Oswald, had known Marcello associates (Figure 4.28).[223]

The House found that Jack Ruby knew associates of Marcello and Florida chieftain Santos Trafficante, a key figure behind the joint CIA-Mafia plots against Castro. The Castro plots tied further into Sam Giancana, the Chicago boss, mob lieutenant Johnny Roselli, and Judith Exner. Jim Garrison's investigation laid some of the groundwork for this conclusion, with the notable exception that the New Orleans probe did not see any relationship with the mob. The House did conclude that Oswald, Ferrie, and Clay Shaw were together in Clinton, Louisiana. The mob theme remains popular in the critical literature, particularly as it ties into the notion of combinations among mafiosos, anti-Castro Cubans, and rogue intelligence agents.[224] There have been a number of secretly taped conversations released in which mob leaders stated that they wanted Kennedy dead.

CUBA

A possible Cuban connection made sense to officials and searchers, particularly after the revelation that the U.S. government engaged in active plots to assassinate Castro during Kennedy's term in office. The Warren Commission did not find any concrete leads, but the House Committee investigated the matter and even went to Cuba and met with Fidel Castro, who—not surprisingly—denied any complicity in the Kennedy assassination. The House panel ruled that the government of Cuba did not play any active role in plotting to kill the American chief executive.[225]

The House Committee did find several leads into anti-Cuban groups in America but did not accuse any individual organization in a conspiracy. Individuals associated with these groups may have done it, said the House. Ties led to Miami or back to New Orleans and the Ferrie-Bannister scenario. Searchers have followed up on a Dallas-Cuban connection as well. Many American Cubans were furious with Kennedy for the Bay of Pigs and for his agreement not to invade the island after the Cuban missile crisis.[226]

Searchers have proposed both pro- and anti-Cuban connections in a possible plot and have named several likely Cuban assassins for the Kennedy murder. The 544 Camp Street address figures prominently in their research. The Church Committee revealed in 1976 that although Kennedy had canceled a CIA-backed anti-Castro campaign, rogue agents kept it active. Researchers have proposed links between disgruntled anti-Castro exiles and these wildcard CIA agents.[227]

U.S. INTELLIGENCE AGENCIES

Texas authorities informed the Warren Commission about persistent rumors that Oswald had been a paid informant for the FBI; the matter was discussed in a special closed-session meeting of the commission in January 1964. The transcript of the meeting was later released to the searchers, causing quite a stir.[228] In part, the commission decided to accept J. Edgar Hoover's denial of the allegations and let the matter drop, after Texas authorities confirmed that a Houston reporter's assertion did not carry the weight that they once believed it had. Later disclosures that a Dallas FBI agent had destroyed a note from Oswald and that the bureau had withheld information from the commission fueled the flames of debate. The House Committee chided the FBI but did not cast blame on the agency or its employees in plotting to kill the president.[229] Critics, however, have not been inclined to acquit the bureau or its agents.[230] Much has been written about an FBI cover-up during the original assassination investigation. In terms of actual plotting, the scene goes to New Orleans and to 544 Camp Street, where ex-FBI agent Bannister kept his office.

The House Committee also cleared the CIA, military intelligence, and the Secret Service, institutionally and individually, of any plots against JFK.[231] The CIA has been a main target for the searchers, who worked off the agency's involvement in the Castro plots during the early 1960's and who developed other potential links between the intelligence unit and the principals in the Kennedy murder. Some searchers have questioned Oswald's Marine service at Atsugi in Japan as a possible CIA link, asserting that the agency had a facility there; George DeMohrenschild, Oswald's best friend in Dallas, has been labeled a CIA informant; and critics maintain that Oswald's "201" CIA file meant that he was employed by the organization.[232]

The five Watergate burglars were all operatives during the Bay of Pigs fiasco, a tie-in that has led to many efforts to connect everything that has gone wrong in the nation since 1963.[233] Anthony Summers and Gaeton Fonzi have written of a CIA agent named Maurice Bishop and have linked him in a complicated network of intrigue.[234] The critics have been vocal in asserting that intelligence agencies covered up facts of the crime and kept these facts from the people. The opening of long-classified files from these agencies in the next few years should throw additional light on critics' claims.

No official agency has ever found any proof that the Dallas Police Department was involved in a plot to kill the president, although the House Committee did suspect that a member of the force might have let Ruby into the basement of police headquarters through a back stairwell. Ruby himself said he went down a ramp at a time when an officer was distracted. Advance planning in the *timing* of the Oswald murder has been impossible to prove. Ruby was wiring money to a stripper in Fort Worth at a nearby Western Union office only four minutes before Oswald appeared in the basement, the transfer of the suspect was running about an hour late when Ruby arrived, and no one has proved that anyone called to alert him.[235] On the other hand, some searchers suspect that Oswald was not moved until Ruby was known to have arrived.

THE RIGHT WING

The idea of a right-wing conspiracy was an early theory that has lost some of its support among searchers. It did not take long for the media spin that "hatred" was responsible for the assassination to formalize into assertions that elements of the right wing had plotted the president's murder. Officials looked into the advertisers behind the black-bordered ad that had appeared in *The Dallas Morning News* on the day of the assassination and also the source of printed "Wanted for Treason" anti-Kennedy handbills that had appeared in the city before the president's arrival. No connections were found.

Searchers, primarily those who were unfamiliar with the layout of Dealey Plaza, have accused the planners of the Dallas motorcade of changing the route at the last minute. (The final route was made public on November 19.) The route was set after advance men arrived in Dallas and discovered that continuing the motorcade on Main Street through Dealey Plaza was not feasible, since a curb on Main Street prevented direct access to the Stemmons Freeway ramp, the most direct route to JFK's next appearance. Nevertheless, the search for a right-wing cause for the murder has continued since the 1960's. The name of Georgia ultraconservative Joseph Milteer has been prominent in claims that the right wing wanted Kennedy dead.[236] This idea dominated the 1973 film *Executive Action.*[237]

VIETNAM

The Vietnam theme is tied closely to the Kennedy myth and might be said to spring from the urge to have Kennedy, posthumously, get the United States out of the war. No official investigation has given credence to searchers' claims that the military or its massive industrial support complex actually planned and executed the murder of the president.

Oliver Stone relied on Fletcher Prouty, a former officer with the Joint Chiefs of Staff, for some of his scripting in the film *JFK*, but the meat of Stone's argument came from military scholar John Newman, whose book outlining a JFK plan for complete withdrawal from Vietnam appeared shortly after the premiere of Stone's Hollywood film.[238] The fictional film character of Mr. X was based on Prouty, but Newman is the strongest proponent of the idea that Kennedy planned to get out of Vietnam. Newman, however, did not allege that this plan caused JFK's death.

THE SOVIETS

The Soviet theme appeared immediately after the assassination, yet the Warren Commission and House Committee probes found no solid leads suggesting ties to the USSR in any plots.[239] The House investigation made use of the CIA defector Yuri Nosenko, a KGB agent who had overseen Oswald's file during part of the time the accused assassin resided in the Soviet Union from 1959 until 1962. Nosenko defected to the United States only two months after the assassination in Dallas, leading officials within the CIA to seriously question his reliability in asserting that the Soviets had not recruited Oswald, that they thought he was mentally unstable, and that the Russians really did not even want to keep him in the country as a token defector.

The House Committee discounted Nosenko as a reliable informer, primarily due to his earlier treatment during the 1960's at the hands of the CIA. The defector was imprisoned without adequate food or care in solitary confinement, badgered to admit he was a liar, and treated so roughly that the committee feared he was forever ruined as a source of information about the Russian residency of Oswald. The issue of Nosenko's reliability caused major dissension within the ranks of the CIA. Nosenko survived his incarceration and still lives, under an assumed identity, in the United States.

The exhumation of Oswald's body undermined searchers' claims that the assassin was an imposter put in place by Russians or another agency. However, the searchers have used Oswald's Soviet defection to argue that he was an agent for U.S. intelligence sent to spy on the Soviets, or the other way around.[240] The United States has formally requested that the Russian government share its KGB files on Oswald. Since the collapse of the Soviet Union, some former officials have come forward to assert that the Russians thought little of Oswald and did not recruit him.[241] Norman Mailer's recent book *Oswald's Tale* supports this conclusion.[242]

MYSTERIOUS DEATHS

When I told my brother in 1987 that I was returning to Dallas to work full time on completing The Sixth Floor Museum, he cautioned me: "Be careful what you say about this thing [Kennedy's death] or someone might chop you up into little pieces and stuff you in an oil drum and drop you overboard." This was the fate of mob lieutenant Johnny Roselli in 1976; a year earlier he was discovered to have played a part in the CIA plots to assassinate Castro during the early 1960's.[243] Obviously my brother believed the theory that strange or violent deaths are a part of the legacy of the Kennedy assassination.

The idea was put forth early by the searchers and continues to flourish today. The theory implies that some giant sinister force is still at work in society, systematically eliminating people who were unlucky enough to become involved with the subject of the assassination. The publicity for the film *Executive Action* included a promotion stating that the odds against the number of claimed Kennedy-related deaths was one hundred thousand trillion to one.[244] The House Committee tried to deflate the theory by producing a letter from the London newspaper that had originally run the statistic; the newspaper admitted that its estimate had been incorrect.[245]

But in 1989, searcher Jim Marrs's *Crossfire* included a list of 103 "convenient" deaths, and the theme reappeared in Oliver Stone's movie in 1991.[246] Marrs's list encompasses natural deaths that one might expect more than two decades after the shooting. Preserver Gerald Posner must have been angered by the persistence of the theory, since he went to great lengths in his book *Case Closed* to try to discount the notion.[247] Both Marrs and Posner provide subtle shadings in their arguments for convenient versus natural deaths.

WHAT NEXT?

The 1992 law calling for the formation of a presidential panel to oversee the declassification of assassination documents may help to resolve the conflicts that persist over the murder of a young and vibrant president. Opening these files will loosen the earlier hold on declassified information held by the searchers, who obtained their material through the tedious process of Freedom of Information Act requests. We would be naive to expect any quick resolution in this incredibly complicated matter. The remaining classified documents may take years for the presidentially appointed panel and its staff to review, and there is no guarantee that these papers will provide significant new information.

The searchers have named more than fifty people who may have been gunmen in Dealey Plaza on November 22, 1963; none of them have gained credence with the public.[248] For the present, we can only regret that Jack Ruby shot down the prime suspect in the murder. A trial might have removed some of the intense speculation that has become a legacy of the crime itself.

In February 1962, John F. Kennedy gave a speech on the twentieth anniversary of the Voice of America broadcasting service. He reminded his audience of one of the unique characteristics of the *practice* of freedom in the United States: "We are not afraid to entrust the American people with unpleasant facts, foreign ideas, alien philosophies, and competitive values. For a nation that is afraid to let its people judge the truth and falsehood in an open market is a nation that is afraid of its people."

Much has changed since 1962. After the collapse of the eastern communist bloc, the role once played by Voice of America shifted. Today we know that our government does not always trust the people to judge the truth in an open market, but we firmly believe that it should. We debate openly on a bewildering variety of issues big and small, and in this way we enjoy practicing freedom in America. Clearly, the debate about the death of President John F. Kennedy has passed, along with his myth, from one generation to another. Some members of the new generation may want to take on the challenge of searching for the "truth," and some will become preservers of the "truth." In either case, the experiences of my generation may encourage you to exercise caution in evaluating the information put forward by authoritative voices.

CHAPTER 5

The Media as Messenger

Try to remember your first encounter with John F. Kennedy. Chances are it was visual, communicated to you by television or some other form of media. Unlike the Founding Fathers, who survive solely in portraits, in myth, and on the printed page, JFK survives also on video, film, and audiotape, and his image has been preserved in countless photographic archives. The media shows us JFK regularly to note anniversaries of his death, to highlight issues during political campaigns, and to gain points during ratings sweeps. Thanks to the media, you can almost sense him as a real person, full of *vigah*—as he pronounced it—witty, sophisticated, handsome, appearing to enjoy being president in an era dominated by crises. The media has been the voice of the collective memory.

This voice from the past may sound like history, but it isn't. The traditional "textbook JFK" is inadequate to meet the informational demands of a generation raised on television, a generation that desires moving images that impart a sense of real experiences.[1] In *The Americans: The Democratic Experience*, historian Daniel Boorstin offered a cautionary tale about the danger of confusing television with history.[2] First, he observed that the experiential format of television creates a *time myopia* that divorces historical people and events from the context of their past. The same can be said of radio: except for the tinny tones that denote old sounds, everything on radio is presented as *now*, stripped of the important meaning that is inherent in its original cultural milieu. Yet historiography relies heavily on context. Kennedy's rhetoric about the threat of nuclear annihilation worked well during the early Sixties, when the memory of Hiroshima was fresh and many people actually believed that we might all be blown to smithereens. It sounds somewhat shrill today. Second, Boorstin warned that whereas the democratization of learning, launched by the invention of the printing press, took four hundred years to liberate the masses from despotism, television has taken over in only one generation. TV has the power to present information that will galvanize public opinion, pro or con, on many issues.

NEWS IN AMERICA

The rules of historical reportage were developed slowly by scholars during the Victorian era to apply to the printed interpretation of the past. This makes sense, since before the communications revolution, books and journals were the primary means for the dissemination of information. Journalism in general and television in particular have not developed any formal educational guidelines to handle the responsibilities that fall into the modern category of information services. There are no strict demands for expertise gained through advanced academic training. In fact, entry to the field of journalism still does not require any form of licensing or testing.

The famous 1962 prophecy "the medium is the message" did not come true. "Marshall McLuhan says the printed word is 'obsolete,'" noted the *Saturday Review* magazine in 1973. "To prove it he wrote fifteen books."[3] Journalists and historians sometimes work according to entirely different rules. When requested to do so, reporters are committed to protecting their sources, whereas historiography requires that writers clearly acknowledge their sources, usually through footnotes. "Journalists," states political scientist Edward Jay Epstein, "cannot even claim the modicum of authority granted to academic researchers because they cannot fulfill the requirement of always identifying their sources, let alone documenting their claims."[4]

The new generation falls into the nebulous zone between the memory of JFK and the history of that memory. My generation had the same experience with World War II, Franklin Roosevelt, and Hiroshima. Television was still a relatively new medium during my formative years, so the printed word carried considerable weight in educating me about these elusive figures and events from the past. In fact, my family watched television mainly for its entertainment value; there was no PBS or CNN, and the news was a brief rehash of daily events. Weekly television news magazines did not exist.

Since 1960, television has assumed awesome power as a medium of communication, and it has played a major role in preserving and reshaping the memory of JFK. It is not my intention to warn you away from the media or from television in particular; I watch the Kennedy documentaries and docudramas, enjoying most of them thoroughly. The question remains: how much of the material on television is entertainment and how much is documentary? In terms of the documentaries, has the material been fairly presented, or has the media shown JFK through a tinted glass? The media's important role in communicating information about JFK to all of us suggests a need to explore its peculiar stewardship over the legacy of the thirty-fifth president.

The media's involvement with John F. Kennedy began before the future president ever ran for office in 1946. According to Kennedy biographer Nigel Hamilton, "For years [Joe Kennedy, Sr.] had bribed a veritable corps of Washington, New York and Boston newspapermen with lavish gifts to write up the Kennedys."[5] (Both Jack and Jackie Kennedy did stints in the field of journalism, which gave them an entrée into the media club.)[6] Toward the end of World War II, the former PT-109 commander's heroism in the Pacific received much attention in the print media. When JFK's political career took on national importance during the 1950's, the media simply continued its practice of focusing on the handsome Democrat. Television embraced him during the 1960 campaign and relished its special role during the Kennedy presidency, when the chief executive held frequent press conferences and gave reporters unusual access to the Oval Office (see image opposite page 101).

Twenty-five years after the assassination, ABC news commentator Peter Jennings admitted that John F. Kennedy was the last president "to seduce the press."[7] Seduce them he did, and the scent of admiration still lingers in the frequent retellings offered by the media today. Journalists in the early 1960's were vastly different from the investigators that emerged from the Watergate scandals. Certain personal subjects—sex in particular—were tacitly kept out of the press in the early 1960's, and no one ventured to predict the outcome of a presidential election before all the polls were closed. The media gave a curious public a healthy daily dose of Kennedy activities, and we responded by watching the television programs and buying the magazines that included feature stories about them. There was a high level of respect for the office of the presidency.

JFK's administration had its share of difficulties, and the media did its job as reporter of events by pointing out his blunders along with his triumphs. Yet the photojournalists rarely caught JFK in a bad pose, and there was a heavy amount of laudatory coverage about his family life. Detailed analysis of JFK's policies and his problems came from the print media; television was still entertainment and was not afforded too much authority on issues of news.

The assassination in 1963 created a new, powerful bond between JFK and the media. One of the great ironies of that era lies in the fact that television news journalism owes its legitimacy to the death of a president.[8] Just a few months before the tragedy in Dallas, the International Press Institute turned down a bid by radio and television news reporters to be admitted to membership; these reporters "did not constitute bona fide journalists," sniffed the institute.[9] During those endless four days in November, radio and television largely scooped print journalism on the Kennedy story, with the result that the once-entertainment reporters were soon admitted into the institute.[10]

Virtually overnight, television news took charge of shaping the collective memory of one of the century's most important events, embracing the subject of Kennedy's life and career along with his death. Since the shooting, radio and print media have also staked a claim to the memory of the youthful president. Media stewardship of the Kennedy legacy has persisted continuously since 1963.

The biggest change occurred in television. Since colonial days in America, print journalism had been the established forum for serious news. The notions of competition for stories and the evolution of the journalistic method of writing developed during the nineteenth century. The nation's first Washington, D.C., correspondent sent in from New York by a major daily did not arrive in the capital until 1822 and then only "for the winter." War correspondents came into being during the Crimean War of 1854, and the use of the pyramid format in presenting news reports was developed during the Civil War to accommodate the technology of the telegraph.[11]

Claims of journalistic impartiality can be traced to the dawn of the era of newspapers; the objective role of reporters as *observers* can be found in accounts in the seven-

teenth century. Radio appeared on the American scene in 1920 when Westinghouse launched station KDKA in Pittsburgh. By 1992 there were 576 stations nationwide; consumers purchased 100,000 radio sets that same year. By 1925 there were 5.5 million sets in use in the United States, accounting for nearly half of all sets in existence. Radio borrowed its news format from print journalism, lured staff away from newspapers, and honed their language to conform to the simple style of the new medium.[12]

Radio dominated all reportage during World War II. I have vague memories of sitting around the radio with my grandparents during the late 1940's, listening to the regular programs. The set was a large veneer affair afforded a prominent place in their living room, and I recall that the sound effects were dramatically *real.*

During the 1950's radio began to see staff desertions from its ranks into the new medium of television.[13] Television had been around since the 1940's, but most of the families in our town did not buy sets until the early 1950's. Initially, television stations had trouble finding visuals. When the Japanese attacked Pearl Harbor in early December 1941, pioneer network CBS in New York City reported the bombing while showing the lonely image of an "undulating American flag blown by a fan in the studio."[14]

The advent of television news dated to the postwar years. By 1949 there were about one hundred stations in the nation and two fifteen-minute news programs, one on CBS and the other on NBC. I was about four years old when my parents got their first TV set, and I dimly recall the adults watching the NBC evening *Camel News Caravan* with announcer John Cameron Swayze. "This is John Cameron Swayze," he would say, night after night. It was obviously the same man who had done the news the night before, and I could not understand why he kept reintroducing himself. Most of the program showed Swayze as a "talking head," reading the news on camera. Soon we were seeing more film footage, flown daily into New York, and I came to know Walter Cronkite as a CBS *anchorman* during the presidential convention coverage in 1952.[15]

Television changed the way that news was reported, inventing the *sound bite* and shoehorning momentous events into two-minute time slots. According to writer Norman Mailer, this habit of severe compression led to a journalistic style of "munching nuances like peanuts."[16] Radio survived the competition of television by targeting its programming to specific audiences—classical music, all news, top 40— while newspapers moved away from pure news to a cosmopolitan smorgasbord of news, features, commentary, and popular sociology. Some papers, like *USA Today,* have borrowed their language and visual format from television.[17] CNN, which was not around during the Kennedy era, launched the first all-news reportage in 1980. Since then, some of the surviving weekly print news magazines—*Time* and *Newsweek,* to name only two—have been redesigned to more closely resemble television.

But in 1963 television was still outside the realm of official news journalism. TV was largely entertainment. Milton Berle and Arthur Godfrey induced us to turn on the set during the early Fifties. By 1963 we tuned in to the nightly news on NBC with Chet Huntley and David Brinkley, but our real interests were *Bonanza,* the *Dick Van Dyke Show,* and the *Beverly Hillbillies.* When the shots were fired in Dallas, the importance of TV news changed virtually overnight.

ASSASSINATION COVERAGE

There were only a few professional journalists at the scene who *saw* Kennedy being shot in 1963. Most members of the White House press corps were in the two press buses near the end of the motorcade. Of the major TV networks, CBS and ABC each had two correspondents in Dallas; NBC had only one.[18] Young audiences who are accustomed to having a TV "witnessing" view of news—multiple cameras showing close-ups of every angle at a sports or political event—find it hard to believe that the networks were not in the park to offer detailed visuals of the assassination and, by today's standards, instant replays of the critical moments of this historic event. It simply did not happen that way.

Plenty of journalists heard the shots, but only Dallas reporters James Altgens from AP, Pierce Allman from WFAA-AM, and a few *Dallas Morning News* reporters, including Mary Woodward, actually saw the assassination. WFAA cameraman Tom Alyea got into the Depository before it was sealed and took historic footage at the major crime scene. Alyea, *Dallas Morning News* reporter Kent Biffle, and Allman were inside the building when all the major evidence was discovered, almost two hours before the rest of the press was admitted. Other photographers who were riding in the press pool cars were able to jump from the vehicles and remained at the scene immediately after the shooting. Few reporters actually saw the damage that was done in the limousine on Elm Street. Altgens and Allman knew that the president had been badly hurt, but they relied on their professional training to limit reports to the fact that shots had been fired. The final count of amateur and professional photographers at the scene during the first ninety minutes after the assassination was more than seventy-five, and these individuals took more than five hundred visuals.[19] But the assassination itself was recorded mainly by amateurs.

Reporters in 1963 knew how to identify what they call a "hot moment," an event "through which a society or culture assesses its significance."[20] All of the elements were there: tension—a young Democratic president cut down by a sniper in a predominantly Republican town; surprise—more than two hundred thousand Dallasites had just given Kennedy his most enthusiastic reception in Texas; suspense—the threat of global conspiracy with half the cabinet flying somewhere over the Pacific; poignancy—the slain leader falling into the arms of a beautiful wife who rarely accompanied him on political trips. Kennedy had always generated excitement among the media. This was the quintessential exciting moment. The *New York Times* got word of the shooting at 12:40 P.M. and had thirty-two reporters assigned to the story within hours; editor Harrison Salisbury recalled that the impetus at the time was "to provide a record for history and for historians."[21] The original emphasis on being the recorders for history would later shift.

John Kennedy was a friend to quite a few journalists, and the members of the White House Press corps on the trip had enjoyed frequent access to the president. Reporting the story was doubly hard because many reporters were mourning a personal loss while they covered the tremendous story of his death.

That the TV networks were somewhat late to the scene of the crime did not particularly matter at the time of the shooting itself, but it came to have significance later. Ask a rememberer which images remain fresh in his or her memory from the weekend, and chances are the footage showing the murder of Oswald and scenes from the memorial services top the list. Television was *there* for those moments, and the networks have replayed them over and over since 1963. The retelling of the events relating to the JFK years has relied heavily on the film footage that was taken at the time. Small wonder that the Oswald shooting and the Nixon-Kennedy debates have been high-ranking programs for decades.[22]

What about magazines? Because of scheduling deadlines the weekly magazines were unable to provide the saturation coverage available to the other forms of media during the four days in November, but they made up for the delay during the months immediately after the state funeral. *Newsweek* produced twenty-five extra pages on the death of the president; *Time* added seventeen.[23] At the time that JFK was killed, the big-format weeklies—*Look*, *Life*, and the *Saturday Evening Post*—were among the most popular journals in American homes. *Life* always included a photographic essay, and its other regular features provided recaps on weekly news, business, and the arts. The advertisements were huge, and the style was easy to digest. Some of the leading photojournalists in the nation worked for these magazines.

The funeral flowers at Arlington National Cemetery had not yet withered when the first memorial magazine features on JFK hit the newsstands. Some were compiled postmortem, whereas other stories ran as if the president were still alive. All of them were poignant and lavish in their praise of JFK. *Look*'s December 3 issue featured a cover and photo essay on "The President and His Son," with pictures taken by Kennedy favorite Stanley Tredick. There was JFK, alive and smiling, playing with his lively little son, who was trying to learn how to salute like a soldier.[24]

Life's December 6, 1963, funeral edition marked the twenty-first time that the Kennedys had appeared on the cover.[25] Inside the magazine were all the visual icons from the weekend: the soldierly salute from little John, the caisson, Jacqueline Kennedy dressed in black.[26] The prose for *Life*'s tribute was rather typical of the time: "A woman knelt and gently kissed the flag. A little girl's hand tenderly fumbled under the flag to reach closer. Thus, in a privacy open to all the world, John F. Kennedy's wife and daughter touched at a barrier that no mortal can ever pass again."[27]

Taking their cue from the newspapers and broadcast media, these magazines also included positive essays on the qualifications of the new president and their own early assessments about the guilt or innocence of Lee Harvey Oswald. *Life*'s LBJ story was titled "The New Chief Moves Boldly to His Big Tasks," with a sidebar on the first lady, "Lady Bird Takes on Her Role with a Sure Hand." "Johnson has been called probably the best-prepared president to enter the White House," said *Life*, "and his Lady Bird also brings her own special flair."[28]

The *Life* murder story ran under the title "End to Nagging Rumors: The Six Critical Seconds."[29] Noting the prevalence of conspiracy rumors about the shooting, *Life* declared that Oswald was the assassin. "The evidence against him is circumstantial," intoned the magazine, "but it appears to be positive." The article stated that three shots had been fired, all from Oswald's rifle. According to *Life*, which possessed the original Zapruder film, the first shot hit President Kennedy "in the throat," the second, 4 seconds later, hit Governor Connally, and an additional 2.66 seconds elapsed before the third shot hit President Kennedy in the head. In an effort to deflate questions about a possible shot from the front, the reporter offered the following: "It has been hard to understand how the bullet could enter the front of his [Kennedy's] throat. Hence the recurring guess that there was a second sniper somewhere else. But the 8mm [Zapruder] film shows the president turning his body far around to the right as he waves to someone in the crowd. *His throat is exposed—toward the sniper's nest—just before he clutches it*" (emphasis added).

The American public did not see the Zapruder film on television until 1975, nearly twelve years after *Life*'s report. Only then did people realize that President Kennedy never turned around toward the Depository building behind him. It was the temper of the times to allay fears about conspiracy, and *Life* certainly did its best to assist. The article assured its readers that Oswald's actions had not been part of a conspiracy.[30]

The December 6 issue of *Life* ended with Theodore White's historic epilogue, the Jackie Kennedy interview that made Camelot the name for an era. White's interview effectively *became* history and injected into the Kennedy equation an entirely new element, one that had never existed before.

The Kennedy assassination gave news journalism added power, and it came to be the benchmark against which the medium judged its subsequent behavior.[31] The result has been both good and bad. On the one hand, few can deny that the media did a fantastic job in reporting on the events of the weekend with incredible diligence and speed. Reporters in Dallas and Washington went for days without sleep, pushing themselves to the limits of endurance, emotionally and physically. The networks garnered an incredible array of manpower to handle coverage of the investigation in Dallas and the funeral in Washington. Reports from abroad came in like clockwork, serving to inform the American people that other nations shared their grief and at the same time reassuring the populace that the world felt confidence in the orderly transfer of power.

Getting the American people, and others, to accept Lyndon Johnson's succession was probably the major contribution that the media made to society at the time.[32] Its efforts to build up the image of the new president were consistent. From the onset, headlines may have screamed "KENNEDY SLAIN," but they also proclaimed "JOHNSON SWORN IN AS NEW PRESIDENT." For nearly every report on aspects of the mourning, there was a counter-report on positive political action being taken by the new chief executive. In a world made anxious by the threat of nuclear war, the reportage was soothing, particularly to nations abroad.

On the negative side, the media's initial reports were filled with errors, some of which became fuel to flame the enduring controversy about the president's death. The article from *Life* about JFK being shot in the throat from the front, cited above, is only one example. But it was the media's interference with the investigation into the crime that led to the loudest accusations that the press was "making news" instead of merely reporting it (Figure 5.1). The chaotic scenes at the Dallas police headquarters during the course of the assassination weekend were bad enough, said the critics, but journalists compounded their error during Jack Ruby's trial, which took place in Dallas during March 1964.

District Attorney Henry Wade overestimated the number of journalists who converged on Dallas in the aftermath

FIGURE 5.1

Oswald's midnight press conference, held early on November 23. Journalists and their equipment jammed the hallways at Dallas police headquarters during the weekend following the assassination, disrupting the investigations into the murders of President Kennedy and Officer Tippit. *Dallas Times Herald Collection, Sixth Floor Museum Archives*

FIGURE 5.2

Jack Ruby during a rare interview. The media attention surrounding
the 1964 Ruby trial was overwhelming. The nightclub owner was given
the death sentence and died of cancer in 1967 pending a new trial.
Tom C. Dillard, courtesy THE DALLAS MORNING NEWS

of the Kennedy slaying; he said 300, but the number was closer to 100. The circus during the Ruby trial consisted of 308 American news reporters and 68 representatives from fourteen foreign countries.[33] Witnesses had to run a gauntlet outside the Criminal Courts Building in order to testify, a repeat of the journalistic harassment that had characterized the Oswald interrogations (Figure 5.2).

Whether or not Jack Ruby had shot Lee Oswald was not an issue at the trial; millions of television viewers had seen him do it. The big question should have been: how much time will he serve? The Ruby family hired flamboyant San Francisco attorney Melvin Belli as the lead defense attorney. Belli, known as the "king of torts," wore elevator shoes and carried a velvet briefcase. He lost no time blaming the city of Dallas and its atmosphere of hatred for the murder and presented a "psycho-motor epilepsy" defense that dragged up sad details from the suspect's childhood and otherwise turned the trial into a tabloid exposé.[34] The media covered every aspect of the circus. A Dallas jury voted the death penalty. Later, Texas defense attorneys won a repeal of the conviction, based on the issues of admission of evidence and change of venue.

Ruby, a Jew, was kept in the Dallas County Jail at Dealey Plaza. Locals believe that the trial unsettled Ruby's mind and that he came to believe there was a national pogrom against American people of his faith. The nightclub owner became ill during the fall of 1966 and was hospitalized for pneumonia at Parkland. There, doctors discovered that he was suffering from cancer of the lymph glands; he died on January 3, 1967, before the new trial was convened. His motive for the murder, according to his trial: a desire

for fame, an urge to avenge the president's death, and a pathetic wish to spare Jacqueline Kennedy the trauma of attending a trial. The media adopted Belli's theme of Dallas hatred during the trial and even blamed the city for Ruby's death. Eric Sevareid announced Ruby's obituary on the CBS-TV News and added, "Dallas officialdom fumbled to the end."[35]

One can make a case against the national press for the diatribes launched against Dallas in the wake of the Kennedy assassination. Social commentator Christopher Lasch asserted that the media, fearing that the accomplishments of JFK's brief term in office would not measure up to those of Lincoln, deliberately tried to focus attention away from politics and turned instead to "speculation about the dark undercurrents in American life, the unsuspected flaws in the national character, that had led to his murder."[36]

Some have suggested that the traditional liberal leanings of the press may have led to a subconscious hesitancy to focus on the actions of Oswald, a man who professed to belong to a radical wing of liberalism. Harrison Salisbury of the *New York Times* heard the news of the Kennedy shooting and thought of a *right*-wing conspiracy: "Dallas . . . Kennedy . . . violence . . . it seemed an almost inevitable pattern, and my mind leaped instantly to the passion in Dallas that had raged. . . . Dallas had seemed like another country, ranting against *everything*."[37] Where was the *left*-wing Oswald in this train of thought?

One local editor summarized the Dallas view of media behavior toward both Oswald and Ruby: "The regiment of newsmen . . . invaded the city rooms of the two Dallas newspapers, tied up local telephone lines, wrecked reference files, and attempted to boss local picture staffs." The State Bar of Texas roundly attacked the media's role in the death of Oswald and the trial of Ruby, asserting that they "forgot the rules of decency and courtesy, respect for due process of law, respect for the judiciary, and respect for the rights of Lee Harvey Oswald and Jack Ruby to fair trials."[38]

During the investigation into the Kennedy assassination, much commentary surrounded the role that the press may have played in creating a hole through police lines and thus allowing Jack Ruby to get close to his targeted victim. The Warren Commission *Report* chastised the Dallas Police Department for not having managed to get the investigation firmly under control, but it went on to state: "A part of the responsibility for the unfortunate circumstances following the president's death must be borne by the news media. The crowd of newsmen generally failed to respond properly to the demands of the police. . . . the news media, as well as the police authorities . . . must share responsibility for the failure of law enforcement which occurred in connection with the death of Oswald."[39]

The commission also urged journalism to adopt voluntary guidelines to establish "a code of professional conduct" and to avoid further interference with due process.[40] Journalists, however, did not see their role in these investigations in quite the same light. "The suggestion," noted one magazine five years later, "ran into a stone wall seven months later at the 1965 annual meeting of the American Society of Newspaper Editors."[41] Immediately after the Oswald slaying the *New York Times* wrote that the blame for the shooting of the prime suspect fell on "the Dallas police force and the rest of its law-enforcement machinery." The paper *did* admit that the problems were "aided and encouraged by the newspaper, TV, and radio press." But "no matter what the demands of reporters and cameramen may have been," boomed the *Times*, the police should have handled the Oswald transfer privately.[42]

The Kennedy assassination weekend was not the first time that journalists had got out of hand. The law banning cameras and microphones from most trials dated to the mid-1930's, after reporters disrupted the trial of Bruno Richard Hauptmann for the kidnap-murder of aviator Charles Lindbergh's baby.[43] Later, so many unruly reporters accompanied Soviet Premier Nikita Khrushchev on his 1959 American visit to an Iowa farm that the incident came to be known as the Battle of Coon Rapids. Even *New York Times* writer James Reston admitted after the Iowa fiasco, "We were not the observers of history, we were the creators of history."[44]

The shift from observer of history to creator of history has important applications to the issue of the legacy of JFK. How many journalists have mentioned the role that the press might have played in interfering with due process in the Oswald investigation and the Ruby trial? This has not been a dominant theme. On the other hand, TV announcers have frequently reminded audiences how the media *was there* as history unfolded. Television, they say, dominated the weekend coverage, losing more than $32 million in advertising revenues, and CBS is still fond of telling its viewers that anchorman Dan Rather *was there* and that the network undertook an investigation into the assassination after it occurred.[45] In fact, when Rather hosted a 1993 CBS program on JFK, the anchorman introduced the documentary by assuring audiences, "In the three decades CBS has never stopped its own independent investigation, never stopped searching for answers."[46]

The print media has often taken the same approach. UPI may have lost its 1960's power, but the wire-service agency has pointed with understandable pride to the fact that Merriman Smith won the Pulitzer Prize for his reporting on that fateful weekend. The two wire-service commemorative books, raced into print immediately after the assassination, share a tone of self-celebration in keeping with a well-done job of reporting at the time. Tom Wicker and other writers from the *New York Times* have spent decades writing byline articles about the Kennedys while reminding us of the role played by themselves and their paper in covering the first moments after the assassination.[47]

The media played the major role in the dissemination of information following the assassination of the president, and it was definitely the positive force that calmed national anxiety and confusion about the future of the country and the qualifications of the new president. Although this may explain how the rememberers developed such a powerful collective memory, it does not explain the role that the media has played *since* 1963 in reshaping our recollections about JFK and his meaning to American society.

In 1992 Dr. Barbie Zelizer, a journalism professor who wrote her dissertation on the media and the Kennedy assassination, published *Covering the Body*, the title taken from the lingo of the press to describe its role in tracking the activities of a president. Her exhaustive research provides the most in-depth examination of why the media acts somewhat protectively about JFK and particularly about the assassination. Her harsh tone reflects the recent trend toward "media bashing," but she proves several of her points well.

Zelizer argues that journalists have indeed claimed ownership of the assassination tale and have made the "assassination story as much a tale about themselves as about the 35th president of the United States, thus strengthening their position as cultural authorities concerning events of the 'real world.'"[48] The shooting in Dallas, says Zelizer, put television news in the spotlight; the events of November 1963 thus became a benchmark in the professional history of that arm of broadcasting. TV has risen steadily in importance since 1963, so that event remains a critical rite of passage, a part of the "roots" that all members of the profession claim as a part of their collective heritage. Hence TV news has a tendency to hark repeatedly back to the event that gave it importance within its own history. Zelizer also believes that reporters use the Kennedy assassination—a great narrative with a powerful collective memory among the journalistic family and among the audiences that it serves—as a way to strengthen the profession. By feeding the collective memory of the public, journalism also feeds itself.[49]

As a rule, institutional and professional histories are somewhat self-congratulatory, so it is hardly surprising that the retellings of the assassination events have developed a tendency to touch lightly on the fact that journalists may have shared some of the blame for the death of Lee Harvey Oswald. On the issue of media authority to claim ownership of the assassination story, the timing was right—well within the context of the 1960's, when the questioning of traditional modes of authority was the norm. "The old order was being challenged," wrote author David Halberstam, "and it was a rich time for journalists."[50]

Using this pretext of doubt against authority, states Zelizer, the press began to assume the role of arbiter in matters cultural, political, social, and eventually, historical.[51] Today we expect to hear a political speech and then a commentary from a journalist about what the speech meant. This practice postdates 1963. Today, the media claims authority and expertise on a vast array of subjects, reflecting our highly specialized society.

Zelizer reasons that the JFK legacy is one of the important subjects on which the media has claimed specialized knowledge. The avenues that journalists have taken to claim hold of the memory of JFK fall into four main categories: eyewitness testimony (I was there); representative testimony (our station or network was there); investigative testimony (we performed an investigation and we know); and interpretive testimony (let us tell you how it was).[52] All of these approaches and combinations of them are used on every television network and in every major American newspaper and magazine.

The assassination had one side effect that no one might have anticipated: the rise of television news reporters to the status of celebrity stars. It has been a common and unfair allegation that Dan Rather's ascent within the ranks of CBS dates to his prominence as a man on the scene in Dallas after the Kennedy assassination. Similarly, many came to regard Walter Cronkite, 1963 anchor at the CBS network, as the stabilizing force that got them through the emotional trauma of the weekend.

Over time, as the role of the celebrity establishment journalists became more prominent in the retelling of the assassination events, the names of other reporters were dropped from the story. Television news, radio, and photojournalism dominated the assassination weekend; radio was the first messenger but has declined in importance over the years during the frequent retellings of the story.[53] Few of the CBS versions of the assassination during recent years have given credit to Dallas CBS-affiliate newsman Eddie Barker, who was the first person to get confirmation that the president was dead; yet Rather himself gave credit to the Dallas newsman in his book *The Camera Never Blinks*.[54]

Rather's well-known book devotes considerable space to his role in Dallas during the weekend of the assassination.[55] The reporter had come to Dallas to drop off an earlier interview with former Vice President John Nance Garner, who was celebrating a birthday on November 22, 1963. At the local affiliate station, KRLD (now KDFW-TV), Rather learned that the network needed someone to cover a film drop at the end of the motorcade, so he went down to Stemmons Freeway, west of the triple underpass, to pick up the footage. "I had not heard a shot," admitted Rather, but he subsequently played a major role in on-the-scene reports from Dallas over the weekend, using the KRLD studios as a base.[56]

In a national piece run on Tuesday, November 26, Rather's team included a story that northern Dallas schoolchildren applauded the news of the assassination when they heard it over the loudspeaker system. Later, many cities would report similar actions by children who focused their attention only on the announcement that school would be closed. Eddie Barker and the other reporters from Dallas were so enraged by the broadcast that they threw Rather and his associates out of the studio. In his book Rather himself admitted that members of the network team had tried to gather up the film footage owned by KRLD to take with them.

But what happened to Jim Underwood, who did the first media interview with Oswald on November 22, or Dallas cameraman Tom Alyea, who was shooting film while investigators were searching for evidence on the sixth floor of the Depository, or Pierce Allman, who broadcast live from the old warehouse moments after the assassination? They have remained shadows in the endless broadcast retellings of the events of 1963.[57] At least *Dallas Times Herald* photographer Bob Jackson has maintained his prominence for capturing the shooting of Oswald; he won the Pulitzer Prize. In November 1993, Southern Methodist University sponsored a reunion of the reporters who had covered the assassination weekend; the seminar, telecast by C-Span, represented the first serious effort to record these important recollections for posterity.[58]

The media's retellings have blurred the lines between the original event and "the event as told."[59] During the years that I worked on organizing The Sixth Floor Museum, many national journalists questioned Dallas's right to play any role in interpreting the 1963 tragedy. A stringer from *Time*, touring the old Depository building during the 1984 Republican National Convention, was genuinely outraged that Dallas claimed any right to talk about the subject of the assassination. I had to remind her that Dallas *had* the actual site where the assassination had occurred and that millions of people—like her—visited it. She persisted in stating that no museum was needed because everyone remembered the shooting; a young reporter from a college newspaper was standing nearby and gently informed the middle-aged journalist that *she* had been born less than a year before the assassination.

The media's claim to the legacy of JFK has extended to the rest of the Kennedy family. Many young people have questioned me about the vast amount of coverage afforded to the Kennedys and their offspring. One reason for the coverage is that the dynasty is well-known and therefore subject to celebrity scrutiny. But a part of today's enduring focus on the family can be traced to that weekend in November 1963, when the Kennedys openly shared their grief with a nation. The public adopted the members of the clan, and the media has kept us abreast of their activities ever since.

Robert Kennedy's 1968 assassination and funeral were featured on the news, and Edward Kennedy's accident at Chappaquidick topped the headlines in 1969. Senator Kennedy's divorce from Joan Kennedy, and her struggle with alcoholism, also took the spotlight. In recent years the media provided unrelenting attention—TV gave live coverage—to the William Kennedy Smith rape trial in Palm Beach, Florida; young Smith, a nephew of JFK, was acquitted.

Then there was Jackie. The death and funeral of Jacqueline Kennedy Onassis in May 1994 showed the tremendous power the media can wield in shaping a collective memory. In the case of Mrs. Onassis, the press was nearly universal in praising her memory as a widowed first lady. She symbolized grace, elegance, and charm, they chorused. Aristotle Onassis—a Greek and not an American—virtually disappeared as the media retold her story, focusing on her years as the regal consort of John F. Kennedy.

I spoke at length with some members of the new generation during the mourning and learned that many were shocked by the media attention. I was surprised that many younger Americans had never heard Jackie Kennedy's voice and knew her only through reruns of home movies, news features, or the 1963 state funeral, where she never spoke an audible word. She had remained almost invisible during most of their lives, and then suddenly, she was everywhere.

The media honored the mourning by issuing a spate of memorial features on Jacqueline Bouvier Kennedy Onassis; these editions bore similarities to those of 1963 in the way that they extolled virtue, never vice, and in the way that rememberers snapped them up as souvenirs of the elusive but illustrious "Jackie O." *Life* magazine ran "Remembering Jackie: A Life in Pictures," reminding its readers that she had been on its cover eighteen times.[60] Women friends of my age group mourned her passing as the death of American elegance; we had abandoned our gloves to pursue careers. She pursued a career with her gloves firmly in place.

One young friend asked me how Jacqueline Onassis managed to avoid criticism by the media for her failed marriage to Onassis and her long relationship with a married man. "She had already paid her dues," I said. She had paid them in 1963. The dignified tone of the media coverage threw the spotlight clearly on Jacqueline Onassis's main legacy, her outstanding courage as a national heroine after the tragedy in Dallas. Had she stumbled then, many might have gone down with her. The collective memory won in the end, and the media gave her credit for her victory. Ari Onassis, JFK's supposed escapades, and all of the other topics paled, then virtually disappeared, against the importance of her awesome display of strength in November 1963. Perhaps the media sensed that she had paid a high enough price for what Edward Kennedy called "the glare of a million lights."[61]

Those lights recorded her struggle to honor her husband and his office and, later, her determination to find herself and lead a normal life. Comments written in The Sixth Floor Museum memory books on the days immediately after her death gave support to the public's insistence on remembering Jacqueline Bouvier Kennedy, not Jackie Onassis. "Together at last," wrote one visitor. From others came, "May you both rest in peace," and finally, "Camelot is over but not forgotten."[62]

THE MEDIA AND THE CRITICS

The *New York Times* conducted its own investigation into the assassination between late November 1963 and early January 1964. In recalling the thrust of the *Times* probe, Harrison Salisbury noted that the paper assumed four major scenarios:

1. Oswald was innocent.
2. Oswald was the lone, deranged killer.
3. Oswald was a communist agent.
4. Oswald was an agent of a right-wing conspiracy.[63]

The prevailing assumption about the cause of the crime began and ended with the person of Lee Harvey Oswald; the field of inquiry into possible conspiracy was narrow, limited to the communists and the right wing. The *Times* satisfied itself that Oswald was the assassin and abandoned its investigation early in 1964. Context is again important here: best-selling spy novels and a general distrust of government intelligence agencies—the investigators for the Warren Commission—did not then reign high among the people.

Context is a major consideration in assessing the media's role in coverage of the work of the Warren Commission. In a way the press became a handmaiden to help the government assure its citizens that order had been restored to the nation. *Time* ran a special feature highlighting the major findings of the commission and summarized, "In its final form, the commission's report was amazing in its detail, remarkable in its judicious caution and restraint, yet utterly convincing in its major conclusions."[64] The *New York Times* not only backed the report but cooperated with the government and Bantam books to rush seven hundred thousand copies of a special-edition volume into print within a matter of hours. Zelizer loses sight of historical context by objecting to the fact that most of the media made little or no effort to stand back from the investigation and comment on it dispassionately.[65]

Long before the Warren Commission issued its final conclusions, most of the details had already been leaked to the press.[66] Magazines like *Time*, *Newsweek*, and *Life* had kept readers abreast of the investigation into the assassination during late 1963 and most of 1964. *Life*'s cover in February 1964 showed the photograph of Oswald holding his weapons; the accompanying story left the suspect's guilt in little doubt. Critics of the government's investigation said the *Life* photo had been altered; *Life* admitted that it had retouched the photo before using it on the cover.[67]

Only months earlier the press had played an exceptionally active role in helping the government soothe the populace about the orderly transfer of power. In my view, this spirit of cooperation with the government dominated the times; it was small surprise that the major media endorsed

a study that promised to lay the troubling matter to rest.

I remember when the Warren *Report* came out. I was satisfied to accept the findings that Oswald, acting alone, had killed the president. The media had been preparing me to accept this conclusion for months. When the *Report* was issued, the press buried us in details about its effectiveness: the FBI had conducted twenty-five thousand interviews; the *Report* alone contained more than eight hundred pages; there were millions of pages of supporting documents; no stone had been left unturned. The niggling questions, said the press, would be of concern only to historians and dramatists. Why worry? After all, the members of the Warren Commission were, in the words of one congressman, "the very best there were."[68]

When questions began to be raised about the quality of the Warren Commission investigation, the nation's major news organizations were defensive and did not support the questioners. This reaction was still within the context of the times. Writers who published books against the official conclusions were branded "critics" or "buffs," and even though newspapers reported on their efforts, some of the commentary was snide and occasionally derisive.

Swipes at the critics of the Warren *Report* have shown up in nearly all forms of media during the years. If today's non-rememberers logically wonder how *Life* magazine managed to buy the single most important piece of visual evidence associated with such a major crime, one must consider the times. *Life* later assured its readers that the government had said it was content to work from a copy, leaving ownership of the original evidence to the private sector.[69] Nevertheless, audiences did not see the Zapruder film on television for nearly twelve years after the shooting; its airing in 1975 was one factor that moved Congress to fund another official investigation into the crime.

Pre-release coverage of Edward Jay Epstein's 1966 *Inquest*, the first real probe into the inner workings of the Warren Commission, was favorable in Dallas; but then a Los Angeles paper tried to tie Epstein to the more controversial author Mark Lane, and the Dallas reporters changed their minds.[70] Epstein, who became a highly respected political scientist, had researched the book for his master's degree at Cornell. His thesis, now largely accepted, was that the Warren Commission searched more for "political" than legal truth, was plagued by internal disputes, and was led by a group of very busy men who did not attend all the work sessions.[71] The notion that Oswald was the shooter, he said, was never really questioned by the government.

The early critical books by foreign-based writers such as Thomas Buchanan and Leo Sauvage had been easier to dismiss—as products for foreigners who were culturally predisposed to believe in the idea of conspiracy. One American news account in 1966 took exactly this view. "In Europe, many people are inclined to think that [it] was a political assassination. . . . But in the United States, one doesn't find the conspiracy element, except in the case of Abraham Lincoln. All of the others . . . were done by 'loners,' the work of a single, disturbed individual."[72]

Epstein's ties to the academy made him much more difficult to discredit and impossible to ignore. Nevertheless, *Look* magazine dismissed the book and warned its readers that *Inquest* might be "dangerously deceptive." The reviewer was "convinced that Epstein was guilty of the very sins of which he accused the Warren Commission: distortion, ignoring testimony, sifting the evidence."[73] *Look*'s reviewer objected to the lack of detail that the author had devoted to the investigative aspects of the case. Yet Epstein's main work had been an examination of the inner workings of the commission itself, not a full-blown investigation of the crime.

In truth, the media had a tendency either to minimize the critics or to ignore them.[74] Attorney Mark Lane's landmark best-seller, *Rush to Judgment*, released in 1966, got poor reviews in the Dallas papers, probably because Lane was already a controversial figure. The conservative *Dallas Morning News* spent much space recounting Lane's role as attorney for Oswald's mother, Marguerite Oswald, and informed readers that Lane had also been arrested during the freedom rides in 1961 and was involved with the NAACP, the American Civil Liberties Union, and Americans for Democratic Action. The *News* repeated the cry from many other journalistic organs of the day in calling on Lane and other writers to come up with another suspect for the murder.[75]

The *Dallas Times Herald* noted somewhat coolly that Lane's book had been turned down by fifteen publishers before Epstein's more academic *Inquest* had opened the door at Holt, Rinehart. Here was a rather subtle attempt to tie Epstein to Lane. The paper duly noted that whereas Epstein's book had sold twenty thousand copies in hardback, Lane's sold thirty thousand copies in two weeks.[76] Lane's conspiracy book became a top best-seller of the year. Despite the put-downs from the media, the critics began to stake a claim as the legitimate spokesmen about the assassination.

Books like *Rush to Judgment* and disclosures like those made by the Clark panels in 1966–68 that the Bethesda doctors had made mistakes in the placement of one of President Kennedy's wounds forced the media to rethink its earlier position about the validity of the original Warren Commission investigation. When the media did get on the "reopen the investigation bandwagon," however, few major journalistic institutions assumed a leadership role. CBS television did a report in 1967, leading to an endorsement of the Warren Commission findings. Dan Rather later recalled: "CBS had spent roughly a half million dollars of their money and a year of my time on a show that set out to disprove the Warren Commission findings. And we could not do so."[77]

Life called for a new probe in 1966 but would not allow Professor Josiah Thompson, author of *Six Seconds in Dallas*, to publish the still photos from the Zapruder film that the magazine kept in its possession. The former philosophy professor had to resort to drawings instead.[78]

The media focused attention on New Orleans District Attorney Jim Garrison's conspiracy investigation in 1967–69, but the tone of some reportage was skeptical. In March 1967, two years before the end of the Garrison inquiry, *Newsweek*, noting the DA's "wide-ranging accusations," assured readers that top federal government officials were leery of Garrison's claims, and predicted that the Louisiana investigation would end up "on a garbage dump."[79]

This provides a clue to the thinking of the day: the reporter assumed that the federal government would not lie to the people; therefore, Garrison's claims must be false. Although the Garrison investigation ended up being something of a fiasco, many readers today would find *Newsweek*'s tone somewhat biased. The Sixties was a very different time. The most interesting early articles about conspiracy theories

appeared in more esoteric journals, including *Minority of One, Ramparts,* and *Esquire.*[80]

Then came Watergate, and the media took a different approach. Separate disclosures during the mid-1970's that the FBI, the Secret Service, and the CIA had withheld information from the Warren Commission fueled the flames of controversy over the questions surrounding the assassination. This and the growing skepticism about government in general gave the critics a forum for their theories. If people in government had lied to Americans about Vietnam, Watergate, and later Iran-gate, said many, then they probably had lied about the Kennedy assassination as well. Ironically, the media's retelling of its important role in the events surrounding the assassination had the side effect of reminding audiences that there were unanswered questions about the death of the president. Eventually the press and the critics declared something of a stalemate, each side claiming a right to tell the story of the Kennedy assassination in its own way.[81]

Although the press did not provide adequate coverage of the findings of the House Select Committee investigation in 1977–79, the media deserves some credit for having a "nose for news."[82] The public interest in an official investigation in 1977 into the assassination was much less than the interest expressed in 1964. Many people had become cynical about government and its ability to function effectively on behalf of the American people. Some of this wariness was undoubtedly leveled at the House Committee probe. The *real* news was in the acoustic analysis that led to a vote in favor of conspiracy, and the media focused on this revelation, almost to the exclusion of much of the rest of the data.

After the 1982 National Academy of Sciences panel dismissed the validity of the House Committee scientist's original acoustical conclusions, the entire congressional investigation practically vanished from the reports about the assassination. The committee had more than the acoustic evidence on which to base its argument for a conspiracy, but the public did not clamor for a deeper probe.[83] Few later media reports relied on the House probe's scientific findings, some of which used techniques that had not been available to the Warren Commission in 1964. Instead, there was a trend toward reasserting the validity of the Warren panel's work, despite the disclosures of its weaknesses during the 1960's and 1970's.

During the years following the Dallas shooting, the media slowly developed a mode of reporting that resembled history. Zelizer asserts that journalists believed "they could play the role of historians better than historians themselves."[84] Yet journalists have been cautious in areas where professional historians have studied, most notably JFK's life and political career. The media has not tried to replace historians, but they roam freely over ground that has not yet been claimed by historiography.

In fact, historians as a group have not yet tried to assume authority for explaining the assassination; they have been waiting for the emotionalism of living memory to die before they launch their examinations into the record. They are also waiting for documents to be declassified and made available for research. As long as papers concerning the assassination remain sealed in government archives, historians will be content to wait.

With some exceptions, the media has always recognized that the legacy of JFK would eventually fall under the stewardship of historians. We are experiencing the awkward transition between recording history and interpreting history. The Kennedy books by Theodore White, Hugh Sidey, Henry Fairlee, Ben Bradlee, and Pierre Salinger will all be a part of the record that historians review in the future.[85]

OLIVER STONE'S *JFK*

Zelizer's thesis that the media was overly protective of its authority to speak on the assassination was tested with the making of Oliver Stone's movie *JFK*. In my view, the establishment (old East Coast) press went too far in its negative coverage of the making and airing of the 1991 Hollywood film. Academy Award–winning director Oliver Stone created an "alternate [conspiracy] myth to the Warren Commission myth," and the media attacked him.[86]

In 1964 the *New York Times*, copublisher of the Warren *Report* Bantam edition, wrote in its introduction to the book that the remaining questions about the assassination would be left to historians and dramatists. When Stone, definitely a dramatist, focused his artistic talents against the Warren *Report* a quarter century later, the *Times* marshaled its forces and devoted nearly "30 articles, op-eds, letters, notes, addenda, editorials and columns to attacks on the film."[87] The media seems to have forgotten that Stone was a dramatist with an artistic vision shaped by his personal needs, a vision that had little or nothing to do with history.

Stone, who was born in 1946, admitted that the film's goal was to "remind people how much our nation and our world lost when President Kennedy died."[88] He was speaking of his own sense of *personal* loss, which he had translated into a major film. To support his right to portray the JFK story in his own way, he quoted Thomas Jefferson: "Eternal vigilance is the price of Liberty."[89] The popular filmmaker became the crusading vigilante, demanding that all records pertaining to the assassination be released. "The real issue is trusting the people with their own history," he wrote. "The real issue is opening all the files . . . only then can we start to have a real democracy."[90]

The controversy over the Stone movie gave nearly every major journalist who had ever been on the scene in Dallas an excuse to repeat the tale of his or her historic role and to use this accident of geography as a qualification to attack or support the film. Stone's decision to base his drama on the New Orleans probe conducted by District Attorney Jim Garrison in the 1960's was enough to dismay most journalists, many of whom had dutifully covered this investigation only to learn during the trial that the major witnesses included a drug addict who had witnessed an important encounter while shooting up on heroin, a man who regularly fingerprinted his child to be sure of the youngster's identity, and an assortment of quasi-misfits who embarrassed everyone involved in, or observing, the case.[91]

The film reopened the public discussion over Kennedy's plans about Vietnam and how they might have led to a plot to assassinate him. Historians and assassination researchers had little proof that Kennedy actually planned to withdraw *all* troops from Southeast Asia; the movie nevertheless tried to make a case that Kennedy wanted to end the war, and it hinted that the military and industrial complex might have killed him for this plan. Oliver Stone had served in Vietnam, and his lingering anger about the war had been expressed earlier both in *Platoon* and in *Born on the Fourth of July*. The Vietnam theme has appeared in other films that postdate *JFK*. Although film critics may have understood Stone's tendency to focus on the war, the news reporters who appointed themselves historians and film critics apparently were unaware of the director's emotional involvement with the Asian conflict.

George Lardner, a *Washington Post* reporter who had covered the Garrison investigation, launched a virulent attack against the movie while it was still being filmed. Lardner's piece, "Dallas in Wonderland," used an early draft of the script provided by a concerned critic and accused Stone of trying to pass himself off as a "cinematic historian."[92] Apparently it never occurred to Lardner that neither he nor the *Post* also had no particular qualifications in the profession of history.

The feisty director took shelter behind his right to freedom of artistic expression and fired off a counterattack on June 2 under the title "A Higher Truth?" He called the movie a "metaphor for all those doubts, suspicions, and unanswered questions" about the crime of the century.[93] The battle was joined. During the ensuing months, and long after the release of the movie nationwide on December 21, 1991, the press was full of attacks and counterattacks, with most of the attackers drawn from the news media and from the ranks of the critics. Both groups clearly resented Stone's invasion into previously protected turf and his arrogant attitude about his rights to treat historical events in accordance with his own personal artistic ideas.

Stone dedicated the film to the nonrememberers, a smart move on his part. Freed from the restraint of memory, this audience was the most susceptible to his message. "History is being distorted, and to many, fiction had become fact," lamented the *American Bar Association Journal*. Stone retorted, "You are defending an indefensible position."[94] The director appeared on television to present his case on morning and evening talk shows. Millions of Americans flocked to see the film, which reportedly grossed more than $196 million worldwide.[95]

The nation engaged in a generational discussion between those who remembered and those who did not about the accuracy of the movie's content and its relevance to history. The nonrememberers led the charge to require an opening of all sealed government files. Stone and the film became a catalyst for change. Norman Mailer, whose recent *Harlot's Ghost* had referenced the JFK assassination, penned a review of the film for *Vanity Fair* proclaiming the assassination "a psychic phenomenon, a creature in the dream life of the nation."[96] In his literary way Mailer recast the media as part of the larger "Washington Club" and chided them all for having "circled their wagons around the lone assassin."[97] The blast against the establishment press had the full force of feeling from the decade of the 1960's.

Well-known media specialist Frank Mankiewicz was hired by Stone to monitor the storm. He summed up the news reporters' objections to the movie rather well. "So long as the criticism was left to those easily criticized by the mainstream press, the Crime of the Century remained below the surface of American mainstream consciousness," Mankiewicz wrote in the introduction to Stone's *JFK: The Book of the Film*.[98] The book included transcripts of ninety-seven printed reactions to the film and many of Stone's rejoinders. Former Warren Commission principals Gerald Ford and David Belin added their opinions, along with such

FIGURE 5.3
Oliver Stone cartoon. ©1995 *DAYTON DAILY NEWS. Distributed by Tribune Media Services. Reprinted with permission.*

notables as Tom Wicker, Arthur Schlesinger, and critic-journalist Robert Sam Anson.

Former President Ford and Belin condemned "the big lie—the assertion that the top echelons of our government were conspiratorially involved in the assassination, and that Lee Harvey Oswald was not the lone gunman. . . . false charges of this kind are a desecration to the memory of President Kennedy."[99] Stone fired back: "Belin and former President Gerald Ford are the last of a dying breed: Warren Commission apologists. Today, not even the government itself contends the Warren Commission investigation . . . was an adequate one."[100]

Stone made a blanket comment to complaints from Wicker, Dan Rather, and news reporters who had a claim to Dallas: "History may be too important to leave to newsmen."[101] The filmmaker consistently chided the media for its adherence to the Warren *Report.* The Warren Commission defense was, he wrote, "obsolete, highly selective information, printed many times before over the past twenty-eight years, not believed by 75 percent of the American people or even supported by the conservative findings of the HSCA that JFK was killed as the result of a 'probable' conspiracy."[102] Stone had at least done his homework; the reportage from some of the media suggested that the journalists were unfamiliar with the work performed by the House Select Committee and had not done much research into the assassination since the 1960's.

Film critic Roger Ebert was among a group of prominent writers who became alarmed at the number of news reporters passing themselves off as qualified cinema experts. Ebert penned a piece for Universal Press Syndicate. "It is always a little daunting," he wrote, "when the deep thinkers of the editorial department venture out to the movies. . . . There is condescension in their voices when they return."[103] Another film critic, for the *Washingtonian,* saw *JFK* and gave it three and one-half stars; the rating so infuriated her editor that he pulled the review, so she resigned in protest.[104]

Too many people lost sight of the fact that *JFK* was a movie, a piece of dramatic art produced and directed by a provocative Hollywood showman. Stone based his authority on his qualifications as an artist and as a baby boomer, a member of the first large youth generation to question government authority. He invented characters and distorted others to fit them into his creative narrative vision.

His portrayal of Garrison as Everyman was clearly metaphoric, in his eyes, of all the ills suffered by individuals at the hands of an evil government aided by a compliant press. The film was high drama to be sure, hinting that blame for the assassination *might* belong to virtually every high organ of government, with big business, the Dallas police force, and even LBJ standing in the wings.

One of the reasons the critics were so upset was the fear that people who did not remember the assassination would believe that *JFK* was documentary history (Figure 5.3). They should not have worried. An unscientific NBC *Today* poll, taken in February 1992, showed that 94% of the survey disbelieved the Warren Commission's conclusion that Oswald was the lone assassin.[105] By 1993, however, a CNN poll found that pro-conspiracy feeling among the public had receded to its more traditional level of 75%. People recognized that *JFK* was not history as an accurate portrayal of proven facts but was a think piece about human disappointments and that it reflected Oliver Stone's personal ideas and frustrations. The film was not a documentary about the work of the critics but was a simplistic tale of the failed quest of one character to right the wrongs in American society. Stone staged the film to take place in 1969, before the disclosures of the 1970's or the House Committee investigation; it was only a windowpane in the larger window into the history of the assassination itself.[106]

Stone's contribution to history did not lie in the film but in what he made of it as a piece of propaganda. He called on *your* generation to end the continued government classification of documents. Journalist Bill Moyers remarked, "I think it is quite interesting that it's Oliver Stone that's forcing Congress to open up the files and not *The Washington Post, The New York Times,* or CBS."[107] One Dallas attorney seconded Moyers's opinion: "If the politicians, pundits and members of the media who have steadfastly remained apologists for the Warren Commission had devoted the same time and energy that they have spent attacking Mr. Stone and the movie 'JFK' in trying to bring the conspirators to justice, the crime of the century might be solved."[108]

By mid-January 1992 the media, and even Gerald Ford, offered their support for the early release of the government files. The documents had been sealed to await the scrutiny of historians.[109] Congress passed the Assassination Materials Disclosure Act in 1992, and the first batch of declassified documents was released late in August 1993.[110] Once the documents are opened for review, more historians may conduct research into this troubling chapter from the past.

On one level the movie *JFK* captured the essence of the rift among rememberers about how they choose to judge the root cause of the death of President Kennedy. The preservers came forth to defend the Warren *Report*, searchers used the movie to condemn it. Clearly, Stone thought the media had swayed too subjectively into the camp of the preservers, so he skewed the film toward the searchers.

Stone's film set off a debate at the actual scene of the crime. Again, the question of stewardship was at the core of the controversy, but this time it was not stewardship of retellings but stewardship of the assassination site itself. Oliver Stone had shot parts of *Talk Radio* and *Born on the Fourth of July* in Dallas, and he returned to the city for a major part of the shooting of *JFK.* He approached the city, the county, and major property owners around Dealey Plaza to obtain permission to restore the assassination scene to its original 1963 appearance. Furthermore, his exacting approach to the re-creation of the murder required that traffic be diverted around the plaza for more than two weeks. The Hollywood director's investment in the local shoot was reputed to be in the area of $10 million, a definite boost to the depressed local economy and to the many technical film professionals based in the Dallas area.

Stone's representatives asked to disassemble all of the exhibits in The Sixth Floor Museum and to film from the sniper's perch there. The county and the museum's board of directors claimed that preservation of the space and ongoing operations of the exhibit for the public had to take precedence over Stone's artistic quest for an accurate reconstruction of the event.[111] The county offered Stone access to the unrestored seventh floor for use as his "set." The museum had taken stock film footage from the sniper's perch and other sixth-floor locations before the space had been transformed into the museum. It offered this footage and the original artifacts from the Depository's second-floor lunchroom as models for the film's re-creation of that space, which was assembled in a nearby building. But the county and the museum held firm against allowing Stone access to the sniper's perch and refused to permit disassembling of the museum exhibits.

Stone abandoned his idea of dismounting the displays, but he persisted in his request to film from the corner window. Local leaders feared that allowing Stone access to the sixth-floor space might be construed as a commercialization of the site or even as an indirect endorsement of the director's "alternate myth to the Warren Commission myth." As the controversy over the assassination had grown during the years since 1963, the community had withdrawn from active debate. The *Dallas Times Herald* now entered the discussion and asked its readers in a call-in poll to comment on the propriety of allowing Oliver Stone to film in the sniper's perch.[112] Three out of four Dallasites said yes. Permission was granted, and the deal was cut. The crew agreed to film from the sniper's perch after visitors' hours.

The unscientific newspaper poll indicated a shift from Dallas's earlier objections to any commercialization of the assassination site. After officials finally agreed to allow access to the sniper's perch, the matter of payment for use of the space was left to museum President Dave Fox to negotiate with Stone's representatives. At that time The Sixth Floor Museum had a five-figure private debt from a loan that had been negotiated in 1989 to cover the shortfall in the fund-raising. Stone made a substantial contribution to the museum, effectively retiring the loan.

Arguments over stewardship rights at historic sites have raged in countless American cities, and it is significant that the Dallas debate, like so many before it, ended up in a workable compromise that did no permanent harm to the premises. The filming itself took on an air that blended carnival and surrealism. One local paper launched a "Kevin Watch" for readers who spotted actor Kevin Costner at local nightspots. Hostesses clamored to get Stone to attend parties and charity benefits. More than ten thousand people responded to the director's call for movie extras.

The active discussion prompted by the controversy was helpful to the community, although there was little agreement. City Councilman Al Lipscomb was in favor of the Dallas film shooting. "We need a good therapeutic . . . ," he said, "to make sure there will be no residue of the past."[113]

Dallas Morning News columnist William Murchison cast the Hollywood intrusion as a "wimp-out" for the city. "Oliver Stone's traffic jams are the abasement we deserve," fumed Murchison. "He gets to block traffic and insult the whole city because . . . we wouldn't want such a man thinking ill of Dallas. . . . How tame, how servile and cringing is the spirit of the Old West."[114]

Set designers trimmed the trees back in Dealey Plaza and even repainted the trim on buildings to match their appearance in 1963. One of the second-floor offices in my office building at 501 Elm—formerly the Dal-Tex building, where Zapruder had his office—was completely refitted as another location for a gunman. A roving "sniper" went from one spot to another to fire his rifle at the motorcade.

Since my office was on the fourth floor at 501 Elm, I had a front-seat view of the Dallas filming. First there were partial reenactments of the motorcade passing through the park, then full-dress rehearsals. Filming often lasted until late in the day to maximize the lighting, so many of the tenants in the building did not try to exit the parking garage until the crews had left. The repeated gunfire set off subliminal reactions in some office workers. Several were lethargic, and others spent more time than usual away from the office during normal working hours. Stone's special effects crew used a nearby parking lot to test a prosthesis of the president's head, which would be worn by the actor playing JFK. During the trials, technicians blew up the false heads to check on authenticity. The West End Pub, located near the movie set, reported a substantial increase in business.

On the day that Stone was scheduled to hold the last dress rehearsal for the motorcade sequence, I got a call from *Dallas Morning News* columnist and humor author Maryln Schwartz. She wanted to see the filming from The Sixth Floor Museum. We went over to the museum and watched the filming from our vantage point overlooking the park. All the characters were there, portrayed by actors and dressed as they had been in 1963. I spotted the Newmans with their sons, Charles Brehm and his little boy, Jean Hill and Mary Moorman, and Abraham Zapruder with his receptionist. Maryln asked where the sniper was, and I looked around. "They're everywhere," I said, noting that Stone had stationed shooters in a variety of locations around Dealey Plaza. When the big blue limousine, flags flying, turned into the park, the extras waved and cheered just as the actual witnesses had done so many years before. Photographers clicked their cameras while President Kennedy and his pink-suited wife waved to the crowd.

We watched the motorcade pass below us twice; each time, the assassination re-creation lasted for mere seconds. It was amazing. I was trying to capture the larger scene and realized that I could not get a grasp of the events as they were unfolding below me (Figure 5.4). On the second pass-through I focused on the limousine itself and was able to recall a few more details of what I had seen.

A FUTURE ROLE?

After *JFK* proved to be a commercial success, the media softened its tone for a while and even openly acknowledged that the public was deeply divided over the issue of who shot JFK. One incident of admirable restraint followed the June 1993 death of John Connally; assassination researchers

FIGURE 5.4
A scene from Oliver Stone's film *JFK*. In 1991 Stone restored Dealey Plaza
and reenacted the assassination for his mammoth conspiracy film.
David Woo, courtesy THE DALLAS MORNING NEWS

requested that the former governor's family arrange to have the remaining bullet fragments in his wrist investigated.[115] Connally had long held to his claim that he had been wounded by a separate bullet from the one that injured President Kennedy in the back and throat; the researchers wanted the procedure to be performed posthumously.

Their timing was terrible. The request went to the Justice Department, and the FBI presented the idea to the grief-stricken Connallys at the very time they were preparing to bury the former governor. The Connallys refused. In an editorial in *The Dallas Morning News* on June 24, 1993, the paper chose to present both sides of the argument for exhumation and only then elected to back the family as the final arbiter in the matter.

During the early fall of 1993, Gerald Posner's *Case Closed* was released. The book's major thesis held that Oswald was the lone assassin. Suddenly, some of the mainstream press resumed its Sixties tone. Before the book's publication date, *U.S. News & World Report's* August 30/September 6 issue devoted its cover and seventeen pages to *Case Closed*.[116] "A brilliant new book . . . makes an airtight case against JFK's killer," proclaimed the magazine.[117] As for Stone and the three decades of critical writings, the magazine dismissed them as "hobbyists and profiteers."[118] The *New York Times* book review for November 21 was titled "The Most Durable Assassination Theory: Oswald Did It Alone."[119] The *Times* even agreed to run a full-page ad for the book by Random House, which viciously attacked several of the leading assassination researchers.

By asserting that there was no evidence tying Oswald to a possible conspiracy, Posner opened up the proverbial Pandora's box of information amassed by the searchers during the two decades since passage of the Freedom of Information Act. Journalists who offered reviews of *Case Closed* needed to be familiar with these hundreds of thousands of pages of documents, plus the independent data gathered by the critics, in order to perform an adequate critique of Posner's work. By 1993 the subject of the assassination was too complex to pass over lightly, yet many in the media did just that.

Posner's book did not receive universal praise among the press. Patricia Holt of the *San Francisco Chronicle* did some checking. Posner's computer analysis, conducted by Failure Analysis of California, was offered up to provide proof for the single-bullet theory and to show that all the trajectories matched up with shots from the Depository. When I read the book, I got the impression that the analysis had been prepared for Posner. So did others. For instance, in "Computer-Aided Probe: Oswald Acted Alone," the *Chicago Sun Times* lauded the book in a reprise of the Reuters wire story and noted that Posner had "used the most advanced computer technologies available" to prove his case.[120] But Holt called the company and discovered that the analysis had been prepared for a mock trial at the 1992 American Bar Association convention.[121] The company had prepared materials for the use of both the prosecution and the defense, said Holt, and the trial had ended with a hung jury. Furthermore, reported the *Chronicle*, Roger McCarthy, the CEO of Failure Analysis, had testified for the defense and later appeared on a California talk show, where he told the host "he thought Oswald did not do it alone."[122] This fact was not widely reported by the media after it was disclosed; Posner clarified the issue in the revised, paperback edition of *Case Closed*, issued in 1994.[123]

A few other journalists questioned aspects of Posner's book.[124] The *Washington Post* summarized *Case Closed* as "another case for the prosecution," and the London *Economist* cautioned its readers, "The book . . . does little more than smugly slant every piece of disputed evidence in favor of the lone-assassin theory."[125] Publications widely read by the assassination research community devoted ample space to denunciations of some of Posner's conclusions, but this literature was largely ignored by the mainstream media.[126]

Regardless of claims of bias and the media's need to exert some authority as official spokesmen on matters of the Kennedys and the assassination, there is growing evidence that Americans take major network journalists' reports with something of a grain of salt. For example, the television news magazine *Prime Time Live* devoted a segment of its program on March 11, 1993, to addressing the eight thousand letters that it had received citing an anti-Bush bias in reporting during the 1992 presidential campaign. The commentator seemed surprised by the public's accusation. *Time*, commenting on the addition of an anchorwoman to join Dan Rather on the *CBS Evening News* in 1993, titled its article "Does Connie Chung Matter?" and cited the fact that only one in thirteen Americans under the age of thirty-five bothered to watch network news at all.[127] The distrust of media news felt by my generation seems to be even stronger in yours. *The Dallas Morning News* ran a headline story, "Media Credibility Sinking," that acknowledged that only 17% of the nation believed the media was doing a "very good job." The reason? The news had become "elitist," with too many celebrity reporters to suit the tastes of average people.[128]

Perhaps it was an accident of history that the death of President Kennedy became one of the keystones around which television news came to define its own profession. We all need roots. The press has a valid claim to speak with authority on the subject of JFK and his legacy, but the media does not *own* the subject. In the long memory of history, the storytellers are never more important than the story itself.

CHAPTER 6

JFK as Commemoration

Our consumer society is fond of historic sites and other tangible relics from yesteryear: they are the past as concrete products that one can see, walk in, feel, touch (sometimes), and "buy into." They are history in a form as experiential as television itself. As participation in academic history has waned since the 1960's, appreciation and consumption of the public history offered at these sites has blossomed.[1] "Heritage tourism" is the name for this type of consumerism, and it is a major U.S. growth industry. Presidential commemorative sites are among the most popular. One historian calls them the "bridges between then and now" and reasons that since 1980, their primary appeal has been nostalgic.[2] Much of public history deals with the interpretation of the relics from the past, be they beds that George Washington slept in, homes that Founding Fathers lived and died in, or battlefields and other sites of tragedy that are deemed to have altered the course of U.S. history.

Like other mythical figures before him, Kennedy has generated his share of commemoration. "What pleases the nostalgist," says historian David Lowenthal, is "not so much the past itself, as its supposed aspirations, less the memory of what actually was, than of what was once thought possible."[3] This is the essence of the Kennedy myth: the elusive but infinitely alluring promise of *what might have been.*[4]

The commemorative trend for things associated or remindful of JFK began shortly after his death. Americans purchased the memorial editions of magazines and carefully squirreled them away for some undetermined tomorrow. Six months after the assassination the *Dallas Times Herald* reported on the incredible number of "shrines" that were being dedicated to the memory of the slain president. There were tributes in more than two dozen West German cities, said the newspaper. Dublin named a concert hall for Kennedy; literally thousands of foreign streets and squares were renamed in honor of the American president. The Turkish Boy Scouts planted four million trees in Istanbul and called the park the Kennedy Forest.[5]

The Steinberg Collection at the John F. Kennedy Library contains perhaps the most extensive record of all the memorials around the world dedicated to the late president. Stamps topped the list; just about every country in the world except China issued a Kennedy commemorative stamp. Schools came next; there were more than forty schools named for Kennedy in Argentina alone. There were mountains, highways, bridges, boats, Knights of Columbus lodges, civic and cultural centers, statues, plaques, and busts dedicated to the late president. The variety was as creative as the human spirit itself (see image on opposite page). The United States issued its own commemorative stamp, selling more than one million of them in Dallas on the first day of issue.[6] Artists paid tribute in oils, wood, and other materials. Decades after the shooting, Kennedy half-dollars are hard to find in circulation. People still collect them.

Some commemorations were lofty; others were more down-to-earth. Less than four months after the funeral, composer Igor Stravinsky announced plans to write a choral tribute to the slain president.[7] In 1964 ten African-American singers and instrumentalists released an album of eleven songs, *Can't Keep from Cryin': Topical Blues on the Death of President Kennedy.*[8] So many poems were written that no one could keep count. Historian Thomas Brown notes that the first wave of commemorations, following closely on the heels of the emotional shock of the assassination, "reflected the desire to honor Kennedy as a symbol of national and universal ideals."[9] There it is: the symbolism of myth, Kennedy as inspirer.

In the United States, four major memorial sites dedicated to JFK were created during the three decades that followed his death. Kennedy's grave site at Arlington National Cemetery was the first to be established and is still visited by millions (Figure 6.1). The John F. Kennedy Center for the Performing Arts in Washington, D.C., was erected later during the 1960's. The John F. Kennedy Library and Museum in Massachusetts opened to the public in 1979, and The Sixth Floor Museum at the assassination site in Dallas opened in 1989.

Of these four it is appropriate that two memorials deal with the enduring, positive qualities associated with Kennedy's life, one is the tomb of the fallen hero, and the last provides historical interpretation at Dealey Plaza, the site of his death. The grave site, the Kennedy Center, and the Kennedy Library were clearly intended as memorials, but the assassination site was transformed into one by the public.

Regarding the Kennedy Center, the connection between JFK and the arts is somewhat ethereal, like its namesake (Figure 6.2). It was Jacqueline Kennedy who brought famous artists to the White House, but John F. Kennedy as president promoted the arts and history and helped lay the groundwork for formal legislation to create the two main federal cultural-support programs: the National Endowment for the Arts and the National Endowment for the Humanities. The law was passed under the stewardship of Lyndon Johnson after Kennedy's death. During the Eisenhower administration in 1958, Congress had authorized the creation of a "National Cultural Center" in Washington. Kennedy extended the legislation, and after the assassination the government decided to name the planned facility for the slain president.[10]

FIGURE 6.1
An early view of JFK's grave, in 1964. Every year, millions of people visit the site at Arlington National Cemetery. *Courtesy, John F. Kennedy Library*

In December 1963, LBJ asked Congress to move forward with the program; within a month Congress approved $15.5 million to match private commitments.[11] Noted American architect Edward Durell Stone was selected to design the facility, and the groundbreaking took place in December 1964. Since its opening in 1971, the Kennedy Center has hosted top talent from around the world; its multiple performance halls accommodate a variety of artistic groups.[12] In a way the Kennedy Center has served as a memorial to the elegance of the Kennedy style, elusive to describe but infinitely appealing to the masses. It is a place of culture and education, two qualities deemed necessary for any mythological American hero of the late twentieth century.

The Kennedy Library and Museum in Massachusetts was originally dedicated to "all those who through the art of politics seek a new and better world" (Figure 6.3).[13] JFK prepared carefully for his eventual role in history. Five days after his inauguration, he deposited 860,000 pages of documents from his early political years in the National Archives.[14] In 1961 he announced plans for the Kennedy Library, which he wanted to be affiliated with a major university. Kennedy anticipated that he would be relatively young when he retired from the presidency (presumably in 1968), and he planned to teach and write. Arthur Schlesinger, as White House historian-in-residence, wrote letters to all of the Kennedy officials and asked them to save their records relating to the administration.[15]

The John F. Kennedy Library Corporation, the private arm of the facility, was born within two weeks of the Dallas shooting.[16] The initial plan for the library called for its placement at Kennedy's alma mater, Harvard, with an affiliated Institute of Politics there. Robert Kennedy took on the job of heading up the Library Corporation, whose stated goal was

to show the public that politics is "not a bad profession."[17] The original $18 million in public contributions to the library came from more than seven million people.[18] In 1966 the National Archives transferred documents to a holding warehouse in Massachusetts. The papers were opened to researchers in 1969, hence the appearance of the first histories of JFK's career during the decade that followed.

By the late 1970's the collection numbered 11 million documents from JFK's life, plus those from his administration. There were 2.5 million pages of letters of condolence sent to the Kennedy family after the assassination. The complete collection, estimated at 30 million pages, included 4,000 doodles penned by the energetic president, 110,000

FIGURE 6.2
The John F. Kennedy Center for the Performing Arts, dedicated in 1971 as the official memorial to Kennedy in the nation's capital. It was designed by Edward Durell Stone. *Joan Marcus, courtesy John F. Kennedy Center for the Performing Arts, Washington, D.C.*

FIGURE 6.3
The John F. Kennedy Library and Museum outside Boston, designed by I. M. Pei and opened in 1979 as a memorial to JFK's political career.
Courtesy, John F. Kennedy Library

photographs, 6 million feet of film, and 1,100 oral histories.[19] The holdings have continued to grow over the years. Robert Kennedy's papers were added to the collection after his assassination in 1968. The papers of American writer Ernest Hemingway were also deposited there.

Politics, aesthetics, ecology, and the myth of JFK combined to interfere with plans for placing the library at Harvard. Kennedy himself had visited the area on two occasions in 1963 and expressed enthusiasm for a 2.2-acre site in Brighton, near Harvard Business School; the university pledged to donate the land.[20] After the assassination, the Library Corporation invited eighteen architects to inspect the site; none of them liked it, including I. M. Pei, who was awarded the design contract. Attention turned to an alternate location owned by the Massachusetts Bay Transit Authority; in 1968 the Library Corporation purchased ten acres of this land from the state and added two more with the understanding that the transit agency would move out by 1970.[21]

After five years of effort, the transit authority could not find an alternate location. In 1973 Pei unveiled his design for the library, which called for a glass pyramid.[22] Timing is everything, they say, and the architect's timing was off. The

problem related to another Pei building, the John Hancock glass tower in Boston. After that ultramodern structure was completed, the huge tinted-glass panels began to pop off at random, threatening the lives of pedestrians below; obviously the Harvard pyramid design caused a few people to wonder about the wisdom of risking decapitation for the sake of art.[23] Pei withdrew the plan and went back to the drawing board.

In 1974 the Library Corporation discovered that the site was on a peat bog; an environmental impact study had to be ordered.[24] Meanwhile Pei submitted a new, scaled-down design that called for two buildings: one would house the museum and library, and the other would contain the school of government.[25] Problems with aesthetics arose. *New York Times* writer Paul Goldberger proclaimed that the design was "not totally successful," and he likened the plan to the idea of a "camel being a horse designed by a committee."[26]

On June 16, 1974, *New York Times* critic Ada Louise Huxtable ran an article on the much-delayed library. In "What's a Tourist Attraction Like the Kennedy Library Doing in a Nice Neighborhood Like This?," Huxtable cited neighborhood concerns that tourism near Harvard Square

FIGURE 6.4

A replica of the Hayes presidential desk that Kennedy had used in the Oval Office. This was the centerpiece of the first museum installation at the Kennedy Library and Museum, 1979–93. Organizers devoted the display to the theme that politics can be a noble profession. *Courtesy, John F. Kennedy Library*

would be "like Goths overwhelming the intelligentsia." She continued, "Harvard Square [isn't] so heavenly now, but Cambridge seems to prefer to let it fall apart in its own way."[27]

It was time to move. The University of Massachusetts offered a site on a point of land at its campus in the Boston neighborhood of Dorchester, and the Library Corporation accepted the offer. The school of government split off from the museum-library and remained at Harvard. The rest of the plan moved out of town. The formal dedication of the John F. Kennedy Library and Museum took place in October 1979. Records and research functions were assigned to the upper levels, with eighteen thousand square feet below dedicated to multimedia exhibits.

The first museum, with exhibits designed by Chermayoff and Geisman Associates, began on the ground floor with a thirty-minute documentary by award-winning filmmaker Charles Guggenheim. Visitors then descended into the basement to the museum itself. The centerpiece display contained a replica of the Hayes presidential desk that JFK had used during his presidency (Figure 6.4). A section of the museum was devoted to the career of Robert Kennedy, but in both cases the dominant theme was one of life rather than death.

The family's commitment to the legend of the living found its ultimate expression in the first museum exhibits. There were 315 objects, 600 documents, 750 photos, 22 rear-lit murals, a massive time line, television monitors show-

ing film clips, and special audio effects, but information about the death of President Kennedy was limited to one plaque that simply stated that he had been assassinated in Dallas on November 22, 1963. Robert Kennedy's death in Los Angeles was handled in the same way. The museum was successful in showing that JFK had thrived in the political arena. The problems that faced the planners in the location and design of the facility were settled by the art of compromise, something of a metaphor for politics itself.

Permanent museum exhibits have a limited life span of about a decade. The original museum at the Kennedy Library was completely revamped during the early 1990's.[28] The new display, eighteen thousand square feet, opened to the public on October 30, 1993. Why the change? Library Director Charles Daly cited a need to appeal to younger audiences who did not remember JFK, and he noted that the first museum installation had been "worshipful."[29]

The new installation features an introductory film by Academy Award–winning filmmaker Peter Davis, with display environments designed by Jeff Kennedy Associates (no relation to JFK) of Somerville, Massachusetts (Figure 6.5). The interpretation is recast with a story line using narration in JFK's own words. The museum contains two large and two smaller theaters and boasts twenty videos dispersed among the period settings. The new interpretive program embraces the theme of the assassination, allowing a broader context for studying JFK's legacy (Figure 6.6).

FIGURE 6.5
The "street of shops" at the second museum at the Kennedy Library.
This environment was used to recapture the essence of the Kennedy presidential
campaign in 1960. The interpretation is guided by JFK's own narration.
Courtesy, John F. Kennedy Library

FIGURE 6.7
A 3.5-ton, twelve-foot chunk from the Berlin Wall. This was installed in the
Kennedy Library museum as a highlight of the "Legacy" section of the display.
Courtesy, John F. Kennedy Library

Unlike traditional museum exhibits, which focus on objects in cases, the Kennedy museum has placed one thousand artifacts in a series of contextual environments that trace JFK's life and career. Objects range from the rocking chair that JFK used in the Oval Office, to Jacqueline Kennedy's Emmy, won for the 1962 "A Tour of the White House," to a 3.5-ton fragment from the Berlin Wall (Figure 6.7). The curators used four hundred photographs to enhance the educational messages conveyed in the exhibits. The $6.9 million renovation was funded by the National Archives and the John F. Kennedy Library Foundation, which had replaced the original Library Corporation in 1984. The foundation sponsors several programs, notably the annual Profile in Courage Award.

By recasting the museum experience as a tour conducted by JFK himself, the museum planners have maximized Kennedy's stylistic qualities, which are a major part of his legacy. The decision to include the assassination in the new exhibits was an accommodation to a new generation that learned of the thirty-fifth president within the context of

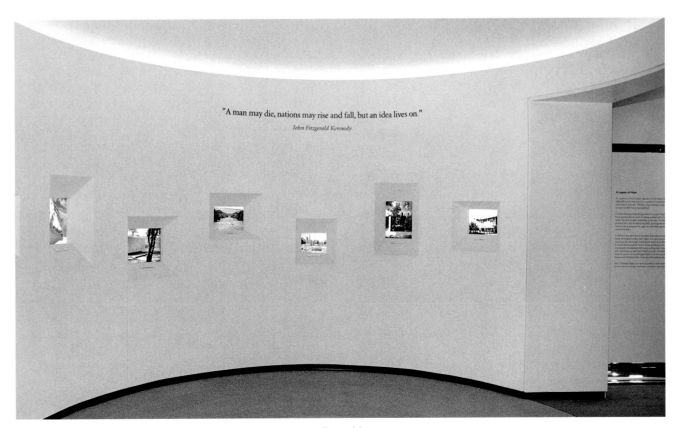

"A man may die, nations may rise and fall, but an idea lives on."
John Fitzgerald Kennedy

FIGURE 6.6
The "Reflection Room," a circular space featuring illustrations of some of the global memorials that were erected in Kennedy's honor.
The 1993 Kennedy Library museum exhibits are the first at that location to include materials on the assassination. *Courtesy, John F. Kennedy Library*

FIGURE 6.8

Dealey Plaza in 1993. Visitors from all over the world began coming to this site shortly after the assassination in 1963; today, the annual number of visitors is in the millions. *Ronald D. Rice, Sixth Floor Museum Archives*

both his life and his tragic death. The library and museum is the largest and most important memorial to JFK in existence, and it properly casts his death in a secondary role.

Unlike Washington, D.C., or the Boston area, Dallas has no claim to the life of John F. Kennedy; its association with the president is his tragic death. Visitors started coming to Dealey Plaza within hours of the shooting in 1963, and they never stopped. One survey taken in 1992—the first professional survey of the site—showed that millions of visitors per year find their way to the three-acre park (Figure 6.8).[30] The number of visitors is remarkable, especially since there is no highway or street sign anywhere in or near Dallas that mentions the name of Dealey Plaza or JFK.[31] Kennedy was alive there, and then, suddenly, he was dead there. The site offers an element of dramatic association and commemoration that is compelling to people from around the world.

Why visit a site of such horrible tragedy? "Commemoration," says former National Park Service Historian Robert Utley, "has always been a powerful motive, perhaps the most powerful. . . . People approach these places not only as vestiges of the past . . . but also as shrines, as temples for veneration."[32] This "shrine" aspect of even the most tragic historic spaces may at first appear bizarre, or at least contradictory, but it shows the American tendency to assign a positive value system to memories that have caused suffering. Some rememberers go to Dealey Plaza and other places that survive in firsthand memory in order to experience catharsis; others go to satisfy nostalgic impulses to return to a simpler and less confusing time; still others visit to learn about and to experience the past. Sites visited in a state of nostalgia have been at least partially cleansed of their negative connotations.

In my view visitors are drawn to Dealey Plaza for a special reason. Lincoln's myth grew up around his past accomplishments as the great emancipator; Ford's Theater, the site of his death, was not directly tied to the sustenance of this ideal. But Kennedy's myth was one of inspiration, symbolic of the country's "thwarted promise"; Dealey Plaza was the place where the promise of what might have been was permanently thwarted.[33] Adherents to the positive legacy of the slain leader come to Dealey Plaza to reflect on what America might have become had Kennedy lived to fulfill his potential. They come to find a source of positive inspiration for their own lives.

As we have seen, various events and shifts in public attitudes since 1963 have led countless Americans to view government as a form of conspiracy against the people. Today we hear talk of America inside the Washington beltway, home of the insiders, and of America itself, home to everyone else. Much of the vast literature about the assassination, pro and con, can be reduced to an argument about what happened in those few seconds in Dealey Plaza on November 22, 1963. The park has become the stepping-off point for those who uphold the government/preserver view of the killing and for those who take the searcher/conspiracy perspective. The site has become a symbol of society's opposing views about the reason that America's promise was so violently thwarted. It is a platform for debate about the value of government in our lives.

Dealey Plaza also serves as a reminder that American history is not made up of good news. George Santayana's famous adage, "Those who cannot remember the past are condemned to repeat it," is a cautionary and timely message to a society increasingly plagued by violence and a growing sense that it is losing its spiritual cohesion.[34] Dealey Plaza maintains a high state of preservation. The site is a symbol that a democratic society has the courage to hold onto its "baneful inheritance," despite an urge to wipe it from the face of the earth, and the foresight to use it instead for guidance in charting an uncertain future. As historian Lowenthal put it, "We subdue an overbearing past by sequestering it."[35]

Dealey Plaza has become a ceremonial site, following in some ways the evolution of the nation's most famous battlefields, ranging from Lexington and Concord to the Alamo and Pearl Harbor. Edward Linenthal's 1991 book *Sacred Ground* offers fascinating insights into how these martial battlegrounds, originally associated with death and slaughter, were transformed through time into symbols of positive American ideals or of the birth of the nation itself.[36] The Alamo was transformed into the birthplace of the Republic of Texas, and Pearl Harbor came to commemorate the rebirth of America after World War II, the place where "a mature nation rose from the . . . prewar years, ready to exercise paternal responsibility for the new world it was destined to help sire."[37]

Linenthal also notes that these sites, after being sufficiently purified, became host to new battles between competing groups who claimed ownership to the ideals that they conveyed. The Texans lost the Alamo to the Mexicans, and the United States was devastated by the Japanese at Pearl Harbor. Yet we do not think of the Alamo as a place where Mexicans congregate to celebrate their great victory; instead, it has traditionally belonged to the memory of the heroes who died defending it. The same thing may be said about Pearl Harbor. In recent years both sites have become more inclusive in their interpretation, but in American mythology they still belong to the heroic losers.

The purification of a negative historic site does not happen all at once. The pain of living memory has so far discouraged people from using Dealey Plaza as an *active* battleground for debate on contemporary issues. The first planned demonstration in Dealey Plaza did not take place until 1993. Predictably, it was a protest against a presumed government cover-up of assassination truths by withholding documents from the public. However, the searchers and the preservers have squared off for years on television and in print to argue about the site. The subliminal idea that Kennedy was slain in battle was planted during the military state funeral in 1963 and was enhanced by the post-assassination writers who set up Kennedy's image as a hero slain by the forces of hatred in society.

During the years that the Kennedy myth took finite shape and the controversy about his death grew, Dallas quietly maintained the site and did its best to stay out of the way. The community dedicated two memorials to the slain president; one was erected outside the Dallas Trade Mart, where JFK had been scheduled to give a speech, and the other was constructed two blocks east of the assassination site in a new park dedicated to and named for JFK (Figure 6.9). Architect Philip Johnson designed the downtown Kennedy Memorial, his first commission of this type. The cenotaph, or roofless, empty tomb, was dedicated in 1970.[38]

The annual anniversary of the assassination in Dallas was commemorated in formal ceremonies for about twenty years; after 1983 the city and county abandoned the rites at the request of the Kennedy family, who asked for com-

FIGURE 6.9
The John F. Kennedy Memorial, dedicated at a site two blocks east of Dealey Plaza in 1970. The cenotaph, or open tomb, was designed by architect Philip Johnson and was a gift of the people of Dallas County. *Courtesy, Robert Louis Staples, Washington, D.C.*

memorations on the date of JFK's birth.[39] Between 1970 and 1983 the Dallas ceremonies took place at the Kennedy Memorial. Nevertheless, on November 22, spontaneous gatherings always occurred in Dealey Plaza. The fifth-year anniversaries drew the largest crowds. In every respect, these assemblies qualified as "happenings."

The assassination critics tended to congregate in the area of the grassy knoll where, as the clock moved toward 12:30 P.M., Penn Jones, author of the *Forgive My Grief* series of critical books, would offer a brief prayer for God to save the country from corrupting influences. Other people simply wandered around the park.

After two decades the city, owner of Dealey Plaza, came to realize that these annual gatherings were going to endure. Now each year the Dallas Park Department cleans the park, touching up the whitewash on the art deco structures and cleaning the reflecting pools. On major anniversaries more elaborate preparations are made. When crowds are large, city police place security nearby, but it is unobtrusive to the point of invisibility. To my knowledge, there has never been an "incident" in Dealey Plaza since shortly after the assassination in 1963 when police promptly arrested a neo-Nazi from Virginia who loudly proclaimed that "Castro Reds" were responsible for the murder.[40]

I watched the ceremony in 1983 from the sniper's perch on the then-unrestored sixth floor of the old Texas School Book Depository building. We were conducting media interviews that day, so the press was allowed entrance to the historic building. People began to move into the park during the morning, and shortly after noon, they formed into loose lines on both sides of Elm Street, the original route of the 1963 motorcade. I learned later that some people came every year from out of state to participate in the event. Then, at 12:30 P.M., everyone stood at the curb and waited for the limousine to miraculously reappear. Of course, it never did.

The same thing happened five years later. In 1988, the twenty-fifth anniversary of the assassination, three thousand people showed up in the park and held an impromptu vigil that lasted from morning until night.[41] Again, the city had spruced up the park. As the crowds swelled during the morning, Dallas sent in its elite mounted police force to quietly monitor events. The troopers lined up behind the

FIGURE 6.10
Elm Street, during the 1988 anniversary of the Kennedy assassination.
Visitors created a shrine in the middle of the street.
Tourists have transformed the site into a memorial to the
positive attributes of JFK. *Sixth Floor Museum Archives*

crowd. At the appointed time, participants lining the curb joined hands. Suddenly, one person walked out into the middle of Elm Street and placed a rose near the spot where the fatal head shot had found its mark. Cars moving west on Elm managed to avoid hitting the pedestrian, but they squashed the flower. Soon, other people followed suit and created a little triangular street shrine, composed of coins, flowers, rosaries, and other mementos. Traffic stopped. Without a word the police quickly moved in and placed protective cones on either side of the street sculpture. Then, as if by signal, cars moved out of the middle lane and traffic continued toward the triple underpass (Figure 6.10).

Locals have always known about these annual happenings in Dealey Plaza, and they learned to accept the phenomenon as a part of the price of stewardship of a site that has been claimed by people from all over the world. The media, the debaters, and the tourists have kept the assassination a living thing for Dallasites. When the government returned to Dealey Plaza to reenact the assassination in 1963, 1964, and 1978, local authorities quietly cooperated. Most independent inquiries, if not too extreme, still find the community willing to help. Attempts to commercialize the area usually meet with strong resistance, however; in 1983 there were no buildings or roads at all, save the two Kennedy memorials, that bore the president's name— no schools, no Knights of Columbus lodges, and most definitely no drugstores, restaurants, or tourist shops.[42]

For nearly three decades after 1963 neither the city nor Dallas County, owner of most of the surrounding buildings, made any effort to draft formal policies that called for the preservation of the site. The area was kept relatively intact in a program of passive preservation. The entire downtown skyline changed drastically, but the assassination site was left pretty much alone. The Dallas Park Department kept it clean, but no drastic alterations were made, except those that related to subtle efforts to protect the tourists who kept flocking to the site.[43]

Dealey Plaza was originally designed as an ornamental thoroughfare for traffic entering and leaving the downtown area. The park acquired its pedestrian function *after* the assassination. In retrospect it is remarkable that tourists, wandering in the streets at night, have not been mowed down by the cars and trucks that speed under the triple underpass, which remains one of the busiest gateways into and out of the city.

After the shooting in 1963 nine out of ten Dallas citizens reported suffering some physical or emotional signs of illness.[44] For two years following the assassination, heart attacks and suicides in Dallas were above average.[45] Accusations against Dallas as the city of hate threatened to destroy the city's spirit, so leaders hastened to urge continued growth and a rededication to community self-confidence.[46] Dallas threw itself into a tremendous building program. While people elsewhere were openly struggling to deal emotionally with the tragedy and to find a sense of peace, Dallasites hid their pain and focused instead on progressive action.

The collective memory in Dallas came to be dominated by shame, defensiveness, and denial. The defensiveness surfaced early. On Sunday, November 24, 1963, Dallas Methodist minister William A. Holmes preached against the hatred in the city; his remarks were broadcast on CBS television on Tuesday night. Immediately, Holmes received death threats and had to take his family into hiding.[47] A few other Dallasites spoke out against the city's extremist attitudes and were chastised by their fellow citizens.

Following the assassination, Dallas became less conservative, and the ultraconservatives went underground. The city built new and impressive structures, and it grew. People did not want to talk about the assassination.[48] Dallas became "the city of the future, and . . . the city without a past."[49] A survey conducted twenty-five years after the shooting showed that Dallasites had not recovered from their sensitivity to the event; in 1988 about 80% of native-born citizens still believed that others blamed the city for President Kennedy's death.[50] Statistically, Dallasites assigned the blame to themselves more than any national poll had assigned blame to the Soviets, the Cubans, the mob, or any other possible conspirators *combined.*

Dallasites who had been around in 1963 still *thought* a great deal about the assassination, but they did not like to *talk* about the tragedy. The suppression of trauma has been shown to be unhealthy, slowing down the normal healing process that discussions about grief and shock often promote. When someone prompted active discussion of the shooting, Dallasites who suffered from denial tended to become defensive.[51]

A Dallas journalist described Dallas's attitude toward the assassination as similar to that of a parent whose child has a terrible birthmark on his or her face. Everyone knows it's there and is reminded of it constantly, but no one wants to mention the blemish aloud.[52] The child might be subject to taunts made by cruel outsiders, but those who love the youngster remain silent.

When I became involved, in 1978, in plans to interpret the assassination at Dealey Plaza, I was shocked by the depth of Dallas's denial and defensiveness. Any change at the park meant that Dallasites would have to openly *discuss* the event that had occurred there in 1963, and few were inclined to deal actively with the spot that had caused the community's most painful memory. Dallas, the city of the future, had little time to deal with its past. In my view, Dealey Plaza also presented Dallas with the unreconcilable conflict of having to address a site that served both as the mid-nineteenth-century "cradle" of the city and county and later as the "grave" of an American president. Local preservation officials had an understandably difficult time accepting recommendations that restoration standards for the site should conform to the 1963 date and not to the 1841–50 era of the founding of Dallas.

The changes to the site, or the urges toward them, happened when the community had to deal squarely with a threat to destroy or commercialize it. First, there was a movement to raze or transform the Texas School Book Depository, Oswald's alleged sniper location. The American impulse to destroy a "baneful inheritance" started early at that particular building and persisted for years.[53]

In 1970 the Texas School Book Depository company left the building and moved to another location in the city. The building owner, Colonel D. Harold Byrd of Dallas, sold the warehouse for $650,000 to Aubrey Mayhew from Nashville, who then announced plans to create a commercial Kennedy museum at the site.[54] Apparently he found no local investors for the plan. In July 1972, one of his warehouse employees was arrested for torching the building. Ten days later, the promoter defaulted on his loan, and the building reverted to the Byrd family.[55]

The attempt to raze the building set off a spirited community debate that hinged on the conflict between emotional hatred of the building—as the site from which shots were fired—and the long-term responsibility to history. "At the heart of the matter," said *The Dallas Morning News* on July 30, "is whether the Depository will remain under private ownership or be taken over by either the State or the City of Dallas for use as a public historical site."[56] Mayhew's plans to commercialize the structure had led many community leaders to cringe; it was time to face the issue of the future of the infamous warehouse.

The owner found a new buyer for the decaying building, but the potential purchaser wanted a permit to tear it down. The debate moved into the city council chambers, since the city had authority to issue all demolition permits. Under the leadership of Mayor Wes Wise, the city voted 9–2 to freeze the issuance of a demolition permit for the Depository building and to encourage placement of the structure on the National Register of Historic Places. Councilman Fred Zeder, who was incensed by the vote, hastily organized a pro-demolition group, raised $100,000, and wrote an article in the paper stating that preservation of the building would create a memorial "to the fanatic foul deed of a sick little man."[57] Mayor Wise prevailed, however, and reminded the detractors that the idea of demolition kept "creeping back to the defensiveness of our citizens."[58]

The defensiveness of the citizenry remained a barricade to any plans to offer educational exhibits to the public anywhere at the assassination site. The debate in 1972 made the community commit in principle to the idea of preserving the main building associated with the assassination. And there the issue remained for five more years. In May 1976,

The Dallas Morning News reported that Dallas County had obtained an option to purchase the building. "The officials' plan," noted reporter Sam Attlesey, "is to renovate all of the floors into office space. . . . All of the floors, that is, except the sixth floor."[59] Finally, after placing the issue in a public bond issue, Dallas County residents voted 2–1 to save the building and remove the potential for commercial exploitation. The county acquired the warehouse in December 1977.[60]

It then became the county's responsibility to come up with a concrete plan to deal with the structure's tragic associations and, by default, to devise a plan to provide some sort of interpretation for the tourists who came to the assassination site. As if by tacit agreement, the community knew that adding a building to the site would change it; the sixth floor was deemed the most likely space for some sort of educational program geared to accommodate visitor demand for information.

In 1977 the volunteer Dallas County Historical Commission was chaired by Lindalyn Adams, the wife of a Dallas physician. Mrs. Adams, who had proved her leadership with a number of other local historical projects, headed the effort to create a historical exhibit on the sixth floor for the educational enrichment of the public. The Sixth Floor Museum was the first national museum to deal with the issue of the death of the president within the context of American history.[61] The job took twelve years to complete.

Denial is the antithesis of activity; the idea of providing interpretation about the assassination at Dealey Plaza was an invitation to action. Ask most native Dallasites how they feel about the Kennedy assassination, then and now, and they will tell you that they wish the subject would just go away. It never has. The proposal to place a museum on the sixth floor of the old Depository building begged the question of how the community could avoid being drawn into the quagmire of debate about the reasons for the crime. Then there was the horrible specter of commercialism; would outsiders accuse the town of exploiting the death of a president?

Mrs. Adams and County Public Works Director C. Judson Shook, who had been instrumental in persuading the county to purchase the old warehouse, tried to turn the interpretive issue over to the federal or state government in 1977–78; they watched doors close from Austin to Washington. "The National Park Service . . . told [Shook] to come back in fifty years," said one report, "then they might be interested."[62] Meanwhile, tourists continued to find the site and to wonder why there was no information, no visitor center, and no museum there. Dallas was forever expanding its convention center and offering every conceivable welcome to its visitors; Dealey Plaza was left out of the loop.

Dallas County had decided to give the rest of the building a positive adaptive reuse by moving county administrative offices into the warehouse and renaming the structure the Dallas County Administration Building.[63] Its transformation of the building accomplished a great deal toward purification of the assassination site. The plan called for a major renovation of the dilapidated warehouse. The project served to change the building and "tame the past by giving its relics a new function."[64]

The county's decision to take over the building provoked local and even national debate. Early in 1978 *Newsweek* reported that Public Works Director Shook was being battered from all sides. "Every time I make a move," admitted Shook, "I get calls—either I'm trying to exploit

FIGURE 6.11
The sixth floor of the old Depository building. The space was adapted in 1988–89 to accommodate a historical museum on the life, times, death, and legacy of JFK. Note that the original space was a large room with no interior partitions. *Sixth Floor Museum Archives*

the building or I'm trying to cover up." The magazine went on to comment, "A proposal to change its [the Depository's] name to the Dallas County Administration Building proved so controversial that only two of the five county commissioners would take a stand on it—one for and one against."[65]

I entered the drama in 1978 and was asked to raise funds to develop an interpretive approach for the sixth floor.[66] Some people had proposed that the space be turned into an art museum, but most Dallasites knew that some direct reference to the historical associations of the site would have to be made.[67]

Dallas County's responsibility to its taxpayers would not allow the government to give away ten thousand square feet of real estate, the size of the sixth floor, without some statistical justification. We asked the Dallas Convention and Visitors' Bureau for visitation figures and discovered that

FIGURE 6.12
The final design for The Sixth Floor Museum, with a visitor center and an elevator tower connecting to the upper floor. The museum plans called for a separate entrance to the sixth floor, apart from the doorway used for regular county business. *Design by James Hendricks, FAIA, photo Sixth Floor Museum Archives*

officially, the assassination site did not exist.[68] The county then organized its own small survey, which showed high visitor interest in the idea of a museum at Dealey Plaza.[69] There was discussion of turning the sixth floor into offices, but the space was historically tainted; on a symbolic level at the very least, it promised to be an unhealthy work environment. Second, the adaptive reuse of the warehouse would transform the old Depository into a public building. All those tourists out in Dealey Plaza would have the right to march through the doors. Conceivably, visitors would find their way up to the sixth floor and disrupt business activities there. No, some form of museum dealing with the assassination was the answer, but there had to be rules (Figure 6.11).

The guidelines for the museum articulated by the Dallas leadership in 1978 never really changed. They were remarkably fair, reflecting the community's desire to deal honestly with history. Since the public was confused enough about the assassination, reasoned the planners, let's not add to it. Mrs. Adams set the tone: the museum would be objective, it would be tasteful, it would be low-key, and it would not be a memorial to anyone, least of all Lee Harvey Oswald. The bulk of the information about the investigations into the assassination would follow the government's findings; tax dollars had paid for the probes, she reasoned, and the public had a right to learn what they had paid for. Government agencies had presumably worked under a set of laws designed to make them accountable to the public; the critics, however, were not required to follow any rules at all. Controversy about these findings would be presented within the framework of the government's original conclusions.

The two main government investigations disagreed with each other on the key issue of conspiracy, so the content of the museum would be able to cover most ground

124

without espousing a particular point of view. By tacit agreement there would be no attempt either to apologize for Dallas or to debunk the memory of the president who died during a visit to the city. Adulation and morbidity were prohibited. Clearly, Mrs. Adams was a preserver, but the rules allowed for the searchers to have their platform.

Initial planning took place between 1979 and 1983.[70] The need to separate county visitors and museum visitors required the addition of another building on the north side of the old Depository, with an elevator tower taking visitors directly to the sixth floor (Figure 6.12). The initial planning team consisted of myself, exhibit designers Staples & Charles of Washington, D.C., Eugene George, AIA of Austin, as restoration architect, and James Hendricks, FAIA of Dallas, as architect for the visitor center, which would provide a separate, noncounty access to the museum. The preliminary designs were presented to the county commissioners in April 1983.[71] "Plans are in the works to give . . . tourists . . . something to do besides stand in the middle of Elm Street," reported *The Dallas Morning News*.[72] *USA Today* set the long-term national spin on the exhibit by describing it as an effort among Dallasites to lay aside local sensitivity to the events of 1963.[73]

The final content of the exhibit was worked out in 1987–88 and engaged the services of two dozen consultants drawn from both sides of the assassination debate and a variety of specialized fields.[74] The team decided to focus on the life, death, and legacy of John F. Kennedy within the broad context of American social history from the late 1950's until the late 1980's. There would be no attempt to solve the crime of the president's death; we would lay out the basics

and then let the public decide for itself. Allen Mondell and Cynthia Mondell of Dallas came in as documentary filmmakers for the project, working in cooperation with award-winning Executive Producer Martin Jurow. Antenna Theater was asked to prepare an audio tour in English, which was later expanded into seven other languages. "It's going to be a rat's maze with film clips," one detractor told the press.[75]

Early names for the museum reflected local uneasiness and denial. At one point it was called "Tragedy in Dealey Plaza" and later "One November Day." Both titles showed extreme urges toward sanitation, and the latter hinted strongly that nothing had ever happened at the site. The name "Sixth Floor" derived from the location of the museum within the larger assassination site itself. We could not use the Texas School Book Depository name because that business was still operating at another location.

The board decided not to exhibit visuals of obvious gore and extreme violence, deemed too influential on impressionable children. Other, less graphic photographs and films of the fatal shot would be used instead.[76] The decision to excise the "head shot" would earn the exhibit some criticism, but statistics later showed that 56% of all visitors were families with young children.[77] The materials were collected with plans to make them available for study in a research center.[78]

The $3.8 million project opened to the public on President's Day, February 20, 1989, to favorable international media reviews. The initial museum exhibits contained 350 photographs and 6 documentary films, with 2 of the latter located in theaters (Figure 6.13). Aside from the

FIGURE 6.13
The exhibit reconstruction of the sniper's perch. The area is enclosed in glass to protect the original flooring; the boxes are reproductions. *Sixth Floor Museum Archives*

FIGURE 6.14
A view of various sections of the museum, allowing visitors to choose different themes to explore.
The exhibits contain 30 original artifacts, 350 photographs, and 6 videos. *Sixth Floor Museum Archives*

original architectural elements already present on the sixth floor, the display included 30 original artifacts, including newspapers, posters, and other items; none of the original physical evidence of the crime was included, since it remained in the National Archives.[79]

The Sixth Floor exhibit was designed to promote catharsis for the rememberers who remained emotionally pained by the assassination (Figure 6.14). At the same time the planners wanted to provide a basic historical overview of events and tried to inject the elements of shock and confusion that characterized the 1963 weekend, so that nonrememberers could "experience" history themselves. The plan manifested itself spatially in the design, interpretively through the selection and arrangement of visuals, and dramatically in the films.

Media coverage of the plans for the exhibit was relentless from 1979 until the completion of the project in 1989. Few historians had exerted authority to speak on the assassination, and a major historical museum, located not only in the former "city of hate" but in the very place where a sniper had fired on the president, was considered newsworthy. Several writers among the traditional authoritative voices on the assassination—official investigators, assassination researchers, and the press—were leery of the Dallas attempt to deal with the subject. Some preservers expressed fears that the museum would veer into the camp of the searchers, and more than one searcher dismissed the Dallas project as the "official version" of events. Seth Kantor, a veteran Scripps-Howard newsman, one of the White House correspondents who had accompanied JFK to Dallas, remarked to me in 1988, "You're gonna get a lot of ink."[80]

As the date for the opening neared, the city grew nervous. One day before the first press preview, *The Dallas Morning News* editorial writer Henry Tatum wrote an article to prepare the community in case of negative reviews. "Texas and events that are transpiring in this state right now," he warned, "are not playing particularly well on the East Coast."[81] Tatum cited the savings-and-loan crisis, which was predicted to cost taxpayers billions, and President George Bush's recent appointments of many Texans into top government positions. It really wasn't Dallas's fault, he reasoned; it was just bad timing that the exhibit was due to open at a time when everyone in the country was sick and tired of Texans.

Since the opening, visitation to the museum has averaged more than one thousand people per day. Many long-term Dallasites still avoid the site of such a painful memory, but visitors from eighty foreign nations find the exhibit every year. The project has won national, state, and local awards. The comments in the memory books range from "I remember where I was when I heard the news" to "I was born in 1967 and never understood before." Evaluations from visitors have had a positive rating in excess of 98%.

As it turned out, the theme of catharsis dominated the media reports about the new museum. Dallas reporters spoke of the exhibit as an effort to help all rememberers in the healing process, and the national media cast the exhibit as an effort for Dallas to heal itself. Everyone was correct, and everyone tended to overlook the educational needs of a new generation of Americans, who had no need to heal. The *Dallas Times Herald*'s banner headline in its afternoon edition on the museum's opening day read, "Today We Stand Whole Again," a line taken from one of the prayers offered at the museum dedication ceremony.

In October 1993, the assassination site was officially designated a National Historic Landmark District by the Secretary of the Interior (Figure 6.15). After three decades the federal government recognized Dallas's efforts to preserve the site and gave official acknowledgment that the place where John F. Kennedy had died was important in commemorating the history of the United States.[82]

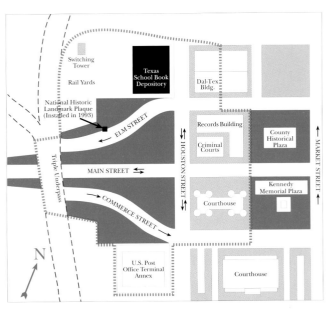

FIGURE 6.15

Plat showing the area included in the Dealey Plaza National Historic Landmark District, approved by the Secretary of the Interior in October 1993. The designation involved the cooperation of seven different property owners: Dallas County, the cities of Dallas and Fort Worth, the federal General Services Administration, Dallas Area Rapid Transit, the Union Pacific Railroad, and West End Historic, Ltd., the owner of 501 Elm Street, the former Dal-Tex building. *Read-Poland, Sixth Floor Museum Archives*

The designation had a positive impact on the local community. Finally, there was outside confirmation that Dallas had made the right decision to commit itself to a 1963 focus on Dealey Plaza; local history could rediscover its place there without risk of conflict with national responsibilities. The creation of the landmark district itself involved the cooperation of seven different property owners. During the years since 1972, the adjoining West End Historic District

had evolved into one of the area's most vibrant entertainment areas; these property owners had agreed that development of that sort at the assassination site was inappropriate.

Official dedication ceremonies were held in Dealey Plaza on November 22, 1993, the thirtieth anniversary of the death of JFK.[83] The entire park was closed to traffic for the occasion. Nellie Connally, widow of former Governor John Connally, returned to the site to perform the honor of dedicating the bronze Landmark plaque. Although international media showed up to cover the event, the community looked on the ceremonies as a local commemoration, and thousands of Dallasites, many of whom had avoided Dealey Plaza for three decades, gathered at the site where the city's most horrible memory had been born (Figure 6.16). Together with descendants of George Bannerman Dealey, with witnesses to the shooting, with representatives from both sides of the assassination debate, with historians and preservationists, with a gospel choir, a wind symphony, and an honor guard, with an assortment of elected officials, these old people and children, these Anglos, African Americans, Hispanics, Asian Americans, and Native Americans all joined peacefully in a united effort to accept and rededicate the site "to future generations of Americans, with the hope that the legacy of John F. Kennedy will inspire them to reach for greatness in their own lives."[84]

Through the slow and painful process of preserving and interpreting the assassination site for the benefit of yours and later generations, Dallasites finally succeeded in taming an "overbearing past." And through that effort, they found a means to commemorate the positive legacy of John F. Kennedy as a symbol of promise and inspiration for the future. The very action of passing the baton to a new generation of Americans was an exercise in the practice of America's civil religion, a small proof that we remain a culture of hope.

FIGURE 6.16

Dedication ceremonies at Dealey Plaza on the thirtieth anniversary of the assassination, November 22, 1993. Nellie Connally, former Texas first lady, officiated at the dedication of the bronze Landmark plaque. Thousands of Dallasites attended the event. *Ronald D. Rice, Sixth Floor Museum Archives*

127

NOTES

KEY TO ABBREVIATIONS

DMN — *The Dallas Morning News*

DTH — *The Dallas Times Herald*

HR — [House Select Committee *Report*] U.S. House of Representatives, Select Committee on Assassinations, *Report* (Washington, D.C.: U.S. Government Printing Office, 1979; Bantam, 1979)

HH — [House Select Committee *Hearings*] U.S. House of Representatives, Select Committee on Assassinations, *Twelve Accompanying Volumes of Hearings and Appendices* (Washington, D.C.: U.S. Government Printing Office, 1979)

SFMA — The Sixth Floor Museum Archives

WR — [Warren Commission *Report*] U.S. President's Commission on the Assassination of President John F. Kennedy, *Report* (Washington, D.C.: U.S. Government Printing Office, 1964; Bantam, 1964; St. Martin's, 1993)

WC — [Warren Commission *Hearings and Exhibits*] U.S. President's Commission on the Assassination of President John F. Kennedy, *Twenty-six Volumes of Supporting Hearings and Exhibits* (Washington, D.C.: U.S. Government Printing Office, 1964)

INTRODUCTION

1. Arthur M. Schlesinger, Jr., *A Thousand Days: John F. Kennedy in the White House* (Boston: Houghton Mifflin, 1965); Lon Tinkle, "Kennedy Career in Picture and Prose," *DMN,* November 28, 1965; "Which Is History?" *DMN,* March 17, 1966.
2. Statisticians do not agree on the effective dates for the boomers; some cut it off at 1964, others at 1962.
3. "TV's Biggest Audience," *Broadcasting,* February 3, 1964, pp. 54–55.
4. Linda Grant DePauw and Conover Hunt, *Remember the Ladies: Women in America, 1750–1815* (New York: Viking Press, 1976). The book accompanied a national bicentennial traveling exhibition on the subject. The project was organized and directed by Mabel H. "Muffie" Brandon of Washington, D.C.
5. James W. Pennebaker, "On the Creation and Maintenance of Collective Memories," manuscript, Research Files, SFMA, p. 7. The paper was published in Spanish in *Psicologia Politica* 6 (1993): 35–51. I wish to thank Dr. Pennebaker for sharing his research findings before they went to press.

CHAPTER 1

1. Unless stated otherwise, all times herein are Central Standard Time, which is one hour earlier than Eastern and two hours later than Pacific time. Since 1963 certain names and titles that were shown in upper case have been altered. President, Presidency, Vice President, Communism, and Communist are now usually depicted in lower case, unless they are directly attached to a name (e.g., "President Kennedy"). I have altered the capitalization in certain quotations to reflect modern usage.
2. James Reston, Jr., *The Lone Star: The Life of John Connally* (New York: Harper and Row, 1989), pp. 238, 263–271, 274; also *The Dallas Morning News, November 22: The Day Remembered* (Dallas: Taylor Publishing Company, 1990), p. 2 (hereafter cited as *November 22*).
3. Richard K. Van Der Karr, "How Dallas Stations Covered Kennedy Shooting," *Journalism Quarterly,* Autumn 1965, pp. 646–648. Also, Richard B. Trask, *Pictures of the Pain: Photography and the Assassination of President Kennedy* (Danvers, MA: Yeoman Press, 1994).

4. Dallas/Fort Worth radio broadcasts of presidential visit, November 22, 1963, audiotape, Audio Collections, SFMA. I am grateful to The Sixth Floor Museum archivist Gary Mack for assistance in identifying the stations and announcers.
5. *November 22*, p. 4.
6. Lawrence Wright, *In the New World: Growing Up with America, 1960–1984* (New York: Alfred A. Knopf, 1988), pp. 29–30.
7. Ibid., pp. 31–47; Warren Leslie, *Dallas Public and Private* (New York: Grossman Publishers, 1964), pp. 87–107; *November 22*, pp. 2–5.
8. Leslie, *Dallas Public and Private,* p. 59, gives a figure of $6,188 for 1964.
9. In 1963 the city had a population of about 130,000 African Americans. Ibid., pp. 71–72. The Citizens' Charter Association was a major factor in Dallas city politics from the early 1930's until the mid-1970's. For a summary history of the association, see Allison Cheney, *Dallas Spirit: A Political History of the City of Dallas* (Dallas: McMullan Publishing Company, 1991), pp. 31–61.
10. Cheney, *Dallas Spirit*; Leslie, *Dallas Public and Private,* pp. 61–86; Wright, *New World,* p. 12.
11. Wright, *New World,* pp. 18–28; Dick West, "Assassination Book Slams Dallas," *DMN,* November 24, 1986, mentions the 60,000-vote margin.
12. Leslie, *Dallas Public and Private,* pp. 90–127; Wright, *New World,* pp. 17–28.
13. See Wright, *New World,* pp. 17–18.
14. Leslie, *Dallas Public and Private,* pp. 179–187, quoted from p. 184; Wright, *New World,* pp. 24–28.
15. Wright, *New World,* pp. 36–41; Leslie, *Dallas Public and Private,* pp. 188–199.
16. Wright, *New World,* pp. 36–37.
17. *November 22*, p. 5.
18. Ibid. Also Jesse E. Curry, *JFK Assassination File* (Dallas: American Poster and Printing Company, 1969), pp. 4–5.
19. Leslie, *Dallas Public and Private,* pp. 199–207.
20. Editorial cartoon by Bob Taylor, *DTH,* November 19, 1963.
21. Reporters provided the estimates on the number of law-enforcement personnel. The afternoon paper, the *Dallas Times Herald,* was working on tight deadlines for its edition and delayed its press time by one hour in order to be able to include coverage of the president's visit. Reporters filed copy all morning long, and the front-page layout had already been designed at the time of the shooting. Everything had to be changed. The original reporters' stories and notes were preserved by publisher Felix McKnight. Original reporters' typescript, file marked "Arrival," November 22, 1962, *Dallas Times Herald* Assassination Collection, Dallas Historical Society.
22. Leslie, *Dallas Public and Private,* p. 203. See also Curry, *JFK,* pp. 17–23.
23. Reports on the actual time of touchdown vary slightly, between 11:36 and 11:37 A.M.
24. The building's atrium, site of the luncheon, was decorated with red carpet beneath the head table, which seated fifteen. The table was draped with avocado-green silk, festooned along the front with garlands of greenery. Texas yellow roses were arranged in vases placed every three feet. The twenty-six hundred guests were seated at twenty-foot tables with white cloths and arrangements that included the six flags of Texas and bowls of yellow roses. The flags were those of Spain, France, Mexico, the Republic, the United States, and the Confederacy, governments that had all ruled Texas. Steak was the main course for the meal. A reporter from the *Dallas Times Herald* noted that about sixty policemen would be stationed in the cavernous hall, with 168 men reserved for the motorcade route. Files 21–23, *Dallas Times Herald* Assassination Collection, Dallas Historical Society. Police Chief Curry later recalled in his book that he had 200 men in or around the Trade Mart. See Curry, *JFK,* pp. 13–15, 23.
25. Files 22–23, *Dallas Times Herald* Assassination Collection, Dallas Historical Society.
26. After the assassination, planners admitted that the end of the motorcade route was considered to be the entry to Dealey Plaza. Police Chief Curry wrote, "Security was comparatively light along the short stretch of Elm Street where the president was shot." Curry, *JFK,* pp. 13, 21.

27. Dallas founder John Neely Bryan came to the area from Arkansas during the late 1830's, and in 1841 he staked a claim to land at the western edge of the modern downtown. He traveled to surrounding settlements to encourage other pioneers to come to Dallas, and he sometimes donated settlement lots to sweeten the offer.

   In 1850 Bryan donated a block of land in his town for a courthouse, and Dallas became the official county seat. The county was named for Vice President George Mifflin Dallas, but no one seems sure where Bryan got the name for the town. Soon, businesses sprang up around the courthouse square, which was only a few blocks from the meandering Trinity River. The river never amounted to much, but Dallas's lack of a usable waterway did not deter the city fathers, who used the railroad, and later aviation, to establish routes of communication with the outside world.

   In 1873, Dallas became the location for the first railroad crossroads in the Southwest. The population mushroomed overnight with the arrival of merchants and new service businesses. By 1890 Dallas was the largest city in the state, a distinction it lost in 1900. When the city's leaders tired of the downtown being flooded by the Trinity, they moved the river and confined it between levees. The erection of Dealey Plaza during the mid-1930's was the final result of that engineering feat. The triple underpass was constructed on the original location of the river bottom. During the twentieth century, Dallas became the major financial and service center in the state. Dallas County never produced any oil, but its banks financed statewide exploration and offered plenty of outlets for newly rich oilmen to spend their money. Neiman-Marcus, the famous retail specialty store, was one of these outlets. Dallas was proud of its entrepreneurial spirit and its growth; in 1954 *Fortune* magazine dubbed the city "a monument to sheer determination." Quoted from Leslie, *Dallas Public and Private*, p. 24.

   For an introduction to the early history of Dallas, see the following: A. C. Greene, *Dallas USA* (Austin: *Texas Monthly* Press, 1984) and *Place Called Dallas* (Dallas: Dallas County Heritage Society, 1975); Sam Acheson, *Dallas Yesterday* (Dallas: Southern Methodist University Press, 1977); and Darwin Payne, *Dallas: An Illustrated History* (Woodland Hills, CA: Windsor Publications, 1982).

28. See "Federal Approval Assures Project Being Completed," *DTH*, March 18, 1934. There are additional letters, photographs, and news clippings in the G. B. Dealey Collection, Dallas Historical Society.

29. The original Elm and Commerce Streets were rebuilt as curving, forty-foot-wide thoroughfares, running 495 feet from Houston Street to the triple underpass. Elm Street was constructed as a one-way street heading west; Commerce Street was one-way heading east, into the downtown. Main Street remained a two-way thoroughfare. WC 17: ex 877.

30. The dates: Post Office Terminal Annex, 1937; Old Red Courthouse, 1892; Dallas Criminal Courts Building, 1915; Dallas County Records Building Annex, 1954; Dal-Tex Building, 1902; Texas School Book Depository, 1901. For a more detailed description of the buildings surrounding the park, see National Historic Landmark Application, "Dealey Plaza Historic District," 1991, typescript, Dealey Plaza National Historic Landmark Collection, SFMA, pp. 5, 11–21. Also, James Steely to Conover Hunt, "Architectural Assessment of 1937 Terminal Annex Building, Dealey Plaza," August 20, 1990, memorandum, Dealey Plaza National Historic Landmark Collection, SFMA.

31. The garden features in the park included twin concrete reflecting pools with fountains running north-south along the west side of Houston Street. To the west of the pools, near Main Street, are concrete colonnades that end in pylons. For the landscaping, see Harry Jebsen, Jr., Robert M. Newton, and Patricia R. Hogan," A Centennial History of the Dallas, Texas, Parks System, 1876–1976," typescript, 1976, Dallas Public Library; also Conover Hunt to Bob Hays, "Memorandum on the History of Plantings in Dealey Plaza," February 18, 1991, letter, Dealey Plaza National Historic Landmark Collection, SFMA. In 1990–91 Phil Huey, then Assistant Director of the Dallas Parks and Recreation Department, traced the evolution of plantings in the park.

32. G. B. Dealey Collection, Dallas Historical Society. See also Ernest Sharpe, *G. B. Dealey of the Dallas News* (New York: Henry Holt and Company, 1955). Dealey was an Englishman who moved to Dallas in 1885 and became known as a progressive leader. He was the father of E. M. "Ted" Dealey, publisher of *The Dallas Morning News* at the time of the assassination, and was the grandfather of Joe M. Dealey, president of the paper in 1963 and later its publisher. Joe Dealey was out of the city when the paper accepted the "Welcome Mr. Kennedy" ad from the American Fact-Finding Committee and was distressed, on his return, to learn of its inclusion. See oral history interview with Joe M. Dealey, 1988, audiotape, Antenna Productions, Oral History Collection, SFMA.

33. Wes Wise, here, and Bob Huffaker of station KRLD were reporting for portions of the parade.

34. According to The Sixth Floor Museum archivist Gary Mack, the Weather Bureau statistics at Love Field showed a temperature of 63 degrees at 11:55 A.M. and 67 degrees at 12:55 P.M. The Hertz sign registered 66 degrees at 12:40 P.M. The House Select Committee estimated that the temperature at the time of the assassination was 65 degrees, so at 12:15 P.M., the temperature would have been 64 or 65 degrees. I am grateful to Mr. Mack for sharing these figures.

35. Statements of Edgar Smith taken July 24, 1964, WC 7: pp. 565–569, and Joe Marshall Smith, taken July 16 and July 23, 1964, WC 7: pp. 531–539 and WC 22: p. 600.

36. Photographic evidence taken at the scene attests to the location of bystanders. For a map of the layout, see Josiah Thompson, *Six Seconds in Dallas* (New York: Bernard Geis Associates, 1967; Berkley, 1976), Appendix A. I have used the Berkley edition herein. Readers are cautioned that no one knows exactly how many people were in Dealey Plaza at the time the shots were fired and that many of the witnesses were in motion at the time of the assassination. Estimates on the number of witnesses vary from a low of about three hundred to a high of seven hundred.

37. Testimony of Abraham Zapruder, WC 7: pp. 569–577. Trask, *Pictures of the Pain*, includes a chapter on Zapruder: see pp. 57–153.

38. Affidavits of William and Gayle Newman taken November 22, 1963, WC 19: pp. 488, 490.

39. Affidavit of Emmett J. Hudson taken November 22, 1963, WC 19: p. 481.

40. See Decker Exhibit 5323, WC 19, for individual affidavits from these witnesses. See also A. L. Miller, WC 6: pp. 223–227; Frank E. Reilly, WC 6: pp. 227–231; E. V. Brown, WC 6: pp. 231–236; Royce G. Skelton, WC 6: pp. 236–239; S. M. Holland, WC 6: pp. 239–248, WC 24: p. 212; J. W. Foster, WC 6: pp. 248–253; Thomas J. Murphey, WC 6: pp. 256–270.

41. Affidavits of Jean Hill and Mary Moorman are included in Decker Exhibit 5323, WC 19; also Jean Hill, WC 6: pp. 205–223.

42. Gary Mack provided the information about the type of Polaroid camera.

43. WR, pp. 31–40, 642–643.

44. The tanning of President Kennedy's skin may have been a side effect of the medication that he took for Addison's disease. However, JFK also paid regular visits to the Kennedy estate in Palm Beach, Florida.

45. AP photographer James Altgens recalled this incident in his oral history interview for The Sixth Floor Museum: 1989, audiotape, Antenna Productions, Oral History Collection, SFMA. See also Trask, *Pictures of the Pain*, especially pp. 307–324.

46. The movement of the limousine and the nature of crowd response were recorded on the 8mm film taken by Abraham Zapruder. See WC 5: pp. 137–142, 151–163, 176–178. Copies of the film are in Assassination Film Collection, SFMA.

47. Jean Hill and Bill Sloan, *JFK: The Last Dissenting Witness* (Gretna: Pelican Publishing Company, 1992) p. 22. Several aspects of Mrs. Hill's story have changed over the years, so I have used information selectively from this volume.

48. The man with the little boy was Charles Brehm, who watched the limousine turn onto Houston from Main and then ran down to Elm to get another look at the motorcade. WC 2022: p. 837. One of the photographers was James Altgens: see WC 6: pp. 515–531.

49. She was Rosemary Willis, ten-year-old daughter of witness Major Phil Willis, who was at the scene with his wife and another daughter, Linda. The movement of the child was recorded on the Zapruder film. The Zapruder frames have been numbered; she halted at frame #197. See David Lui, "The Little Girl Must Have Heard," *DTH*, June 3, 1979. For additional information about Phil Willis, see Trask, *Pictures of the Pain*, especially pp. 167–182.

50. Most witnesses believed that the first shot sounded more like a firecracker or a backfire; the weight of testimony was overwhelming in this regard. Nearby witnesses Abraham Zapruder, William Newman, and Newman's wife at first believed it was someone playing a joke. See Zapruder interview, WFAA-TV, November 22, 1963, reel 5, video, Assassination Film Collection, SFMA; interview with Gayle Newman, WFAA-TV, reel 4, video, Assassination Film Collection, SFMA; and affidavit of William Newman, November 22, 1963, WC 19: p. 490.

51. Testimony of John B. Connally, WC 4: pp. 129–146. Connally recalled yelling "Oh, no!" followed by "They're going to kill us all!"

52. Close-ups of the Zapruder film show that a large flap of flesh-covered skull fell over President Kennedy's right ear, obscuring it from view. Witness Bill Newman thought that the shot had blown off the ear. See William and Gayle Newman interview, March 10, 1993, audiotape, Oral History Collection, SFMA.

53. Ibid. Mr. Newman's exact words to his wife vary from one account to another; however, the essence of his message has remained the same.

54. It was a piece of her husband's head, which she retrieved and later handed to Dr. Marion T. "Pepper" Jenkins at Parkland Hospital.

55. Statement of motorcycle officer Clyde Haygood, April 8, 1964, WC 6: pp. 296–302. Haygood was also recorded in several films and photographs taken at the scene.

56. Statement of Gayle Newman, November 22, 1963, WC 19: p. 488. Also, William and Gayle Newman interview, March 10, 1993, audiotape, Oral History Collection, SFMA. Photographers took pictures of the Newmans still lying on the ground. NBC News cameraman David Weigman was in one of the pool cars and started filming before the fatal head shot. NBC reporter Robert MacNeil jumped off one of the press buses as it passed through the park. See Tom Pettit, "The Television Story in Dallas," in Edwin B. Parker and Bradley S. Greenberg, eds., *The Kennedy Assassination and the American Public: Social Communications in Crisis* (Stanford, CA: Stanford University Press, 1965), pp. 61–66. AP photographer James Altgens, WFAA-Radio reporter Pierce Allman, and WFAA-TV cameraman Thomas Alyea were present at the assassination. Allman saw the shooting; Alyea did not see or hear it. *Times Herald* reporter James Featherston began taking interviews immediately. See Darwin Payne, *The Press Corps and the Kennedy Assassination* ([Lexington, KY]: Association for Education in Journalism, 1970), pp. 3–8. Photographers in the press cars and buses left the motorcade and took pictures also. See statement of Mal Couch, WC 6: pp. 153–162. For additional information on the photographers and cameramen, see Trask, *Pictures of the Pain.*

57. Statement of Zapruder taken July 22, 1964, WC 7: pp. 569–577.

58. See statements/affidavits of the following Sheriff's Department personnel: Roger Craig, April 1, 1964, WC 6: pp. 260–272, and affidavit dated November 22, 1963, WC 6: p. 524; Harold E. Elkins, November 26, 1963, WC 19: p. 540; Luke Mooney, November 22, 1963, WC 19: pp. 528–529; Buddy Walthers, November 22, 1963, WC 19: pp. 518–520; and Seymour Weitzman, April 1, 1964, WC 7: pp. 105–109.

59. *November 22*, p. 19. Brehm gave an emotional interview from the sheriff's office to an NBC reporter; the interview was filmed by NBC-affiliate WBAP-TV/Channel 5 photographer Jimmy Darnell. The interview took place shortly after the shooting and aired on NBC and Channel 5 simultaneously. See KXAS-Channel 5 assassination footage, video, Assassination Film Collection, SFMA. I am grateful to Gary Mack for identifying the photographers.

60. Recorded in a home movie taken at the scene by witness F. Mark Bell, November 22, 1963, video copy, Assassination Film Collection, SFMA.

61. United Press International and *American Heritage* Magazine, *Four Days* (New York: UPI and *American Heritage*, 1964), pp. 22–23 (hereafter cited as UPI, *Four Days*). This announcement was broadcast on radio and television.

62. Assassination Audio Collection, SFMA.

63. Associated Press, *The Torch Is Passed . . .* (New York: Associated Press, 1963), pp. 14–15.

64. UPI, *Four Days*, p. 22.

65. Assassination Audio Collection, SFMA.

66. Payne, *Press Corps*, pp. 1–4.

67. UPI, *Four Days*, pp. 22–23, 32–33; Associated Press, *Torch Is Passed*, pp. 13–15.

68. Quoted from UPI, *Four Days*, pp. 32–33.

69. Associated Press, *Torch Is Passed*, pp. 13–15, 16–17.

70. CBS News, broadcast for November 22, 1963, video copy, Assassination Film Collection, SFMA. There is confusion as to which wire service Cronkite used. In an interview aired on television in November 1993, Cronkite stated that he was standing over the UPI machine and went on the air with a voice-over with the Merriman Smith announcement. The televised, on-camera announcement that he made of the president's death used the AP wire story. See Discovery Channel, "The End of Camelot," video, November 21, 1993.

71. WFAA-TV, video, reel 3, Assassination Film Collection, SFMA.

72. The photo ran in the Sunday edition of the paper.

73. "Candid Snapshot Picture of Death," *DTH*, November 22, 1963.

74. The article stated incorrectly that Hargis rode to the right rear of the president; he was to the left, nearer Mrs. Kennedy. "Dallas Policeman Recounts Instant Assassin Struck," ibid.

75. For additional information on Jackson, see Trask, *Pictures of the Pain*, especially pp. 432–470.

CHAPTER 2

1. Kurt Lang and Gladys Engeland, "Collective Memory and the News," *Communications* 11, no. 2 (1989): 123–140, quoted from p. 124.

2. Ibid., pp. 125–132.

3. Ibid., p. 125.

4. Author interview with Sally Groome Powell, August 2, 1993.

5. Elizabeth F. Loftus, *Eyewitness Testimony* (Cambridge: Harvard University Press, 1979), p. 53.

6. Ibid., pp. 31–35.

7. Loftus also points out that witnesses have a tendency to overestimate the amount of time that it takes for an event to occur. Ibid., pp. 36–50.

8. Ibid., pp. 53–55, 63.

9. WC 19, p. 490.

10. WC 22: ex 1425, p. 827.

11. WC 19: p. 490.

12. WC 7: pp. 569–577.

13. WC 6: pp. 205–223; WC 19: ex 5323, p. 479.

14. WC 19: ex 5323, p. 487.

15. WC 4: pp. 129–146.

16. Hill and Moorman heard this.

17. Altgens, WC 7: pp. 515–525; Nellie Connally, WC 4: pp. 146–149.

18. WC 18: ex 1024, pp. 724–727.

19. Lang and Engeland, "Collective Memory," p. 123.

20. Pennebaker, "Collective Memories," p. 2.

21. Ibid.

22. Quoted from Doris Kearns, *Lyndon Johnson and the American Dream* (New York: Harper and Row, 1976), p. 170.

23. Charles M. Bonjean, Richard J. Hill, and Harry W. Martin, "Reactions to the Assassination in Dallas," in Parker and Greenberg, *Communications in Crisis*, pp. 178–198.

24. Bradley S. Greenberg, "Diffusion of News of the Kennedy Assassination," *Public Opinion Quarterly* 28 (Summer 1964): 225–232.

25. WFAA's live feed to ABC in New York was set up within this time frame. See WFAA-TV, video, reel 4, Assassination Film Collection, SFMA.

26. Greenberg, "Diffusion of News," p. 227.

27. Ibid., pp. 225–232. The percentage was 99.8% of all Americans. Paul B. Sheatsley and Jacob J. Feldman, "A National Survey on Public Reactions and Behavior," in Parker and Greenberg, *Communications in Crisis*, pp. 149–177.

28. Frank C. Costigliola, "Like Children in the Darkness: European Reaction to the Assassination of John F. Kennedy," *Journal of Popular Culture* 20, no. 3 (Winter 1986): 115–124.

29. Mollie Panter-Downes, "Letter from London," *New Yorker*, December 7, 1963, pp. 196–198.

30. Costigliola, "Children in the Darkness," p. 118.

31. "The World Resounds: A Tribute," *America: National Catholic Weekly Review* 109, no. 24, (December 14, 1963): 767–771.

32. Ibid., p. 769.

33. James W. Pennebaker, *Opening Up: The Healing Power of Confiding in Others* (New York: William Morrow and Company, 1990), pp. 108 ff. See also Greenberg, "Diffusion of News," p. 230.

34. Wilbur Schramm, "Introduction," in Parker and Greenberg, *Communications in Crisis*, pp. 1–28.

35. Some assassination researchers have made much of the fact that phone lines in the nation's capital went dead around 2:00 P.M. (EST) on the day of the shooting. This author credits the problem to the frenzy of calling that people made after learning the shocking news for the first time. Dallas experienced similar failures. For the Washington and Dallas telephone problems, see William Manchester, *The Death of a President* (New York: Harper and Row, 1967), pp. 253–254. Although the book expresses an anti-Dallas bias, I have relied heavily on Manchester's account of the weekend for the material in this summary.

36. "TV's Biggest Audience," p. 54.

37. Between 12:30 and 12:45 P.M. on Friday, viewers jumped from 23.4% of U.S. home sets to 30.2%. By 1:30, 45.4% of sets had tuned in to television. Viewing on Friday peaked at 6:15–6:30 P.M. (CST) with 67% watching. The largest viewing audience was on Monday, just before the end of the mass at St. Matthew's Cathedral; at that time 79.5% of

all television sets were tuned in to the funeral coverage. Ibid., pp. 54–55. See also Roberta S. Sigel, "Television and the Reaction of School Children to the Assassination," in Parker and Greenberg, *Communications in Crisis*, pp. 199–219.

38. "Paper Sales Soared When JFK Died," *Editor & Publisher*, April 18, 1964, p. 22.

39. Edwin B. Parker and Bradley S. Greenberg, "Newspaper Content on the Assassination Weekend," in Parker and Greenberg, *Communications in Crisis*, pp. 46–50.

40. Ibid., p. 50.

41. "A World Listened and Watched," *Broadcasting*, December 2, 1963, pp. 36–46.

42. Some networks recouped a part of their losses by rescheduling. Ibid., pp. 36–40. Not all network affiliates canceled advertising during the weekend. For an interesting study, see Karl J. Nestvold, "Oregon Radio-TV Response to the Kennedy Assassination," *Broadcasting* 8, no. 2 (Spring 1964): 141–146.

43. "A World Listened and Watched," pp. 36–40.

44. Quoted in Manchester, *Death of a President*, p. 531.

45. Author interview with Jim Anderson, Dallas, August 1993.

46. "TV's Biggest Audience," p. 54.

47. Readers who wish to get a visual and audio sense of the weekend are encouraged to view David L. Wolper's masterful "Four Days in November," originally released in the U.S. in 1964 and now an MGM/UA Home Video. Wolper gathered extensive film and sound footage for this documentary. Although I have tried to document the actual sequence of disclosures as they were aired by the media, the record is contradictory. The weekend reportage was followed immediately by an avalanche of magazine articles that corrected or expanded the initial coverage. Readers should assume that most of the information included herein was known to most Americans within sixty to ninety days of the shooting.

48. Curry, *JFK*, p. 30, includes one version of this announcement. There were discrepancies in the transcripts of the police transmissions submitted to the Warren Commission. I have relied on Mary Ferrell, "Transcripts of Dallas Police Radio Logs, Channels #1 and 2," Dallas, n.d., typescript, Research Files, SFMA.

49. The dispatcher recording suggests the time as 12:30 P.M., but the exact time may have been closer to 12:31. The Sixth Floor Museum archivist Gary Mack was kind to bring up this point.

50. Testimony of Senator Ralph Yarborough, July 10, 1964, WC 7: pp. 437–439.

51. Testimony of Rufus Youngblood, WC 2: pp. 144–155; testimony of Lyndon B. Johnson, WC 5: pp. 561–564.

52. The Warren Commission obtained statements from 190 witnesses, but the assassination researchers have identified many more people during the years since 1963. See File 15, *Dallas Times Herald* Assassination Collection, Dallas Historical Society.

53. Statement of Sheriff Bill Decker, WC 19: pp. 457–465; also Ferrell, "Dallas Police Radio Logs," Log 1.

54. A number of eye- and earwitnesses at the scene believed that shots had been fired from the direction of the grassy knoll. For a summary of witnesses who said they saw smoke under the trees at the knoll, see Jim Marrs, *Crossfire: The Plot That Killed Kennedy* (New York: Carroll and Graf, 1989), pp. 56–60.

55. Jean Hill said she saw a policeman, WC 19: p. 479; traffic officer Joe Marshall Smith said a Secret Service man behind the fence showed him official identification, WC 7: pp. 531–539 and WC 22: p. 600.

56. About half a dozen witnesses saw a gun or gunman at the actual time of the assassination. Others saw one or more armed men in the area before the shooting and assumed that they were security agents. Howard Leslie Brennan, WC 3: pp. 140–161, 184–186, 211–212; Malcolm O. Couch, WC 6: pp. 153–162; Mrs. Earle Cabell, WC 7: pp. 485–492; James N. Crawford, WC 6: pp. 171–174; Tom Dillard, WC 6: pp. 162–167; Robert E. Edwards, WC 6: pp. 200–205, WC 19: p. 473; Amos Lee Euins, WC 19: p. 474; Ronald B. Fisher, WC 6: pp. 191–200, WC 19: p. 475; Arnold Rowland, WC 19: ex 5323, p. 494; Beverly Rowland, WC 6: pp. 177–191; Carolyn Walther, WC 24: p. 522; James Richard Worrell, WC 16: p. 959.

57. Ferrell, "Dallas Police Radio Logs," Log 2.

58. Ibid. Curry, *JFK*, pp. 43–44, lists the time as one minute later.

59. Howard Brennan, with J. Edward Cherryholmes, *Eyewitness to History* (Waco, TX: Texian Press, 1987), pp. 1–17.

60. Ibid. Brennan's account was told to his preacher and was published several years after the steamfitter died in 1983. See also Ferrell, "Dallas Police Radio Logs," Log 2.

61. File 15, *Dallas Times Herald* Assassination Collection, Dallas Historical Society.

62. Baker FBI affidavit, WC 26: p. 679. Parts of the original staircase were removed during a renovation of the building performed in phases between 1979 and 1987; the staircase between the fifth and seventh floors was preserved in place.

63. Mooney affidavit taken November 23, 1963, WC 19: pp. 528–529. Investigators disturbed the original arrangement of boxes at the corner window. All photographs taken on November 22, 1963, showed reconstructions. Tom Alyea of WFAA-TV shot film of the original arrangement of boxes before they were disturbed by investigators.

64. Affidavit of E. L. Boone, November 22, 1963, WC 19: p. 507.

65. Curry, *JFK*, quoted from p. 32.

66. Testimony of Clinton Hill, WC 2: pp. 132–144.

67. Statements of Parkland doctors, WC 6: pp. 1–115; nurses and orderlies, WC 6: pp. 115–153.

68. At 1:18 P.M. the Associated Press issued a report that LBJ had been wounded. Secret Service Agent Youngblood had briefly forced LBJ into a crouching position during the shooting; the vice president was probably flexing a cramp in his arm. See Manchester, *Death of a President*, p. 244.

69. Ibid., pp. 176–177.

70. WC 6: pp. 1–155.

71. Manchester offers an excellent summary of Mrs. Kennedy's activities at Parkland: see *Death of a President*, pp. 289 ff.

72. Ibid., pp. 213–219, 243–244. See also WC 6: pp. 1–115. The priest who performed the final rites was Oscar Huber.

73. Manchester, *Death of a President*, pp. 225–228.

74. Manchester states that LBJ was informed of President Kennedy's death at 1:13 P.M. and that he left for Love Field at 1:26 P.M. Ibid., pp. 219–220, 230–234, 237–239. Ferrell, "Dallas Police Radio Logs," Log 2, places the time of arrival at around 1:37 P.M.

75. Associated Press, *Torch Is Passed*, p. 19. See also Manchester, *Death of a President*, pp. 194–195 and 224 ff.

76. Author interview with Ms. Carter, July 19, 1993.

77. The Dallas CBS affiliate's News Director Eddie Barker got the story first. For an account of the CBS announcement, see Dan Rather, with Mickey Herskowitz, *The Camera Never Blinks* (New York: William Morrow, 1977), pp. 116–120.

78. Manchester, *Death of a President*, pp. 220–222. The local reaction at the hospital was recorded by Dallas reporters. See Tom Milligan, "200 Outside Hospital Gasp at Death Word," *DMN*, November 23, 1963. Some of the film footage of the reaction is included in Wolper's video "Four Days in November."

79. File 7, *Dallas Times Herald* Assassination Collection, Dallas Historical Society.

80. On the matter of authority, see Manchester, *Death of a President*, pp. 273–274. Also Curry, *JFK*, quoted from p. 72.

81. I am grateful to Dr. Marian Ann Montgomery for clarifying this issue.

82. LBJ testimony, WC 5: pp. 561–564; also *November 22*, p. 31.

83. The casket was placed aboard at 2:20 P.M. Manchester, *Death of a President*, p. 309. See also *November 22*, pp. 39–40.

84. Manchester, *Death of a President*, pp. 311–326, 348. Also *November 22*, p. 40.

85. Manchester, *Death of a President*, quoted from p. 348.

86. For a discussion of events that took place aboard *Air Force One* en route to Washington, see ibid., pp. 348–395. Note that Manchester's treatment of the Johnson followers was somewhat harsh. Lyndon Johnson's exact words after the oath have been reported with variations. This account of the swearing-in was taken from the live radio report given in Dallas by Walter Evans from Love Field. See Assassination Audio Collection, SFMA.

87. I am grateful to The Sixth Floor archivist Gary Mack for clarifying this issue.

88. Domingo Benavides heard the shots, saw the assailant leave the scene, and then ran over to the police car. He tried to call in the report but could not work the equipment. T. F. Bowley finally made the call. WC 24: pp. 202, 254. Many books and manuscripts incorrectly state that Benavides made the call. See Ferrell, "Dallas Police Radio Logs," Log 1. Also Payne, *Press Corps*, p. 8.

89. WR, pp. 166–171, 651; also WC 3: pp. 306–321, 322–335, 343–354; WC 4: pp. 166–176, 212,; WC 6: pp. 446–451, 455–464,; WC 7: pp. 68, 83–85, 153, 167–168, 250, 252–254, 263–266, 274, 395–400, 500–506, 594,; WC 11: pp. 434–437; WC 12: pp. 199, 201–205; WC 15: pp. 703, 744–745.

90. Ferrell, "Dallas Police Radio Logs," Log 1.

91. Johnny Brewer, manager of a shoe store on Jefferson Avenue, heard the radio announce the shooting of a police officer. Soon thereafter, a man appeared in the outside entryway to his store and waited there until a police car had passed. When the man moved on, Brewer followed him and saw the suspect enter the Texas Theater without buying a ticket. Brewer notified the theater cashier, who phoned the police. See WR, pp. 176–180, 654–655; WC 3: pp. 295–304, 463–464; WC 4: pp. 151, 206, 461–462; WC 5: pp. 34–35, 215, 220; WC 7: pp. 1–104, 111–118, 163, 248, 261–263, 276, 309, 312, 481, 547, 551; WC 15: pp. 349, 591.

92. Quoted from *November 22*, p. 31. Also Ferrell, "Dallas Police Radio Logs," Log 2.

93. See Manchester, *Death of a President*, p. 284.

94. Reiland was unlucky. He set his camera to the wrong setting inside the theater, and the footage came out dark; he switched the setting when he got outside, and it was overexposed. WFAA-TV, video, reel 5, Assassination Film Collection, SFMA.

95. Payne, *Press Corps*, p. 9, states that there were three reporters at the police station when Oswald was brought in to headquarters. KRLD's Jim Underwood, who rode in the motorcade, was there and filmed Oswald on the elevator.

96. Ibid., pp. 8–12.

97. Quoted from Manchester, *Death of a President*, p. 386, and see also pp. 385–395. Wolper's "Four Days in November" includes most of this film footage.

98. The decision to have the autopsy performed at Bethesda Naval Hospital was made by Mrs. Kennedy during the flight from Dallas to Washington. See Manchester, *Death of a President*, p. 349.

99. Ibid., p. 401.

100. Television reports related evidence as it was brought in to headquarters. Most newspapers included it in accounts printed on Saturday morning. The details of the evidence will be discussed in detail in chapter 4.

101. KRLD-TV, Tape 54, Film Collections, SFMA. I am indebted to archivist Gary Mack for sharing this information with me.

102. Payne, *Press Corps*, pp. 9–12.

103. Manchester, *Death of a President*, pp. 331–332.

104. Accounts vary. Dallas District Attorney Henry Wade stated that he contacted Abt. Others insist that it was the media who finally reached the ACLU lawyer. In any case, Abt declined to represent Oswald, citing a heavy caseload. *November 22*, pp. 64–65.

105. Ibid., p. 55. There is doubt among some Kennedy assassination researchers that the arraignment actually took place.

106. For the Tippit murder, see WR, pp. 166–171, 651; WC 3: pp. 306–321, 322–335, 343–354; WC 4: pp. 166–176, 212; WC 6: pp. 446–451, 455–464; WC 7: pp. 68, 83–85, 153, 167–168, 250, 252–254, 263–266, 274, 395–400, 500–506, 594; WC 11: pp. 434–437; WC 12: pp. 199, 201–205; WC 15: pp. 703, 744–745. Also WR, pp. 161, 169, 625, 651; WC 3: pp. 147; WC 11: p. 206.

107. On aliases, see WR, pp. 16, 121, 181, 233, 292, 312–315, 570–577, 602, 614, 636, 644–645, 723, 728.

108. WR, pp. 122–124, 135, 140–141, 249, 563–566, 646–647.

109. WR, pp. 131–134, 247–248, 604–605, 626, 636. Testimony of Frazier, WC 2: pp. 224–229; Randall testimony, WC 2: pp. 248–251. There is controversy about the location of the paper bag, which the Warren Commission stated was found on the floor in the far corner near the window. There are news photographs that show the Dallas Police removing a bag from the Depository, but no films or photos were taken of the artifact in its original location. Frazier re-created the drive to Dallas for Wolper in "Four Days in November."

110. The lunch was eaten by another Depository employee, Bonnie Ray Williams; see WC 3: pp. 161–186.

111. WR, pp. 125–128, 592–597, 607–610, 625, 628–629, 647. Quotation from *November 22*, p. 65. For the quotation from Oswald, see Seth Kantor, WC 20: ex 3, p. 366.

112. WR, pp. 81–85, 118–121, 235, 553–555, 569, 661, 645.

113. WFAA-TV, video, reels 12 and 14, Assassination Film Collection, SFMA. The controversy over the paraffin tests will be discussed in chapter 4.

114. Associated Press, *Torch Is Passed*, p. 36; Manchester, *Death of a President*, pp. 440–442.

115. Manchester, *Death of a President*, pp. 459–464, 466–469.

116. Associated Press, *Torch Is Passed*, p. 37; Manchester, *Death of a President*, pp. 372–373.

117. The ring was later returned to her. Manchester, *Death of a President*, pp. 293–294.

118. The family spent considerable time debating between Boston and Arlington as the most appropriate resting place. Ibid., pp. 490–500.

119. Ibid., pp. 460, 475–477.

120. See WFAA-TV, video, reel 14-2, Assassination Film Collection, SFMA, and *November 22*, p. 66.

121. Payne, *Press Corps*, p. 12; also WFAA-TV, video, reel 8, Assassination Film Collection, SFMA.

122. Associated Press, *Torch Is Passed*, pp. 70–71.

123. Payne, *Press Corps*, p. 12.; WR, pp. 209–210, 213–216, 225–231, 630. Wolper's "Four Days in November" shows this historic footage.

124. Ike Pappas broadcast, November 24, 1963, audiotape, Assassination Audio Collection, SFMA.

125. The knifing of Japanese leader Inejiro Asanuma had been taped in 1960 and was aired ten minutes later. The NBC coverage was live. See "A World Listened and Watched," p. 42.

126. Quoted in Manchester, *Death of a President*, p. 543.

127. Drums are muffled by loosening the heads to deaden the sound. Then they are covered. They are a traditional feature at major military funerals. Most of the description of the procession was taken from ibid., pp. 536–541, 562–564. Wolper's "Four Days in November" includes the sights and sounds from the Sunday procession.

128. Quoted from *November 22*, p. 92. For the text of all speeches given at the rotunda, see UPI, *Four Days*, p. 130.

129. Manchester reported that the Joint Chiefs of Staff wept at the sight. See *Death of a President*, pp. 542–543.

130. Details of the public viewing at the rotunda are summarized in ibid., pp. 562–564.

131. WC 6: pp. 1–153.

132. Payne, *Press Corps*, p. 13; Associated Press, *Torch Is Passed*, pp. 76–78.

133. Brennan, *Eyewitness*, quoted from p. 34.

134. Wolper's footage of the viewing is particularly poignant. See "Four Days in November."

135. Author interview with W. P. Hunt, Jr., August 1, 1993.

136. Many of the people who converged on Washington were young. Manchester, *Death of a President*, pp. 562 ff.

137. Quoted in *November 22*, p. 96.

138. Manchester's description of the anxieties surrounding the march is superb: ibid., pp. 485, 570–575.

139. For listings of the order of procession and names of dignitaries who attended the funeral for President Kennedy, see UPI, *Four Days*, pp. 139–141.

140. Manchester, *Death of a President*, pp. 578–582, eloquently describes the procession; Wolper, "Four Days in November," includes the footage.

141. Author interview with W. P. Hunt, Jr., August 1, 1993.

142. Mrs. Kennedy's handwritten instruction is illustrated in UPI, *Four Days*, p. 142, along with the text of the funeral eulogy.

143. Quoted in Manchester, *Death of a President*, p. 589.

144. Ibid., pp. 584–590.

145. Quoted in *November 22*, p. 109.

146. Manchester, *Death of a President*, pp. 599–600, 550, 600–602.

147. Ibid., quoted from p. 611.

148. Ibid., pp. 606 ff.

149. Ibid., pp. 604–605.

150. *November 22*, pp. 110–111.

151. Ibid., pp. 100–102, 114–115.

152. Ibid., pp. 114–116.

153. Fred I. Greenstein, "College Students' Reactions to the Assassination," in Parker and Greenberg, *Communications in Crisis*, pp. 221–239, quoted from p. 231.

154. Sheatsley and Feldman, "National Survey," p. 154.

155. Previously, Theodore Roosevelt was the youngest to assume the presidency, but he had moved up from the vice presidency after the assassination of McKinley.

156. Michael Barone and Katia Hetter, "The Lost World of John Kennedy," *U.S. News & World Report*, November 15, 1993, pp. 38–44, quoted from p. 44.

157. Sheatsley and Feldman, "National Survey," p. 156, and Sigel, "Reaction of School Children"; also Bonjean, Hill, and Martin, "Reactions to the Assassination in Dallas."

158. The following information about reaction to the loss of a "presidential" figure is taken from Fred L. Greenstein, "Popular Images of the President," *American Journal of Psychiatry*, November 1965, pp. 523–529.

159. Barone and Hetter, "Lost World of John Kennedy," p. 44.

160. William A. Mindak and Gerald D. Hursh, "Television's Func-

tions in the Assassination Weekend," in Parker and Greenberg, *Communications in Crisis*, pp. 131–141.

161. Ibid., p. 136.

162. Lee F. Anderson and Emerson Morran, "Audience Perceptions of Radio and Television Objectivity," in Parker and Greenberg, *Communications in Crisis*, pp. 142–146.

163. Mindak and Hursh, "Television's Functions," p. 137.

164. WFAA-TV, video, reel 5–2, Assassination Film Collection, SFMA.

165. See Wolper, "Four Days in November," and Manchester, *Death of a President*, pp. 562 ff.

166. Some 44% of adults and 62% of children surveyed expressed fear for the future of the country. See Sigal, "Reaction of School Children," pp. 206–208.

167. Mindak and Hursh, "Television's Functions," p. 138.

168. Sigal, "Reaction of School Children," pp. 206–208; Sheatsley and Feldman, "National Survey," pp. 162–166.

169. See Sheatsley and Feldman, "National Survey," p. 155, and Sigal, "Reaction of School Children," pp. 206, 208–210. Adults: 33%; children, 15%. Children laid the blame directly on Oswald as an individual by 73%. Adults were not asked that question.

170. Only 16% of the adults and a mere 6% of the children thought that communism was behind the assassination. Sigal, "Reaction of School Children," p. 208.

171. Sheatsley and Feldman, "National Survey," pp. 173–174.

172. Ibid., pp. 164–166.

173. Ibid., p. 138–140. Also Christopher J. Hurn and Mark Messer, "Grief and Rededication," in Parker and Greenberg, *Communications in Crisis*, pp. 336–349.

174. Panter-Downes, "Letter from London."

175. Loosely translated, this means, "I am a Berliner."

176. For the German and other tributes, see Associated Press, *Torch Is Passed*, pp. 46–47, 49.

177. Quoted in Manchester, *Death of a President*, p. 556.

178. Max Lerner, "The World Impact," *New Statesman*, December 23, 1963, p. 769.

179. Costigliola, "Children in the Darkness," pp. 118–119.

180. Manchester offers a summary of tributes: *Death of a President*, pp. 584–585.

181. Wright, *New World*, quoted from p. 298.

182. Sheatsley and Feldman, "National Survey," p. 166; also Greenstein, "College Students' Reactions," pp. 221–223.

183. Andrzej Siginski, "Dallas and Warsaw: The Impact of a Major National Political Event on Public Opinion Abroad," *Public Opinion Quarterly*, Summer 1969, pp. 190–196.

184. Costigliola, "Children in the Darkness," pp. 121–124.

185. "The World Resounds," pp. 768–769.

186. Karl Meyer, "History as Tragedy," *New Statesman*, November 29, 1963, pp. 766–768; *New York Times*, November 25, 1963, reprinted in *DTH*, November 26, 1963.

187. Bonjean, Hill and Martin, "Reactions to the Assassination in Dallas," pp. 183–184.

188. "City Stunned after JFK's Death," *DMN*, November 24, 1963.

189. An enterprising groundskeeper in Dealey Plaza saved some of the cards from these tributes. There are ten volumes of them stored in the Dealey Plaza Memorial Card Collection, Dallas Public Library.

190. *DTH*, Editorial, November 24, 1963.

191. Articles in *DTH*, afternoon of November 22, 1963, and in both Dallas papers, November 24 and 25, 1963.

192. "Dallas Citizens Still Stunned," *DTH*, November 23, 1963, includes a statement by Mayor Cabell that the assassination was the work of one man, Oswald; also see Francis Raffeto, "Act of Maniac Not Tied to City: Cabell," *DMN*, November 23, 1963.

193. Even 82% of children expressed anger. See Sigel, "Reaction of School Children," pp. 206–207.

194. "Threats Follow Oswald Slaying," *DTH*, November 25, 1963.

195. "Telegrams to City Mostly Abusive," *DTH*, November 25, 1963.

196. *November 22*, pp. 151–154, quoted from p. 154.

197. *DTH* reprint of the *New York Times* editorial, November 26, 1963.

198. "Why Did It Happen Here? Residents of Dallas Ask," *DMN*, November 30, 1963.

199. James W. Pennebaker and Rhonda Polakoff, "The Effects of the John F. Kennedy Assassination on Dallas," Southern Methodist University, 1988, typescript, Research Files, SFMA, p. 1. This same material is summarized in Pennebaker, *Opening Up*, pp. 169 ff. The statement quoted was made to Lindalyn Adams.

CHAPTER 3

1. Theodore Roosevelt, at forty-two, assumed the presidency after the assassination of William McKinley in 1901. At forty-three, JFK was the youngest man *elected* to the office.

2. All Kennedy quotations, unless otherwise noted, are taken from John F. Kennedy, *Public Papers of the Presidents of the United States* (Washington, D.C.: U.S. Government Printing Office, 1962–64).

3. David Lowenthal, *The Past Is a Foreign Country* (Cambridge: Cambridge University Press, 1985), p. xvi. The quotation came from L. P. Hartley.

4. Bill Moyers, introduction to Harris Wofford, *Of Kennedys and Kings: Making Sense of the Sixties* (Pittsburgh, PA: University of Pittsburgh Press, 1980), quoted from p. x.

5. David Halberstam, *The Best and the Brightest* (New York: Random House, 1969), pp. 8–39.

6. The information on JFK's youth is taken from Herbert S. Parmet, *Jack: The Struggles of John F. Kennedy*, 2 vols. (New York: Dial Press, 1980).

7. Nigel Hamilton, *JFK: Reckless Youth* (New York: Random House, 1992), quoted from p. 680.

8. Countless books have been written about every aspect of the 1960's and every major leader during that period. For a good, brief overview of the era, see Norman Rosenberg and Emily S. Rosenberg, *In Our Times*, 2d ed (Englewood Cliffs, NJ: Prentiss-Hall, 1982).

9. Much of the information about the Kennedy presidency was taken from Schlesinger, *Thousand Days*.

10. Barone and Hetter, "The Lost World of John Kennedy," *U.S. News & World Report*, p. 40.

11. Quoted from the debates, as shown in ABC News, "JFK Remembered," with Peter Jennings (New York: ABC Television Video, 1988).

12. Nixon later ran for governor of California and lost. In his farewell speech to the media, the crusty politician pledged, "You won't have Nixon to kick around anymore." Lois Gordon and Alan Gordon, *American Chronicle, 1920–1980* (New York: Atheneum, 1987), quoted from p. 401.

13. Theodore C. Sorensen, *Kennedy* (New York: Harper and Row, 1965), quoted from p. 268. Robert Kennedy had worked on the McClellan Committee examining corrupt labor practices during the 1950's and then went to work for his brother in the White House. See Sorensen, *Kennedy*, pp. 51 ff. Later, he stepped down and ran for the Senate as a representative from New York. He was a senator when he launched his bid for the White House in 1968 and was killed in June, after winning the California primary.

14. Quoted in Schlesinger, *Thousand Days*, p. 733.

15. "Minimum Wage Bill," *U.S. News & World Report*, May 15, 1961, pp. 109–110.

16. For information on the Peace Corps, see Gerald T. Rice, *The Bold Experiment: JFK's Peace Corps* (Notre Dame, IN: University of Notre Dame Press, 1985), pp. 10 ff.

17. Nancy Shute, "After a Turbulent Youth the Peace Corps Comes of Age," *Smithsonian*, February 1986, pp. 81–89.

18. "Alliance for Progress," *Fortune*, May 1961, pp. 87, 90.

19. Quoted from Schlesinger, *Thousand Days*, p. 289.

20. The comment was made to Lyewellyn Thompson, who replied, "Par for the course." See ibid., p. 365.

21. Ibid., quoted from pp. 812–813.

22. "Vietnam's Many-Sided War," *Newsweek*, December 10, 1962, pp. 32–38.

23. "We Wade Deeper into Jungle War," *Life*, January 25, 1963, pp. 22, 31.

24. "The 'Hot' War U.S. Seems to Be Losing," *U.S. News & World Report*, January 21, 1963, pp. 46–48.

25. "Space," *U.S. News & World Report*, June 5, 1961, pp. 76–79.

26. "Space," *Time*, February 20, 1962, pp. 11–14.

27. For information about the life and career of Lyndon Johnson, see Kearns, *Lyndon Johnson*.

28. Richard Wilson, "What Happened to the Kennedy Program," *Look*, November 17, 1964, pp. 11–14.

29. Ibid., quoted from p. 12.

30. "Text of 25th Amendment," *New York Times*, February 11, 1967. The measure was sent to the states for ratification in July 1965 and was approved on February 10, 1967.

31. Editorial, *New York Times*, November 22, 1973.

32. Tom Schachtman, *Decade of Shocks: From Dallas to Watergate, 1963–1975* (New York: Poseidon, 1983), pp. 285–294. I have borrowed

Schachtman's use of the terms *preserver* and *searcher* as useful in describing the public approach toward the Kennedy assassination.

33. Quoted from Joan Morrison and Robert K. Morrison, *From Camelot to Kent State* (New York: Time Books, 1987), p. 3.

34. For a discussion of music of the period, see Charles Hamm, *Yesterdays: Popular Song in America* (New York: W. W. Norton and Company, 1979), pp. 454–459.

35. See Serge R. Denisoff, *Sing a Song of Social Significance*, 2d ed. (Bowling Green, OH: Bowling Green State University Press, 1983), pp. 120–127.

36. For a discussion of general trends, see Rosenberg and Rosenberg, *In Our Times*, pp. 249–252.

37. Quoted from Gordon and Gordon, *American Chronicle*, p. 455.

38. Quoted from *1968 Time Capsule* (New York: *Time-Life* Books, 1969), p. 85.

39. For a brief summary of the Vietnam War during LBJ's administration, see Rosenberg and Rosenberg, *In Our Times*, pp. 133–147.

40. Wright, *New World*, quoted from p. 207.

41. Bruce Bauer, "Whatever Happened to Doris Day?" In Terry Teachout, ed., *Beyond the Boom* (New York: Poseidon, 1990), pp. 15–153.

42. *1968 Time Capsule*, p. 126.

43. Quoted from Schachtman, *Decade*, p. 163.

44. Interview with Jerry Rubin: see Morrison and Morrison, *Camelot to Kent State*, quoted from p. 284.

45. Interview with Berkeley leader Jack Weinberg: ibid., p. 230.

46. Interview with Craig McNamara: ibid., quoted from p. 163.

47. Ibid., pp. 284–285.

48. Quoted from Wright, *New World*, p. 129.

49. Rosenberg and Rosenberg, *In Our Times*, p. 280.

50. Wright, *New World*, p. 188.

51. Ibid., pp. 170–172, 189–204, quoted from p. 170.

52. Wendell Garrett, former editor of *Antiques*, made the remark in January 1971.

53. Interview with Charles O'Connell, former dean of students at the University of Chicago, quoted from Morrison and Morrison, *Camelot to Kent State*, p. 244.

54. Barbara Ehrenreich, "Living Out the Wars of 1968," *Time*, June 7, 1993, p. 74.

55. *1968 Time Capsule*, pp. 117 ff.

56. Rather, *Camera Never Blinks*, quoted from p. 123.

57. Thomas Brown, *JFK: History of an Image* (Bloomington: Indiana University Press, 1988), p. 2. I have relied heavily on Brown's work on the subject of JFK's image in the American mind.

58. Ibid., quoted from p. 2.

59. Ibid., quoted from p. 3.

60. Theodore White, "An Epilogue," *Life*, December 6, 1963, pp. 158–159.

61. Alice Payne Hackett and James Henry Burke, *Eighty Years of Best Sellers, 1895–1975* (New York: R. R. Bowker Company, 1977), p. 192.

62. The Dallas Library listing is by no means complete but was used to get a rather typical selection of titles that might be found in the major library of a large city. See Cynthia Nichols, comp., "Kennedy Bibliography by Year, 1960–1992," 1993, Research Files, SFMA.

63. The book makes interesting reading because it was written before the assassination colored views about Kennedy and his accomplishments. It was reissued in 1966 and again as a Dell paperback in 1977. See Victor Lasky, *JFK: The Man and the Myth* (New York: Dell, 1977). For the quotation, see "Presses Halted on Book Sharply Critical of JFK," *DMN*, November 24, 1963.

64. Jim Bishop, *A Day in the Life of President Kennedy* (New York: Random House, 1964).

65. Benjamin Bradlee, *That Special Grace* (Philadelphia: Lippincott, 1964); Hugh Sidey, *JFK Presidency* (New York: Atheneum, 1964); *New York Times, Kennedy Years* (New York: Viking Press, 1964).

66. Others: Evelyn Lincoln, *My Twelve Years with John F. Kennedy* (New York: D. McKay, Company, 1965); Sorensen's *Kennedy* came out in 1965; Paul Burgess Fay, *The Pleasure of His Company* (New York: Holt and Rinehart, 1966); Pierre Salinger, *With Kennedy* (New York: Doubleday, 1966). Schlesinger's *Thousand Days* made the best-seller listings in both 1965 and 1966. See Hackett and Burke, *Best Sellers*, pp. 195–196.

67. Brown, *Image*, pp. 6 ff.

68. Ibid., p. 7.

69. Ibid.

70. Quoted from "Author Claims Attempt to Stop Book on JFK," *DMN*, September 18, 1966.

71. John Corry, *The Manchester Affair* (New York: G. P. Putnam's Sons, 1967).

72. "Author Claims Attempt to Stop Book on JFK," *DMN*, September 18, 1966.

73. Quoted from Jim Shevis, "Manchester Not Only Author to Feel Kennedy's Pressure," *DMN*, September 18, 1966.

74. Brown, *Image*, pp. 8–9.

75. See ibid., pp. 34 ff., for an excellent discussion of this matter.

76. Ibid., pp. 9–28 et passim.

77. Wright, *New World*, quoted from pp. 227–228.

78. Agnew gave the speech on October 19, 1969.

79. *1968 Time Capsule*, pp. 128–136.

80. "Magic of Camelot Fades," *New York Times*, November 22, 1973.

81. Ibid.

82. Andrew J. Edelstein and Kevin McDonough, *The Seventies* (New York: Dutton, 1990), pp. 2–4.

83. Lowenthal, *Foreign Country*, p. 12.

84. See Edelstein and McDonough, *The Seventies*, pp. 100–104.

85. Quoted from Wright, *New World*, p. 186.

86. Quoted from Edelstein and McDonough, *The Seventies*, p. 105.

87. Ibid., pp. 110–113. Mark Lane, author of *Rush to Judgment*, served as Jones's attorney.

88. Edelstein and McDonough, *The Seventies*, p. 112.

89. Charles Hamm, *Yesterday's Popular Song in America* (New York, London: W. W. Norton and Co., 1979), pp. 454–459.

90. Edelstein and McDonough, *The Seventies*, pp. 10–27, quoted from p. 21.

91. Arthur Bremer stalked Governor Wallace and then shot and wounded him in Laurel, Maryland, on May 15, 1972. The Alabama leader suffered partial paralysis and was permanently confined to a wheelchair as a result of the attack. Franklin L. Ford, *Political Murder: From Tyrannicide to Terrorism* (Cambridge: Harvard University Press, 1985), p. 357.

92. Edelstein and McDonough, *The Seventies*, pp. 2–59, quoted from p. 43.

93. Bauer, "Doris Day," pp. 149–223, quoted from p. 164.

94. For a general discussion, see Edelstein and McDonough, *The Seventies*, pp. 182–209.

95. Ibid., p. 207.

96. Ibid, pp. 121–126.

97. Vincent Virga, *The Eighties* (New York: Harper Collins, 1992).

98. The series ran on June 13, 14, 15, and July 1, 1971.

99. For a discussion of Vietnam, see Schachtman, *Decade*, pp. 188 ff., quoted from p. 195.

100. Bauer, "Doris Day," pp. 222–223.

101. Schachtman, *Decade*, pp. 158–161.

102. For the impacts of Vietnam, see Rosenberg and Rosenberg, *In Our Times*, pp. 149 ff.

103. Christopher Booker, *The Seventies* (New York: Stein and Day, 1980), p. 53.

104. Schachtman, *Decade*, quoted from p. 274.

105. Ibid., pp. 273 ff.

106. Michael Shudson, *Watergate in American Memory* (New York: Basic Books, 1992), quoted from p. 58.

107. Ibid., quoted from p. 162.

108. Ibid., pp. 103 ff. See also Edward Jay Epstein, "Journalism and Truth," in George Rodman, ed. *Mass Media Issues: Analysis and Debate* (Chicago: Science Research Associates, 1981), pp. 89–98.

109. Shudson, *Watergate*, p. 117.

110. Ibid., pp. 155–156.

111. For a discussion of the Ford administration, see Rosenberg and Rosenberg, *In Our Times*, pp. 214–216, quoted from p. 214.

112. Lynette Alice Fromme tried to shoot President Ford at the California State Capitol on September 5, and Sara Jane Moore fired at him in San Francisco on September 22. See J. Bowyer Bell, *Assassin!* (New York: St. Martin's Press, 1979), pp. 71–73.

113. Shudson, *Watergate*, pp. 44 ff.

114. Ibid.

115. "Leaving Murky Waters to the Senate," *Time*, June 16, 1975, pp. 9–10; U.S. Commission on CIA Activities within the United States [Rockefeller Commission], *Report to the President* (Washington, D.C.: U.S. Government Printing Office, 1975; New York: Manor Books, 1976).

116. Shudson, *Watergate*, pp. 45–46; U.S. Senate Select Committee to Study Governmental Operations with Respect to Intelligence Activities [Church Committee], *Alleged Assassination Plots Involving Foreign Leaders: Interim Report* (Washington, D.C.: U.S. Government Printing Office, 1975).

117. U.S. Senate Select Committee to Study Governmental Operations with Respect to Intelligence Activities [Church Committee], *Investigation of the Assassination of President John F. Kennedy, Book V, Final Report* (Washington, D.C.: U.S. Government Printing Office, 1976).

118. Shudson, *Watergate*, pp. 45 ff.
119. For a discussion of the Carter years, see Rosenberg and Rosenberg, *In Our Times*, pp. 216–231.
120. Wright, *New World*, quoted from p. 283.
121. Ibid., pp. 230–231.
122. Ibid., quoted from p. 275.
123. Schachtman, *Decade*, pp. 239–256.
124. Wright, *New World*, p. 217.
125. Barbara Ehrenreich, *The Worst Years of Our Lives* (New York: Harper's Perennial Edition, 1991), pp. 211–217.
126. Ibid., p. 197.
127. Booker, *Seventies*, pp. 22–26.
128. See Schachtman, *Decade*, pp. 203–227.
129. Ibid., pp. 228–234.
130. Rosenberg and Rosenberg, *In Our Times*, pp. 278 ff.
131. Ibid, p. 280.
132. 1993 Report, Department of Education: see "Dumber Than We Thought," *Newsweek*, September 20, 1993, pp. 44–45.
133. Ehrenreich, *Worst Years*, p. 200.
134. Ibid., pp. 196 ff.
135. Ibid., p. 202.
136. Ibid., p. 200.
137. Rosenberg and Rosenberg, *In Our Times*, pp. 238–240.
138. Edelstein and McDonough, *The Seventies*, pp. 98–99.
139. Quoted from *Camelot to Kent State*, p. 291.
140. Ibid., quoted from p. 236.
141. Rosenberg and Rosenberg, *In Our Times*, pp. 273–276.
142. Ibid., p. 277.
143. Theodore White, *America in Search of Itself* (New York: Harper and Row, 1982), pp. 10–32.
144. Ibid., pp. 35–67.
145. Ibid., pp. 121–122.
146. Ibid., pp. 124–128.
147. Ibid., pp. 100 ff.
148. Ibid., p. 71.
149. Wright, *New World*, quoted from pp. 298–299.
150. Quoted from Booker, *Seventies*, p. 105.
151. White, *America in Search*, quoted from p. 5.
152. Ehrenreich, *Worst Years*, pp. 121–137, offers information about the "new man" who appeared in response to women's demands for improved domestic relationships.
153. Ibid., p. 32.
154. Ibid., p. 32 ff.
155. Ibid., pp. 204 f.
156. Ibid., p. 201.
157. Ibid., p. 217.
158. Ibid., p. 206.
159. Ibid., pp. 197 ff.
160. Ibid., quoted from p. 20.
161. Edelstein and McDonough, *The Seventies*, quoted from p. 105.
162. Ehrenreich, *Worst Years*, quoted from p. 34.
163. Ibid., p. 206.
164. Ibid., quoted from p. 80.
165. Lowenthal, *Foreign Country*, quoted from p. 44.
166. Phyllis K. Leffler and Joseph Brent, *Public and Academic History: A Philosophy and Paradigm* (Malamar, FL: Robert E. Krieger Publishing Company, 1990), pp. 13 ff.
167. Ibid., quoted from p. 13.
168. Ibid., p. 14.
169. Pennebaker, *Opening Up*, p. 122.
170. Shudson, *Watergate*, quoted from p. 1.
171. Ehrenreich, *Worst Years*, quoted from pp. 16–17.
172. For a discussion of the left and the right, see Brown, *Image*, pp. 45–50.
173. Ibid., quoted from p. 45.
174. Ibid., quoted from p. 47.
175. Brown offers a summary of the first revisionist movement: ibid., pp. 50–65.
176. Within the context of his era, Kennedy may be credited with authorship of the book; he had the creative vision for the overall concept, used outside researchers on content and inside speechwriters for style, but apparently exercised intellectual control over the project.
177. Brown, *Image*, pp. 61–63. Henry Fairlee, *The Kennedy Promise: The Politics of Expectation* (New York: Dell Publishing, 1973); Nancy Gager Clinch, *The Kennedy Neurosis* (New York: Grosset and Dunlap, 1973).

178. Brown, *Image*, quoted from p. 65.
179. The book remains a steady seller. Kenneth O'Donnell and Dave Powers, *Johnny, We Hardly Knew Ye: Memories of John Fitzgerald Kennedy* (New York: Little Brown, 1972).
180. John F. Kennedy Library, *JFK: A Reading List* (Boston: John F. Kennedy Library, 1975).
181. Thomas N. Downing, oral history interview, November 2, 1992, audiotape, Oral History Collection, SFMA.
182. Quoted from Brown, *Image*, p. 70.
183. Ibid., pp. 71–73.
184. Ibid., pp. 73 ff., and Michael John Sullivan, *Presidential Passions* (New York: Shapolsky Publishers, 1991), pp. 47–56.
185. Brown, *Image*, p. 73.
186. Judith [Campbell] Exner, *My Story* (New York: Grove Press, 1977).
187. Sullivan, *Presidential Passions*, pp. 49–50.
188. Ibid., pp. 55–57.
189. Ibid., p. 53.
190. Brown, *Image*, p. 75.
191. Ibid., p. 77.
192. "An Evening with Hugh Sidey," lecture at the Sixth Floor Museum, November 20, 1995, video, Film Collections, SFMA.
193. Anthony Summers, *Goddess: The Secret Lives of Marilyn Monroe* (New York: New American Library, 1986) pp. 210–352; Sullivan, *Presidential Passions*, pp. 29–46.
194. Brown, *Image*, quoted from p. 81.
195. Brown calls this the balanced view of JFK. For a discussion, see ibid., pp. 82–92.
196. Ibid., quoted from p. 92.
197. Parmet, *Jack*, and Parmet, *JFK: The Presidency of John F. Kennedy* (New York: Dial Press, 1983).
198. Brown, *Image*, pp. 97 ff; Garry Wills, *The Kennedy Imprisonment: A Meditation on Power* (Boston: Little Brown and Company, 1981).
199. Brown, *Image*, quoted from p. 76.
200. Jacques Lowe, *Kennedy: A Time Remembered* (New York: Quartet Books, 1983).
201. William Manchester, *One Brief Shining Moment: Remembering Kennedy* (New York: Little Brown, 1983).
202. John H. Davis, *The Kennedys: Dynasty and Disaster* (New York: McGraw-Hill, 1984).
203. Doris Kearns Goodwin, *The Fitzgeralds and the Kennedys* (New York: Simon and Schuster, 1987).
204. Richard Reeves, *President Kennedy* (New York: Simon and Schuster, 1993).
205. Brown, *Image*, quoted from p. 101.
206. Ibid., quoted from p. 5.
207. James O. Robertson, *American Myth, American Reality*(New York: Hill and Wang, 1980), pp. 18 ff. I have relied on Robertson's work heavily herein.
208. For an interesting series of essays on the nature of myth, see Joseph Campbell, *Myths to Live By* (New York: Viking Press, 1972; Bantam, 1988). I have used the Bantam edition herein.
209. Margaret Brown Klapthor and Howard Alexander Morrison, *G. Washington: A Figure upon a Stage* (Washington, D.C.: National Museum of American History, Smithsonian Institution, 1982), quoted from p. 13.
210. Ibid., quoted from p. 11.
211. The definition came from Robert Bellah. See Shudson, *Watergate*, quoted from p. 24.
212. Ibid., p. 66.
213. Eulogy delivered by Senator Edward Kennedy at her funeral on May 23, 1994.
214. Statement made to the media by John F. Kennedy, Jr., on May 20, 1994.
215. Robertson, *American Myth*, pp. 1–14, quoted from p. 13.
216. Ibid., pp. 56–62.
217. Ibid., pp. 148–160.
218. Ibid., p. 196.
219. Campbell, *Myths to Live By*, quoted from p. 9.
220. Robertson, *American Myth*, quoted from p. 199.
221. Ibid., p. 209.
222. Brown, *Image*, p. 9.
223. Robertson, *American Myth*, p. 207.
224. "We have all become Hamlets in our country—children of a slain father-leader whose killers still possess the throne. The ghost of John F. Kennedy confronts us with the secret murder at the heart of the

American dream." See Oliver Stone and Zachary Sklar, with Jane Rusconi, *JFK: The Book of the Film* (Santa Barbara: Applause Books, 1992), quoted from p. 176.

225. Robert Sam Anson, "The Shooting of JFK," *Esquire*, November 1991, pp. 93–98, 100, 102, 174–176, quoted from p. 102.

CHAPTER 4

1. Editorial, *DTH*, December 4, 1963.
2. Editorial, *DMN*, November 21, 1967.
3. WR, p. xi. The early FBI and Secret Service reports were turned over to the Warren Commission and absorbed into its investigation.
4. Ibid., p. xii.
5. The files of the Texas investigation are kept in the State Archives in Austin. In 1964 the state attorney general published a supplemental report.
6. DeLoyd J. Guth and David R. Wrone, *The Assassination of John F. Kennedy: A Comprehensive Historical and Legal Bibliography* (Westport, CT: Greenwood Press, 1980).
7. Gerald Posner, *Case Closed* (New York: Random House, 1993; Anchor, 1994), p. ix. I have used the Random House edition herein.
8. Norman Mailer, quoted from Stone and Sklar, *JFK: The Book*, p. 444.
9. The investigation took the testimony of 552 individuals. WR, p. xiii. See also Edward Jay Epstein, *Inquest: The Warren Commission and the Establishment of Truth* (New York: Bantam, 1966; Viking, 1966), for a detailed discussion of the inner workings of the commission.
10. The commission stated in its report that it allowed people giving testimony to have an attorney present and that questions could be submitted by said counsel. It also asked American Bar Association President Walter E. Craig to participate in the hearings to make sure that the work was fair. WR, pp. xiv–xv. Epstein's book *Inquest* suggests that the case for the defense never really developed as proposed.
11. Tom Wicker, "Does 'JFK' Conspire against Reason?" *New York Times*, December 15, 1991, in Stone and Sklar *JFK: The Book*, pp. 241–246, quoted from p. 245.
12. Quoted from Schachtman, *Decade*, p. 286.
13. See David R. Wrone, ed., *The Freedom of Information Act and Political Assassinations*, vol. 1 (Stevens Point: University of Wisconsin Press, 1978). Posner also offers a good summary of the early sharing of information among the searchers: see *Case Closed*, pp. 412–424.
14. The newsletter has around one thousand subscribers, according to publisher Dr. Jerry D. Rose, a sociology professor at State University College, Fredonia, New York. The annual ASK (Assassination Seminar on Kennedy), held in 1990 through 1993 in Dallas, attracted an initial group of three hundred, which swelled to more than six hundred in its final year. Norman Mailer was the keynote speaker for the 1993 conference, which offered talks on both sides of the debate; however, the main work of the searchers is still slanted toward conspiracy as a root cause for the murder.
15. A case in point was Bonar Menninger, *Mortal Error: The Shot That Killed JFK* (New York: St. Martin's Press, 1992), which asserted that President Kennedy was accidentally killed by Secret Service agent George Hickey, who was riding in the follow-up car. The Bronson film shows that Hickey was not in a position to fire any shots.
16. Christopher Lasch, "The Life of Kennedy's Death," *Harpers*, October 1983, quoted from p. 34.
17. Members who served included Senators Richard B. Russell and John Sherman Cooper, Representatives Hale Boggs and Gerald R. Ford, former CIA Director Allen Dulles, and former World Bank president John J. McCloy. J. Lee Rankin acted as general counsel.
18. Harrison Salisbury, "The Editor's View in New York," in Parker and Greenberg, *Communications in Crisis* pp. 37–45, see pp. 41–44.
19. WR, Bantam, introduction.
20. Bantam did the printing job in less than three days. The copies sold for $1.00 each.
21. HR, p. xxviii.
22. For a summary of the decline in credibility, see G. Robert Blakey and Richard N. Billings, *The Plot to Kill the President* (New York: Times Books, 1981), pp. 41–61.
23. "Sale of Warren Commission Sets," *DTH*, November 4, 1976.
24. See Jack Minnis and Stoughton Lind, "Seeds of Doubt: Some Questions about the Assassination," *New Republic*, December 21, 1963, pp. 14–20.
25. Buchanan was based abroad. Some of his questions were answered by the *Report*. See Thomas Buchanan, *Who Killed Kennedy?* (New York: G. P. Putnam's Sons, 1964).

26. Calvin Trillin, "The Buffs," *New Yorker*, June 10, 1967, pp. 41–71.
27. Dallas authorities and the local bar association offered assistance in obtaining counsel for Oswald, but the suspect refused to accept anyone except New York attorney John Abt, who declined to represent him.
28. Epstein, *Inquest*.
29. G. Robert Blakey, introduction to HR, p. xxvix. Epstein's book was well received. See "Offers Yet Another Book for the Assassination Shelf," *DTH*, June 15, 1966; Jim Featherston, "Bringing Doubts to Warren Report," *DTH*, June 26, 1966; and Larry Howell, "Second Assassin?" *DMN*, June 10, 1966.
30. Penn Jones, *Forgive My Grief*, 4 vols. (Midlothian, TX: Midlothian Press, 1966–76). This work is out of print but is available in secondhand bookstores.
31. Richard H. Popkin, *The Second Oswald* (New York: Avon Library, 1966).
32. Leo Sauvage, *Oswald Affair: An Examination of the Contradictions and Omissions of the Warren Report* (New York: World Publications, 1966), See also James Lahar, "Lee Harvey Oswald; Beyond Legal Doubt?" *DTH*, September 4, 1966.
33. Harold Weisberg, *Whitewash* (New York: Dell Publishing Company, 1966).
34. Mark Lane, *Rush to Judgment* (Austin: Holt and Rinehart, 1966). The book was the #8 top seller in 1967; see Hackett and Burke, *Best Sellers*, p. 198.
35. Larry Howell, "The Doubters Get a Third Helping," *DMN*, August 6, 1966. Also A. C. Greene, "Another Story of Warren Critique," *DTH*, December 14, 1966.
36. Thompson, *Six Seconds*.
37. John B. Connally, "Why Kennedy Went to Texas," *Life*, November 24, 1967, pp. 86 ff.
38. Meagher's name was pronounced "Mar." Sylvia Meagher, *Subject Index to the Warren Report and Hearings and Exhibits* (New York: Scarecrow Press, 1966); reissued and updated as Sylvia Meagher and Gary Owens, *Master Index to the J.F.K. Assassination Investigations* (Metuchen, N.J. & London: Scarecrow Press, 1980); Sylvia Meagher, *Accessories after the Fact: The Warren Commission, the Authorities, and the Report* (New York: Bobbs-Merrill, 1967; Vintage, 1976). Although the *Index* contains some errors, anyone wanting to make a study of the official literature of the assassination should have a copy of this work on hand.
39. "A Matter of Reasonable Doubt," *Life*, November 25, 1966, pp. 39–48, 53; also Fletcher Knebel, "The Warren Commission Report on the Assassination Is Struck by a New Wave of Doubts," *Look*, July 12, 1966, p. 66; "A Taste For Conspiracy," *Newsweek*, March 20, 1967, p. 76; Edward Jay Epstein, "Who's Afraid of the Warren Report? A Primer of Assassination Theories," *Esquire*, December 1966, pp. 204 ff., 334 f.; Edward Jay Epstein, "A Second Primer of Assassination Theories," *Esquire*, May 1967, pp. 104–107.
40. See "Author Seeks Assassination Film Release," *DTH*, December 13, 1967; Thompson, *Six Seconds*, p. 11.
41. "Magazine Asks New Probe of Kennedy Assassination," *DTH*, November 21, 1966.
42. CBS News, *Transcript of CBS News Inquiry: The Warren Commission* (New York: CBS, 1967); Editorial, *DMN*, November 21, 1967.
43. *Panel Review of Photographs, X-Ray Films, Documents, and Other Evidence Pertaining to the Fatal Wounding of President John F. Kennedy on November 22, 1963, in Dallas, Texas* (Washington, D.C.: U.S. Government Printing Office, 1968) [Clark Panel].
44. President Johnson threw his full support behind passage of the act.
45. For two opposing accounts of the Garrison investigation, see Jim Garrison, *On the Trail of the Assassins: My Investigation and Prosecution of the Murder of President Kennedy* (New York: Sheridan Square Press, 1988), and Milton E. Brener, *The Garrison Case: A Study in the Abuse of Power* (New York: Clarkson N. Potter, 1969). Brener worked with Garrison on the New Orleans investigation. See also James Kirkwood, *American Grotesque* (New York: Simon and Schuster, 1970).
46. Sheatsley and Feldman, "National Survey," pp. 163–166.
47. Murray Edelman and Rita James Simon, "Presidential Assassinations: Their Meaning and Impact on American Society," *Ethics* 79, no. 3 (April 1969): 199–221, quotation from p. 200.
48. Ibid., pp. 201–202. See also Bell, *Assassin!*, especially pp. 67–87.
49. Edelman and Simon, "Presidential Assassinations," p. 201 ff.
50. Ibid., pp. 199–221, especially pp. 201 ff. Also William S. Crotty, "Presidential Assassinations," *Society*, May 1972, pp. 18–25, especially pp. 19 ff.
51. National Commission on the Causes and Prevention of Violence, *Report*, October 1969.

52. See William Hanchett, *The Lincoln Murder Conspiracies* (Urbanna: University of Illinois Press, 1986), pp. 65 ff.

53. Lincoln was a Baptist, but some authors have doubts about his religiosity. See Thomas Reed Turner, *Beware the People Weeping* (Baton Rouge: Louisiana State University Press, 1982), pp. 26–46, 77–100; also see Lloyd Lewis, *Myths after Lincoln* (Gloucester, MA: Peter Smith, 1973), pp. 58–129.

54. See Turner, *Beware the People Weeping*, chapter 6, for a discussion of the sermons and the attempt to spread the blame for the assassination on a larger group.

55. See Lewis, *Myths after Lincoln*, pp. 108–129.

56. Ibid, pp. 129–259.

57. Ibid., pp. 259 ff.

58. S. Elizabeth Bird, "Media and Folklore as Intertextural Processes: John F. Kennedy and the Supermarket Tabloids," *Communications Yearbook* 10 (Newbury Park, CA: Sage, 1987), pp. 758–772, quoted from p. 761.

59. Ibid., pp. 761–762.

60. Osborn H. Oldroyd, *The Assassination of Abraham Lincoln* (Washington, D.C.: O. H. Oldroyd, 1901), quoted from p. 385.

61. The trial included defense representatives for the accused, but most writers do not believe they did a very good job. For a discussion of the trials, see Turner, *Beware the People Weeping*, pp. 125–154.

62. Oldroyd, *Assassination of Abraham Lincoln*, p. 324, and see also pp. 323–381.

63. Quoted from Turner, *Beware the People Weeping*, p. 124. See also Lewis, *Myths after Lincoln*, pp. 350–356.

64. Hanchett, *Lincoln Murder Conspiracies*, pp. 2–4.

65. Ibid., pp. 241 ff., quoted from p. 241.

66. Turner, *Beware the People Weeping*, p. xii.

67. There are some academic historians who have written on the subject. See, for example, Michael L. Kurtz, *Crime of the Century: The Kennedy Assassination from a Historian's Perspective* (Knoxville: University of Tennessee Press, 1982). David Wrone, whose work is cited elsewhere in this book, is another historian involved in assassination research.

68. Hanchett, *Lincoln Murder Conspiracies*, quoted from p. 7.

69. Ibid., pp. 82 ff. Congress even convened a special assassinations committee to look into the allegations against President Andrew Johnson. See ibid., pp. 84 ff.

70. Ibid., p. 92.

71. Ibid., pp. 96 ff., quoted from p. 106.

72. Ibid., pp. 135–157.

73. Otto Eisenschiml, *Why Was Lincoln Murdered?* (New York: Grosset and Dunlap, 1937). Also Hanchett, *Lincoln Murder Conspiracies*, quoted from p. 209 and pp. 158–184. For problems with other conspiracy books, see pp. 228 ff.

74. For a summary, see Anthony Summers, *Conspiracy* (New York: McGraw-Hill, 1980; Paragon, 1991), pp. 369–374. I have used the Paragon edition.

75. George O'Toole, "The Assassination Probe," *Saturday Evening Post*, November 1975, pp. 45–48, 112.

76. Representative Stewart B. McKinney, quoted in ibid., p. 112.

77. Itek Corporation did enhancement work on the film in 1967 and 1975. The Geraldo Rivera show aired in March 1975.

78. See, for example, Harold Weisberg, *Oswald in New Orleans: Case of Conspiracy with the CIA* (New York: Canyon Books, 1967). In 1975 Michael Canfield and Alan J. Weberman published *Coup d'Etat in America: The CIA and the Assassination of John F. Kennedy* (New York: Third Press), which had a substantial readership.

79. The initial authorization was passed by House Resolution 1540, which expired with the end of the 94th Congress in January 1977. The committee was then reestablished under HR 222, passed in February 1977, which gave the investigation two months of life before HR 433, passed in March, allowed the committee to function until January 3, 1979, a period of less than two years. See HR, introduction, p. xxxi.

80. For a summary of the House investigation's internal workings, see Blakey and Billings, *Plot to Kill the President*, pp. 61–70.

81. The actual fact-finding phase of the investigation took place in a period of only six months. HR, p. xxxvi.

82. In 1980 the FBI issued a report on the House committee's acoustic work, which was roundly condemned by assassination researchers. See Federal Bureau of Investigation, "Acoustic Gunshot Analysis: The Kennedy Assassination and Beyond," *FBI Law Enforcement Bulletin* 52, no. 11 (November 1983) and 53, no. 12 (December 1983).

83. National Research Council, *Report of the Committee on Ballistics Acoustics* (Washington, D.C.: Department of Justice, 1982).

84. Video copies of both programs, Film Collections, SFMA.

85. Summers, *Conspiracy*.

86. David Lifton, *Best Evidence: Disguise and Deception in the Assassination of John F. Kennedy* (New York: Macmillan, 1980; Dell Publishing, 1982). The book was reissued in 1988 by Carroll and Graf.

87. Robert Groden and Harrison Livingston, *High Treason: The Assassination of John F. Kennedy* (Baltimore: Conservatory Press, 1989).

88. Garrison's book, *On the Trail of the Assassins*, was published by Sheridan Square Press in New York in 1988; Marrs's *Crossfire* came out in 1989 under the auspices of Carroll and Graf in New York; the paperback is the first edition to contain an index.

89. Peter Dale Scott, Paul R. Hoch and Russell Stetler, *The Assassination: Dallas and Beyond* (New York: Random House, 1976).

90. John M. Newman, *JFK and Vietnam: Deception, Intrigue, and the Struggle for Power* (New York: Warner Books, 1992). The movie *JFK* was also a Warner production.

91. Mark North, *Act of Treason: The Role of J. Edgar Hoover and the Assassination of President Kennedy* (New York: Carroll and Graf, 1991); Anthony Summers, *Official and Confidential: The Secret Life of J. Edgar Hoover* (New York: G. P. Putnam's Sons, 1993).

92. Summers, *Official and Confidential*, quoted from p. 316.

93. Ibid., quoted from p. 317.

94. Gaeton Fonzi, *The Last Investigation* (New York: Thunder Mouth Press, 1993).

95. Bob Callahan, *Who Shot JFK?* (New York: Simon and Schuster, 1993). The book contains a listing of major sources by chapter, which is helpful to students of the subject.

96. David W. Belin, *Final Disclosure: The Truth about the Assassination of President Kennedy* (New York: Scribner's, 1988); Moore's *Conspiracy of One*, published in 1990 by the Summit Group in Fort Worth, was critical of the way that the Warren Commission arrived at its conclusions about a lone gunman, but the book backed the panel's findings.

97. Quoted in Samuel Adams, "One Man's Obsession," *Waco Tribune-Herald*, September 3, 1990.

98. Posner theorizes that the first shot was fired at Zapruder frame 160 and missed; the second, which passed through Kennedy and also wounded Connally, hit at frame 223–224, and the fatal shot hit at frame 313. See *Case Closed*, pp. 319 ff.

99. Dick Hitt, "A Distorted Window into Dallas' Soul," *DTH*, August 7, 1988.

100. Larry Powell, "Looking Back on JFK Theories and Ugly '60s Shoes," *DMN*, September 2, 1993.

101. See Anthony Frewin, comp., *The Assassination of John F. Kennedy: An Annotated Film, TV, and Videography, 1963–1992* (Westport, CT: Greenwood Press, 1993), which lists nearly three hundred films relating to the president.

102. The show aired on November 15, 1988: Film Collections, SFMA.

103. London, 1988, Film Collections, SFMA.

104. ABC/*Washington Post*. A 1966 Gallup poll asked the same question, and 63% said they did not want another probe.

105. CBS/*New York Times*, taken October 8–10, 1988.

106. Quoted from Pennebaker, *Opening Up*, p. 102.

107. Ibid., pp. 103 ff.

108. David Jackson, "JFK: An Eternal Flam," *DMN*, November 21, 1993.

109. WR, pp. 254–423, 598–636, 669–778.

110. See Edelman and Simon, "Presidential Assassinations," pp. 199 ff.

111. Posner, *Case Closed*, pp. 3–197.

112. This is a complicated topic; for a simple summary, see Callahan, *Who Shot JFK?* pp. 101–111.

113. Marrs states that Oswald had a relatively normal childhood: *Crossfire*, pp. 90–112.

114. WR, pp. 156–180.

115. Oswald was not living permanently with his wife and children at the time of the assassination. Marina and the two infants were residing with Ruth Paine at her home in Irving. Oswald rented his room in Dallas using the alias O. H. Lee. He usually caught a ride to visit his family on weekends.

116. HR, pp. 56–59. For a concise discussion of the case against Oswald in the Tippit murder, see Posner, *Case Closed*, pp. 273–282.

117. Many of the searchers have worked on this matter over the years; books readily available at bookstores provide the gist of their arguments. See Marrs, *Crossfire*, pp. 340–350; also Garrison, *On the Trail*, pp. 193–203; Summers, *Conspiracy*, pp. 84–98.

118. WR, pp. 183–186.

119. The House Committee concluded that there was veracity to the claims of more than one gunman at the Walker shooting. Summers

provides a good summary of the controversy in *Conspiracy*, pp. 205–217. For the prosecution, see Posner, *Case Closed*, pp. 99–121; for the defense, see Marrs, *Crossfire*, pp. 255–265.

120. PBS, "Frontline," Invision Productions, Ltd., which aired on November 16, 1993.

121. Marrs charges that Oswald's communist tendencies were a cover for government work. *Crossfire*, pp. 90–112; Edward Jay Epstein, *Legend: The Secret World of Lee Harvey Oswald* (New York: *Reader's Digest* Press, 1978; Ballantine, 1979), says Oswald *was* a communist and was recruited as an agent for the Soviets during his defection. Summers, *Conspiracy*, offers a good summary of the Oswald "double" issue: pp. 368–393.

122. Garrison, *On the Trail*, especially pp. 44–54.

123. See Summers, *Conspiracy*, pp. 413–414.

124. Edelman and Simon, "Presidential Assassinations," pp. 199–201.

125. For the Connally theory, see Reston, *Lone Star*, pp. 218 ff.

126. Summers's book, *Conspiracy*, makes a good case for cover-up, after the fact, by government agencies.

127. Leffler and Brent, *Public and Academic History*, pp. 65–68.

128. Posner offers a summary of the misreading claim in *Case Closed*: see pp. 308 ff.

129. For the House work, see HR, pp. 63–103; Summers, *Conspiracy*, pp. 14–17, 20–21, backs up the House interpretations, while Posner, *Case Closed*, pp. 239–245, asserts that the National Academy of Science panel completely discredited the congressional findings. For another view, see Gary Mack, "Eyes Closed: The Case against Gerald Posner," *Fourth Decade* 1, no. 1, (November 1993): 16.

130. For the debate on the witnesses, see WR, pp. 61–78; HR, pp. 43, 56, 94–99; Summers, *Conspiracy*, pp. 22–29; Marrs, *Crossfire*, pp. 17–27; and Posner, *Case Closed*, pp. 236–238, 245–262. Both sides of the debate overstate the accuracy of witness accounts.

131. Thompson noted that the Warren Commission did not question either Merriman Smith or Tom Alyea about their recollections of the shooting. The author's list includes a chart on the number of shots, timing, etc.; the chart was compiled from the comments of the 190 witnesses who provided testimony to the Warren Commission. See *Six Seconds*, Appendix A.

132. Loftus, *Eyewitness*, pp. 29 ff. She also warns that "testimony about an emotionally loaded incident should be treated with greater caution than testimony about a less emotional incident" (p. 32).

133. The oral history interview of Bill and Gayle Newman taken by The Sixth Floor Museum in 1993 showed that Bill Newman has downplayed, but not denied, his original opinion that the shots came from the top of the hill behind them. See interview, March 10, 1993, audiotape, Oral History Collection, SFMA.

134. Consider, for example, the mystery of the "babushka lady," the scarfed woman who stood on the south side of Elm Street near the location of Jean Hill, Mary Moorman, and the Brehms. Beverly Oliver came forward long after the assassination and claimed to be the woman in the scarf. Oliver says that the FBI confiscated her film and never returned it, that she knew Jack Ruby, and that Ruby introduced her to Oswald. Some searchers believe her story, but others do not. See Marrs, *Crossfire*, pp. 35–39, and more recently Gary Mack, book review, *DMN*, December 18, 1994, p. 9J.

135. Researchers urged two witnesses to come forward years after the assassination to support the idea of a gunman at the grassy knoll. Ed Hoffman, a deaf-mute since birth, told author Jim Marrs in 1985 that he was standing two hundred yards west of the parking lot behind the cedar fence and that he saw two men, one with a rifle, involved in the shooting. He said he tried to tell his story to the authorities immediately after the shooting, again in 1967, and in 1977. See Marrs, *Crossfire*, pp. 81–85. Gordon Arnold came forward reluctantly years later to state that he had been standing beneath the large tree near the corner of the cedar fence on the grassy knoll at the time of the assassination. Arnold said that he had a camera and that he fell to the ground when he heard shots coming from behind him. His account states that two policemen appeared, one with a gun, and confiscated the film. Support for his account may have come from the recollection of Senator Ralph Yarborough, who said in 1978 that he had seen a man on the hill drop to the ground. Marrs, *Crossfire*, pp. 78–80. Some of the searchers have doubts about the stories told by both men, and Posner dismisses their testimony completely. See *Case Closed*, pp. 257–258, 484.

136. Compare Thompson's analysis in *Six Seconds*, appendix A, which argues that a majority of the witnesses believed a shot came from the knoll, with the thesis put forth by Posner, *Case Closed*, pp. 236–262.

137. Testimony of S. M. Holland, WC 6: pp. 239 ff, and WC 24: ex 2003, p. 2003.

138. Another important early article was Harold Feldman's "Fifty-One Witnesses: The Grassy Knoll," *Minority of One*, March 1965, pp. 15–25. Feldman interviewed 121 witnesses and concluded that 52% believed a shot had come from the knoll.

139. See Marrs, *Crossfire*, pp. 57–60; Thompson, *Six Seconds*, chapter 2; and Feldman, "Fifty-One Witnesses."

140. See WR, pp. 79–83, 118–156, 547–566, 580–592; HR, pp. 31–36, 44–56, 103.

141. WR, pp. 76–77, 116–117, 641; HH I: pp. 495, 513, 515; HH II: p. 200; HH VII, pp. 356, 360, 365–366, 368, 380, 385.

142. WR, pp. 245–248; HR, pp. 227–230.

143. Jarman did not recall details of the shooting. Harold Norman, statement taken March 18, 1964, WC 22: ex 1381, p. 666; Bonnie Ray Williams, March 19, 1964, WC 22: pp. 681–682; James Earl Jarman, March 18, 1964, WC 22: p. 655.

144. WR, pp. 64–65; WC 2: pp. 155–165.

145. WR, pp. 63–64; WC 3: pp. 140–161, 184–186, 211–212. See also Brennan, *Eyewitness*.

146. See Summers, *Conspiracy*, pp. 55–83. Marrs, *Crossfire*, pp. 448–449, states that the presence of the blanket fiber is meaningless because the paper bag was photographed by the Dallas police when it was touching the blanket. Marrs also cites discrepancies in FBI reports about the analysis of the paper. Note that the fiber was found *inside* the paper bag, so the issue of touching is irrelevant.

147. Marrs, *Crossfire*, pp. 437–439.

148. Nearly all searchers point to problems with the rifle identification: ibid., pp. 439–443.

149. Ibid., pp. 363–367. The searchers' case was helped by the testimony of the late veteran newsman Seth Kantor, who said that he knew Jack Ruby and had seen Ruby at Parkland on November 22 around 1:20 P.M., before the bullet was discovered. WR, pp. 335–336.

150. WR, p. 81. The government was weak on this point.

151. Marrs, *Crossfire*, pp. 442–443.

152. Researcher Mary Ferrell's study of the witness testimony and the whereabouts of all known Depository employees after the shooting suggests that several people did not return to the building. See Ferrell, "Texas School Book Depository," 1988, typescript, Research Files, SFMA.

153. Summers, *Conspiracy*, pp. 41–48.

154. See Brennan, *Eyewitness*, for his own account, printed years after the shooting. Brennan maintained that he had not identified Oswald in the lineup because he was afraid for himself and his family's safety. For the doubters, see Summers, *Conspiracy*, pp. 78–79, and Marrs, *Crossfire*, pp. 25–27.

155. Summers, *Conspiracy*, pp. 41–48, discusses the two-gunman problem.

156. Marrs, *Crossfire*, pp. 45–55.

157. Ibid., p. 49; Summers, *Conspiracy*, pp. 77–80.

158. Marrs, *Crossfire*, p. 50.

159. For arguments favoring adequate time for Oswald to descend, see WR, pp. 151–155, 648; and Posner, *Case Closed*, pp. 264–266; those against include Marrs, *Crossfire*, pp. 50–51; Summers leaves it as a matter of serious doubt, *Conspiracy*, pp. 80–81.

160. WR, pp. 182–183.

161. On the issue of the FBI's reluctance to look into the matter of the chipped curb, both sides of the debate are in accord. Posner thinks that the first shot hit a tree, then traveled down toward the underpass and caused the ricochet that wounded Tague: *Case Closed*, pp. 324–326; see also Marrs, *Crossfire*, pp. 60–64.

162. Marrs, *Crossfire*, pp. 449–450.

163. After the NAA confirmed that the fragments from Kennedy's brain originated with a bullet fired from the Mannlicher-Carcano, the searchers turned their focus more to the disputed wrist fragments from Connally. Summers accepts the validity of the NAA tests: *Conspiracy*, pp. 33–37; Marrs has doubts on the matter of the wrist: *Crossfire*, pp. 446–450.

164. For the case in favor of two shots from the rear, see summary discussions of the problems with the medical controversy in Posner, *Case Closed*, pp. 286–313; the House Committee medical panel conclusions can be found in HH VII; medical opinions about the evidence include John K. Lattimer, "Could Oswald Have Shot President Kennedy?" *Bulletin of the New York Academy of Medicine*, 2d ser., 48, no. 3 (April 1972): 113–124; John K. Lattimer, "Observations Based on a Review of the Autopsy Photographs, X-Rays, and Related Materials of the Late President John F. Kennedy," *Resident and Staff Physician*, May

1972, pp. 34–64; and Dennis L. Breo, "JFK's Death: The Plain Truth from the MD's Who Did the Autopsy," *Journal of the American Medical Association* 267, no. 20 (May 27, 1992): 2800 ff. Those who question the evidence include David Welsh and David Lifton, "The Case for Three Assassins," part 1, *Ramparts* (January 1967), pp. 77–87; Summers, *Conspiracy*, pp. 8–13; Marrs, *Crossfire*, pp. 361–380; Lifton, *Best Evidence*; Groden and Livingston, *High Treason*, pp. 25–100. Medical opinion has come from Dr. Robert J. Joling, "The JFK Assassination: Still an Unsolved Murder Mystery," part 3, *Saturday Evening Post*, December 1975, pp. 44–46, 120. Articles both pro and con are included in an issue of the *Journal of the American Medical Association* 269, no. 12 (March 24/31, 1993): 1507, 1540–1552, with R. R. Artwohl, Cyril Wecht, J. K. Lattimer, and Charles Petty. Major dissent is found in Cyril H. Wecht, "Pathologist's View of JFK Autopsy: An Unsolved Case," *Modern Medicine* 40 (November 1972): 28–32, and Cyril H. Wecht, "The Medical Evidence in the Assassination of President John F. Kennedy," *Forensic Science* 3 (April 1974): 105–128.

165. *Panel Review of Photographs.*

166. U.S. Commission on CIA Activities [Rockefeller Commission], *Report* (1975).

167. Wecht, "Pathologist's View," pp. 28–32.

168. His dissent is included in an appendix to HH VII.

169. HSCA Director G. Robert Blakey told me in 1979 that Robert Kennedy may have buried or otherwise disposed of JFK's brain to prevent its eventual display in some sort of museum.

170. The agents were Sibert and O'Neill, quoted from Lifton, *Best Evidence*, p. 172.

171. Only a portion of the photographs have circulated among the searchers. Groden and Livingston's *High Treason* included the photos, as did the 1991, updated version of Anthony Summers's *Conspiracy* and as did Robert Groden's *The Killing of a President* (New York: Viking Penguin, 1993).

172. Charles A. Crenshaw, with Jens Hansen and J. Gary Shaw, *JFK: Conspiracy of Silence* (New York: Penguin, 1992). Some of the information in this book has been seriously questioned by official and unofficial investigators alike.

173. Posner offered a summary of the treatment at Parkland based on more recent interviews with some of the doctors: see *Case Closed*, pp. 286 ff. He also made a case against Crenshaw on pp. 313–315. Compare his argument with the one made by Crenshaw. See also David Real, "Questions Linger after Doctor Airs His JFK Theory," *DMN*, April 9, 1992.

174. See Michael Riley, "Tales from the Crypt," *Time*, September 14, 1992.

175. Popkin, *The Second Oswald*. For the preservers, see Posner, *Case Closed*, pp. 174–182; for the searchers, see Summers, *Conspiracy*, pp. 368–386.

176. The testimony of Cuban-born Sylvia Odio is a case in point. Odio and her sister testified that two Cubans accompanied by "Leon Oswald" visited their Dallas home in September 1963, at the same time that the Warren Commission concluded Oswald was traveling to Mexico City. Odio had a follow-up call with the Cubans, and she and her sister recognized Oswald's photo when they saw it on television after the Kennedy shooting. The House Committee gave credence to her testimony: see HR, pp. 163–166; also Blakey and Billings, *Plot to Kill the President*, pp. 162–165, and Summers, *Conspiracy*, pp. 386–393.

177. This was a key thesis of Michael Eddowes in his *Oswald File* (New York: Clarkson N. Potter, 1977).

178. Eddowes's initial request, through county officials, was rejected. See Dan van Cleve, "British Author Says Oswald Really a Russian Imposter," *DTH*, January 10, 1979; "Briton's Bid to Open Oswald's Grave Rejected," *DMN*, June 2, 1979.

179. Posner summarizes the exhumation in *Case Closed*, p. 346.

180. Groden and Livingston, *High Treason*, pp. 295–296.

181. WR, pp. 96–110, 152, 163, 648–650.

182. HR, pp. 41–44, 48, 51, 82.

183. WR, pp. 96–117; HR, pp. 36–46.

184. WR, pp. 193–194.

185. HR, p. 185.

186. Posner, *Case Closed*, offers a good summary of the official conclusions: pp. 317 ff.

187. Groden and Livingston question how this shot could have been fired in such a short reload time and with the tree in the way: see *High Treason*, pp. 189–191.

188. Dr. Michael Baden, chairman of the forensic pathology panel, testified that there was a possibility that the shot from the grassy knoll had hit the president in the head, with evidence of this shot obliterated by the large exit wound caused by the head shot from the Depository. If the knoll shot was the fatal head shot, then the sequence of shots would have conformed to Zapruder frames 170, 200, 312, and 321. The House Committee discounted this possibility: see HR, pp. 85 ff.

189. Epstein offers a clear account of the development of the single bullet theory in *Inquest*, pp. 21, 94, et passim.

190. J. K. Lattimer asserts that the bullet hit Connally before Zapruder frame 220. The study done on the Zapruder film by Itek Corporation in 1967 suggested that the bullet made contact at frame 223 or 224. The Failure Analysis Association in 1992 said Connally was hit at frame 224. Lattimer notes that Kennedy's arm starts to rise at frame 225, the onset of a the neck wounds putting him in the "Thorburn position." See "Additional Data on the Shooting of President Kennedy," *Journal of the American Medical Association* 269, no. 12 (March 24/31, 1993): 1544–1547. Dr. Charles Petty ascribes the lack of damage to the near pristine bullet at least in part to the fact that it traveled along Connally's rib, causing a "slap fracture." See "JFK: An Allonge," *Journal of the American Medical Association* 269, no. 12 (March 24/31, 1993): 1552–1553.

191. HR, pp. 33–46, 82, 484, 493, 504.

192. Summers provides a good summary of this in *Conspiracy*, pp. 484–486.

193. John K. Lattimer, *Kennedy and Lincoln: Medical and Ballistic Comparisons of Their Assassinations* (New York: Harcourt Brace Jovanovich, 1980).

194. See Marrs, *Crossfire*, pp. 454–457.

195. CBS News used marksmen who fired a Mannlicher-Carcano rifle; the average was 5.6 seconds for three shots, without maximum accuracy. The program hypothesized that the first shot missed, and it suggested that the total sequence took 7 to 8 seconds. This analysis was influenced by work done by Dr. Luis Alvarez at the University of California, Berkeley, who noticed a jiggle pattern in the Zapruder film; he surmised that the pattern might have been caused by the sounds of gunfire alarming the cameraman. CBS News used photo expert Charles Wyckoff to test the notion, with the result that Wyckoff found significant jiggles at frames 190, 227, and 318 of the Zapruder film. CBS News, *The Warren Commission*.

196. Simplicity is impossible on the matter of the bullet. See preserver Posner's account in *Case Closed*, pp. 317–342, as opposed to searcher Marrs's version in *Crossfire*, pp. 485–493.

197. Posner, *Case Closed*, totally condemns this assertion: pp. 339 ff.

198. Author interview with Rodney Mills, September 1993.

199. Thompson, *Six Seconds*.

200. For some recent commentary from a physician, see R. R. Artwohl, "JFK's Assassination: Conspiracy, Forensic Science, and Common Sense," *Journal of the American Medical Association* 269, no. 12 (March 24/31, 1993): 1540–1543.

201. Groden and Livingston have been adamant in this regard: see *High Treason*, pp. 25 ff; see also Lifton, *Best Evidence*, pp. 33–54, 70–146, 308–379, et passim. Summers, in *Conspiracy*, pp. 479–486, offers an excellent summary of the controversy about the head wound and concludes that the official medical conclusions were correct.

202. Posner, *Case Closed*, pp. 286–304, 307–316.

203. WR, pp. 97, 109–110, 112, 115, 147, 644; HR, pp. 44–45, 55–56, 58, 82–87, 91–92.

204. The House Committee photographic analysis was presented in HH VI.

205. The Warren Commission worked with only two images of the backyard photo; another print was discovered in the collections of George DeMohrenschildt shortly before the House Committee did its investigations.

206. For the searchers' view, see Marrs, *Crossfire*, pp. 450–454, and Groden and Livingston, *High Treason*, pp. 171–180.

207. HR, pp. 635–637.

208. Groden and Livingston discuss the Bronson film and other photographic evidence that might contain clues in *High Treason*, pp. 195–195 et passim.

209. HR, pp. 65–83; Blakey and Billings, *Plot to Kill the President*, pp. 91–93.

210. HR, pp. 39, 63–103; HH V, VIII.

211. National Research Council, *Report*.

212. For a defense, see Summers, *Conspiracy*, pp. 474–477.

213. WR, pp. 248–374.

214. HR, pp. 104–288.

215. This scenario is summarized in Blakey and Billings, *Plot to Kill the President*, pp. 367–398.

216. Epstein, "Who's Afraid?" pp. 205–210, 334–335, and Epstein, "A Second Primer." For the "umbrella man" theory, see Robert B. Cutler,

The Flight of CE-399: Evidence of Conspiracy (Beverly, MA: Cutler Designs, 1970).

217. Louis Steven Witt was his name; see HH IV: pp. 428–453. Marrs still does not believe his story: *Crossfire*, pp. 31–32.

218. Marrs, *Crossfire*, pp. 289–298.

219. WR, pp. 333–374.

220. HR, pp. 180–193 et passim. The House investigation into the connections with Marcello and Trafficante led to a formal recommendation that the Justice Department look more deeply into these mob operations. The Justice Department did not follow up on the suggestion.

221. See Marrs, *Crossfire*, pp. 325, 327–328, 365–373, 380–414. Also Seth Kantor, *Who Was Jack Ruby?* (Costa Mesa, CA: Everest House, 1978).

222. John Davis, *Mafia Kingfish: Carlos Marcello and the Assassination of John F. Kennedy* (New York: Times Books, 1981).

223. HR, pp. 177–223. See also Blakey and Billings, *Plot to Kill the President*, pp. 135–367.

224. David Scheim, *Contract on America: The Mafia Murders of John and Robert Kennedy* (New York: Shapolsky Books, 1988). Summers sees a Mafia, intelligence agency, and Cuban connection, *Conspiracy*, pp. 489–504 et passim; see also Marrs, *Crossfire*, pp. 156–179.

225. HR, pp. 116–152.

226. Ibid., pp. 153–176.

227. See Summers, *Conspiracy*, pp. 223–342, and Marrs, *Crossfire*, pp. 135–155.

228. Wrone, *The Freedom of Information Act*, deals with the suit over this classified memo and analyzes its contents.

229. HR, pp. 230–246.

230. See Marrs, *Crossfire*, pp. 211–240, as an example.

231. HR, pp. 246–288 and 224–230, and see also pp. 289–338.

232. See Summers, *Conspiracy*, pp. 223–242, and Marrs, *Crossfire*, pp. 181–202.

233. Canfield and Weberman, *Coup d'Etat*.

234. Summers, *Conspiracy*, pp. 504–519: Fonzi, *Last Investigation*. Fonzi's book goes into the subject in great detail.

235. Summers, *Conspiracy*, sees a connection through the mob to the police and Jack Ruby.

236. Marrs, *Crossfire*, pp. 253–278.

237. This film is available on video at national rental outlets.

238. Newman, *JFK and Vietnam*.

239. See HR, pp. 109–116.

240. Epstein's *Legend* proposes that Oswald was an agent for the Soviets. See also Marrs, *Crossfire*, pp. 113–130, and on Nosenko, pp. 130–133; Summers, *Conspiracy*, pp. 111–222.

241. See interviews on two TV specials that aired in mid-November 1993: CBS News, "Who Shot JFK? The Final Chapter," and Discovery Channel, "The End of Camelot."

242. Mailer, *Oswald's Tale* (New York: Random House, 1995).

243. See Summers, *Conspiracy*, pp. 495–496.

244. Promotional advertisement on view at The Sixth Floor Museum.

245. HH IV: pp. 464–465.

246. Marrs, *Crossfire*, pp. 555–566.

247. Posner, *Case Closed*, appendix B, pp. 483–499.

248. Posner stated that the critics had produced thirty suspects: ibid., pp. 466–468; the identification of fifty people came from Dave Perry, 1994, unpublished manuscript, Research Files, SFMA.

CHAPTER 5

1. John Berendt, "Ten Years Later, A Look at the Record: What School Books Are Teaching Our Kids about JFK." *Esquire*, November 1973.

2. Daniel J. Boorstin, *The Americans: The Democratic Experience* (New York: Random House, 1973), pp. 392–397.

3. Quoted from Gordon and Gordon, *American Chronicle*, p. 509.

4. Epstein, "Journalism and Truth," quoted from p. 92.

5. Quoted from Hamilton, *Reckless Youth*, p. 663, and see also p. 211.

6. Ibid., pp. 687 ff.

7. ABC News, "JFK Remembered," narrated by Peter Jennings (New York: ABC Television Video, 1988).

8. Since 1987, I have been researching the role of the media in the Kennedy legacy; this chapter is one result of my research. Journalism Professor Barbie Zelizer published *Covering the Body: The Kennedy Assassination, the Media, and the Shaping of Collective Memory* (Chicago: University of Chicago Press, 1992). Dr. Zelizer researched the subject to complete her doctorate at the University of Pennsylvania; I am indebted to some of her work.

9. Ibid., p. 27.

10. Ibid., pp. 21–28.

11. Mitchell Stephens, *A History of News* (New York: Viking Press, 1988), pp. 226–254.

12. Ibid., pp. 256–277.

13. Television technology dates back to the 1920's, but the medium did not become popular until after World War II.

14. Stevens, *History of News*, pp. 277–281.

15. Ibid., p. 282.

16. Ibid., quoted from p. 255.

17. Ibid., pp. 279, 287.

18. Van Der Karr, "How Dallas Stations Covered Kennedy Shooting," pp. 646–648.

19. Richard Sprague, "The Application of Computers to the Photographic Evidence," *Computers and Automation*, May 1970, includes a list of the photographs and most names of photographers on pp. 52–56.

20. Zelizer, *Body*, quoted from p. 4.

21. Salisbury, "Editor's View," pp. 37–45, quoted from p. 38.

22. Statistics for 1976—provided in 1983 by the Museum of Broadcasting in New York—showed that the Oswald shooting was the #5 top current-affairs show, with the Nixon-JFK debates ranked as #7. For 1980, the shooting ranked #2, the debates were #5, and Jacqueline Kennedy's tour of the White House came in at #6. Typescript, Research Files, SFMA.

23. William L. Rivers, "The Press and the Assassination," in Parker and Greenberg, *Communications in Crisis*, pp. 51–60.

24. "The President and His Son," *Life*, December 3, 1963, pp. 26–36.

25. Philip B. Kunhardt, Jr., ed., *Life in Camelot: The Kennedy Years* (Boston: Little, Brown and Company, 1988), pp. 318–319. *Life*'s November 29 edition was devoted to the crime.

26. *Life*, Memorial Issue, November 29, 1963, pp. 38–57.

27. Ibid., quoted from p. 38.

28. Ibid., pp. 50–52, quotation from p. 52.

29. Ibid., pp. 52 f.

30. See also Schramm, "Introduction."

31. Zelizer, *Body*, p. 5.

32. See, for example, John B. Mayo, Jr., *Bulletin from Dallas: The President Is Dead* (Norris, TN: Exposition Press, 1967), which heaps praise on the media in this regard.

33. "ASNE Speakers Condemn 'Mass Coverage' in Dallas," *Editor & Publisher*, April 18, 1964, pp. 15, 151.

34. Belli recounted his own theatrical role in Melvin Belli, with Maurice S. Carroll, *Dallas Justice: The Real Story of Jack Ruby and His Trial* (New York: McKay, 1964); for Dallas's viewpoint about the affair, see Barry Boesch, "Jack Ruby," in *November 22*, pp. 127–135.

35. Editorial defending treatment of Ruby: *DMN*, January 5, 1967.

36. Lasch, "Kennedy's Death," quoted from p. 34.

37. Harrison Salisbury, *A Time of Change* (New York: Harper and Row, 1988), quoted from p. 68.

38. "ASNE Speakers," quoted from p. 151.

39. WR, pp. 241–242.

40. Ibid., p. 242.

41. Gilbert Cranberg, "Voluntary Press Codes," *Saturday Review*, May 10, 1969, quoted from p. 73.

42. Editorial, *New York Times*, November 25, 1963, reprinted in the *Dallas Times Herald* on November 26, 1963.

43. Charles Lindbergh won fame for his 1927 solo flight across the Atlantic in the *Spirit of St. Louis*.

44. Apparently, reporters roosted in the trees and so angered the owner of the farm that he threw silage at them and kicked several reporters in the backsides. Herbert Brucker, "When the Press Shapes the News," *Saturday Review*, January 11, 1964, p. 76.

45. Rather, *Camera Never Blinks*, chapter 5.

46. Quoted from CBS News, "Who Killed JFK?"

47. See for example, Tom Wicker, "That Day in Dallas," in Parker and Greenberg, *Communications in Crisis*, pp. 29–36, and Salisbury, "Editor's View."

48. Zelizer, *Body*, quoted from pp. 1–2.

49. Ibid., pp. 4–5, 170, et passim.

50. Ibid., quoted from p. 20.

51. Ibid., pp. 17–20.

52. Ibid., pp. 137–141.

53. Ibid., pp. 172–173.

54. See Van Der Karr, "How Dallas Stations Covered Kennedy Slaying," pp. 647–648, and Rather, *Camera Never Blinks*, chapter 5.

55. Rather, *Camera Never Blinks*, chapter 5.

56. Ibid., quoted from p. 115.

57. Zelizer, *Body*, p. 138.

58. Film Collections, SFMA.

59. Zelizer, *Body*, quoted from p. 158.

60. "Remembering Jackie: A Life in Pictures," *Life*, June 1994.

61. Funeral eulogy delivered by Senator Edward Kennedy on May 23, 1994, transcript, Research Files, SFMA.

62. Comments from May 20–21, 1994, Memory Book Collection, SFMA.

63. "The Warren Commission Report," *Time*, October 2, 1964, pp. 45–55, quoted from p. 45.

64. Zelizer, *Body*, p. 137; see also Robert Hennelly and Jerry Policoff, "JFK: How the Media Assassinated the Real Story," *Village Voice*, March 31, 1992, pp. 33–38.

65. "The Warren Commission Report," *Time*, October 2, 1964.

66. The House Committee had to perform detailed tests on the original negative to prove that it was genuine. See chapter 4 for details.

67. Oral history interview with former Congressman Thomas N. Downing, November 2, 1992, audiotape, Oral History Collection, SFMA.

68. Compare Richard Stolley, "Editor's Note," *Life*, November 1983, p. 4, with Hennelly and Policoff, "JFK," p. 35.

69. Larry Howell, "The Doubters Get a Third Helping," *DMN*, August 6, 1966.

70. The average commissioner heard 43% of the testimony taken during hearings: Epstein, *Inquest*, pp. 89 ff.

71. "The Truth about the Kennedy Assassination," *U.S. News & World Report*, October 3, 1966, pp. 44–47, quoted from pp. 44–45.

72. Knebel, "The Warren Commission Report," *Look*, July 12, 1966, pp. 66–70, quoted from p. 66.

73. Salisbury, "Editor's View," p. 40.

74. Zelizer, *Body*, pp. 137–140.

75. Howell, "Third Helping," *DMN*.

76. A. C. Greene, "Another Story of Warren Critique," *DTH*, December 14, 1966.

77. Rather, *Camera Never Blinks*, quoted from p. 128. Hennelly and Policoff argue that CBS did not really try: see "JFK," p. 36.

78. Thompson, *Six Seconds*, pp. 7–21.

79. "Assassination: History or Headlines?" *Newsweek*, March 13, 1967, pp. 44–45.

80. This trend began with Mark Lane, who could not find a major American magazine to publish his first article questioning the investigations. See Mark Lane, "A Defense Brief for Lee Harvey Oswald," *National Guardian*, December 19, 1963; see also interview with Mark Lane, February 1988, transcript, Oral History Collection, SFMA; Welsh and Lifton, "Three Assassins."

81. Zelizer, *Body*, p. 175.

82. Ibid., p. 137.

83. Brown notes, "Perhaps the belief in a conspiracy was so widely held that the committee's findings came as no shock" (*Image*, pp. 79–81).

84. Zelizer, *Body*, pp. 176, 186.

85. Zelizer believes that the media is actively barring the entry of historians into the subject: ibid., pp. 177–184.

86. Ibid., pp. 138, 202 ff.

87. Frank Mankiewicz, commentary at introduction to Stone and Sklar, *JFK: The Book*, quoted from p. 187.

88. Oliver Stone, "Stone's JFK: A Higher Truth?" *Washington Post Outlook*, June 2, 1991, quoted from ibid., p. 199.

89. Ibid.

90. Stone, "Who Is Rewriting History?" *New York Times*, December 20, 1991.

91. Garrison, *On the Trail*.

92. George Lardner, *Washington Post*, May 19, 1991.

93. Quoted from Stone and Sklar, *JFK: The Book*, p. 199.

94. Two articles: Richard M. Mosk and counter by Oliver Stone, both in *American Bar Association Journal*, April 1992, pp. 36–37.

95. Gerald Parshall, "The Man with a Deadly Smirk," *U.S. News & World Report*, August 30/September 6, 1993, pp. 62–72, quoted from p. 71.

96. Norman Mailer, "Footfalls in the Crypt," *Vanity Fair*, February 1992, reprinted in Stone and Sklar, *JFK: The Book*, pp. 438–448, quoted from p. 439.

97. The club, according to Mailer, includes the *Washington Post*, *Newsweek*, *Time*, the FBI, the CIA, the Pentagon, the White House, and the TV networks "on those occasions when they wish to exercise their guest privileges" (ibid., quoted from p. 440).

98. Ibid., quoted from p. 187.

99. The article, titled "Kennedy Assassination: How about the Truth?" appeared in the *Washington Post* on December 17, 1991, and was reprinted in many American newspapers. Quoted in ibid, pp. 253–254.

100. Oliver Stone, "The JFK Assassination: What about the Evidence?" *Washington Post*, December 24, 1991, reprinted in ibid., pp. 257–261, quoted from p. 257.

101. "Who Is Rewriting History?" appeared in the *New York Times* on December 20, 1991. Quoted from ibid, p. 276.

102. Ibid., quoted from p. 261.

103. Ibid., p. 419.

104. AP ran the story: ibid., pp. 421–422.

105. See D. Bradley Kizzia, "Film Renews Public Interest in Assassination," *DMN*, March 29, 1992.

106. Readers should note that some of the information shown in *JFK* was not released until after 1969, so the film was not entirely a period piece.

107. Quoted from Hennelly and Policoff, "JFK," p. 38.

108. Kizzia, "Film Renews Public Interest."

109. Professor G. Robert Blakey, former chief counsel and staff director for the House Select Committee investigation, offered this reason for the fifty-year seal on the records of that probe (telephone interview with the author, 1993).

110. See Jim Lesar, "Free the JFK Papers," *Washington Post*, January 8, 1992; Steve McGonigle, "Into the Light," *DMN*, February 10, 1992; George Lardner, "Panel Creates Exemption to Disclosure of JFK Files," *Washington Post*, July 6, 1992; Steve McGonigle, "Files to Be Opened Today on JFK Death," *DMN*, August 23, 1993. The last article estimated that up to three million documents would end up in the National Archives. The CIA initially withheld 160,000 of its 300,000 pages of material pending formal review by the presidential panel appointed to oversee the final declassification process. President Clinton did not appoint the panel until early September 1993. The executive director was hired in July 1994.

111. See the following articles for a summary of the debate: Pete Slover, "Sixth Floor Sought for JFK Movie," *DMN*, March 1, 1991; "You Spotted Kevin Where?" *DMN*, April 22, 1991; "The Sixth Floor," *DTH*, April 20, 1991.

112. Media clippings about the Dallas debate are in the SFMA Media Files for March and April 1991.

113. "Can Hollywood Solve JFK's Murder?" *Texas Monthly*, December 1991, pp. 128–133, quoted from p. 133.

114. Ibid.

115. See Steve McGonigle, "Bullet Fragments Sought from Connally's Wrist," *DMN*, June 17, 1993; "Connally Won't Be Exhumed, *DMN*, June 19, 1993.

116. "Case Closed," *U.S. News & World Report*, August 30/September 6, 1993, pp. 62–98, including a cover story and two excerpts by the author.

117. Ibid., quoted from inside cover.

118. Ibid., quoted from p. 71.

119. Geoffrey C. Ward, "The Most Durable Assassination Theory: Oswald Did It Alone," *New York Times Book Review*, November 21, 1993, pp. 15–18.

120. Arthur Spiegelman, "Hi-Tech Author Debunks JFK Conspiracy," *Chicago Sun Times*, August 23, 1993.

121. Patricia Holt, "Assassination Enigma Endures," *San Francisco Chronicle*, September 5, 1993.

122. The show, "On the Money," aired on July 31 on the West Coast: ibid.

123. Posner, *Case Closed* (Anchor edition, 1994).

124. The lack of up-to-date research affected several of the reviewers of Posner's book. For example, Mary Perot Nichols of the *Philadelphia Inquirer* did a review in which she noted the author's strong prosecution slant but lauded Posner for his interview with Yuri Nosenko, a Soviet defector who had once handled Oswald's file. Nichols may not have been familiar with the work on Nosenko performed by the House Select Committee on Assassinations during its 1976–78 probe, which was reported in detail in HH 12A: pp. 475–644. A CBS Reports 1993 documentary featured an interview with Nosenko, presenting him as an expert witness. Nosenko is living in the United States under an assumed name. See Mary Perot Nichols, "RIP Conspiracy Theories?" *Philadelphia Inquirer*, August 29, 1993, and CBS News, "Who Shot JFK?"

125. Jeffrey A. Frank, "Who Shot JFK? The 30-Year Mystery," *Washington Post*, October 31, 1993; "The Death of a President," *Economist*, October 9, 1993.

126. See, for example, JFK Assassination Information Center, *Dateline Dallas*, November 1993, with essays from various researchers, and

Fourth Decade 1, no. 1 (November 1993), both located in Research Files, SFMA. The Assassination Archives and Research Center in Washington, D.C., has a special compendium of media articles about *Case Closed*, which is available for a nominal fee.

127. Kurt Anderson, "Does Connie Chung Matter?" *Time*, May 31, 1993, p. 71. Connie Chung was released from her job as anchor during the spring of 1995.

128. David Shaw, "Media Credibility Sinking," *DMN*, June 20, 1993.

CHAPTER 6

1. Leffler and Brent, *Public and Academic History*, pp. 12–13.
2. Lowenthal, *Foreign Country*, p. xxiii; see also pp. 6 ff.
3. Ibid., quoted from p. 8.
4. Columnist James Reston offered the "what might have been" name for the Kennedy legend in "What Was Killed Was Not Only the President but the Promise," *New York Times Magazine*, November 15, 1964, pp. 24–25, 126–127.
5. "World Remembers JFK with Memorial Projects," *DTH*, April 22, 1964.
6. John Geddie, "1,000,000 Stamps Bought First Day," *DMN*, May 30, 1964.
7. "Stravinsky Ode to JFK after Verse of Auden," *Variety*, March 11, 1964.
8. Robert Shelton, "President's Death Is Folk-Disk Dream," *New York Times*, October 11, 1964.
9. Brown, *Image*, quoted from p. 4.
10. See William Payne, "Cultural Center in Washington Would Be Fitting JFK Memorial," *DMN*, November 27, 1963.
11. "Bill to Rename Center Approved," *DMN*, December 12, 1963.
12. The cost of the structure ran over budget. See "JFK Center to Be International Showplace," *DTH*, November 25, 1967, and Leslie Carpenter, "Center for Performing Arts May Be Delayed by Cost Hike," *DTH*, September 16, 1968.
13. William Davis and Christina Tree, *The Kennedy Library* (Exton, PA: Schiffer Publishing Company, 1980), quoted from p. v.
14. Ibid., pp. 79 ff.
15. Ibid., p. 80.
16. See "Kennedy Memorial Library Announced," *Topeka Daily Capital*, December 6, 1963.
17. Davis and Tree, *Kennedy Library*, quoted from p. 99.
18. Ibid., pp. v, 115.
19. Ibid., pp. vi, 80 ff.
20. Ibid., p. 115.
21. Ibid., pp. 115–116. See also "Group Presents 10 Acres of Land for JFK Library," *DTH*, February 18, 1968.
22. Robert Reinhold, "Kennedys Ready a Library Model," *New York Times*, April 8, 1973.
23. Davis and Tree, *Kennedy Library*, pp. 116 f.
24. Ibid., p. 116.
25. "Kennedy Library Plan Scaled Down Greatly," *New York Times*, May 7, 1974. The new structure was estimated to cost $15 million and would not have had space to hold more than six million documents. The rest of the papers would have had to remain in warehouse storage. See "Scale-Down Plans for Kennedy Library Unveiled," *New York Times*, June 8, 1974.
26. Paul Goldberger, "New Library Plan," *New York Times*, June 8, 1974.
27. Ada Louise Huxtable, "What's a Tourist Attraction Like the Kennedy Library Doing in a Nice Neighborhood Like This?" *New York Times*, June 16, 1974.
28. Information taken from the official press kit issued by the library, in Research Files, SFMA.
29. Quoted from Patti Hartigan, "JFK for a New Generation," *Boston Globe*, October 19, 1993.
30. Promark Marketing Survey performed for the Dallas Convention and Visitor Bureau, 1992, in Research Files, SFMA.
31. The city placed signs in the downtown area only a few years ago; these include arrows to The Sixth Floor Museum, but many people do not associate that name with JFK.
32. Foreword to Edward Tabor Linenthal, *Sacred Ground* (Urbana: University of Illinois Press, 1991), p. x.
33. The thesis that the Kennedy legend is one of thwarted promise came from Christopher Lasch: see "Kennedy's Death," quoted from p. 32.
34. Santayana wrote these words in his *Life of Reason* in 1905, quoted in Lowenthal, *Foreign Country*, p. 47.
35. Ibid., pp. 66–69, quoted from p. 69.
36. Linenthal, *Sacred Ground*, discusses the following sites: Lexington and Concord, the Alamo, Gettysburg, Little Bighorn, and Pearl Harbor.

37. Ibid., quoted from p. 213; see also pp. 53–86 on the Alamo and pp. 173–212 on Pearl Harbor.
38. The Kennedy family suggested the architect but did not participate in any formal approval process for the memorial. See Lorraine Haacke, "Design Guided by Simplicity," *DTH*, June 25, 1970.
39. For several years the nurses at Parkland Hospital placed a wreath on the door of Trauma Room #1 on the anniversary date. See Tom Johnson, "Prayers Said at JFK Site," *DMN*, November 23, 1968, and "JFK Memorial Crowd Sparse," *DTH*, November 23, 1970. Once the ceremonies were officially moved to the Kennedy Memorial, interest in attending waned; see Dotty Griffith, "Memories Clear as Dallas Skies," *DMN*, November 22, 1973, which noted that only fifty people attended the ceremony. The Greater Dallas Council of Churches threatened to cancel the ceremony in 1976, but public outcries led the local Democratic party to take it on; see "Traditional JFK Service Canceled," *DTH*, November 16, 1976, and "Memorial Services for JFK Canceled in Dallas," *DMN*, November 18, 1976. Dallas had plans to switch the service to May 29, the date of JFK's birth, but they never materialized; see Sam Attlesey, "Date of JFK Service May Change," *DMN*, October 4, 1983. There was no service in 1984; see "Anniversary of JFK Death Downplayed," *DMN*, November 22, 1984.
40. "Police Arrest `Nazi' at Site of JFK Death," *DMN*, December 8, 1963.
41. The afternoon edition of the *DTH* on November 22, 1988, estimated attendance at 1,500; the *DMN* account on the following day doubled the figure.
42. Pennebaker researched the number of JFK sites in 1989. See *Opening Up*, p. 170. There *was* a small commercial, for-profit "JFK Museum" that operated from 1970 to 1981 from the first floor and basement of the old Dal-Tex Building at 501 Elm Street, just across Houston Street from the Depository. The museum, which featured a small colonial-style sign with its name, was ignored by local residents. When the building changed owners, the operator lost his lease and closed the museum.
43. Shortly after the assassination, the state highway department replaced the Stemmons Freeway sign on the north side of Elm Street with the triple overhead sign above the intersection of Elm and Houston Streets. Other ground-mounted signs were removed later. During the mid-1960's the street lamps were moved from the sidewalks onto the grass, and additional lights were added. At the same time the city added a bronze tablet near Houston Street, with a map of the presidential motorcade route. Two pioneer historical markers were added to the site during the Bicentennial in 1976, and twin memorial flag-poles were placed in the park in 1985. Dealey Plaza today differs little in appearance from 1963: the layout of the park, its major structures and landscape features, the plantings and all of the surrounding buildings were present at the time of the assassination. The former Texas School Book Depository was altered by Dallas County after 1978 by the removal of some additions, and the railroad track that dominated the rail yards has been removed and the ground paved for public parking. The Sixth Floor Museum preserves many of the old Depository elements in its collections.
44. The actual statistic was 96%. Bonjean, Hill, and Martin, "Reactions to the Assassination in Dallas," p. 185.
45. Pennebaker and Polakoff, "Effects of John F. Kennedy Assassination on Dallas," pp. 2 ff.
46. See "Thornton Calls for New Faith," *DMN*, November 28, 1963, and "City Leaders Urge Unity, Dedication" *DTH*, December 1, 1963.
47. For a discussion on the defensiveness, see *November 22*, pp. 144–150.
48. Pennebaker, "Collective Memories," p. 4. See also *November 22*, pp. 144–150.
49. Quoted from Pennebaker, "Collective Memories," pp. 3–4.
50. Ibid.
51. Pennebaker, *Opening Up*, pp. 168–174.
52. Blackie Sherrod, "Shadows: Dallas' Dark Journey," in *November 22*, pp. 151–154.
53. Lowenthal comments on the American urge toward destruction of negative relics from the past: *Foreign Country*, pp. 47–68, quoted from p. 66.
54. Aubrey Mayhew purchased the building at public auction on April 16, 1970, and opened a souvenir shop in the lobby, which operated for about a year. See "The Site of JFK's Death Stands Idle and Unwanted Today," January 6, 1974, Texas School Book Depository Files, Texas/Dallas History and Archives Division, Dallas Public Library. The Byrd family had acquired the structure during the 1930's and leased it to a variety of businesses, including the Texas School Book

Depository Company. See [Shirley Caldwell], "Texas School Book Depository: Application for an Official Texas Historical Marker," typescript, November 6, 1980, Files of the Dallas County Historical Commission. Colonel Byrd, a well-known oilman, had invested in his cousin Richard E. Byrd's Antarctic expedition and founded the Texas Civil Air Patrol during World War II. He removed the original window from the sniper's perch within weeks of the assassination and stored it at home to protect it. The artifact was returned to The Sixth Floor Museum in 1994 by his son, Caruth C. Byrd.

55. See Mike Fresques, "Depository Hit by Arson Blaze," *DMN*, July 21, 1972, which noted that the fire affected two floors, with gasoline cans found on five of the seven levels of the structure. Also "Arson Studied," *DMN*, July 22, 1972; "Employee Charged in Fire," *DMN*, July 27, 1972; Tony Castro, "Mayhew to File Fire Suit," *DMN*, July 30, 1972; Julian Bishop, "Jury May Probe Depository Fire," *DTH*, August 1, 1972; George Proctor, "Grand Jury to Get Arson Testimony," *DMN*, August 1, 1972.

56. Castro, "Mayhew to File Fire Suit."

57. See Fred M. Zeder II, "A Memorial to What?" *DTH*, September 10, 1972.

58. Jerry McCarthy, "Depository Demolition Ruled Out," *DTH*, September 12, 1972.

59. Byrd regained the building in the foreclosure for $471,000. See "Tragic Sensations Haunt Historical Site," *DMN*, May 2, 1976.

60. The county got the option at a price of $400,000; rapid growth in the region indicated that the municipal agency would need 250,000 square feet of additional office space by the year 2000. The bond election set aside $1.4 million for renovation to the old warehouse. See Don Mason, "Depository Renovation Planned," *DMN*," November 5, 1977. See also "County Buys Book Depository," *DTH*, December 6, 1977.

61. In 1983 Mrs. Adams completed the incorporation of a nonprofit organization, the Dallas County Historical Foundation, to oversee the completion of the museum and to operate it for the educational enrichment of the public. The foundation continues to oversee the operation of the museum. By definition, a "museum" is a nonprofit organization devoted to the education of the public.

62. Quoted from the *Texas Humanist*, May 1979, in Texas School Book Depository Files, Dallas Public Library.

63. Dallas County is a large land area comprising twenty-seven municipalities. Dallas is the largest city.

64. Lowenthal, *Foreign Country*, quoted from p. 67.

65. *Newsweek*, February 27, 1978, in Texas School Book Depository Files, Dallas Public Library.

66. I kept an informal diary of my work on the project from 1978 through mid-July 1989, when my work as project director for the exhibit was complete. From June 1987 through July 1989, I kept a detailed diary. Adah Leah Wolf, who joined the project as administrative assistant early in 1987 and was the first staff member hired by the foundation, also kept a daily diary during the final two years of the effort. I compared the two records. My diary remains in my possession; Ms. Wolf's daily record is in the business files of the foundation. The following brief history of the organization of The Sixth Floor Museum is based on these notes and on my personal recollections of events. Quotations, unless footnoted, are approximations.

67. Editorial, *DMN*, February 23, 1978, cites the notion of an art museum. The paper, however, cautioned: "Whatever use is decided upon, the floor's significance in this nation's history should be noted." During the period between 1978 and 1987 the community urge toward extreme purification was dominant.

68. The city did not ask the question, so there were no figures available. When I called in the summer of 1978, I was given detailed statistics about visitation at Southfork, the so-called Ewing Ranch of the television series *Dallas*; Southfork is not even located in Dallas County.

69. Dealey Plaza Visitor Survey, 1978, typescript, Research Files, SFMA.

70. The primary leaders in the Dallas effort were Mrs. Adams, museum President David G. Fox, and County Judge Lee Jackson.

71. See *DTH*, April 20, 1983, in Media Files, SFMA.

72. Laura Miller, *DMN*, April 20, 1983, in Media Files, SFMA.

73. *USA Today*, August 4, 1983, in Media Files, SFMA.

74. Dallas historian Jackie McElhaney was a key member of the research team. Staples & Charles coordinated inquiries at the National Archives using Chuck Briggs, former staff director of the CIA, and Abby Porter. Major consultants included Bob Blakey, photo experts Gary Mack, Jack White, and Robert Groden, assassination specialist Mary Ferrell, box manufacturer Rick Lane, and assassination researchers Jim Moore, Farris Rookstool, and J. Gary Shaw. Others who were called in for professional advice included a team of academics from Southern Methodist University. The team, organized by foundation board member and historian Dr. Glenn Linden, included SMU psychology professor Dr. James Pennebaker, art historian Dr. Mary Vernon, dean and historian Dr. R. Hal Williams, historian Dr. Tom Knock, and political scientist Dr. Dennis Simon. Urban studies professor and sociologist Dr. Paul Geisel from the University of Texas at Arlington offered many insights.

75. Robert Wurmstedt, "The Sixth Floor: Designed to Bring a Tragic Piece of Dallas' Past to Life," *Fort-Worth Star Telegram*, September 1987, in Media Files, SFMA.

76. Several photographers recorded the actual assassination or parts of the shooting. The Zapruder film "head shot," frame #313, is the most graphic depiction.

77. Cheryl Price, "Visitor Evaluation, Sixth Floor Exhibit," 1989, typescript, Business Files, SFMA.

78. The board approved plans for the construction of a four-thousand-square-foot fireproof area beneath the visitor center. The space, designated for use as a public archive and research center, was constructed, but the completion was delayed by the Dallas recession. The archive is scheduled to be finished in 1997–98.

79. In 1989 the historic space could not easily be refitted to reach museum-quality climatic conditions. For this reason the planners limited artifacts. Since 1995 the original window from the sniper's perch and the FBI model of the site, prepared in 1963–64 for use by the Warren Commission, have been placed on loan to the museum. Other original artifacts are being donated regularly to the museum and will be placed on display in changing exhibits on the seventh floor, which Dallas County allocated for museum usage late in 1995.

80. Author's conversation with Seth Kantor, 1988.

81. Henry Tatum, "Sixth Floor's Fragile Lesson," *DMN*, February 16, 1989.

82. The National Historic Landmark program dates from 1935; there are more than eighteen hundred designated landmarks in the United States, of which fewer than one hundred are districts. The Dealey Plaza National Historic Landmark is such a district and includes the park, all surrounding buildings, the triple underpass, and the rail yards north of the park extending to the switching tower.

83. Foundation board member Meg Read chaired the planning and organized a special community task force to handle the logistics.

84. Remarks by Nellie Connally at the dedication ceremony, November 22, 1993, typescript, Dealey Plaza National Historic Landmark Collection, SFMA.

BIBLIOGRAPHY

PRIMARY SOURCES

Dallas County Historical Commission
  Dealey Plaza Buildings Files
  John Sissom Collection
  The Sixth Floor Musuem Files, 1977–83
Dallas Historical Society
  Artifact Collections
  Dallas Times Herald Assassination Collection
  G. B. Dealey Collection
  Jack Ruby Collection
Dallas Public Library, Texas/Dallas History and Archives Division
  Dealey Plaza Buildings Files
  Dealey Plaza Memorial Card Collection
  Kennedy Assassination Files [Extensive]
  Kennedy Books Files
  John F. Kennedy Center for the Performing Arts File
  John F. Kennedy Library File
  Kennedy Memorial Files
  Magazine Collections
  Photographic Collections
  The Sixth Floor Museum Files
  Texas School Book Depository Files
DeGolyer Library, Southern Methodist University
  Dealey Plaza Photographic Collection, 1934–35
John F. Kennedy Library and Museum
  Art Collections
  Miscellaneous Files
  Photographic Collections
  Steinberg Collection
The Sixth Floor Museum Archives
  Artifact Collections
  Assassination Audio Collection
  Assassination Film Collection
  Audio Collections:
    Antenna Productions, audio interviews, 1988–89
    Broadcast documentaries and news programs, selected,
  1963–present
    CBS-TV (New York) selected assassination coverage, video copies
    Dallas radio and TV coverage, November 1963, video and
      audio copies
    Oral History Collection
    Research video and audio for Sixth Floor Films
    Witness assassination film footage for: Abraham Zapruder (various
      states), Orville Nix, Marie Muchmore, Mark Bell, and others
  Business Files
  Dallas Times Herald Collection
  Dealey Plaza National Historic Landmark Collection
  Exhibit Files
  Film Collections
  Media Files
  Memory Book Collection
  Newspaper Collections
  Oral History Collection
  Photographic Collections
  Research Files

GOVERNMENT PUBLICATIONS

*Unless noted otherwise, all publications were issued by
the U.S. Government Printing Office.*

Federal Bureau of Investigation. "Acoustic Gunshot Analysis: The
  Kennedy Assassination and Beyond." *FBI Law Enforcement Bulletin* 52,
  no. 11 (November 1983); 53, no. 12 (December 1983).
National Commission on the Causes and Prevention of Violence. *Report.*
  Washington, D.C., 1969.

National Research Council. *Report of the Committee on Ballistics Acoustics.*
  Washington, D.C.: Department of Justice, 1982.
*Panel Review of Photographs, X-Ray Films, Documents, and Other Evidence
  Pertaining to the Fatal Wounding of President John F. Kennedy on November
  22, 1963, in Dallas, Texas.* Washington, D.C., 1968. [Clark Panel]
Texas Attorney General's Office. *Texas Supplemental Report on the
  Assassination of John F. Kennedy and the Serious Wounding of Gov. John B.
  Connally.* Austin: Texas Attorney General's Office, 1964.
U.S. Commission on CIA Activities within the United States. *Report to the
  President.* Washington, D.C., 1975; New York: Manor Books, 1976.
  [Rockefeller Commission]
U.S. House of Representatives, Select Committee on Assassinations.
  Report and Twelve Accompanying Volumes of Hearings and Appendices.
  Washington, D.C., 1979; *Report*, Bantam edition, 1979.
U.S. President's Commission for a National Agenda for the Eighties.
  Report. Washington, D.C., 1980.
U.S. President's Commission on the Assassination of President John F.
  Kennedy. *Report and Twenty-six Volumes of Supporting Hearings and
  Exhibits.* [Warren *Report*]. Washington, D.C., 1964; *Report*, Bantam edi-
  tion, 1964; St. Martin's Press edition, 1993.
U.S. Senate Select Committee to Study Governmental Operations with
  Respect to Intelligence Activities [Church Committee]. *Alleged
  Assassination Plots Involving Foreign Leaders: Interim Report.* Washington,
  D.C., 1975.
————. *Investigation of the Assassination of President John F. Kennedy, Book V,
  Final Report.* Washington, D.C., 1976.

BOOKS, ARTICLES, AND VIDEOS

ABC News. "Goodnight America." With Geraldo Rivera. March 26, 1975.
  Video, Film Collections, SFMA.
————. "JFK Remembered." Narrated by Peter Jennings. New York: ABC
  Television Video, 1988.
Acheson, Sam. *Dallas Yesterday.* Dallas: Southern Methodist University
  Press, 1977.
Adams, Samuel. "One Man's Obsession." *Waco Tribune-Herald*, September
  3, 1990.
"Alliance for Progress." *Fortune*, May 1961, pp. 87–88, 90.
Anderson, Lee F., and Emerson Morran. "Audience Perceptions of Radio
  and Television Objectivity." In Parker and Greenberg, *Communications
  in Crisis*, pp. 142–146.
"The Annual Questionnaire Returns." *Consumer Reports*, January 1963.
Anson, Robert Sam. "The Shooting of JFK." *Esquire*, November 1991.
Appelbaum, Stephen A. "The Kennedy Assassination." *Psychoanalytic
  Review* 53, no. 3 (Fall 1966): 69–80.
Artwohl, R. R., MD. "JFK's Assassination: Conspiracy, Forensic Science,
  and Common Sense." *Journal of the American Medical Association* 269,
  no. 12 (March 24/31, 1993): 1540–1543.
Asbell, Bernard. "A Legacy of Torment Haunts Those Closest to the JFK
  Assassination." *Today's Health*, October 1973, pp. 56–65.
"ASNE Speakers Condemn 'Mass Coverage' in Dallas." *Editor & Publisher*,
  April 18, 1964, pp. 15, 151.
Associated Press. *The Torch Is Passed. . . .* New York: Associated Press,
  1963.
Attwood, William. "In Memory of JFK." *Look*, December 31, 1963, pp.
  11–12.
Bauer, Bruce. "Whatever Happened to Doris Day?" In Terry Teachout,
  ed., *Beyond the Boom*, pp. 149–223. New York: Poseidon, 1990.
Belin, David W. *Final Disclosure: The Truth about the Assassination of President
  Kennedy.* New York: Scribner's, 1988.
————. *Nov. 22, 1963: You Are the Jury.* New York: Quadrangle, 1973.
Bell, J. Bowyer. *Assassin!* New York: St. Martin's Press, 1979.
Belli, Melvin, and Maurice S. Carroll. *Dallas Justice: The Real Story of Jack
  Ruby and His Trial.* New York: McKay, 1964.
Berendt, John. "Ten Years Later, A Look at the Record: What School
  Books Are Teaching Our Kids about JFK." *Esquire*, November 1973,
  pp. 140, 263–265.

Bird, S. Elizabeth. "Media and Folklore as Intertextural Processes: John F. Kennedy and the Supermarket Tabloids." *Communications Yearbook* 10:758–772. Newbury Park, CA: Sage, 1987.

Bishop, Jim. *A Day in the Life of President Kennedy*. New York: Random House, 1964.

———. *The Day Kennedy Was Shot*. New York: Funk and Wagnalls, 1968.

Blakey, G. Robert, and Richard N. Billings. *Fatal Hour*. New York: Berkley, 1992.

———. *The Plot to Kill the President*. New York: Times Books, 1981.

Bonjean, Charles M., Richard J. Hill, and Harry W. Martin. "Reactions to the Assassination in Dallas." In Parker and Greenberg, *Communications in Crisis*, pp. 178–198.

Booker, Christopher. *The Seventies*. New York: Stein and Day, 1980.

Boorstin, Daniel J. *The Americans: The Democratic Experience*. New York: Random House, 1973.

Bradlee, Benjamin. *That Special Grace*. Philadelphia: Lippincott, 1964.

Brandimarte, Cynthia A. "The Sixth Floor." *Journal of American History*, June 1991, pp. 268–274.

Brener, Milton E. *The Garrison Case: A Study in the Abuse of Power*. New York: Clarkson N. Potter, 1969.

Brennan, Howard, with J. Edward Cherryholmes. *Eyewitness to History*. Waco, TX: Texian Press, 1987.

Breo, Dennis L. "JFK's Death: The Plain Truth from the MD's Who Did the Autopsy." *Journal of the American Medical Association* 267, no. 20 (May 27, 1992): 2800 ff.

Brown, Thomas. *JFK: History of an Image*. Bloomington: Indiana University Press, 1988.

Brucker, Herbert. "When the Press Shapes the News." *Saturday Review*, January 11, 1964, pp. 75–77, 85.

Buchanan, Thomas. *Who Killed Kennedy?* New York: G. P. Putnam's Sons, 1964.

[Caldwell, Shirley.] "Texas School Book Depository: Application for an Official Texas Historical Marker." Typescript. Dallas County Historical Commission, 1980.

Callahan, Bob. *Who Shot JFK?* New York: Simon and Schuster, 1993.

Canfield, Michael, and Alan J. Weberman. *Coup d'Etat in America: The CIA and the Assassination of John F. Kennedy*. New York: Third Press, 1975.

"Can Hollywood Solve JFK's Murder?" *Texas Monthly*, December 1991, pp. 128–133.

CBS News. "Four Days in November." With Dan Rather. November 17, 1988. Video, Film Collections, SFMA.

———. *Transcript of CBS News Inquiry: The Warren Commission*. New York: CBS, 1967.

———. "Who Shot JFK? The Final Chapter." With Dan Rather. November 19, 1993. Video, Film Collections, SFMA.

Cheney, Allison A. *Dallas Spirit: A Political History of the City of Dallas*. Dallas: McMullan Publishing, 1991.

Clinch, Nancy Gager. *The Kennedy Neurosis*. New York: Grosset and Dunlap, 1973.

Condon, Richard. *Winter Kills*. New York: Dial, 1974.

Corry, John. *The Manchester Affair*. New York: G. P. Putnam's Sons, 1967.

Costigliola, Frank C. "Like Children in the Darkness: European Reaction to the Assassination of John F. Kennedy." *Journal of Popular Culture* 20, no. 3 (Winter 1986): 115–124.

Cranberg, Gilbert. "Voluntary Press Codes." *Saturday Review*, May 10, 1969.

Crenshaw, Charles A., MD, with Jens Hansen and J. Gary Shaw. *JFK: Conspiracy of Silence*. New York: Penguin, 1992.

Crotty, William S. "Presidential Assassinations." *Society*, May 1972, pp. 18–25.

Curry, Jesse E. *JFK Assassination File*. Dallas: American Poster and Printing Company, 1969.

Cutler, Robert B. *The Flight of CE-399: Evidence of Conspiracy*. Beverly, MA: Cutler Designs, 1970.

Dallas County Historical Foundation. "Application for Designation of Dealey Plaza as a National Historical Landmark." 1991. Typescript, Dealey Plaza National Historic Landmark Collection, SFMA.

The Dallas Morning News. November 22: The Day Remembered. Dallas: Taylor Publishing Company, 1990.

The Dallas Morning News. November 22–26, 1963, issues.

The Dallas Morning News: Articles

"[Adlai Stevenson:] Our Apologies." October 26, 1963.

"Advisor Wants to Know How Many See JFK Site." September 9, 1978.

"After 200 Years It's Still Big News." December 1, 1976.

Anders, John. "We've Waited 30 Years for This Moment." April 18, 1993.

"Arson Studied." July 22, 1972.

Attlesey, Sam. "Date of JFK Service May Change." October 4, 1983.

"Author Claims Attempt to Stop Book on JFK." September 18, 1966.

Aynesworth, Hugh, and James Ewell. "Slaying Reviewed: Probers at Scene." May 8, 1963.

Bernarbo, Marc. "Council Rejects Razing." September 12, 1972.

"Bill to Rename Center Approved." December 12, 1963.

Borges, Walter, and Barry Boesch. "Depository was Torched, Officials Say." August 24, 1984.

"Brief Service to Note JFK Assassination." November 22, 1978.

"Briton's Bid to Open Oswald's Grave Rejected." June 2, 1979.

Castro, Tony. "Mayhew to File Fire Suit." July 30, 1972.

"Chamber of Commerce Head Says Dallas Treated with Vengeance." February 23, 1964.

Chism, Olin. "The Travails of a JFK Biographer." December 13, 1992.

"City to Take No Part in Kennedy Ceremonies." July 8, 1983.

"Connally Won't Be Exhumed." June 19, 1993.

Editorial. December 8, 1963.

Editorial. January 5, 1967.

Editorial. November 21, 1967.

Editorial. February 23, 1978.

"Employee Charged in Fire." July 27, 1972.

"Federal Approval Assures Project Being Completed." March 18, 1934.

"Few Attend Memorial for JFK." November 22, 1978.

Fresques, Mike. "Depository Hit by Arson Blaze." July 21, 1972.

"Full Text of Statement by Mayor Cabell Given." November 27, 1963.

Geddie, John. "1,000,000 Stamps Bought First Day." May 30, 1964.

Golz, Earl. "Assassin of JFK a European, Author of Best-Selling Book Says." January 18, 1976.

———. "New Book Alleges Body of Assassin Not Oswald." November 23, 1975.

———. "New Views of the Assassination." July 6, 1980.

Griffith, Dotty. "Memories Clear as Dallas Skies." November 22, 1973.

Hess, John L. "New Book Out on JFK Death." January 2, 1969.

"Historic Meeting Set for Memorial." November 21, 1964.

Housewright, Ed. "Building's Use in JFK Film Backed." March 6, 1991.

Howard, Judy. "Ex-JFK Aide Calls Project 'Morbid.'" June 1, 1988.

Howell, Larry. "The Doubters Get a Third Helping." August 6, 1966.

———. "Second Assassin?" June 10, 1966.

Jackson, David. "JFK: An Eternal Flame." November 21, 1993.

Johnson, Tom. "JFK Honored Today." June 24, 1970.

———. "Monument to Kennedy Dedicated." June 25, 1970.

———. "Prayers Said at JFK Site." November 23, 1968.

"Jonsson Hopes Hate Myth Ended." September 28, 1964.

"Kennedy's Life an Open Book." November 21, 1993

Kizzia, D. Bradley. "Film Renews Public Interest in Assassination." March 29, 1992.

Mack, Gary. Book review. December 18, 1994.

Mason, Don. "Depository Renovation Planned." November 5, 1977.

"Mayor Jonsson Proposes Minute's Silence on Sunday." November 21, 1964.

McGonigle, Steve. "Bullet Fragments Sought from Connally's Wrist." June 17, 1993.

———. "Files to Be Opened Today on JFK Death." August 23, 1993.

———. "Into the Light." February 10, 1992.

"Memorial Services for JFK Canceled in Dallas." November 18, 1976.

"Memorial's Start, Dedication Slated." June 20, 1969.

Miller, Laura. "Anniversary of JFK Death Downplayed." November 22, 1984.

"New Study Claims 3 Shot at Kennedy." November 16, 1967.

Payne, William. "Cultural Center in Washington Would Be Fitting JFK Memorial." November 27, 1963.

"Police Arrest 'Nazi' at Site of JFK Death." December 8, 1963.

Powell, Larry. "Looking Back on JFK Theories and Ugly '60s Shoes." September 2, 1993.

Proctor, George. "Grand Jury to Get Arson Testimony." August 1, 1972.

Quinn, Mike. "Civic Leaders Wire Apologies to Adlai." October 26, 1963.

Rabe, Stephen G. "JFK: Evaluating His 1,000-Day Term as President." June 5, 1983.

Real, David. "Questions Linger after Doctor Airs His JFK Theory." April 9, 1992.

Shaw, David. "Media Credibility Sinking." June 20, 1993.

Shevis, Jim. "Manchester Not Only Author to Feel Kennedy's Pressure." September 18, 1966.

Slover, Pete. "Sixth Floor Sought for JFK Movie." March 1, 1991.

Sumner, Jane. "JFK: The Mystery Becomes the Movie." April 14, 1991.

Tatum, Henry. "Sixth Floor's Fragile Lesson." February 16, 1989.

Thornton, Joe. "Notion of Dallas' Guilt Debunked by Attorney." February 21, 1964.

"Thornton Calls for New Faith." November 28, 1963.

Tinkle, Lon. "Kennedy Career in Picture and Prose." November 28, 1965.

"Traditional JFK Service Canceled." November 18, 1976.

"Tragic Sensations Haunt Historical Site." May 2, 1979.

West, Dick. "Assassination Book Slams Dallas." November 24, 1986.

"Which Is History?" March 17, 1966.

"Why Did It Happen Here? Residents of Dallas Ask." November 30, 1963.

"You Spotted Kevin Where?" April 22, 1991.

Dallas Times Herald. November 19–26, 1963, issues.

Dallas Times Herald: Articles

"Assassination Books Due." July 19, 1979.

"Attacks on Adlai Scored." October 25, 1963.

"Author Seeks Assassination Film Release." December 13, 1967.

Bishop, Julian. "Jury May Probe Depository Fire." August 1, 1972.

Brown, Jeff. "Kennedy Museum Still Stuck in Planning Stage." August 19, 1984.

Carpenter, Leslie. "Center for Performing Arts May Be Delayed by Cost Hike." September 16, 1968.

Chism, Olin. "The Assassination: Defense for Warren Report." December 12, 1973.

"The Citizens of Dallas Honor the Memory of John F. Kennedy." August 26, 1964.

"City Leaders Urge Unity, Dedication." December 1, 1963.

"County Buys Book Depository." December 6, 1977.

"County Officials Favor Garage for JFK Exhibit." May 19, 1987.

Dudney, Bob. "Helms Says Documents Disappeared from Oswald's File." September 23, 1978.

Editorial. November 27, 1963.

Editorial. December 4, 1963.

Featherston, Jim. "Bringing Doubts to Warren Report." June 26, 1966.

"Former Caretaker Indicted in Fire." September 19, 1972.

Greene, A. C. "Another Story of Warren Critique." December 14, 1966.

———. "The Best Picture of Oswald." June 13, 1965.

———. "Better Hear the Critics Out." April 19, 1964.

———. "What Adlai Gave Dallas." July 18, 1965.

———. "Why Do So Many Hate the Kennedys?" November 20, 1963.

"Group Presents 10 Acres of Land for JFK Library." February 18, 1968.

Gunn, Steve. "Eddowes Fighting Tough Odds." October 22, 1979.

Haacke, Lorraine. "Design Guided by Simplicity." June 25, 1970.

Henderson, Jim. "'Climate of Hate' Ruled City in 1963." November 17, 1983.

———. "Intolerance Bred Dallas' Disgrace." November 18, 1983.

Hitt, Dick. "A Distorted Window into Dallas' Soul." August 7, 1988.

"JFK Center to Be International Showplace." November 25, 1967.

"JFK Memorial Crowd Sparse." November 23, 1970.

Lahar, James. "Lee Harvey Oswald: Beyond Legal Doubt?" September 4, 1966.

Lardner, George, Jr. "Does Mark Lane Direct JFK Probe?" March 15, 1977.

Lui, David. "The Little Girl Must Have Heard." June 3, 1979.

Lyons, Douglas C. "Judge Wants to Complete JFK Exhibit." January 3, 1987.

"Magazine Asks New Probe of Kennedy Assassination." November 21, 1966.

McCarthy, Jerry. "Depository Demolition Ruled Out." September 12, 1993.

"Methodists Plan Good Will Move." November 30, 1963.

"NBC Remote Pickup from Dallas Monday." November 16, 1975.

"Offers Yet Another Book for the Assassination Shelf." June 15, 1966.

Parks, Scott. "Panel Calls for JFK Assassination Memorial." April 13, 1979.

"Photos of Kennedy's Body Stir Up Fresh Controversy." October 26, 1988.

Porter, Bob. "JFK Memory Dance Ballet Tribute Abuzz." November 26, 1964.

Pusey, Allen. "Epstein Book Probes Lee H. Oswald's Secret Life." March 29, 1978.

"Sale of Warren Commission Sets." November 4, 1976.

"The Sixth Floor." April 20, 1991.

"A Statement about Michael Eddowes." September 14, 1977.

"Stevenson Voices Shock over Near-Riot after Talk." October 25, 1963.

"Stop Worrying about Image, Dallasites Told." March 27, 1964.

Taylor, Bob. Editorial cartoon. November 19, 1963.

"Texas Caricature Drawn in Speech." March 27, 1964.

"Traditional JFK Service Canceled." November 16, 1976.

Van Cleve, Dan. "British Author Says Oswald Really a Russian Imposter." January 10, 1979.

Von Zelfden, Alan. "County Again Shuts Window on Stone's Request." March 27, 1991.

"World Remembers JFK with Memorial Projects." April 22, 1964.

Zeder, Fred M., II. "A Memorial to What?" September 10, 1972.

Davis, John H. *The Kennedys: Dynasty and Disaster*. New York: McGraw-Hill, 1984.

———. *Mafia Kingfish: Carlos Marcello and the Assassination of John F. Kennedy*. New York: Times Books, 1981.

Davis, William, and Christina Tree. *The Kennedy Library*. Exton, PA: Schiffer Publishing Company, 1980.

Dealey Plaza Historic District. "Application for Designation as a National Historic Landmark." Typescript. National Park Service, Washington, D.C., 1991.

"The Death of a President." *Economist*. October 9, 1993, p. 9.

DeLillo, Don. *Libra*. New York: Penguin, 1989.

Denisoff, Serge R. *Sing a Song of Social Significance*. 2d ed. Bowling Green, OH: Bowling Green State University Press, 1983.

DePauw, Linda Grant, and Conover Hunt. *Remember the Ladies: Women in America, 1750–1815*. New York: Viking Press, 1976.

Discovery Channel. "The End of Camelot." November 21, 1993. Video, Film Collections, SFMA.

Eddowes, Michael. *Oswald File*. New York: Clarkson N. Potter, 1977.

Edelman, Murray, and Rita James Simon. "Presidential Assassinations: Their Meaning and Impact on American Society." *Ethics* 79, no. 3 (April 1969): 199–221.

Edelstein, Andrew J., and Kevin McDonough. *The Seventies*. New York: Dutton, 1990.

Ehrenreich, Barbara. *The Worst Years of Our Lives*. New York: Harper's Perennial Edition, 1991.

Eisenschiml, Otto. *Why Was Lincoln Murdered?* New York: Grosset and Dunlap, 1937.

Epstein, Edward Jay. *Inquest: The Warren Commission and the Establishment of Truth*. New York: Bantam, 1966; Viking, 1966.

———. "Journalism and Truth." In George Rodman, ed., *Mass Media Issues: Analysis and Debate*, pp. 89–98. Chicago: Science Research Associates, 1981.

———. *Legend: The Secret World of Lee Harvey Oswald*. New York: *Reader's Digest* Press, 1978; Ballantine, 1979.

———. "A Second Primer of Assassination Theories." *Esquire*, May 1967.

———. "Who's Afraid of the Warren Report? A Primer of Assassination Theories." *Esquire*, December 1966.

Ewen, David. "Rebels with a Cause." *In All the Years of American Popular Music*, pp. 640–657. New York: Prentiss-Hall, 1977.

Exner, Judith Campbell. *My Story*. New York: Grove Press, 1977.

Fairlee, Henry. *The Kennedy Promise: The Politics of Expectation*. New York: Doubleday, 1973; Dell Publishing, 1973.

Fay, Paul Burgess. *The Pleasure of His Company*. New York: Holt and Rinehart, 1966.

Feldman, Harold. "Fifty-One Witnesses: The Grassy Knoll." *Minority of One*, March 1965, pp. 15–25.

Fensterwald, Bernard. "A Legacy of Suspicion." *Esquire*, November 1973.

Ferrell, Mary. "Texas School Book Depository." Dallas, 1988. Typescript, Research Files, SFMA.

———. "Transcripts of Dallas Police Radio Logs, Channels #1 and 2." Dallas, n.d. Typescript, Research Files, SFMA.

Fonzi, Gaeton. *The Last Investigation*. New York: Thunder Mouth Press, 1993.

Ford, Franklin L. *Political Murder: From Tyrannicide to Terrorism*. Cambridge: Harvard University Press, 1985.

Ford, Gerald R., and John R. Stiles. *Portrait of an Assassin*. New York: Simon and Schuster, 1965.

Fox, Sylvan. *The Unanswered Questions about President Kennedy's Assassination*. New York: Award Books, 1975.

Frank, Jeffrey A. "Who Shot JFK? The 30-Year Mystery." *Washington Post*, October 31, 1993.

Freed, Donald, and Mark Lane. *Executive Action: Assassination of a Head of State*. New York: Dell, 1973.

———. *Executive Action*. 1973. Video, Film Collections, SFMA.

Freeman, John. "The Man We Trusted." *New Statesman*, November 29, 1963.

Frewin, Anthony, comp. *The Assassination of John F. Kennedy: An Annotated Film, TV, and Videography, 1963–1992*. Westport, CT: Greenwood Press, 1993.

Garber, Judy, and Martin E. P. Seligman, eds. *Human Helplessness: Theory and Applications.* New York: Academic Press, 1980.

Garrison, Jim. *On the Trail of the Assassins: My Investigation and Prosecution of the Murder of President Kennedy.* New York: Sheridan Square Press, 1988.

Goodwin, Doris Kearns. *The Fitzgeralds and the Kennedys.* New York: Simon and Schuster, 1987.

Gordon, Lois, and Alan Gordon. *American Chronicle, 1920–1980.* New York: Atheneum, 1987.

Greenberg, Bradley S. "Diffusion of News of the Kennedy Assassination." *Public Opinion Quarterly* 28 (Summer 1964): 225–232.

Greene, A. C. *Dallas USA.* Austin: *Texas Monthly* Press, 1984.

———. *A Place Called Dallas.* Dallas: Dallas County Heritage Society, 1975.

Greenstein, Fred I. "College Students' Reactions to the Assassination." In Parker and Greenberg, *Communications in Crisis,* pp. 221–239.

Greenstein, Fred L. "Popular Images of the President." *American J Iournal of Psychiatry,* November 1965, pp. 523–529.

Groden, Robert. *The Killing of a President.* New York: Viking Penguin, 1993.

Groden, Robert, and Harrison Livingston. *High Treason: The Assassination of John F. Kennedy.* Baltimore: Conservatory Press, 1989.

Guth, DeLoyd J., and David R. Wrone. *The Assassination of John F. Kennedy: A Comprehensive Historical and Legal Bibliography.* Westport, CT: Greenwood Press, 1980.

Hackett, Alice Payne, and James Henry Burke. *Eighty Years of Best Sellers, 1895–1975.* New York: R. R. Bowker Company, 1977.

Halberstam, David. *The Best and the Brightest.* New York: Random House, 1969.

Halbwachs, Maurice. *The Collective Memory.* New York: Harper and Row, 1980.

Hamilton, Nigel. *JFK: Reckless Youth.* New York: Random House, 1992.

Hamm, Charles. *Yesterdays: Popular Song in America.* New York: W. W. Norton and Company, 1979.

Hanchett, William. *The Lincoln Murder Conspiracies.* Urbana: University of Illinois Press, 1986.

Hardy, James. "Subtle Challenge for America." *Music Educators Journal,* June-July 1965, p. 98.

Hartigan, Patti. "JFK for a New Generation." *Boston Globe,* October 19, 1993.

Hennelly, Robert, and Jerry Policoff. "JFK: How the Media Assassinated the Real Story." *Village Voice,* March 31, 1992, pp. 33–38.

Heyman, David C. *A Woman Named Jackie.* New York: Lyle Stewart/Carrol Communications, 1989.

Hill, Jean, and Bill Sloan. *JFK: The Last Dissenting Witness.* Gretna: Pelican Publishing Company, 1992.

Holt, Patricia. "Assassination Enigma Endures." *San Francisco Chronicle,* September 5, 1993.

Horowitz, Mardi Jon, MD. *Stress Response Syndromes.* New York: Jason Aronson, 1976.

Hosmer, Charles B., Jr. *Presence of the Past.* New York: G. P. Putnam's Sons, 1965.

Hunt, Conover. *The Sixth Floor: John F. Kennedy and the Memory of a Nation.* Dallas: Dallas County Historical Foundation, 1989.

———. *A Visitor's Guide to Dealey Plaza National Historic Landmark.* Dallas: The Sixth Floor Museum, 1995.

Hurn, Christopher J., and Mark Messer. "Grief and Rededication." In Parker and Greenberg, *Communications in Crisis,* pp. 336–349.

Hurt, Henry. *Reasonable Doubt.* New York: Holt, Rinehart, and Winston, 1985.

Institute for Earth and Man, Southern Methodist University. "Archaeological Resources Impact: Potential of P100 Alternatives, CBD, Dallas." Report prepared for Dallas Area Rapid Transit. Dallas, March 22, 1988. Typescript, Research Files, SFMA.

Jebsen, Harry, Jr., Robert M. Newton, and Patricia R. Hogan. "A Centennial History of the Dallas, Texas, Parks System, 1876–1976." Typescript. Texas Tech University, Lubbock, 1976. Dealey Plaza Buildings Files, Dallas Public Library.

Jellicoe, G. A. "Landscape Memorial [Runnymede]." *Architectural Review* 138 (October 1965).

JFK Assassination Information Center. *Dateline Dallas.* Dallas: JFK Assassination Information Center, 1993.

"John F. Kennedy Center for the Performing Arts in Retrospect." *Choral and Organ Guide* 19 (October 1966).

John F. Kennedy Library. *JFK: A Reading List.* Boston: John F. Kennedy Library, 1975.

Johnson, Lyndon Baines. *The Vantage Point.* New York: Popular Press, 1971.

Joling, Robert J., JD. "The JFK Assassination: Still an Unsolved Murder Mystery." Part 3. *Saturday Evening Post,* December 1975.

Jones, Penn. *Forgive My Grief.* 4 vols. Midlothian, TX: Midlothian Press, 1966–76.

Kantor, Seth. *Who Was Jack Ruby?* Costa Mesa, CA: Everest House, 1978.

Kearns, Doris. *Lyndon Johnson and the American Dream.* New York: Harper and Row, 1976.

Kennedy, John F. *Public Papers of the Presidents of the United States.* Washington, D.C.: U.S. Government Printing Office, 1962–64.

"Kennedy Memorial Library Announced." *Topeka Daily Capital,* December 6, 1963.

"Kennedy Pro Art . . . et Sequitur?" *Art News* 62, no. 1 (January 1964): 23, 46.

"Kennedy's Death Causes Tour and Concert Cancellations." *Down Beat* 31, no. 1 (January 2, 1964).

Ketchum, Richard M., ed. *The World of George Washington.* New York: McGraw-Hill, 1974.

Kirkwood, James. *American Grotesque.* New York: Simon and Schuster, 1970.

Klapthor, Margaret Brown, and Howard Alexander Morrison. *G. Washington: A Figure upon a Stage.* Washington, D.C.: National Museum of American History, Smithsonian Institution, 1982.

Knebel, Fletcher. "The Warren Commission Report on the Assassination Is Struck by a New Wave of Doubts." *Look,* July 12, 1966.

Kruger, Barbara, and Phil Mariana, eds. *Remaking History.* Seattle: Bay Press, 1989.

Kunhardt, Philip B., Jr., ed. *Life in Camelot: The Kennedy Years.* Boston: Little, Brown and Company, 1988.

Kurtz, Michael L. *Crime of the Century: The Kennedy Assassination from a Historian's Perspective.* Knoxville: University of Tennessee Press, 1982.

Lane, Mark. "A Defense Brief for Lee Harvey Oswald." *National Guardian,* December 19, 1963.

———. *Rush to Judgment.* Austin: Holt and Rinehart, 1966.

Lang, Kurt, and Gladys Engeland, with Thomas J. Johnson and Peggy E. Roberts. "Collective Memory and the News." *Communications* 11, no. 2 (1989): 123–140.

Lardner, George. "Panel Creates Exemption to Disclosure of JFK Files." *Washington Post,* July 6, 1992.

Lasch, Christopher. "The Life of Kennedy's Death." *Harpers,* October 1983.

Lasky, Victor. JFK: *The Man and the Myth.* New York: Dell, 1977.

Lattimer, John K., MD., with Gary Lattimer and Jon Lattimer. "Additional Data on the Shooting of President Kennedy." *Journal of the American Medical Association* 269, no. 12 (March 24/31, 1993): 1544–1547.

———. "Could Oswald Have Shot President Kennedy?" *Bulletin of the New York Academy of Medicine,* 2d ser., 48, no. 3 (April 1972): 113–124.

———. *Kennedy and Lincoln: Medical and Ballistic Comparisons of Their Assassinations.* San Diego: Harcourt Brace Jovanovich, 1980.

———. "Observations Based on a Review of the Autopsy Photographs, X-Rays, and Related Materials of the Late President John F. Kennedy." *Resident and Staff Physician,* May 1972, pp. 34–64.

"Leader of the West." *Economist,* November 30, 1963.

Leffler, Phyllis K., and Joseph Brent. *Public and Academic History: A Philosophy and Paradigm.* Malamar, FL: Robert E. Krieger Publishing Company, 1990.

"Legacy of Style." In Washington Home, *Washington Post,* May 26, 1994.

Lerner, Max. "The World Impact." *New Statesman,* December 23, 1963.

Lesar, Jim. "Free the JFK Papers." *Washington Post,* January 8, 1992.

Leslie, Warren. *Dallas Public and Private.* New York: Grossman Publishers, 1964.

Lewis, Lloyd. *Myths after Lincoln.* Gloucester, MA: Peter Smith, 1973.

Life. Articles
    Assassination Issue. November 29, 1963.
    Connally, John B. "Why Kennedy Went to Texas." November 24, 1967.
    "The Early Bird Gets the Word." May 7, 1965.
    "Four Days That Stopped America." November 29, 1963.
    Grunwald, Lisa. "Why We Still Care." November 1991.
    John F. Kennedy Memorial Edition. December 6, 1963.
    "A Matter of Reasonable Doubt." November 25, 1966.
    "The President and His Son." December 3, 1963.
    "Remembering Jackie: A Life in Pictures." June 1994.
    Stolley, Richard. "Editor's Note." November 1983.
    "We Wade Deeper into Jungle War." January 25, 1963.
    White, Theodore. "An Epilogue." December 6, 1963.

Lifton, David. *Best Evidence: Disguise and Deception in the Assassination of John F. Kennedy.* New York: Macmillan, 1980; Dell Publishing, 1982; Carroll and Graf, 1988.

Lincoln, Evelyn. *My Twelve Years with John F. Kennedy.* New York: D. McKay, Company, 1965.

Linenthal, Edward Tabor. *Sacred Ground.* Urbana: University of Illinois Press, 1991.

Loftus, Elizabeth F. *Eyewitness Testimony.* Cambridge: Harvard University Press, 1979.

London Weekend Television. "On Trial: Lee Harvey Oswald." 5-part series, 1986.

Lowe, Jacques. *Kennedy: A Time Remembered.* New York: Quartet Books, 1983.

Lowenthal, David. *The Past Is a Foreign Country.* Cambridge: Cambridge University Press, 1985.

Lyons, Gene. "Conspiracy Killer." *Entertainment Weekly,* September 24, 1993, pp. 82–84.

Mack, Gary. "Eyes Closed: The Case against Gerald Posner." *Fourth Decade* 1, no. 1 (November 1993): 15–18.

Mailer, Norman. *Oswald's Tale.* New York: Random House, 1995.

Manchester, William. *The Death of a President.* New York: Harper and Row, 1967.

———. *One Brief Shining Moment: Remembering Kennedy.* New York: Little Brown, 1983.

Marrs, Jim. *Crossfire: The Plot That Killed Kennedy.* New York: Carroll and Graf, 1989.

Mayo, John B., Jr. *Bulletin from Dallas: The President Is Dead.* Norris, TN: Exposition Press, 1967.

Meagher, Sylvia. *Assessories after the Fact: The Warren Commission, the Authorities, and the Report.* New York: Bobbs-Merrill, 1967; Vintage, 1976.

———. "Notes for a New Investigation." *Esquire,* December 1966.

———. *Subject Index to the Warren Report and Hearings and Exhibits.* New York: Scarecrow Press, 1966; Vintage Books, 1976.

Meagher, Sylvia, and Gary Owens. *Master Index to the J.F.K. Assassination Investigationss.* Metuchen, N.J.: Scarecrow Press, 1980.

Menninger, Bonar. *Mortal Error: The Shot That Killed JFK.* New York: St. Martin's Press, 1992.

Meyer, Karl. "History as Tragedy." *New Statesman,* November 29, 1963.

———. "The World and the White House." *New Statesman,* December 23, 1963.

Mindak, William A., and Gerald D. Hursh. "Television's Functions in the Assassination Weekend." In Parker and Greenberg, *Communications in Crisis,* pp. 131–141.

Minnis, Jack, and Stoughton Lind. "Seeds of Doubt: Some Questions about the Assassination." *New Republic,* December 21, 1963.

Moore, Jim. *Conspiracy of One.* Fort Worth, TX: Summit Group, 1990.

Morrison, Joan, and Robert K. Morrison. *From Camelot to Kent State.* New York: Times Books, 1987.

National Park Service. "Reconnaissance Report on Dealey Plaza." December 1987. Typescript, Dealey Plaza National Historic Landmark Collection, SFMA.

NBC News. "The Week We Lost John F. Kennedy." With John Chancellor. March 1989. Video Series, Film Collections, SFMA.

Nestvold, Karl J. "Oregon Radio-TV Response to the Kennedy Assassination." *Broadcasting* 8, no. 2 (Spring 1964): 141–146.

Newman, John M. *JFK and Vietnam: Deception, Intrigue, and the Struggle for Power.* New York: Warner Books, 1992.

Newsweek: Articles

"Assassination: History or Headlines?" March 13, 1967.

"Dumber Than We Thought." September 20, 1993.

"Jacqueline Kennedy Onassis, 1929–1994." May 30, 1994.

"Long Live Telstar II." May 20, 1963.

"The Peace Corps Grows Up." March 10, 1986.

"Rifles: Target for Control?" December 28, 1964.

"Taking a Flyer in Outer Space." March 16, 1964.

"A Taste for Conspiracy." March 20, 1967.

"Vietnam's Many-Sided War." December 10, 1962.

"Why? Because It's There." September 24, 1962.

New York Times. Kennedy Years. New York: Viking Press, 1964.

New York Times. November 23–26, 1963, issues.

New York Times: Articles

"Anniversary of Kennedy's Death Is Noted Quietly in Dealey Plaza." November 23, 1984.

"Army-Navy Game Postponed." November 27, 1963.

Daniel, Clifton. "Kennedy, Nixon: Two Faces of One Era." November 22, 1973.

DeMohrenschildt, George. "Couple Tie Death of Kennedy Whose Kin They Also Know, to a Domestic Quarrel." December 12, 1966.

"Doubt on Warren Report." March 7, 1967.

Dowd, Maureen. "City Tour: A Trauma as Legend." August 22, 1984.

Editorial. November 22, 1973.

Hamilton, Thomas J. "Security Council Is Asked to Meet: U.S. Seeks Session Today for Resolution in Cuba." October 23, 1962.

Huxtable, Ada Louise. "What's a Tourist Attraction Like the Kennedy Library Doing in a Nice Neighborhood Like This?" June 16, 1974.

Kappett, Leonard. "Decision Is Made by the Pentagon." November 27, 1963.

"Kennedy Library Plan Scaled Down Greatly." May 7, 1974.

Kenworth, W. E. "Plans to End Blockade as Soon as Moscow Lives Up to Vow." October 29, 1962.

King, Wayne. "Building That Hid Oswald Hit by Fire." August 24, 1984.

"Magic of Camelot Fades." November 22, 1973.

"New Library Plan." June 8, 1974.

"Pentagon Papers." June 13–15, July 1, 1971.

"Polls Say [Manchester] Dispute Hurt Mrs. Kennedy." February 1, 1967.

Reinhold, Robert. "Kennedys Ready a Library Model." April 8, 1973.

———. "Kennedy's Role in History: Some Doubts." November 22, 1973.

Ripley, Anthony. "Change, More Than a Sense of Tragedy, Now Dominates Dallas." November 24, 1973.

"Scale-Down Plans for Kennedy Library Unveiled." June 8, 1974.

Shelton, Robert. "President's Death Is Folk-Disk Dream." October 11, 1964.

"66% in Poll Accept Kennedy Plot View." March 30, 1967.

Stone, Oliver. "Who Is Rewriting History?" December 20, 1991.

"Ten Years Later." November 22, 1973.

"25th Amendment Gains Approval" and "Text of 25th Amendment." February 11, 1967.

Nichols, Mary Perot. "RIP Conspiracy Theories?" *Philadelphia Inquirer,* August 29, 1993.

1950–1960: This Fabulous Century. New York: *Time-Life* Books, 1970.

1968 Time Capsule. New York: *Time-Life* Books, 1969.

North, Mark. *Act of Treason: The Role of J. Edgar Hoover and the Assassination of President Kennedy.* New York: Carroll and Graf, 1991.

NOVA. "Who Shot President Kennedy?" WGBH, PBS, 1988.

O'Donnell, Kenneth, and Dave Powers. *Johnny, We Hardly Knew Ye: Memories of John Fitzgerald Kennedy.* New York: Little Brown, 1972.

Oglesby, Carl, and Jeff Goldberg. "Did the Mob Kill Kennedy?" *Washington Post,* February 25, 1975.

Oldroyd, Osborn H. *The Assassination of Abraham Lincoln.* Washington, D.C.: O. H. Oldroyd, 1901.

O'Toole, George. "The Assassination Probe." *Saturday Evening Post,* November 1975.

Panter-Downes, Mollie. "Letter from London." *New Yorker,* December 7, 1963.

"Paper Sales Soared When JFK Died." *Editor & Publisher,* April 18, 1964, p. 22.

Parker, Edwin B., and Bradley S. Greenberg. "Newspaper Content on the Assassination Weekend." In Parker and Greenberg, *Communications in Crisis,* pp. 46–50.

———, eds. *The Kennedy Assassination and the American Public: Social Communications in Crisis.* Stanford, CA: Stanford University Press, 1965.

Parmet, Herbert S. *Jack: The Struggles of John F. Kennedy.* 2 vols. New York: Dial Press, 1980.

———. *JFK: The Presidency of John F. Kennedy.* New York: Dial Press, 1983.

Payne, Darwin, *Dallas: An Illustrated History.* Woodland Hills, CA: Windsor Publications, 1982.

———. *The Press Corps and the Kennedy Assassination.* [Lexington, KY]: Association for Education in Journalism, 1970.

Pennebaker, James W. "On the Creation and Maintenance of Collective Memories." Manuscript, Research Files, SFMA. Published in Spanish in Psicología Politica 6 (1993): 35–51.

———. *Opening Up: The Healing Power of Confiding in Others.* New York: William Morrow and Company, 1990.

Pennebaker, James W., and Rhonda Polakoff. "The Effects of the John F. Kennedy Assassination on Dallas." Southern Methodist University, Dallas, 1988. Typescript, Research Files, SFMA.

Pettit, Tom. "The Television Story in Dallas." In Parker and Greenberg, *Communications in Crisis,* pp. 61–66.

Petty, Charles, MD. "JFK: An Allonge." *Journal of the American Medical Association* 269, no. 12 (March 24/31, 1993): 1552–1553.

Popkin, Richard H. *The Second Oswald.* New York: Avon Library, 1966.

Posner, Gerald. *Case Closed.* New York: Random House, 1993; Anchor, 1994.

Rather, Dan, with Mickey Herskowitz. *The Camera Never Blinks.* New York: William Morrow, 1977.

Reeves, Richard. *President Kennedy*. New York: Simon and Schuster, 1993.

Reston, James, Jr. *The Lone Star: The Life of John Connally*. New York: Harper and Row, 1989.

———. "What Was Killed Was Not Only the President but the Promise." *New York Times Magazine*. November 15, 1964.

Rice, Gerald T. *The Bold Experiment: JFK's Peace Corps*. Notre Dame, IN: University of Notre Dame Press, 1985.

Rivers, William L. "The Press and the Assassination." In Parker and Greenberg, *Communications in Crisis*, pp. 51–60.

Robertson, James O. *American Myth, American Reality*. New York: Hill and Wang, 1980.

Rosenberg, Norman, and Emily S. Rosenberg. *In Our Times*. 2d ed. Englewood Cliffs, NJ: Prentiss-Hall, 1982.

Rosenstone, Robert H. "JFK: Historical Fact/Historical Film." *American Historical Review*, April 1992, pp. 506–511.

Salinger, Pierre. *With Kennedy*. New York: Doubleday, 1966.

Salisbury, Harrison. "The Editor's View in New York." In Parker and Greenberg, *Communications in Crisis*, pp. 37–45.

———. *Time of Change*. New York: Harper and Row, 1988.

Sauvage, Leo. *Oswald Affair: An Examination of the Contradictions and Omissions of the Warren Report*. New York: World Publications, 1966.

Schachtman, Tom. *Decade of Shocks: From Dallas to Watergate, 1963–1975*. New York: Poseidon, 1983.

Scheim, David E. *Contract on America: The Mafia Murders of John and Robert Kennedy*. Lakewood, CO: Argyle Press, 1983; New York: Shapolsky Books, 1988.

Schlesinger, Arthur M., Jr. *A Thousand Days: John F. Kennedy in the White House*. Boston: Houghton Mifflin, 1965.

Schramm, Wilbur, "Introduction." In Parker and Greenberg, *Communications in Crisis*, pp. 1–28.

Scott, Peter Dale, Paul R. Hoch, and Russell Stetler. *The Assassination: Dallas and Beyond*. New York: Random House, 1976.

———. "The Longest Cover-up." *Ramparts*, November 1973, pp. 12–20, 53–54.

Sharpe, Ernest, *G. B. Dealey of the Dallas News*. New York: Henry Holt and Company, 1955.

Shaw, J. Gary, and Larry R. Harris. *Cover-up: The Governmental Conspiracy to Conceal the Facts about the Public Execution of John Kennedy*. Cleburne, TX: Privately printed, 1976.

Sheatsley, Paul B., and Jacob J. Feldman. "A National Survey on Public Reactions and Behavior." In Parker and Greenberg, *Communications in Crisis*, pp. 149–177.

Showtime Television. "Inside Oliver Stone." April 14, 1992.

Shudson, Michael. *Watergate in American Memory*. New York: Basic Books, 1992.

Shute, Nancy. "After a Turbulent Youth the Peace Corps Comes of Age." *Smithsonian*. February 1986.

Sidey, Hugh. *JFK Presidency*. New York: Atheneum, 1964.

Sigel, Roberta S. "Television and the Reaction of School Children to the Assassination." In Parker and Greenberg, *Communications in Crisis*, pp. 199–219.

Siginski, Andrzej. "Dallas and Warsaw: The Impact of a Major National Political Event on Public Opinion Abroad." *Public Opinion Quarterly*, Summer 1969, pp. 190–196.

"6th Floor Shrine a Smelly, Sick Plan." Editorial. *Bryan (Texas) Eagle*, December 1, 1979.

"Slow Progress for the Alliance." *Business Week*, March 31, 1961.

Sorensen, Theodore C. *Kennedy*. New York: Harper and Row, 1965.

Spiegelman, Arthur. "Hi-Tech Author Debunks JFK Conspiracy." *Chicago Sun Times*, August 23, 1993.

Sprague, Richard. "The Application of Computers to the Photographic Evidence." *Computers and Automation*, May 1970.

Stephens, Mitchell. *A History of News*. New York: Viking Press, 1988.

Stone, Oliver, and Zachary Sklar, with Jane Rusconi. *JFK: The Book of the Film*. Santa Barbara, CA: Applause Books, 1992.

———. "Stone Shoots Back." *Esquire*, December, 1991.

Suinn, Richard M. "Note: Guilt and Depth of Reaction to the Death of a President." *Psychoanalytic Review* 53, no. 3 (Fall 1966): 81–82.

Sullivan, Michael John. *Presidential Passions*. New York: Shapolsky Publishers, 1991.

Summers, Anthony. *Conspiracy*. New York: McGraw-Hill, 1980; Paragon, 1991.

———. *Goddess: The Secret Lives of Marilyn Monroe*. New York: New American Library, 1986.

———. *Official and Confidential: The Secret Life of J. Edgar Hoover*. New York: G. P. Putnam's Sons, 1993.

Teachout, Terry, ed. *Beyond the Boom*. New York: Poseidon, 1990.

Texas State Journal of Medicine. *Three Patients at Parkland*. Austin: Texas State Journal of Medicine, 1964.

"That Nations May Know." *Saturday Review*, December 3, 1966.

Thelen, David. "Memory and American History." *Journal of American History* 75, no. 4 (March 1989): 1117–1129.

Thompson, Josiah. "The Cross Fire That Killed President Kennedy." *Saturday Evening Post*, December 2, 1967.

———. *Six Seconds in Dallas*. New York: Bernard Geis Associates, 1967; Berkley, 1976.

Time. Articles

    "All Out against Fallout." August 4, 1961.

    "America's First Lady." May 30, 1994.

    Anderson, Kurt. "Does Connie Chung Matter?" May 31, 1993.

    Ehrenreich, Barbara. "Living Out the Wars of 1968." June 7, 1993.

    "Leaving Murky Waters to the Senate." June 16, 1975.

    Nelan, Bruce. "Back to the New Frontier." October 18, 1993.

    Riley, Michael. "Tales from the Crypt." September 14, 1992.

    "Space." February 20, 1962.

    "The Succession." February 20, 1967.

    "The Warren Commission Report." October 2, 1964.

"To John F. Kennedy: Homage by Artists." *Art in America* 52 (October 1964).

"To John F. Kennedy: Homage by Artists." *Art News* 62 (January 1964).

Toscano, Vincent L. *Since Dallas: Images of John F. Kennedy in Popular and Scholarly Literature, 1963–1978*. San Francisco: R&E Research Association, 1978.

Trask, Richard B. *Pictures of the Pain: Photography and the Assassination of President Kennedy*. Danvers, MA: Yeoman Press, 1994.

Trillin, Calvin. "The Buffs." *New Yorker*, June 10, 1967.

Tribune Entertainment. "On Trial: Lee Harvey Oswald." Five-part series, 1988.

———. "On Trial: Lee Harvey Oswald." Press Kit. September 1988.

Turner, Thomas Reed. *Beware the People Weeping*. Baton Rouge: Louisiana State University Press, 1982.

"TV's Biggest Audience." *Broadcasting*, February 3, 1964, pp. 54–55.

United Press International and *American Heritage* Magazine. *Four Days*. New York: UPI and *American Heritage*, 1964.

United States Information Agency. "Years of Lightning, Day of Drums." 1964. Video, Film Collections, SFMA.

U.S. News & World Report: Articles

    Barone, Michael, and Katia Hetter. "The Lost World of John Kennedy." November 15, 1993.

    "Before You Get Too Excited about the New Telstar." May 20, 1963.

    Boorstin, Daniel, "JFK, His Vision: Now and Then." October 24, 1988.

    "Case Closed." August 30/September 6, 1993.

    "The Changed Mood of America." April 30, 1962.

    "The 'Hot' War U.S. Seems to Be Losing." January 21, 1963.

    "If Anything Happens to a President." February 27, 1967.

    "Minimum Wage Bill." May 15, 1961.

    Parshall, Gerald. "The Man with a Deadly Smirk." August 30/September 6, 1993.

    "Space." May 15, 1961.

    "Space." June 5, 1961.

    "A 10-Year 'Marshall Plan' to Build Up Latin America." March 27, 1961.

    "The Truth about the Kennedy Assassination." October 3, 1966.

    "What Jacqueline Kennedy Onassis Meant to America." May 30, 1994.

Van Der Karr, Richard K. "How Dallas Stations Covered Kennedy Shooting." *Journalism Quarterly*, Autumn 1965, pp. 646–648.

Variety: Articles

    "JFK's Arts Gestures Okay by LBJ: More Fed Nods to All of Show Biz." January 13, 1965.

    "Stravinsky Ode to JFK after Verse of Auden." March 11, 1964.

    "392 Verses on Death of JFK Wins a Sicilian Top Balladeer Honors in Italy." August 5, 1964.

Virga, Vincent. *The Eighties*. New York: Harper Collins, 1992.

Ward, Geoffrey C. "The Most Durable Assassination Theory: Oswald Did It Alone." *New York Times Book Review*, November 21, 1993, pp. 15–18.

Watson, Mary Ann. *The Expanding Vista*. New York: Oxford University Press, 1990.

The Way We Were: 1963, The Year Kennedy Was Shot. New York: Carroll and Graf, 1988.

Wecht, Cyril H., MD. "JFK Revisited." *Journal of the American Medical Association* 269, no. 12 (March 24/31, 1993): 1507.

———."The Medical Evidence in the Assassination of President John F. Kennedy." *Forensic Science* 3 (April 1974): 105–128.

———. "Pathologist's View of JFK Autopsy: An Unsolved Case." *Modern Medicine* 40 (November 1972): 28–32.

Weinstein, Edwin A, and Olga G. Lyerly. "Symbolic Aspects of Presidential Assassination." *Psychiatry* 32, no. 1 (February 1969): 1–11.

Weisberg, Harold. *Oswald in New Orleans: Case of Conspiracy with the CIA.* New York: Canyon Books, 1967.

———. *Whitewash.* New York: Dell Publishing Company, 1966.

———. *Whitewash II: The FBI-Secret Service Cover Up.* New York: Dell, 1966/67.

Welsh, David, and David Lifton. "The Case for Three Assassins." Part 1. *Ramparts,* January 1967, pp. 77–87.

West End Historic District. "Application for Inclusion on the National Register of Historic Places." City of Dallas, 1978. Typescript, Research Files, SFMA.

"What Ever Happened to the Peace Corps?" *Senior Scholastic,* February 8, 1971, pp. 9–15.

"Where Were You?" *Esquire,* November 1973, pp. 136–137.

White, Theodore. *America in Search of Itself: The Making of the President, 1956–1980.* New York: Harper and Row, 1982.

Wicker, Tom. "That Day in Dallas." In Parker and Greenberg, *Communications in Crisis,* pp. 29–36.

Wills, Garry. *The Kennedy Imprisonment: A Meditation on Power.* Boston: Little Brown and Company, 1981.

Wilson, Richard. "What Happened to the Kennedy Program." *Look,* November 17, 1964, pp. 11–14.

Winters, Willis. "Exhibit Helps Heal 25-Year-Old Wound." *Texas Architect,* May 1, 1989.

Wofford, Harris. Of Kennedys and Kings: Making Sense of the Sixties. Pittsburgh: University of Pittsburgh Press, 1980.

Wolper, David L. (producer). "Four Days in November." MGM/UA Home Video, 1964.

"A World Listened and Watched." *Broadcasting,* December 2, 1963, pp. 36–46.

"The World Resounds: A Tribute." *America: National Catholic Weekly Review* 109, no. 24 (December 14, 1963): 767–771.

Wright, Lawrence. *In the New World: Growing Up with America, 1960–1984.* New York: Alfred A. Knopf, 1988.

Wrone, David R., ed. *The Freedom of Information Act and Political Assassinations,* vol. 1. Stevens Point: University of Wisconsin Press, 1978.

Wurmstedt, Robert. "The Sixth Floor: Designed to Bring a Tragic Piece of Dallas' Past to Life." *Fort-Worth Star Telegram,* September 1987.

Zelizer, Barbie. *Covering the Body: The Kennedy Assassination, the Media, and the Shaping of Collective Memory.* Chicago: University of Chicago Press, 1992.

INDEX

NOTE: Italicized page numbers refer to illustrations.

A native of Hampton, Virginia, CONOVER HUNT is a public historian who has consulted nationally to museum and historical organizations since 1975. A graduate of Newcomb College, Tulane University, she holds a Master of Arts from the Winterthur Museum Program at the University of Delaware. Hunt served as the project director and chief curator organizing The Sixth

Howard Hackney Photo

Floor Museum from 1978 until it opened in 1989, and prepared the draft application for the designation of Dealey Plaza as a National Historic Landmark. *JFK for a New Generation* is her third book on the life, death, and legacy of President John F. Kennedy. She divides her time between Dallas and Caddo Lake in East Texas.

HUGH SIDEY has written about the American presidency for thirty-five years. He began covering Dwight Eisenhower for the weekly *Life* magazine in 1957, and later became *Time*'s political and White House correspondent. A former Washington bureau chief, Sidey is now Washington contributing editor for *Time* magazine. He is the author of *Time*'s column "The Presidency," which he started in *Life* in 1966.